Rethinking Criminal Justice

For 200 years, the penal equation 'crime plus blame equals punishment' has meant prison crises, a permanent crime problem, violent and damaged lives. The retributive theory of punishment supports this; fully developed, it could transform it. A moral psychology of violation distinguishes primitive and mature retributivism, explaining punishment's necessary failure and guilt, forgiveness and reconciliation's power. 'Atonement' means both punitive 'payback' and being 'at one' again with self and others. Reconciliation for offender, victim and society leads to punishment's deep, tendential abolition.

Intellectually innovative and bold, Alan Norrie's mature retributivism is rooted in human ontology, in the metaphysical animal that thinks and loves. Speaking to law, philosophy, criminology and criminal justice, his moral psychology considers victims who victimise, grief at violation, denial and mourning and the loving prison. Exploring ethics, psychoanalysis, social theory, testimony and film, his psychologically developed moral philosophy challenges basic assumptions about punishment and the penal equation.

Alan Norrie is Professor of Law and former Head of Warwick Law School. He is a Fellow of the British Academy and the author of *Crime, Reason and History* in the Cambridge Law in Context series, among many books and articles.

Law in Context

Since 1970, the Law in Context series has been at the forefront of a movement to broaden the study of law. The series is a vehicle for the publication of innovative monographs and texts that treat law and legal phenomena critically in their cultural, social, political, technological, environmental and economic contexts. A contextual approach involves treating legal subjects broadly, using materials from other humanities and social sciences, and from any other discipline that helps to explain the operation in practice of the particular legal field or legal phenomena under investigation. It is intended that this orientation is at once more stimulating and more revealing than the bare exposition of legal rules. The series includes original research monographs, coursebooks and textbooks that foreground contextual approaches and methods. The series includes and welcomes books on the study of law in all its contexts, including domestic legal systems, European and international law, transnational and global legal processes, and comparative law.

Books in the Series

Acosta: *The National versus the Foreigner in South America: 200 Years of Migration and Citizenship Law*
Alaattinoğlu: *Grievance Formation, Rights and Remedies*
Ali: *Modern Challenges to Islamic Law*
Alyagon Darr: *Plausible Crime Stories: The Legal History of Sexual Offences in Mandate Palestine*
Anderson, Schum & Twining: *Analysis of Evidence, 2nd Edition*
Ashworth: *Sentencing and Criminal Justice, 6th Edition*
Barton & Douglas: *Law and Parenthood*
Baxi, McCrudden & Paliwala: *Law's Ethical, Global and Theoretical Contexts: Essays in Honour of William Twining*

Beecher-Monas: *Evaluating Scientific Evidence: An Interdisciplinary Framework for Intellectual Due Process*
Bell: *French Legal Cultures*
Bercusson: *European Labour Law, 2nd Edition*
Birkinshaw: *European Public Law*
Birkinshaw: *Freedom of Information: The Law, the Practice and the Ideal, 4th Edition*
Blick: *Electrified Democracy: The Internet and the United Kingdom Parliament in History*
Broderick & Ferri: *International and European Disability Law and Policy: Text, Cases and Materials*
Brownsword & Goodwin: *Law and the Technologies of the Twenty-First Century: Text and Materials*
Cane & Goudkamp: *Atiyah's Accidents, Compensation and the Law, 9th Edition*
Clarke: *Principles of Property Law*
Clarke & Kohler: *Property Law: Commentary and Materials*
Collins: *The Law of Contract, 4th Edition*
Collins, Ewing & McColgan: *Labour Law, 2nd Edition*
Cowan: *Housing Law and Policy*
Cranston: *Making Commercial Law Through Practice 1830–1970*
Cranston: *Legal Foundations of the Welfare State*
Darian-Smith: *Laws and Societies in Global Contexts: Contemporary Approaches*
Dauvergne: *Making People Illegal: What Globalisation Means for Immigration and Law*
David: *Kinship, Law and Politics: An Anatomy of Belonging*
Davies: *Perspectives on Labour Law, 2nd Edition*
Dembour: *Who Believes in Human Rights?: Reflections on the European Convention*
de Sousa Santos: *Toward a New Legal Common Sense: Law, Globalization, and Emancipation*
Diduck: *Law's Families*
Douglas-Scott: *Brexit, Union, and Disunion: The Evolution of British Constitutional Unsettlement*
Dowdle: *Transnational Law: A Framework for Analysis*
Dupret: *Positive Law from the Muslim World: Jurisprudence, History, Practices*
Emon: *Jurisdictional Exceptionalisms: Islamic Law, International Law, and Parental Child Abduction*
Estella: *Legal Foundations of EU Economic Governance*
Fortin: *Children's Rights and the Developing Law, 3rd Edition*
Garnsey: *The Justice of Visual Art: Creative State-Building in Times of Political Transition*
Garton, Probert & Bean: *Moffat's Trusts Law: Text and Materials, 7th Edition*
Ghai & Woodman: *Practising Self-Government: A Comparative Study of Autonomous Regions*
Glover-Thomas: *Reconstructing Mental Health Law and Policy*
Gobert & Punch: *Rethinking Corporate Crime*
Goldman: *Globalisation and the Western Legal Tradition: Recurring Patterns of Law and Authority*
Haack: *Evidence Matters: Science, Proof, and Truth in the Law*
Harlow & Rawlings: *Law and Administration, 4th Edition*

Harris: *An Introduction to Law, 8th Edition*
Harris, Campbell & Halson: *Remedies in Contract and Tort, 2nd Edition*
Harvey: *Seeking Asylum in the UK: Problems and Prospects*
Herring: *Law and the Relational Self*
Hervey & McHale: *European Union Health Law: Themes and Implications*
Hervey & McHale: *Health Law and the European Union*
Holder & Lee: *Environmental Protection, Law and Policy: Text and Materials, 2nd Edition*
Jackson & Summers: *The Internationalisation of Criminal Evidence: Beyond the Common Law and Civil Law Traditions*
Jeutner: *The Reasonable Person: A Legal Biography*
Kennedy: *Inducing Intimacy: Deception, Consent and the Law*
Kostakopoulou: *The Future Governance of Citizenship*
Kreiczer-Levy: *Destabilized Property: Property Law in the Sharing Economy*
Kubal: *Immigration and Refugee Law in Russia: Socio-Legal Perspectives*
Lewis: *Choice and the Legal Order: Rising above Politics*
Likosky: *Law, Infrastructure and Human Rights*
Likosky: *Transnational Legal Processes: Globalisation and Power Disparities*
Lixinski: *Legalized Identities: Cultural Heritage Law and the Shaping of Transitional Justice*
Loughnan: *Self, Others and the State: Relations of Criminal Responsibility*
Lunney: *A History of Australian Tort Law 1901–1945: England's Obedient Servant?*
Maughan & Webb: *Lawyering Skills and the Legal Process, 2nd Edition*
McGaughey: *Principles of Enterprise Law*
McGlynn: *Families and the European Union: Law, Politics and Pluralism*
Mertens: *A Philosophical Introduction to Human Rights*
Miller: *An Introduction to German Law and Legal Culture: Text and Materials*
Moffat: *Trusts Law: Text and Materials*
Monti: *EC Competition Law*
Morgan: *Contract Law Minimalism: A Formalist Restatement of Commercial Contract Law*
Morgan & Yeung: *An Introduction to Law and Regulation: Text and Materials*
Nash: *British Islam and English Law: A Classical Pluralist Perspective*
Ng: *Political Censorship in British Hong Kong: Freedom of Expression and the Law (1842–1997)*
Nicola & Davies: *EU Law Stories: Contextual and Critical Histories of European Jurisprudence*
Norrie: *Crime, Reason and History: A Critical Introduction to Criminal Law, 3rd Edition*
O'Dair: *Legal Ethics: Text and Materials*
Oliver: *Common Values and the Public–Private Divide*
Oliver & Drewry: *The Law and Parliament*
Palmer & Roberts: *Dispute Processes: ADR and the Primary Forms of Decision-Making, 1st Edition*
Palmer & Roberts: *Dispute Processes: ADR and the Primary Forms of Decision-Making, 3rd Edition*
Picciotto: *International Business Taxation*

Pieraccini: *Regulating the Sea: A Socio-Legal Analysis of English Marine Protected Areas*
Probert: *The Changing Legal Regulation of Cohabitation, 1600–2010: From Fornicators to Family, 1600–2010*
Qiao: *The Authoritarian Commons: Neighborhood Democratization in Urban China*
Radi: *Rules and Practices of International Investment Law and Arbitration*
Reed: *Internet Law: Text and Materials*
Richardson: *Law, Process and Custody*
Roberts & Palmer: *Dispute Processes: ADR and the Primary Forms of Decision-Making, 2nd Edition*
Rowbottom: *Democracy Distorted: Wealth, Influence and Democratic Politics*
Sauter: *Public Services in EU Law*
Scott & Black: *Cranston's Consumers and the Law*
Seneviratne: *Ombudsmen: Public Services and Administrative Justice*
Seppänen: *Ideological Conflict and the Rule of Law in Contemporary China: Useful Paradoxes*
Siems: *Comparative Law, 3rd Edition*
Stapleton: *Product Liability*
Stewart: *Gender, Law and Justice in a Global Market*
Tamanaha: *Law as a Means to an End: Threat to the Rule of Law*
Taylor: *Fortin's Children's Rights and the Developing Law, 4th Edition*
Tuori: *Properties of Law: Modern Law and After*
Turpin & Tomkins: *British Government and the Constitution: Text and Materials, 7th Edition*
Twining: *General Jurisprudence: Understanding Law from a Global Perspective*
Twining: *Globalisation and Legal Theory*
Twining: *Human Rights, Southern Voices: Francis Deng, Abdullahi An-Na'im, Yash Ghai and Upendra Baxi*
Twining: *Jurist in Context: A Memoir*
Twining: *Karl Llewellyn and the Realist Movement, 2nd Edition*
Twining: *Rethinking Evidence: Exploratory Essays, 2nd Edition*
Twining & Miers: *How to Do Things with Rules, 5th Edition*
Wan: *Film and Constitutional Controversy: Visualizing Hong Kong Identity in the Age of 'One Country, Two Systems'*
Ward: *A Critical Introduction to European Law, 3rd Edition*
Ward: *Law, Text, Terror*
Ward: *Shakespeare and Legal Imagination*
Watt: *The Making Sense of Politics, Media, and Law: Rhetorical Performance as Invention, Creation, Production*
Wells & Quick: *Lacey, Wells and Quick: Reconstructing Criminal Law: Text and Materials, 4th Edition*
Woodhead: *Caring for Cultural Heritage: An Integrated Approach to Legal and Ethical Initiatives in the United Kingdom*
Yeung and Ranchordás: *An Introduction to Law and Regulation: Text and Materials, 2nd edition*
Young: *Turpin and Tomkins' British Government and the Constitution: Text and Materials, 8th Edition*
Zander: *Cases and Materials on the English Legal System, 10th Edition*
Zander: *The Law-Making Process, 6th Edition*

International Journal of Law in Context: A Global Forum for Interdisciplinary Legal Studies

The *International Journal of Law in Context* is the companion journal to the Law in Context book series and provides a forum for interdisciplinary legal studies and offers intellectual space for ground-breaking critical research. It publishes contextual work about law and its relationship with other disciplines including but not limited to science, literature, humanities, philosophy, sociology, psychology, ethics, history and geography. More information about the journal and how to submit an article can be found at http://journals.cambridge.org/ijc.

Rethinking Criminal Justice

Punishment, Abolition and Moral Psychology

ALAN NORRIE
University of Warwick

CAMBRIDGE
UNIVERSITY PRESS

CAMBRIDGE
UNIVERSITY PRESS

Shaftesbury Road, Cambridge CB2 8EA, United Kingdom

One Liberty Plaza, 20th Floor, New York, NY 10006, USA

477 Williamstown Road, Port Melbourne, VIC 3207, Australia

314–321, 3rd Floor, Plot 3, Splendor Forum, Jasola District Centre, New Delhi – 110025, India

103 Penang Road, #05–06/07, Visioncrest Commercial, Singapore 238467

Cambridge University Press is part of Cambridge University Press & Assessment, a department of the University of Cambridge.

We share the University's mission to contribute to society through the pursuit of education, learning and research at the highest international levels of excellence.

www.cambridge.org
Information on this title: www.cambridge.org/9781108478878

DOI: 10.1017/9781108781329

When citing this work, please include a reference to the DOI 10.1017/9781108781329

First published 2025

A catalogue record for this publication is available from the British Library

A Cataloging-in-Publication data record for this book is available from the Library of Congress

ISBN 978-1-108-47887-8 Hardback

For Gwen with love

Philosophers have … written exhaustively on … punishment and responsibility … [but] … little attention has been paid to the concepts of guilt and guilt feelings, and … the rich assortment of related concepts such as remorse, repentance, contrition, forgiveness, and shame. The complex world of moral feelings … so central to our lives … has attracted … little attention ….

Herbert Morris (1976: viii)

A truthful ethical life … can include … our psychological life … [one that] is compatible with naturalistic explanation.

Bernard Williams (1995b: 19–20)

SOCRATES: I am still unable … to know myself; and it really seems to me ridiculous to look into other things before I have understood that …. Am I a beast more complicated and savage … or am I a tamer, simpler animal with a share in a divine and gentle nature?

Plato, *Phaedrus*, 230a

How could vomiting be 'thinking'?
This is the mystery Freud sets out to solve: the mystery of the flesh made word.

Jonathan Lear (1990: 7, xii)

Since we cannot atone you, we shall see
Justice design the victor's chivalry.

Shakespeare, *Richard II*, i.1

[I]t is quite reasonable to maintain, as Plato did, that in a perfect state no punishment at all would be necessary.

Immanuel Kant (1993: 246)

Contents

Preface
For the Metaphysical Animal that Thinks and Loves

This preface provides a brief summary of the argument of this book and how it develops. My original title was *Criminal Justice and the Blaming Relation*, but the idea of a blaming relation needed deeper investigation than I had realised. As the final title suggests, I was led into questions about moral psychology, which make a blaming relation possible. Eventually I came to the book's underlying idea and its substantive conclusion. The main idea is that criminal justice should be designed to reflect our nature as human beings, as 'the animal that thinks and loves'. Though it covers a lot of ground, its main conclusion is that the retributive philosophy usually understood as criminal punishment's main justification in fact requires its abolition.

A Philosophical Argument

The argument is that existing penal theory leads to an abolitionist conclusion even if it might seem in its essence to reject it. Penal abolition is not hugely popular in criminal justice circles despite the system's obvious failures. This may be the result of an inability to think beyond the current ways of doing things. It may be the result of a turf war in which political theorists of punishment defend 'their' theory against critics. It may also be that there are good reasons for rejecting existing abolitionist approaches as undercooked or impractical. Whatever the reason, this book's aim is to show the heretofore hidden connection between law's retributive theory of punishment and an abolitionist penal practice that is normally seen as its negation.

How is it possible both to reject criminal punishment and see that a fully developed retributivism is abolitionist in its implications? The answer lies in what I call a deep or tendential abolitionism which lies within the theory of punishment itself. Through moral psychology, we find an immanent abolitionist direction of travel that emerges from the 'mature' retributive theory developed here. Importantly, this argument does not herald a takeover of the philosophy of punishment by another discipline (moral psychology). It is a philosophical argument *in its own right* once philosophy is understood, as I believe it should be, in the fuller Socratic manner that I argue for in the text.

Types of Critique

The book starts with questions of method. Chapter 1 outlines seven different kinds of critique relevant to my argument. From these, two are immanent and ontological critique, and a third and fourth stem from them. The book works, first, as immanent critique through the problems and impasses of existing criminal justice theory. It develops, second, as ontological critique in the form of a substantive moral psychology of guilt, responsibility, mourning, forgiveness, reconciliation and denial, terms which reflect how human beings operate when faced with violation. The essence of human being is that we are metaphysical animals capable of thought and love, and this is at the root of our moral psychology. This psychology is, third, the basis for a further critique contrasting the way human beings are with how they are understood theoretically in an institutional practice such as criminal justice. It gives rise to what I call an 'ethically real and institutionally critical' position (or an 'ERIC' critique for short). This is a realist-based critique of existing practice which then generates a fourth emancipatory critique in the form of a way of thinking about violation that is practically (deeply and tendentially) abolitionist, in its implications.

The argument is commenced in Parts I and II, probing our existing knowledge immanently and ontologically. It is then stated most fully in Part III before being developed in Part IV and concluded in Part V. The abolitionist conclusion emerges as the work proceeds. It comes both immanently from penal theory's existing premises and ontologically from the moral psychology developed alongside these. Chapter 1 starts with dissatisfaction with existing enquiry, indications of possible ways forward, elaboration of different kinds of critique and a brief sketch of my own pre-project starting point centred on love. It moves in Chapter 2 to an introductory prototype argument comparing the young and older Hegel (whom, for reasons to be seen, I refuse to call 'mature'). It then picks up (Chapter 3) the perennial criminal justice problem of 'just deserts in an unjust society' and thinks about the guilt of victims who victimise others in the different registers of political theory and moral psychology.

Moral Psychology and Love

These early chapters begin to argue for the importance of a moral psychology based on love as a critical rejoinder to the problems of criminal justice. The young Hegel had written of love as the core of human ethical life, and this provided an important starting point. Chapter 2 contrasts young Hegel's account of love, grief and injury with his later work on law and right as a point of embarkation for the project as a whole.

Chapter 3 on just deserts then starts a deeper foray into love and moral psychology through psychoanalytic thought. It contrasts guilt in liberal political theory with an understanding of what is at work when people feel moral guilt for harming others. It begins to explore love and moral psychology through two bold and illuminating works, Jessica Benjamin's *The Bonds of Love* (1988), and Jonathan Lear's *Love and Its Place in Nature* (1990). As their titles suggest, these help us understand love as a ground of human being and I see them as establishing the deeper foundations for ideas and feelings of guilt, forgiveness and blame. If the young Hegel is one initial philosophical route, Benjamin's work on love and recognition is a second which helps deepen our orientation. It is a first step into moral psychology in its relation to human metapsychology in the tradition started by Sigmund Freud. Lear's work, with its connection to Freud through the psychoanalyst Hans Loewald, will engage us later, as the analysis progresses.

As the project was taking shape, two further encounters emerged. The first (Chapter 4) was with Martha Nussbaum's *Anger and Forgiveness* (2016), which came at the right time but with for me the wrong argument. She had previously pressed the importance of love and psychoanalysis for political theory (Nussbaum 2004, 2014), but on guilt and forgiveness in her 2016 work, she held to philosophical love while stepping back from Freud. Nussbaum's emphasis on love is important, but I found her step back from Freud's metapsychology helpful in a different way. It made me consider critically and defend my view that Freudian metapsychology was important.

The second encounter (Chapter 5) was different again. Marina Cantacuzino's *The Forgiveness Project* (2015) is a collection of personal accounts of forgiveness and guilt which I read alongside Marian Partington's *If You Sit Very Still* (2012), her memoir of her sister Lucy's murder by the serial killers Fred and Rose West. Writing about the 'blaming relation', I wanted to reflect on the position of both perpetrators and victims of violent crimes. These works in their emotional immediacy took me into questions of forgiveness and the position of the victim.[1] *The Forgiveness Project* and Partington convinced me that there was an ethical experience of forgiveness based in love that needed to be brought into the discussion. Here, indeed, was the basis for a blaming relation incorporating victims and perpetrators. Interestingly, however, this was more about reconciliation than blame in the punitive and retributive way normally understood, and it was based on the love of family members grieving their loss.

Love, then, was at the root of the analysis in all four of these substantive chapters, whether about guilt or forgiveness, or perpetrators or victims; and whether in the young Hegel, Benjamin's metapsychology, Nussbaum's splitting of love from its psychoanalytic grounds, or the testimony of victims who forgive. Yet these different starting points point beyond themselves to a

[1] I use terms such as 'perpetrator' and 'victim' with hesitation because they can be contested (the perpetrator may also be a victim; the victim is also, or rather, a survivor; perpetrator and victimhood may be politically organized in a hierarchy: McEvoy and McConnachie 2012, 2013; Hearty 2016). They are somewhat legalistic but they remain important. In a more ethical mode, I talk of 'violation' instead of violent crimes, and what Benjamin calls the positions of the 'doer' and the 'done to' (Benjamin 2018), in place of perpetrator and victim.

further question. Some are emotional, some philosophical, some ethical, some psychoanalytical, some contesting the terrain, some contesting the law. They suggest the need for an overall understanding of how these different aspects of moral psychology can be combined.

For the Metaphysical Animal That Thinks and Loves

This brings me to the book's underlying theoretical question, which is how to link love, ethics, psychology (psychoanalysis) and law in an inclusive moral psychology. Its motto is 'for the metaphysical animal that thinks and loves', but this might be thought rhetorical unless the challenge it reflects is addressed. This is to establish and connect the two sides of human nature as both the emotional animal with feelings and the ethical being. How does this work?

A similar way of describing human being as the 'metaphysical animal' comes from the Oxford philosopher Donald MacKinnon.[2] I argue that this involves two things. One is 'the metaphysical' in a narrower sense, meaning the capacity for ethical reflection on moral issues such as right and wrong, and the panoply of philosophical terms that accompanies this (including guilt, forgiveness and so on). This is essentially a philosophical meaning, emphasising the side of us that thinks, and, in thinking, expresses ourselves ethically. The second meaning comes from the animal side of our nature, meaning the human as a kind of animal with natural powers and tendencies, and that is both feeling and intelligent. This is the human *animal*, an embodied, somatic being capable by virtue of its species being of both thought and love. The challenge, then, is to connect these two sides, mind and body. In the phrase 'metaphysical animal', both aspects, metaphysical and animal, must play their part to provide a broader meaning of the term. The argument is that our minds are embodied just as our bodies are 'enminded' so that we are both metaphysical (in the narrower sense of having capacities for ethical thought) and animal (in the sense of living and being through feeling and emotion which may be expressed in ethical terms). This unified being is the metaphysical animal in a broader sense.

Human being then involves both the possibility of metaphysical experience and reflection *and* that this is grounded in our human, embodied, psychological being. The underlying need is to understand how these two come together in the metaphysical animal, how, as Lear succinctly puts it, the flesh can become word (Lear 1990: xii). Bringing them together is the way to understand our human moral psychology as feeling, thinking, loving creatures capable of ethical action, but also of failing in such action. This then becomes in relation to violation the basis for thinking about how we might best deal with situations where humans violate others. It provides a way of

[2] From MacKinnon's term comes the title of a book considering his influence on women philosophers in postwar Oxford: Mac Cumhaill and Wiseman (2022), discussed in Chapter 1.

understanding our emotional and ethical reactions to violation and how we might best process these. It enables us, more particularly, to understand why we might value seeing another punished, why that value might be limited and even counterproductive, and how other emotional processes might help us move forward. This is not just a matter of a better or worse philosophy but of how we might live better in the world. It leads us to distinguish our more primitive from our mature emotional reactions and how both become translated into better or worse ethical sentiments. Moral psychology as the reality of the metaphysical animal, the one that thinks and loves, provides in this book a perspective on criminal punishment and why mature retributivism and ensuing abolition represent a real and generally better way to deal with violation.

The Moral Psychology of Violation

If Parts I and II work towards a moral psychology of violation, Chapters 6–8 consolidate it by showing three things. First, they show that this moral psychology of the metaphysical animal that thinks and loves does not impose an external critique on legal theory, political philosophy or the philosophy of punishment. Rather, understood in Socratic philosophical terms, this approach represents a key and enriching contribution to what philosophy is, or should be (Chapter 6). Second, substantively, they show that psychoanalysis in the work of both Freud and Melanie Klein distinguishes primitive (punitive) and mature (restorative, reconciliative) ways of dealing with violation and blame. These are relevant to thinking about better and worse ways of dealing with situations where one person violates another. Freud's account of guilt is critically analysed in these terms in Chapter 7, and here, the work of Lear and Loewald is key, while Klein's parallel account is seen in Chapter 8, and I bring them together to argue for what I call mature retributive thinking.

Third, and engaging fully with criminal justice theory, they show that we can identify law's retributive philosophy of punishment with a primitive and persecutory moral psychology, but we can also use it to develop a mature retributivism, one that is restorative and reconciliative in its approach (Chapter 8). I draw here, among other ideas, on that of atonement, which can be understood either in primitive and punitive terms ('paying back') or maturely, as a form of being 'at one' (reconciled) with oneself and others after violation. This is atonement as 'at-one-ment' and is true for both the perpetrator (a doer) and the victim (a done to). In this way, the metapsychological grounds underlying our different kinds of ethical experience provide the ontological basis for a mature retributivism. This suggests how it would be best to deal with violation for the kind of metaphysical animal that human beings are. Most importantly, we find in mature retributivism the ethically real ontological basis for critique of existing penal practices. This is an ERIC critique that takes the form of deep or tendential penal abolitionism.

From Moral Psychology to Penal Abolition

Chapters 9–11 extend the analysis in three chapters which begin by considering additional categories in the blaming relation which are central to the metaphysical animal that thinks and loves. The first two consider denial or disavowal by perpetrators (Chapter 9) and mourning or melancholia in victims (Chapter 10). Both accounts pair moral psychology and film to develop theoretical discussion with a 'case study' showing its relevance.[3] They stress the importance of psychoanalytic thinking alongside metaphysical (philosophical and aesthetic) experience and link the analysis back to the discussion of atonement as non-punitive at-one-ment developed in Chapters 6 and 7.

Chapter 11 then engages not with film but prison autobiography, Jimmy Boyle's *A Sense of Freedom* (2016), on his time in Barlinnie Special Unit, Glasgow, in the 1970s. It identifies moral and psychological ideas of freedom and reconciliation as these may emerge even in a prison setting. This chapter takes us back to Chapter 8 with its argument that a mature alternative to punishment is possible even in the dark heart of the penal system. The Special Unit represented mature retributivism in action, and it provides the example in practice of an abolitionist approach to punishment in what I call, with a small measure of provocation, the 'loving prison'. It is noted, however, that the possibilities of developing a mature approach to violation depend on broader structural commitments. These must be both to social change and to addressing the overall 'structure in dominance' of the penal system which I describe as persecutory (primitive) in the major key and reparative (mature) in the minor. Throughout the book, the argument is that individual and social change must come together in order for either to be possible.

The final chapter takes up the book's argument as a whole and especially that of Chapters 8 and 11. A developed moral psychology of the human metaphysical animal, the animal that thinks and loves, provides us with an ontology of and for being human. That ontology distinguishes primitive, persecutory and punitive responses from mature, restorative and reconciliatory ones for dealing with violation. The resulting mature retributive theory makes abolition of punishment a real human possibility. Various implications of thinking about a mature retributive response to violation are explored, and some issues with abolitionist argument are addressed. This is a deep or tendential abolitionism which grounds abolition in human ontology as its immanent power, whether it is exercised or not. While the argument is theoretical rather than practical, it offers an ethically real basis for asserting an institutional (ERIC) critique of the present system of criminal punishment. It refuses to be cowed by objections based on what Immanuel Kant called 'adverse experience' (Kant 1993: 246), though these should be addressed. Against sceptics, there is an ontological

[3] Joshua Oppenheimer's *The Act of Killing* (2014) on denial; Patricio Guzmán's *Nostalgia for the Light* (2010) on mourning.

basis for holding to a real utopian position, that is, one that is ontologically grounded even if it appears utopian under present social conditions. Against existing abolitionist positions, its deep and tendential form provides grounds for distinguishing between an immanent (latent and real) demand and an imminent (immediate) demand for penal reform. The slogan 'Abolition now!' (Davis et al. 2022) can be interpreted both ways.

In the end, we have what is outlined in Chapter 1, an immanent and ontological critique based on the moral psychology of the metaphysical animal that thinks and loves. This is an ethically real approach that provides the ground on which to be critical of our legal (and other) institutions. The moral psychology of the blaming relation based on the ontology of the metaphysical animal provides (ERIC) grounds for criticising existing social, political and institutional practices and the possibility of emancipatory alternatives. It provides a basis both for identifying fundamentally different and better ways of dealing with violation through rational *philosophical* (Socratic, post-Freudian) criticism of present penal practices.

Acknowledgements

The initial work for the book was conducted under a Leverhulme Trust Major Research Fellowship (MRF-2014-122), and I acknowledge the Trust's support with gratitude.

I should like to thank the following friends and colleagues who read and commented on papers or discussed issues, either at a workshop supported by Warwick Law School in April 2023 or at other times: Sam Ashenden, Carl Auerbach, Zenon Bankowski, Henrique Carvalho, Halil Cesur, Davina Cooper, Mark Drumbl, Antony Duff, Lindsay Farmer, David Gurnham, Nicola Lacey, Sandra Marshall, BB Pande, George Pavlich, Peter Ramsay, Craig Reeves, Victor Tadros, Scott Veitch, Fabienne Viala and Amanda Wilson. I truly valued and benefitted from their thoughts and I am sorry if I missed anyone out. I would especially like to thank Henrique Carvalho for organising the workshop and for his thoughtfulness, energy, friendship and support at Warwick. I thank Amanda Wilson similarly and for working closely with me in recent years as a postdoctoral fellow and now associate professor at Warwick. Her views on abolition and restorative justice helped me press this work to its conclusion. I look forward to seeing her striking articles on restorative justice in book form. I thank Bel Rawson for helping to assemble the final manuscript so promptly, thoroughly and amicably.

I also thank Craig Reeves for intellectual and personal friendship over many years. Craig first directed me to the connection between psychoanalytic and liberal political theory in the work of Bernard Williams, Herbert Morris, Jessica Benjamin, Jonathan Lear and Martha Nussbaum, and thence to Sigmund Freud, Melanie Klein and Hans Loewald. This was somewhat new territory, and I confess to anxiety that I tread ground of which others have much deeper knowledge. When in doubt, I have taken courage from Williams's preface to his *Shame and Necessity*, where he notes that if scholarship is to be bold and interesting it 'cannot travel entirely on its own credentials' (Williams 1993: x). The risk of being superficial is the price of pushing one's limits and trying to say something new. The intellectual backdrop to these interests remains, as the book makes clear, the philosophy of critical realism and the work of Roy Bhaskar. The tenth anniversary of Roy's death was in November 2024, and I hope this book is a tribute to his philosophy.

During the time of my Leverhulme, I gave research papers at Kent Law School, Oxford Transitional Justice Research Group, Institut d'Etudes Avancées de Nantes, National Law University Delhi, Indian Law Institute Delhi, National Law University Orissa, University of Cambridge, Cornell University, University of Stockholm, Universidad Libre Bogota, Pontificia Universidad Catolica de Valparaiso, Birkbeck Institute for Social Research, London School of Economics, Yale University, Indira Gandhi National Open University Delhi, Yale Center for Faith & Culture at University of Fribourg, Switzerland, University of Ulster, Edinburgh Law School, University of Alberta and University of Toronto. I thank all those who organised these visits and for their hospitality at the time.

Personally, as ever, I owe so much to my wife, Gwen. A lengthy book project, carried well beyond its original finish date, takes up mental and emotional space. Gwen was always completely supportive, and I thank her for that as well as for everything else. Life is a long song. Stephen and Richard, Sachiko, Eleanor (my favourite granddaughter), Peter and Jennifer all bring the complex experience of love to me, as I to them. I remember with love my parents Tom and Gerry, my grandparents Ernest and Winifred Myles and a great aunt, Ada Jaffray, thereby keeping a promise from when I was very small that has stayed with me.

The cover of this book is also in part an act of memory. A copy of *The Hunters in the Snow* by Pieter Bruegel the Elder hung in my grandparents' house in Arbroath, which was a place for me of great warmth and love. Nearby was a skating pond with a hill on one side, and as a small child I initially imagined the painting to be a local scene. With this sense of immediacy, I was quite troubled by the dark hunters in the foreground with what I saw as their air of threat and violence. They seemed far removed from the happy skaters below with whom I readily identified. A child's emotional experience is hardly a complete guide to adult life, nor a medieval scene a guide to modern concerns. Yet I find the painting represents a tension, between love and reconciliation and fear and aggression, and one that is still unresolved in our society. I see punishment as a prominent site of such a tension and law as playing a complicated part in dealing with it, as suggested by Shakespeare in the book's prefatory quote.

Earlier versions of chapters, significantly reworked and developed for publication here, have appeared in the following publications: Norrie, A. (2019). Love in law's shadow: political theory, moral psychology and young Hegel's critique of punishment. *Social & Legal Studies*, 28(1), 10–30. https://doi.org/10.1177/0964663918758512 (Chapter 2); Norrie, A. (2022). Victims who victimise: guilt in political theory and moral psychology, in *The Criminal Law's Person*. Edited by Claes Lernestedt and Matt Matravers. Hart Publishing, an imprint of Bloomsbury Publishing Plc (Chapter 3); Norrie, A. (2018). Love and justice: can we flourish without addressing the past? *Journal of Critical Realism*, 17(1), 17–33. https://doi.org/10.1080/14767430.2018.1426525, reprinted by permission of Taylor & Francis Ltd (Chapter 4); Norrie, A. (2018). Love actually: law and the moral psychology of forgiveness. *Journal of*

Critical Realism, 17(4), 390–407. https://doi.org/10.1080/14767430.2018.1472409 (Chapter 5), reprinted by permission of Taylor & Francis Ltd; Norrie, A. (2019). Animals who think and love: law, identification and the moral psychology of guilt. *Criminal Law and Philosophy* 13, 515–44. https://doi.org/10.1007/s11572-018-9483-8 (Chapters 6 and 7); Norrie, A. (2021). Taking guilt seriously, in *On Crime, Society, and Responsibility in the Work of Nicola Lacey*. Edited by Iyiola Solanke. Oxford University Press, 119–44. https://doi.org/10.1093/oso/9780198852681.003.0007a (Chapter 8), with permission of the Licensor through PLS clear; Norrie, A. (2019). Identification, atonement and the moral psychology of violation: on Patricio Guzman's *Nostalgia for the Light*. *Journal of Critical Realism*, 18(4), 383–401. https://doi.org/10.1080/14767430.2019.1656922, reprinted by permission of Taylor & Francis Ltd (Chapter 10); Norrie, A. (2022). Restoration, abolition and the loving prison: Jimmy Boyle and Barlinnie Special Unit. *Howard Journal of Crime and Justice*, 61, 103–16. DOI: 10.1111/hojo.12457 (Chapter 11).

1

Criminal Justice and the Metaphysical Animal

> Morality, the Peculiar System: a special system, a particular variety of ethical thought.
>
> Bernard Williams (2011, 193)

> Mary and Iris were heading south. A pair of metaphysical animals on their way to Westminster.
>
> Clare Mac Cumhaill and Rachael Wiseman (2022, 98)

This book is a study of criminal justice theory. In an overworked field, it may be thought there is little more to say. Yet the crisis in criminal justice systems and the repetitiveness of stock solutions indicate the need for a new perspective. This is an attempt to think deeply and radically about taken-for-granted assumptions and to offer an alternative. In this introductory chapter, I set out a way of thinking about criminal justice which proposes a new ontology of violation with two aims. The first is to think seriously about how society should treat people who violate or are violated by others. The second is to think critically about our existing forms of criminal justice.

One reach-me-down solution to the general problem of crime and criminal justice is less criminalisation and increased resources in the penal establishment. Alternatively, society should do more of what it already does with more punishment and prisons, and this will somehow fix the problem. Neither solution questions the basic premises of the system. The deep issue that is not faced is that criminal justice thinking and the resulting practice is out of sync with human nature. This book suggests that we should identify more clearly what human beings are and how they work and then act accordingly. It is not about penal and criminal justice policy narrowly conceived, nor is it a work in political philosophy which seeks to justify or redesign something like our current systems. Nor is it a work of historical explanation as to why we have the practices we have, or a call to instigate something 'much better' without much idea as to what that might be. It is a work in moral psychology which asks what human beings are like in their nature as 'animals who think and love',[1] or as

[1] The title of a recent essay (Norrie 2019), which I develop here in Part III, and which expresses my underlying position.

'metaphysical animals'.[2] That humans are a particular species with powers and capacities for good and ill is everywhere to be seen, and this includes in our criminal justice system. Yet as a society, we continue to act as if understanding such powers and capacities, our human ontology, is irrelevant. Criminal justice theory offers little help in this regard. It is time to think differently.

This chapter begins by describing an impasse in criminal justice theory between those whose position is one of political or liberal normativism and those who take up an historical or genealogical critique. It then draws upon the work of the philosopher Bernard Williams to raise questions about what is wrong with our current ways of thinking and to identify a way forward through what he called naturalistic moral psychology. Along with Herbert Morris, whom we meet later, Williams identified a crucial absence in how we think about concepts such as guilt and responsibility and proposed a naturalistic moral alternative.[3] For Morris, there is a strange imbalance between the way philosophers of punishment and responsibility talk and the ways in which ordinary people think about these things. Williams similarly saw a gap between the modern morality which dominates and shapes our concepts and a naturalistic moral alternative. He provocatively termed this system 'peculiar' (see the prefatory quote to this chapter). He linked this, we shall see, to 'a certain political theory of freedom in the modern state', and not to the 'moral refinement of the very conception of responsibility' (Williams 1993: 66). Williams acts as a bridgehead for my argument by suggesting we link the nature of human being, moral psychology and our ethics, while inviting us to think beyond the standard moral categories which lack an important connection to human nature.

This introductory chapter provides the basis for the argument to follow. It begins by outlining an impasse in modern criminal justice thinking between two approaches, the politically normative and the historically critical. It then draws on Williams's approach to start to move beyond the impasse. It develops an account of a moral psychology that is naturalistic and relates this to the notion of an ontological critique. Such a critique is part of a chain of critiques and I set out how these critiques inform this work. Thereafter, I outline how I came to think that an *ontology of love* should provide a starting point for my

[2] I borrow the phrase from a recent book on those Oxford women philosophers (Elizabeth Anscombe, Philippa Foot, Mary Midgely and Iris Murdoch) who sought new ways of moral thinking after the Second World War (Mac Cumhaill and Wiseman 2022). The last two are the Mary and Iris in my prefatory quote, which I chose for its jaunty image. The authors identify the phrase with the women's Oxford teacher, Donald MacKinnon, and the 'need to speak about the transcendent, about the human spirit and the infinite' (Mac Cumhaill and Wiseman 2022: 91). As we shall see, I use it similarly to reflect on the nature of moral discourse around violation, but I include a further sense of violation associated with psychoanalytical thought. The main theoretical goal in Parts I–III is to show how the human really is a particular kind of *animal* in the phrase 'metaphysical animals'. The idea of the metaphysical is deepened to include a metapsychological ground.

[3] See the prefatory quotes from Williams and Morris which introduce this book.

enquiry. This is central to developing the idea of the human being as an animal that thinks and loves. Overall, my aim is a deeper understanding of how we might deal better with acts of violation than the dominant approach in the criminal justice system achieves, and this chapter indicates my methodological and substantive starting points.

Impasse in Criminal Justice Thinking

The broad nature of criminal justice theory will be known to many who come to this book. Here I outline two approaches, the politically normative and the critical-historical, and point to a way beyond their impasse.

Two Approaches to Criminal Justice Theory

The normative approach is primarily associated with modern liberal political theory in its various guises. From modern retributivism drawing on classical Enlightenment statements by Kant and Hegel, through to utilitarian and more broadly consequentialist positions, and onto communitarian, preventive (Ashworth and Zedner 2014) and political (Chiao 2018) variants, there is significant diversity of standpoint. Yet this is diversity within a recognisable and self-contained field, where it is possible to identify a range of well-known 'moves'. Modern political theory dictates the parameters. Its concern boils down to justifying state or sovereign practices around crime and punishment and relating these to the idea of responsible citizens or subjects who get what they deserve. These are normative questions about what ought to happen in a relationship between persons and political authority. How and why ought 'we' to punish offenders? The whole material is woven around questions of political normativity and what is normatively justified in sovereign–subject relations. It would be as impossible to deny the thoroughness and energy invested in this 'oughtification' of the penal field as it would the continuity of the questions asked. These concern generally the nature and value of punishment in a way that suggests that, whatever solution is proposed, the basic unquestionability of this practice is maintained. A 'definitional stop' argument supports this, claiming that since criminal justice is necessarily a state function, it is impossible to avoid the validity of a political theory approach. Other approaches may be more or less interesting but are optional to the main business.

That implies however that thinking about the state and criminal justice involves giving primacy to one method over others, that of political theory. What would happen if it turned out that the questions posed were the wrong ones, or that they could be answered in a very different way? In opposition to the standard normative models, critical approaches consider questions of punishment to be of a different order. Though hegemonic, liberal political theory is a relatively recent phenomenon developing from the seventeenth century. Packaged as Whig philosophy, as the outcome of an enlightened and timeless process, critics argue per contra that criminal justice is emergent under particular social, political and cultural conditions which fundamentally shape its practice (Ramsay 2009; Norrie 2014, 2017b; Farmer 2016; Lacey 2016; Carvalho 2017). The normative approach obscures social functions and interests which criminal justice's forms reflect in often contradictory ways. Legal practices do not lack contestable political goals which they also obscure. The legal form of responsibility, based on the abstraction of individuals from their social context, covers up social injustice. If these underlying functions changed, it could be that many assumptions about what is normatively compelling are wrong. There is a challenge to the oughtification project here: issues of normative political principle should be seen as both historically produced and flawed, as partisan rather than universal. Political normativity justifies the unjustifiable and should be submitted to a critical historical analysis which reveals the underlying truth and untruth.

In this debate, the politically normative and the critically social-theoretical and historical bounce off each other without finding a way forward. They generally compete by speaking past each other. Yet criticisms levelled at normative theory and the need for alternatives have become more salient in recent times. Its high-minded language of punishment and responsibility legitimates profound injustice concerning crime linked to social, racial and gendered disparities. Against claims that criminal justice delivers justice – even potentially, or only in principle, historical changes in advanced capitalist societies reveal increasingly the underlying systemic or structural violence that underpins it. Authoritarian political ('law and order') developments which accompany social and economic degradation sharpen the problem by exacerbating conflict. Social movements born from the experience of criminal justice failures register and protest the outcomes. Liberal criminal justice theory is charged with complicity and hypocrisy. These changes render normative political theory more vulnerable to the claim that the world it imagined is past, if it were ever present, in societies marked by class, misogyny, racism and their colonial history. The unquestioning affirmation of liberal norms begins to look impotent, a matter of diminishing returns, in a political world bent on their denial. There is a breach in the status quo critics would wish to face, but how and with what end in sight?

Beyond Impasse: Abolition and Moral Psychology

The critical view is that criminal justice is in social, political and legal disarray and in need of change. Society is in upheaval and political systems do not provide justice to the poor, minorities or women. Instead, they defend existing systems leading to the repetition of problems and failed solutions. One such case in point concerns the prison, where, from a critical standpoint, abolition is in the air. Normative theorists respond by distancing themselves from actual outcomes with 'in principle' or 'better the devil you know' arguments, but this is at best a partial defence when criminal justice systems are on a downward slide to 'more of the same', or worse, with less resource. Yet critique is hard-pressed to say what should replace the present and the past. Liberal theorists ask fairly, what do *you* think ought to happen? 'Abolition' of the criminal justice system seems a rallying cry for a very different future across the board, but it invites questions about what it means and what happens after abolition. Critics, it should be noted, also find it hard to reject entirely the language of responsibility and penal justice, wishing to see the powerful (the police, men assaulting women) arraigned before courts to get their 'just deserts'. Social organisation 'from below' in communities of the dispossessed is seen as providing alternative forms of social control. This may indeed provide sightings of genuine alternatives to criminal justice, but it has its own dangers and, indeed, needs its own moral understanding of how it should operate both on the small scale and were it to be developed generally. Abolition looks like a radical call for change, but it needs to be examined more thoroughly, especially in theoretical terms, if it is both to be understood and to stand as a defensible position in a time of political flux.

In the standoff between political normativists reconfiguring the status quo and critics imagining very different futures, I propose a further position from which to examine the problem. My own past work has been on the side of critical theory and for social and legal change (e.g. Norrie 2000, 2014), but more is needed and possible. Maintaining these older commitments, I suggest a critical step-change to find the way forward, through the different means of moral psychology. Such an approach has something to say about moral questions and the criminal justice field for it sets human ethical being (the 'animal that thinks and loves') at the heart of what ought to be done. Yet it does not lose sight of either the social problems that generate crime or the historical critique of law and its forms. It suggests that underneath these we also need a different way of thinking about how human beings live together and deal with each other. It recognises the importance of dealing with the ways humans violate each other through a moral language of violation, but it declines to think of this in the standard terms of criminal justice. An alternative approach points beyond the limits of political theory, criminal justice thinking and penal institutions to how humans could address wrongdoing in ways that are open to individual and social change. This offers the possibility we could find means to abolish criminal justice 'from within', at least in the sense that we develop a different and better understanding of what criminal justice claims to do but does badly. We can use a moral psychological critique of criminal justice's own moral psychology to think about how to move beyond it.

These are big issues and I hope to deal with them in ways that are sufficiently complex to capture what is most deeply at stake. However, it may be possible to state the issues simply to help us proceed. At the bottom, I want to raise and provide answers to five questions: (1) what is wrong with existing criminal justice concepts and practices? (2) what is the nature of the human agency and suffering to which they relate, and relate badly? (3) why do we remain stuck with what we have? (4) what could make things better for all concerned? and (5) given where we are, how do we relate critically to existing criminal justice practices? These questions, to which I return in what follows in exploring different kinds of critique, lie at the core of the argument I shall develop in this chapter and the book as a whole.

A Very Peculiar Practice

Critical approaches to criminal justice theory can be developed in different ways. My approach draws on moral psychology to produce a critical ontology of law. I see liberal normative theory generally as an important historical and political project shaped by the social relations of the modern nation-state. It is this linkage that provides it with its achievements and its limits (Norrie 2000, 2005, 2014, 2017c). One important limit is the structural gap that it develops between individual and social justice (to be discussed in Chapter 3). A second limit is that it provides only an abstract conception of the human subject, which enables it to link with a primitive moral psychology based on blame and punishment but finds no way of developing the psychological position of a perpetrator or of genuinely supporting the victim of a serious crime. That is a large part of what I will argue through the critique I develop in this book as a whole. In this section, I lay the foundation for this argument by sketching a critique of legal and political theory drawn from Bernard Williams to identify what is wrong with the political normativist approach and to indicate a way beyond it. Some of this reflects themes in my own earlier work on what I call law's 'morality of form' (Norrie 2000, 2014), but I find Williams helpfully provides a good way of condensing the issues and directing us towards the moral psychology I want to develop here.

Against the 'Morality System'

Williams was a moral philosopher who wrote of the 'morality system' as what he called a 'peculiar institution'. This work chimes with a critique of law in two ways. First, it views modern liberal philosophy as a strange or 'peculiar' way of looking at moral issues.[4] Second, it opens the door to thinking about a different approach to modern ethics through moral psychology. This groundbreaking work has generally been bypassed by criminal justice theorists, save where it could be fitted into mainstream assumptions.[5] Avoiding it was made

[4] See, for example, my discussion of individual justice in *Crime, Reason and History*: 'Legal individualism affixes a badge to our clothing or a mask to our face which has nothing to do with what we really are … with the real needs and attributes of human beings', and of legal theory as a 'praxiology' (Norrie 2014: 15, 379).

[5] For example, Williams's work on 'moral luck' (Williams 1981), which extends the understanding of liability to include outcomes associated with a person who lacked mental awareness, has been influential.

easier by the fact that Williams did not develop his ideas, sometimes only gesturing at them. Nonetheless, they provide an initial bridge to a new direction of travel.

In *Ethics and the Limits of Philosophy* (2011), Williams described what he called 'Morality' as 'The Peculiar Institution', by which he meant 'a special system, a particular variety of ethical thought' (Williams 2011: 193). His target was the idea of moral obligation, which he linked substantively to blame and guilt, and philosophically to Kant; more broadly, Williams saw these ideas as 'part of the outlook of almost all of us' in modern liberal society (Williams 2011: 194). People were trapped by a way of thinking which had the effect of securing social order, but which made people subservient to moral command and obligation in a way that involved illusion, fiction and myth. It gave the 'morality system' power to control people by laying stress on the idea that they ought to act in certain ways. When they did, they were responsible because they acted 'voluntarily'. This was an 'official' moral concept supporting the state but was too general and crude to explain how people in fact reflect ethically on their lives. The idea of voluntary moral obligation appeared to describe human powers, but in reality it decontextualised human actions. It was entirely helpful to the state and legal order, but it was disempowering for ordinary, human ethical experience. It lined us up as abstract agents submitted to state and social control. Williams wondered whether the morality system, being essentially fictional, 'could survive a clear understanding of how it works' (Williams 2011: 215) and thought 'we would be better off without' it (Williams 2011: 192).

The Morality System and Criminal Justice

The morality system qua peculiar institution is at play in normative criminal justice theory. In *Shame and Necessity* (1993), Williams developed his critique of modern ethics especially in the form of guilt and blame. He looked at how such ideas were historically shaped and different among the Greeks and the moderns. He showed how moral language had been conditioned by historical and political forms rather than by disinterested philosophy. He distinguished proper ethical enquiry from its political expression, arguing that modern normative theory distorted ethics in favour of politics. The following quote makes the point:

> We have handed many of the responses to a very special formation, the modern state, and we have principles governing what such a state can and should do. An important ideal that helps shape those principles is that an individual should, so far as possible, have control over his or her life, in relation to the power of the state.... To the extent that our ideas about legal responsibility are shaped by that ideal, they are governed by a certain political theory of freedom in the modern state, not by a moral refinement of the very conception of responsibility. (Williams 1993: 66)

He also wrote in an appendix to *Shame and Necessity* of 'guilt-centred, autonomous, moralities' in which 'guilt is pictured as an emotion experienced in the face of an abstraction, the moral law, which has become part of the subject himself'. This generates an 'idealised picture' in which 'guilt comes to be represented simply as the attitude of respect for an abstract law, and it then no longer has any special connection with victims' (Williams 1993: 219–22). Note here the concern about abstraction in punishment theory, and the wish to speak in a different mode about the experience of victims. Of course, the modern political theory of punishment pushes in different directions – towards communitarianism, Aristotle, Hegel or consequentialism – and not just what might be thought to be Williams's Kantian target here. But his aim was not just at broadening political theory. It was to take our understanding of punishment's terms to a deeper level, one in which we could understand in human, naturalistic, not merely normative, terms the psychological as well as the moral experience of guilt or being a victim. Modern normative philosophy around issues of guilt and responsibility was political ventriloquy, a philosophical *trahison des clercs*. Williams's argument is severely deflationary for liberal criminal justice theory, emphasising its historical, political, *non-ethical* and fictional nature.

Criminal justice thinking reflects and legitimates state practices,[6] but this leaves two questions. The first concerns what the idea of a deeper, naturalistic basis for guilt means. This needs considerable development, which it receives below but also throughout this book and especially as we develop the account of guilt in Part III. The second question concerns how we understand the ethics in legal practices of blame, guilt and responsibility. Are these *only* the expression of historical and political standpoints, so that they might be abandoned (as Williams appeared to suggest in *Ethics and the Limits of Philosophy*), or might they be reconfigured (as he appeared to suggest in *Shame and Necessity*)? Take the idea of 'the voluntary'. If it is over-emphasised and misrepresented by a peculiar morality, should it be discarded or should it be reworked to do better or even radically different, ethical work? If the latter, how should we take it so as not just to revise the present concept, and how would such a radically reworked concept relate to history and politics, the nature of the state and its law? Williams had no ready answers to these questions. He wrote that it would be better to do without morality as this peculiar institution, but he also wrote that there was a 'much larger question of what needs to be, and what can be, restructured in the light of a reflective and nonmythical understanding of our ethical practices' (Williams 2011: 215). What looks initially like a shut-out reveals something more complicated, a quest to understand how human ethical experience, falsely shaped by the peculiar morality system, might be different.

[6] Compare this with my *Punishment, Responsibility and Justice*, where I link 'criminal justice thinking' as a specific form of thinking to 'identity thinking' in Adorno's work (Norrie 2000).

If this is so, however, it raises a third question. If we could develop a deeper understanding of our moral concepts away from the peculiarities of the morality system, how should this relate to what we have now with its links to state and law? Would it imply their abolition, and, alternatively, if abolition proved presently impossible, how would an ethical practice based on human moral psychology relate to one based on law? Such questions are entailed by Williams's challenge to think through a moral psychology grounded in human nature rather than political artifice. They occupy us in this book and Williams did not provide ready answers. We should begin, however, by sketching out a general position in moral psychology before pursuing it in a particular case.

For Moral Psychology

Williams argues that we need an ethical position that lies beyond the peculiar morality of modern political theory shaped by modern politics, law and the state. What should it look like? He did not work out a full answer and he shifted over time. When writing *Shame and Necessity*, he began to develop the idea of 'moral psychology' or 'a naturalistic psychology of ethics' (Williams 1995: 203). He meant by this an account of ethics that was related to human psychology and nature. Detail was light though the overall direction was clear. Breaking away from the peculiar morality would lead to an ethics directly related to the everyday psychology of human motives, desires and meanings:

> A non-moralised, or less moralised, psychology uses the categories of meaning, reasons, and value, but leaves it open, or even problematical, in what way moral reasons and ethical values fit with other motives and desires, how far they express those other motives, and how far they are in conflict with them. (Williams 1995: 202)

Human beings relate their moral experience to other mental states (meaning, reasons, values, motives or desires), all as part of their general psychology. As we already have seen, Williams believed we best understand a person's ethical life in relation to her general human psychology:

> A truthful ethical life is, and always has been, one that can include our best understanding of our psychological life, and we know that such an understanding is compatible with naturalistic explanation. (Williams 1995: 19–20)

Note the idea of a 'naturalistic' explanation, to which we shall return. Williams is pointing a path here to moral psychology, meaning that ethics are just one part of normal human psychology. Conceding that what this meant was 'not at all perspicuous' (Williams 1995: 203), he related his thought to a psychoanalytical approach. Basic human drives are developed and shaped in the psyche into moral emotions. For example, a relationship is posited between a basic psychology of fear and anger and an elaborate ethics of blame and guilt:

> At the most primitive level, the attitude of the internalised figure is anger, while the reaction of the subject is fear. The fear, most primitively, is *fear at anger*.... From this primitive basis, it is possible, by what is sometimes called 'bootstrapping', to develop the model to allow for reactions that are progressively more structured by social, ethical, or moral notions. So mere fear at mere anger becomes fear of recrimination, and this can develop into a reaction that is restricted to what the subject regards as justified recrimination. (Williams 1993: 219, emphasis added)

The idea in this passage (which appears as an endnote to *Shame and Necessity*) is that there are basic, non-ethical drives like fear which convert primitive psychological forces via social interactions into ethical forms. We thus picture a moral psychology built in human development from biological, psychological and social forces. In a process of mental development involving the mind and society, ethical responses are fashioned and people become moral actors. Biology and history are relevant, but the mind and psyche retain sui generis qualities. In thinking about this idea of a naturalistic moral psychology, three points may help us see what is at stake. They concern, first, a basic question about the method, second, an example of Williams's substantive argument, and third, an anticipatory rejoinder to criticism.

Linking Different Levels

First and briefly, there is a general point about moving from a primitive individual drive and emotion like fear and anger to something more complex, social and ethical, like justified self-anger or self-recrimination (guilt), as in the above quote. It is not apparent from Williams how this occurs. How the forming of the more complex ethical idea operates is clearly important, but what does 'bootstrapping' mean? It looks like a metaphor in place of an explanation.[7] The work needed to be done on how moral emotions emerge from psychological ground states is addressed in the next section.

Identifying Different Underlying Forces

This leads, second, to a substantive point in the same quote, concerning what is linked with what when we connect primitive drives or emotions to complex elements in moral psychology. Williams's observation here is that *fear and anger* underlie guilt and recrimination. This argument will be something I explore later (in Part III on the psychology of guilt). I believe Williams identifies a valid link, but one that misses the main point in how human psychology develops. The complex of emotions around fear, anger, recrimination and guilt is certainly important to the human mind, and also in criminal justice settings.

[7] As per Jonathan Lear: 'it is crucial to recognise that "bootstrapping" does not itself name any determinate psychological phenomena or theory. It is rather *serving as a placeholder* for that theory' (Lear 2004: 519).

Fear and anger, we might say, stalk the penal system's practices as these emotions are directed at offenders as a means of control. Criminal justice *means* to make people feel fearful and bad about themselves, and no doubt often succeeds. Guilt works through anger and fear in citizens who have broken the law, but there is more to human psychology than this. Perhaps the following (somewhat isolated) quote indicates Williams knew this. As before, he builds a moral psychology from basic drives and emotions, but here he finds a different source for internalised moral recrimination:

> As soon as we look at blame not as a uniquely appropriate expression of truly moral judgement, and not, on the other hand, simply as an instrument of social control, but see it as part of a concrete ethical life, we shall be helped to understand the other psychological forces (*such as love, perhaps*) that are needed to make blame possible as a manifestation of the ethical dispositions. (Williams 1995: 16, emphasis added)

Williams's claim here that recrimination and guilt may stem from the basic drive and emotion of love contrasts remarkably with his earlier claim about fear and anger. Two very different moral psychologies jostle with each other here. Importantly, this seems to me also to be true in criminal justice systems. There are ways in which these seek to impose fear, anger and guilt on people who pass through the system and experience these emotions. There are also however people who must deal with self-generated anguish and guilt about having violated another. Many prisoners feel this with regard to serious crimes, even if prisons do not help them deal with it and encourage its denial. They too engage with the criminal justice system, and I think we get nearer to their emotions through the basic human experience of loving identification with another. Should we then build our moral psychology of blame, guilt and recrimination out of fear and anger or out of a basic motivation of love?

Note that this gives rise to a further question. If two different motivations with different kinds of psychological outcomes are possible, how can we accommodate such opposing positions in our analysis? These are fundamental questions of moral psychology to be explored for themselves and their implications in this book. My point here is to note the basic psychological mechanisms Williams links to moral experience and the different kinds of drives and emotions that these open. These need to be explored if moral psychology in a criminal justice setting is to tell.

The Individual and the Social

The third thing to note anticipates an objection that will come from sociologically minded critics of the criminal justice system. It is that any argument from moral psychology is reductive since it locates the problems of criminal justice at the level of the individual. This however would involve misunderstanding. Williams does not seek to read moral psychology simply in individual terms, and nor do I. He relates developing human emotions to broader social settings. His focus in *Shame and Necessity* is on the development of a 'concrete ethical life' which includes interaction between individual psychology and social context. The Greeks emphasised shame over guilt because of the nature of social relations in ancient Greek society. Moral psychology *does* involve individual ethical reactions but not in a reductive, individualised account of ethical life. It locates ethical reactions in individuals, but they always exist in and develop out of social settings. Moral psychology sits between different levels in the building of human being: biology (the basic human drives), psychology (how those drives become shaped and articulated in human minds) and society (how social life interacts with and informs human capacities for mental life). The psychological level in human being is always both individually located *and* socially developed albeit in minds which possess their own sui generis powers. The animal that thinks and loves is inherently a social animal.

We might say that love, fear, anger and guilt are propensities in the human mind arising from basic drives, but how these are expressed in the individual psyche also depends on the social world in which the mind develops. For example, a world in which conflict, exploitation and repression are prominent is likely to be one that lacks kindness in its interactions and relies on fear, anger and self-hate for social control. Conversely, a society that is in its essence consensual and harmonious will encourage relationships that are at their core based on love and mutual respect. The human psyche, grounded in basic drives, accommodates both and develops in different ways as it reacts to the social world about it.

To sum up, the passages quoted earlier about fear, anger and love encapsulate Williams's direction towards moral psychology: the avoidance of the peculiar morality system involving abstract ethical obligation, the identification of grounds of ethical experience in human psychology and the development of such psychology to social settings which generate concrete ethical life. The references to *fear at anger* or *love* as the basic emotion that 'bootstraps' into a moral reaction suggest how a moral psychology might commence, though we need to know what bootstrapping means. The reference to love might seem counter-intuitive with regard to criminal justice, but I shall argue that Williams's brief observation will be vindicated. Developed ethical and psychological emotion includes guilt and blame, but also, I shall argue, forgiveness and other emotions relevant to violation. Love is crucial here but both fear and anger as well as love are important to the moral psychology of individuals in social contexts and thus to the criminal justice system. However, the two basic emotions are very different in their implications and how they sit in the human mind. They inform ethical judgment in very different ways. Of the two, love is the more developmentally important, but we cannot avoid fear and anger as much as we should want to (see below, Chapter 8).

On Naturalism and Ontology

In this section, I explore the underlying theory on which my analysis operates. Williams wrote of the need for a 'naturalistic' moral psychology, a term that is important but means different things to different people. For some, the very idea of linking ethics to human nature will seem fundamentally problematic, to others only obvious. Much depends on what we mean by the term. If naturalism reduces our understanding to something like cause and effect relations in the natural sciences, we will go horribly wrong. In this section, I consider what a naturalistic moral psychology might entail, linking Williams with Roy Bhaskar's work on critical realist philosophy, *The Possibility of Naturalism* (1979), and then introducing thought on psychoanalytic theory on which I draw in the book.

Williams's Naturalism

What did Williams mean in claiming that moral psychology should be 'naturalistic'? Naturalism is sometimes associated with a strongly reductionist tendency to explain all life in terms of physical mechanisms in nature, but this is not what is involved in developing a naturalistic moral psychology. Such a psychology involves explaining how it is possible for human beings 'to live under rules and values and to shape their behaviour in some degree to social expectations' (Williams 2002: 24). Societies vary according to time and place as to what they require of people but living under rules, as Williams has it, involves living in ethical systems according to 'a certain psychology' (Williams 2002: 24). Living in ethical systems presupposes a particular psychological capacity, and a naturalistic approach involves understanding the relationship between that capacity and other psychological dimensions of human beings which make the specifically moral dimension possible. Accordingly, 'the naturalist question about ethics will emerge as the question of how closely the motivations and practices of the ethical are related to other aspects of human psychology' in the context of 'the rest of human nature' (Williams 2002: 26).

These comments from 2002 distinguish naturalistic psychology from reductionisms which deny the importance of moral psychological agency, but they may encourage another reduction, of moral psychological life to the life of a liberal political order. 'Living under rules' sounds uncomfortably close to the peculiar morality against which Williams had earlier railed. Nonetheless, they do affirm the need to take naturalistic human psychology seriously. What might this mean in practice? In the last section, we saw that Williams identified basic human drives or emotions as the grounds on which guilt and blame develop, and this approach reflected a psychoanalytical understanding of the mind. A strong case has been made by Jonathan Lear that the moral psychology Williams put to work in *Shame and Necessity* opens moral philosophy's door to psychoanalysis (Lear 2003, 2004) by linking it to the idea of natural drives and the building of emotional identities in the human psyche. The root of a human being (its ontology – a term explained in what follows) lies in how an animal species with basic drives and developed organic brain-based capacities can develop an advanced psychological level of being through social relationships. This is the underdeveloped basis for Williams's naturalistic moral psychology,[8] and I see it as the starting point for a theoretical critique of criminal justice. Before continuing, however, I want to develop and defend more fully the naturalist position.

Naturalism in the Human Sciences

This takes me to Roy Bhaskar's critical realist account of philosophical naturalism in the social sciences (Bhaskar 1979). Bhaskar's aim was to address the differences between the natural and the social sciences. The latter may be seen as qualitatively different from the former because they deal with meaning and interpretation rather than the explanation of cause and effect. Only the natural sciences operate with a conception of 'natural necessity'. Bhaskar's argument was that it was essential that social sciences acknowledge the centrality of both conscious and unconscious intentions and motives to human agency in explanations of social life. Human meaning, reasons and actions are irreducible to social conditions or causes and integral to social reproduction or change, so the social sciences differ from the natural sciences. This does not however mean one cannot speak of a naturalistic social science, only that naturalism in the social sciences is more complex than in the natural sciences. Reason and meaning represent central features in human life and are the medium through which causation operates. Reasons can be causes so that human meaning is essential to explaining how natural necessity works in the social sciences.

This is crucial for understanding moral psychology's naturalism. Any suitably developed naturalistic account in the social sciences must acknowledge the significance of human meaning and agency and therefore must seek to understand how such agency is possible in social and psychological terms. Bhaskar argued for a series of emergent levels or strata in the constitution of human life from the physical, chemical and biological to the psychological and sociological. Each level is dependent on the lower level for its possibility but emerges

[8] Williams's thinking was not always consistent, shifting elsewhere to what he called 'a realistic, rather than a naturalistic, moral psychology' (Williams 1995: 68). In this usage, Williams's focus moved away from a proto-psychoanalytic approach towards Nietzsche's concept of *ressentiment* as the main support for his critique of morality (Williams 1995: ch 6). Such a commitment cannot satisfy the requirement of naturalism, leading rather to a sceptical approach towards human motivations, a 'hermeneutics of suspicion' rather than an account based on human nature. 'Realism' means here scepticism about truth claims rather than naturalism in the sense of identifying things that are true about human being. Scepticism is generally good and wise, but a moral psychology such as Williams canvassed in his work on *Shame and Necessity* offers a different level of critique, one based on the possibility of naturalism.

from it with its own powers and potentials. These can only exist at the higher constitutive level. Thus, mind is *emergent* from embodied matter, requires such matter in order to exist, enjoys a range of psychic capacities only possible at its own level and requires social interaction so that its capacities may be developed and exercised. Linked to the different ontological strata of human being is the need for a range of sciences to explore them. Different sciences must address explanation at the physical and chemical levels of human being, as well as at physiological, psychological and sociological levels to explain how human life operates at higher levels. We also need such sciences to understand how these different levels interconnect to produce individual and social outcomes, generating the need for interdisciplinarity in our studies and explanations.

A naturalistic moral psychology must accordingly be able to make sense of the psychological level in human social life as the level at which meaning, emotion and other psychological features exist. That level is emergent from the biological drives given to humans and is related to the social and cultural relations which activate its possibilities. Explaining human agency thus involves two things. It involves first understanding how this level of the psyche is related to the biological level out of which it is emergent and to the social level with which it interacts in complex ways (Lear 1990; Norrie 2020). Second, and explored in this book, it involves identifying how a sui generis level of moral psychology links to general capacities at the psychological level in a science of the psyche.

Naturalism and Human Psychology

This sketch of how we should explore and explain human being in naturalistic terms then takes us from a general philosophical naturalism to the kind of specifically psychological naturalism found in the work of Freud and his metapsychology. Here my debt is to Freud and to writers broadly linked to the 'object relations' approach. Writers like Jessica Benjamin, Melanie Klein, Jonathan Lear, Hans Loewald and Donald Winnicott appear at different points, though the sources for my main argument in Part III are Loewald and Klein. In *Love and Its Place in Nature* (1990), Lear shows how Sigmund Freud translates biological drives into psychological states with their own emergent properties. Mind develops out of matter in a process whereby 'the flesh becomes word' (Lear 1990: xii). The title of his book indicates two things. The first is that human psychology in Freud's understanding is rooted in a naturalistic process which sees human psychic motivations as emergent from natural biological processes to which they are irreducible. This kind of psychological approach aligns with Bhaskar's critical realist approach and is well-placed to explain Williams's reflection on how moral psychology should be built up from basic motivations like love or anger and fear (Norrie 2020).

Second, this work is important substantively because it depicts *love* as at the core of human nature. Lear argues that love, also referred to by Freud as libido,

Eros and the life instinct, was the key to his metapsychology. Drawing on Loewald, Lear offers a bridge between moral philosophy and psychology constructed out of love. Love in Freud is 'a basic developmental force in nature' (Lear 1990: 12) which drives the human psyche as it develops capacities for a range of emotions and rational capacities. In this book, I link this to Jessica Benjamin's *The Bonds of Love* (1988), her feminist psychoanalytical account of the developing mother–child relation and the possibility of autonomous and responsible personhood emerging from a loving relation. Returning to Williams, we saw that he suggests love may underlie the analysis of blame and guilt (recrimination). To those I would add the whole gamut of psychological states associated with situations in which one person has wronged, harmed or violated another: grief, responsibility (in a psychological sense), forgiveness, mourning, denial and freedom. Humans are capable of possessing these developed moral emotions because their emotional lives have evolved out of strong basic emotions formed from libido or love. Becoming a person with moral emotions emerges from processes of social interaction with parents and others by means of which one becomes 'enformed'. A key psychological mechanism here is that of identification with another, from which we learn, and from which we see the other as like us, and with an important ethical connection to us. From this derives the ability to achieve a sense of responsibility and agency, and the reflexive autonomy to relate it to the contexts from which we were formed.

What though of that other strand of thought in Williams, concerning fear and anger? These too, I shall argue, are present in Freud's naturalist account of human emotions, and I shall link what he says to Melanie Klein's account of love and anger in infanthood as another important basis on which to build a naturalistic account of moral psychology. It will turn out to be important to understand the relationship between fear and anger on the one hand and love on the other in a developing moral psychology in which love proves the basis for mature emotional reactions while anger plays an often negative role as an early or primitive reaction which we cannot always escape. Regrettably, I shall argue that modern criminal justice systems permit significantly greater importance to primitive than to mature moral emotions. Indeed, the argument of this book will be that a reversal of this prioritisation provides a different vision of what we now call criminal justice might entail.

Naturalistic Moral Psychology as Human Ontology

To tie these elements together, one way of unifying a philosophical account of naturalism with a naturalist moral psychology is through the idea of human ontology (being) as involving a *natural kind*. The human species has much in common with other animal species but also differs. Williams suggests that the significant difference between humans and other animals is they are capable of 'non-genetic learning', though this seems too broad. Other animals learn by way of cognitive process and experience too. Nonetheless, as he says, '[e]very species has an ethological description' (Williams 2002: 23), and we could say that key features in the human species being would include psychological powers that are cognitive, intellectual, reflexive, emotional and moral. An element central to human experience, certainly in relation to violation, but also more generally, would be the ability to think metaphysically about the human condition. This is Donald MacKinnon's 'need to speak about the transcendent, about the human spirit and the infinite' (Mac Cumhaill and Wiseman 2022: 91) mentioned earlier.[9] Such a need reflects all the other psychological powers and is a key element in being a metaphysical animal, one that can think and love. It does not however come alone, but as part of a package of potentials that stem from our animal nature.

However ultimately described, these powers make the human species a natural kind. They give it a specific ontology. Human powers are specific to humans, existing differently in them compared to other species. Powers for psychological growth in human babies exist as potentials which may or may not be exercised but exist differently when compared to the powers and potentials of other species. They stem from our biology and are channelled through our genetic capacity into our social animality as beings capable of thought and love. Human ontology involves the latent capacity to generate psychological out of biological life, and as part of that, ethical life. It does this in social and cultural settings which 'bring out' the potential of each human individual to be a powerful particular. Of course, social and cultural settings vary in their ability to enable this to happen, but each human infant represents its own 'generative mechanism' capable with the aid of other human beings of developing a complex moral psychology and acting on it.

This idea of the specific ontology of human being as a natural kind with specific generative powers that are psychological provides the foundation on which to develop a naturalistic moral psychology built on basic human emotions like love (and anger/fear) and leading to complex and differentiated ethical outcomes.[10] This is the psychological ontology of the animal that thinks and loves. But how does this ontological foundation for a naturalistic moral psychology relate to criminal justice? It does so by way of critique, to which I now turn.

On Critique

In considering the nature of humankind, we arrive at the possibility of a critique of criminal justice, but I need to explain why. How does an account of human ontology feed into the possibility of critique, and how does it relate to

[9] See text at Note 2.

[10] In this way, moral psychology works as both the ground for emergent ethical experience to be possible and a way of describing how that experience develops, through specific categories like grief, guilt, denial, mourning and forgiveness, and not missing the ways in which these may be expressed such as through metaphysical thought.

different kinds of critique? To answer these questions, we need to be clear on what we mean by critique and how it relates to the field of criminal justice.

Six Kinds of Critique

Ontological critique is initially part of a group of six (eventually seven) kinds of critique relevant to legal and philosophical enquiry. I begin by setting these out and showing where the specifically ontological sits in the range of critiques. (1) An *internal critique* takes principles identified as existing in the legal field and applies them to that field. (2) A *reconstructive critique* is dissatisfied with existing principles, finding them to be inadequately identified or developed. It reconstructs such principles as the basis for reforming the field. Broadly speaking, internal and reconstructive critiques draw upon concepts or practices immanent to the field, but the idea of (3) an *immanent critique* per se involves more, identifying elements perhaps systematically obscured or blocked in the existing field. Such elements may be suppressed and when identified may disclose deep-seated contradictions constitutive of the field. These are emergent from theory and/or practice and may be unseen by participants. They may involve a theory/practice split. Immanent critique is associated with finding something which undermines the existing claims and pretensions of the field, calling into question the possibility of internal and reconstructive critiques. Things are not as they seem. What was thought to be inevitable and taken for granted as such is not necessarily so. Uncovering what was missed, immanent critique identifies important new aspects of the object under study.

Immanent critique in this strong sense abuts (4) *ontological critique*. What has been shown to be hidden in the field now constitutes a part of it, and this deepens our understanding of the thing under investigation. Immanent critique develops by disclosing a more complex sense of an object's being, that is, its ontology. Next, there is (5) *explanatory critique*, which develops the findings of immanent and ontological critique to identify the reasons *why* important things about the object under study were systematically missed. This may be because, for example, there was a social, political or psychological interest in seeing things one way rather than another. Conceptions of ideology in Marxism and phantasy in psychoanalysis are relevant to this. We have here a logical chain of critiques. Something important that has been missed and exposed (immanent critique) is revealed as a further truth about the object under investigation (ontological critique) and it is possible to explain why it was missed (explanatory critique). Following these, there is then the possibility of (6) *emancipatory critique*, which takes what has been discovered as hidden and important in the sequence of immanent–ontological–explanatory critiques, frees up our understanding of what is at stake and seeks to show how the world could be changed by enacting what was systematically or structurally suppressed. These critiques thus combine to form an immanent–ontological–explanatory–emancipatory axis in critical activity. They operate in sequence by breaking free from and moving beyond the more simple internal-reconstructive approach, which stays with what is given.

Williams's Critique

Six different critiques (with a seventh promised) may seem a challenge, but in fact these play out in Williams's account of the peculiar morality in a straightforward way. Williams was an ambivalent theorist, but at his boldest he was not interested in an internal or reconstructive critique, at least if the latter stays with or tries to renew the existing materials.[11] His work is more squarely in the other kinds of critique: there is something missing and deeply wrong with how morality is formulated, and the search is to find out why this might be. This involves analysing systematic defects in a particular kind of community. He is also interested, as we have seen, in what really underlies issues of moral recrimination (fear and anger, love), thus taking him into moral psychology. The method is essentially based on *immanent* detection and *ontological* exploration. An *explanation* is then to be found both in the workings of the modern liberal state and its moral grammar of voluntariness and in an underlying human nature which needs to be explored. Humankind would be freer (*emancipated*) without the 'peculiar' moral system and if a naturalist moral psychology was given fuller rein. I do not claim that Williams saw or developed his work significantly in these terms, but this sequence of critiques (immanent–ontological–explanatory–emancipatory) is implicit in his work on moral psychology in the late 1980s and early 1990s.

Critique and Criminal Justice

The sequence of critiques in Williams's work helpfully introduces what a critical project around criminal justice might entail. I will be working with the immanent–ontological–emancipatory–explanatory critical axis described here. Relating different critiques to the normative and historical modes of thinking about criminal justice discussed earlier, the liberal, normatively assertive, oughtificatory approach follows the routes of internal and reconstructive critique. It looks for principles that it finds are present in legal practice and seeks to rationalise these or develop them better to formulate principles and understanding of the criminal justice field. On the other hand, those who develop a critical historical method are interested in forms of immanent and explanatory critique. They look for patterns of systematic failure in legal thinking and the normative political approach which seeks to rationalise it. They question its ability to see how the law really operates, finding contradictions which are otherwise explained away. They then seek historical explanations

[11] His final work (Williams 2002) which draws on Nietzsche and social contractarianism is more in the way of reconstructive critique.

as to how these forms of law evolved and why they are maintained. My own earlier work largely follows this pattern (Norrie 1991, 2000, 2014) of immanent and explanatory critique. Now, I wish to complete the critical project by filling out the ontological and emancipatory implications of the earlier critique. I do this by developing a naturalistic moral psychology of the kind gestured at by Williams to set against criminal justice theory and practice.

Here is a simplified illustration. In the orthodox normative view, we have a model of the responsible subject who is entitled to be blamed and punished for freely willed violations of law. We have a range of normative concepts in both philosophy (e.g. retributive or rights-based accounts of punishment) and more strictly legal theory (e.g. the requirements for mens rea and actus reus, a guilty mind and act) which rest on this premise. As Williams suggested, they are all broadly related to the idea of what it means to be a voluntary, and therefore blameworthy, agent. *Immanent critique* picks apart the existing model of the responsible subject and the wrong done and finds it wanting and contradictory. *Ontological critique* suggests that there is a truer account in moral psychology of how humans may feel when they violate or are violated by another. Against the moral grammar of law, an alternative moral language stemming from naturalistic moral psychology is developed. This is the basis for exploring and explaining why false, ideological or phantastic ('peculiar') forms of thinking and practice dominate the field (*explanatory critique*). It is also the basis for identifying different and better ways of dealing with people in situations of violation, as either victims or perpetrators, and this is an *emancipatory critique* for such people and for society as a whole.

Ethically Real/Institutionally Critical ('ERIC')

We are almost but not quite done. There is a seventh critique which stems from the previously discussed 'immanent-ontological-explanatory-emancipatory' axis, which I shall call (7) *institutional critique.* The aim is to use the development of a naturalistic moral psychology in actual institutional settings to provide a standpoint from which one can assess what legal and philosophical principles reflected in institutions achieve in practice. Of course, actually existing criminal justice institutions deal with human beings so they have some relationship to the psychology of mind and action, but a fuller understanding of human moral psychology may reveal how criminal justice theory and practice fail because it excludes elements of that psychology (hence Williams's sense of its 'peculiarity'). The stage is set by ontological critique (what humans and their moral psychology are like) for an institutional critique of actually existing legal and moral forms.

An ontology adequate to the critique of legal institutions will do two things. First, it will establish its (ontological) basis in naturalistic moral psychology, generating a moral language adequate to the experience of people who inflict or suffer violation. Second, it will relate this to how existing institutional legal forms operate in social settings. Combining these, it will produce an understanding of the legal and moral institutional field that brings together the *ethically real* (because based on a naturalistic account of human ontology and moral psychology) and the *institutionally critical* (because showing the limits of existing legal and moral forms and what lies beyond them). This Ethically Real/Institutionally Critical approach provides a useful summary acronym (ERIC) that I will use in various parts of the book to speak about this seventh important critique. An ERIC critique represents the point of purchase between an understanding of what is and what could be.

In this section, I have identified seven kinds of critique. The focus has been on looking at how these are reflected in the standard normative and historical approaches, and, in developing the latter, to bring out the full potential of critique. In drawing these seven forms out, I can now identify the two sides of my approach in this work: to be *ethically realistic* (through an ontological critique based on moral psychology) and *institutionally critical* (relating ontological to institutional critique). To do so also involves drawing on immanent and explanatory methods and emancipatory themes. The sequence of critiques in the critical approach may seem daunting but could be summarised more simply by relating it to the five brief questions introduced earlier in the chapter: (1) What is wrong with existing criminal justice concepts and practices? This involves an immanent critique. (2) What is the nature of the human agency, suffering and violation to which they relate, and relate badly? This involves an ontological critique. (3) Why do we remain stuck with what we have? This takes us to an explanatory critique. (4) What could make things better for all concerned? This involves an emancipatory critique. (5) Given where we are, how do we relate critically to actually existing criminal justice practices? This involves an institutional in-the-light-of an ontological and ethical (an ERIC) critique.

The Road to Love

I have been exploring a critical method for thinking about criminal justice that has emphasised ontological critique, but what would be its substantive starting point? We saw that Williams was ambivalent between anger generating fear and love as the root of guilt. These represented possible base elements behind blame and guilt which become developed ('bootstrapped' is his term) into moral categories like for example 'justified recrimination'. I suggested that both love and anger will play a part in establishing a moral psychology and language to deal with violation and its consequences. I now want to argue that an ontology of love, developed through moral psychology, lies at the core of how humans react to violation. It is the basis for an ethically real critical account. I accept that we must also make sense of the role of emotions like fear and anger which seem to point away from love. We must account for both, but my starting point is an ontology of love.

Making this argument is in large part the work of this book. However, I want to introduce the topic by at least sketching how love came to be central to the argument. A way in involved thinking through that centrepiece of any modern account of moral guilt, Hannah Arendt's *Eichmann in Jerusalem* (1964). I linked this, oddly it may seem, to a more recent and 'domestic' pair of criminal law cases on mercy killing that came before the English and Welsh courts in the first decade of this century. Together, these cases on good and evil gave me an initial track to love by thinking about how its presence or absence underlay them.

Good and Evil

The route involved Arendt's claim about the 'banality of evil', that evil under the Nazis had an everyday, accepted quality which rendered it banal. The Nazis, she said, felt they did no wrong. That evil could be described as banal is of course controversial, and subject to misunderstanding, but the controversy seems to hide a prior question. What did Arendt mean not by 'banality' but by 'evil'?

If we wish to understand evil, we should couple it with a discussion of its opposite, good. When I was thinking about Arendt, two cases had just made their way through the English criminal justice system dealing with mothers involved in the mercy killing of their children.[12] I initially examined these cases in terms of the law's discomfort at deploying mens rea terms like intention to establish culpability. The cases varied in detail and outcome but these mothers had both claimed to act with the intention to kill while possessing a good, even admirable motive for their actions. Law's abstract, formal morality expressed in mens rea terms struggled to address situations where an actor's intention was clear but her motive was said to be good. This was a situation where law's 'peculiar' morality in Williams's terms, its 'morality of form' of intention and voluntariness in my own (Norrie 2000, 2014), collided with a parent's loving commitment to do best by their child. The outcome in Kay Gilderdale's case in particular depended not on stating and applying the law but on judge and jury taking positions against it. Law indicated conviction but the judge bridled and the jury refused to convict. Both relied on an underlying moral judgment that the defendant had acted from an essentially good motive whatever the law of intention said. The analysis focused on a tension between legal form and moral substance in legal practice (Norrie 2011, 2017c: ch 5), but it raised a question: what was meant by 'good' in such a case?

Underlying Good and Evil

How can the cases of Kay Gilderdale and Adolf Eichmann be compared? In moral terms, they are starkly different, yet they raise a similar question: what

[12] The cases of Frances Inglis and Kay Gilderdale, reported in *Guardian*, 21 and 26 January 2010. The detail and different outcomes in these cases is discussed in Norrie 2011, 2017c: ch 5.

do the opposed substantive terms good and evil mean? It is tempting to think such concepts represent raw ethical primitives open only to subjective assessment, or that they disclose dogmatic religious commitments. They seemed to me however to lead to a deeper legal enquiry than we usually pursue. From the point of view of ethical experience, I began to think what such categories might say about human being. Behind discussions of good and evil, one could find ethical values relating to real human powers concerning freedom, solidarity and flourishing (Norrie 2016, 2017c: ch 8). Possibilities for human freedom and flourishing are of course identified as goods by many philosophers. Solidarity involves the good of commitment to another even at serious cost to oneself. In Gilderdale's case, both judge and jury took the view that hers was an essentially good act in loving solidarity with her daughter's tragic wish to end her life. What lay behind the good act was that the mother had acted out of love, loving identification or loving solidarity, with her daughter. With a sense of real loss and serious legal risk to herself, the mother's good act had come from a sense of loving commitment. It was this expression of human love that the law's formal categories struggled to address.

What of evil? Mercy killing from genuine loving commitment is the longest possible way from Nazi genocide, yet there is an underlying ontological continuity. The former embodies the highest forms of human freedom, flourishing and solidarity by acting out of love or loving identification. The latter involving the concentration and death camp attacks the most basic forms of freedom and solidarity. The camp inmate is stripped of all respect. The slaughter of children in front of their parents is the denial of the very possibility of loving identification. Behind the evil act lies the complete negation of love, care and solidarity with another. Here, loving identification with another is again at stake, but this time by its most complete repudiation (Norrie 2016, 2017c: ch 8).

Looking at these very different cases concerning good and evil, love began to seem like the elemental key to human moral being, the plausible object to be investigated as the ground on which ethical categories are built.[13] Thinking this way spurred me to explore those psychoanalytic writers Jessica Benjamin and Jonathan Lear, mentioned earlier, who had written of the central role of love in human development. Of course, the love of a mother for her child is a specific form of love, and it might not be obvious how this should be related to conduct in other relationships. Nonetheless, here is a form of love which suggests an indication of its general significance. When I began to explore the moral psychology of violation, as in Chapter 5, dealing with *The Forgiveness Project*, I found that it was often the mothers of children who had been killed who spoke

[13] A second route to love involved Karl Jaspers's account of metaphysical guilt which I have used previously to explain why someone like Eichmann who cannot see that he has done wrong can be held to moral account. Jaspers's understanding of metaphysical guilt as involving a universal responsibility for, and solidarity with, the other links up with an understanding of universal love (see Norrie 2017c: chs 7, 10). I return to this in Chapter 4.

most clearly about how love related to violation. However, all I am doing for now is explaining my route into love; how I followed it is the work of this book.

Critique and the Metaphysical Animal

We have moved from consideration of an impasse in criminal justice theory between normative and critical historical accounts to consider a different and novel way of developing a critique. The argument has focused on Williams's account of the 'peculiar' nature of ethics deployed in the modern 'morality system' and pursued his suggestion that a moral psychology based on a naturalistic understanding of what human beings are like would be a better way of thinking about what it means to violate or be violated by another. This idea of basing our understanding of violation on a grasp of what it means to be human takes us to ontology and to ontological critique as a pivotal moment in a sequence of four critiques, moving from immanent to explanatory to ontological and then to emancipatory. This then provides the possibility of a further ethically real/ institutionally critical (ERIC) position which brings together the fruits of ontological naturalism and ethical realism.

The starting point for this moral psychology is the human animal which thinks and loves, and which is capable of ethical thought. To be human is to be a metaphysical animal. A human ontology of love underlies our efforts to make moral sense of the world, though we have noted that other emotions such as fear and anger can act as drivers. How all this plays out through the language of violation and through the law and criminal justice is explored in what follows. It will take us to a position where we can develop a critical position on criminal justice and punishment as they standardly operate in our penal system and make a theoretical case for something rather different. To identify the human as the metaphysical animal is eventually to argue for what I shall call, later in this book, a deep or tendential abolition.

Part I
Two Routes Beyond Political Theory

Introduction to Part I: Two Beginnings

I wanted to think critically about the ethics of criminal justice in a way that went beyond the standard terms, whether these were of normative political theory or, in the critical field, of historical critique. I started with Bernard Williams's account of modern legal and political morality as a 'peculiar' practice. This is an ethical and historical approach which chimed with my own previous work, but which needed developing. My springboard was the thought that the key to criminal justice ethics might be understanding love as a natural human emotion. More than that, it could be the basis for thinking about the human being as a 'metaphysical animal'. Linked to a sense of human being in its naturalistic form, love could be the ethical basis for criminal justice: a matter of basic drives which transmute into emotional feelings and philosophical thoughts. It could provide an understanding per Jonathan Lear of 'the mystery of the flesh made word' (Lear 1990: xii; Norrie 2020). Human beings would be animals with natural psychological powers to think and act according to a metaphysical understanding of themselves, their place in the world and how they ought to act. Such metaphysical powers would be grounded in human metapsychology making the human a metaphysical animal, one that thinks and loves.

From here, I was drawn to two different starting points. One, the young Hegel's inspiring account of violation, fate and love, was dominated by metaphysics in the sense of metaphysical ethics (Chapter 2). The other, Melanie Klein's account of love as a complex natural feature of human development, was based on Freudian metapsychology. I put this together with Jessica Benjamin's account of how subjects develop through recognition in her *The Bonds of Love* (Benjamin 1988). I drew on Klein and Benjamin to think about guilt as a moral and psychological experience emerging out of complex love, recognition and misrecognition (Chapter 3). Through these two different starting points, there emerges the metaphysical animal that thinks and loves, understood both in ethical and metapsychological terms. The two approaches are not at this stage synthesised; eventually, I will see the latter as constituting the ground which makes the former possible for the human animal. These chapters work as two distinct prototypes for developing an overall human ontology as the basis for naturalistic moral psychology.

Whether through the young Hegel or Klein and Benjamin, I wanted to establish naturalistic ethics that would enable the critique of theories that rationalise and defend existing institutional ('peculiar') practices despite their manifest deficiencies. These were my first efforts to build an ethically real and institutionally critical (ERIC) approach out of the range of available critiques mentioned in Chapter 1. Chapter 2 came to me ready-made, as it were, since the young Hegel's contrast of love and law could be used as a powerful ethical critique of his own older self in *The Philosophy of Right*. Chapter 3 submits the idea of guilt in modern normative legal and political theory to the moral psychological critique I develop from Klein and Benjamin. These two essays in moral psychological critique, in either ethical or metapsychological vein, are prototypes for a new approach to dealing with violation. They point beyond the law, blame and punishment towards healing and reconciliation for an animal that thinks and loves as the basis for a critique of our actually existing institutional practices.

2

Young Hegel, Love and the Critique of Punishment

> ...the trespasser['s] ... feeling of a life disrupted become[s] a longing for what has been lost.
>
> GWF Hegel (1948: 230)

> ... one of the most ... corrupt maxims ... [is] to imagine bad subjects with well-meaning hearts.
>
> GWF Hegel (2008: 124)

This chapter pursues an historical route to upturn a standard assumption and find an early prototype for my approach. Georg Wilhelm Friedrich Hegel is recognised as a founder of the modern retributive theory of punishment in his *Philosophy of Right* (1821; Hegel 2008). There he synthesises an ethical understanding of the rational free will with modern legal, political and social institutions. Hegel shows how a rational individual's will comes to confront the reality of other such wills and to see the need to reconcile its freedom with theirs. Of course, his account of retributive punishment as a right demanded by the criminal looks psychologically unrealistic, for how many actually demand it? It reveals however the profoundly political nature of his theory. It is the political logic of living under modern social and institutional conditions that is explained, with law and punishment playing a central role. This makes Hegel's retributive theory of punishment a prime example of modern normative political and legal theory.

As a young radical of the 1790s, Hegel had taken a different position on the nature of crime and punishment. In his early so-called theological writings, he focused on the ethical and metaphysical nature of violation and its consequences for both perpetrator and victim. In *The Spirit of Christianity and Its Fate* (1798; Hegel 1948), we find stark criticism of law and punishment for denying the human in an ethics of violation. Hegel's ideas anticipate the kind of moral psychology I wish to develop. This chapter is therefore an essay in interpretive reversal. Rather than seeing Hegel's mature work as resolving the problems of his youth, the young Hegel offers an approach that is validly critical of what he would go on to write, even if he would later reject the earlier view. In a psychological sense, it is the young Hegel who offers the beginnings of what I will call mature philosophical insight through a moral psychology of guilt, violation and love. Writing before moral psychology could develop its metapsychological register (i.e. before the time of psychoanalysis), the young Hegel nonetheless introduced a metaphysics of violation for the animal that thinks and loves. He casts an anticipatorily critical eye on how he would later view violation as legal punishment and political theory in the *Philosophy of Right*. Retrieving the early 'failed' philosophy and opposing it critically to his later 'success' offers a prototype of the 'ethically real institutionally critical' (ERIC) approach outlined in Chapter 1.

The two quotations at the head of the chapter mark the difference between early and late Hegel. The first from *The Spirit of Christianity and Its Fate* notes the role of moral conscience in bringing about reconciliation after violation and without law, while the second from the *Philosophy of Right* justifies legal punishment by denying the relevance of moral conscience in crime. The second position repudiates the first, so what did this change in view signify and how should we take it today? This chapter has three main sections. In the first, I begin by laying out Hegel's early account of love and violation and how in metaphysical terms a violator's guilt is overcome. I consider the negative role law plays in such a process. In the second main section, I consider the place of the victim of a violation in this account and seek to remedy a weakness in Hegel's position. Having set out the young Hegel's position, I then contrast it in the third main section with Hegel's 'mature' work on retributivism in modern political and legal theory. I then draw some conclusions concerning criticism of criminal justice from young Hegel's position in terms of an ERIC standpoint.

Love against Law: Young Hegel on Guilt, Violation and Reconciliation

We know Hegel as a founder of the modern classical retributive theory of punishment, the political and legal theorist of punishment par excellence in his *Philosophy of Right* (PR).[1] There is however a young Hegel who wrote profoundly and movingly of the moral psychology of violation, which he called 'trespass', of the grief it caused and the reconciliation it required. This account of violation and its relationship to love, ethics and law appears in *The Spirit of Christianity and Its Fate* (SCF).[2] In this section, I consider this early thought starting with the general contrast Hegel creates between an ethics of love and life and one incorporating law and punishment. I then consider one main development of that account, an understanding of guilt at violation and reconciliation.

[1] For recent attempts to develop a Hegelian account of punishment, see Brudner 2009 and Brooks 2021. On Brudner's approach, see my review in Norrie 2017c: ch 6.

[2] The title indicates the strong Christian element of Hegel's early thought. God is the locus of unity and wholeness. The key example therein of the beautiful soul who submits and forgives is Jesus (Norrie 2005). My view is that the young Hegel's account of violation, grief and reconciliation has moral significance beyond its particular religious setting.

Love, Life and Law

In SCF, Hegel seeks to move beyond the Kantian division between duty and inclination through a further unifying element that transcends both. This is of course an enduring theme in Hegel, but in the early thought the englobing element is not reason or rational spirit. Rather it is provided by the 'richness and fullness of life', a love of its wholeness beyond all separation. Separations include those established by law and rights, which Hegel sees as on the side of Kantian division, and therefore a sign of an incomplete life. Love is a 'sensing of life … which finds itself again' leading to a sense of reconciliation and living in unity and wholeness. This is a human being's ultimate 'fate' (Hegel 1948: 232), and it is linked to love as 'the complement of the virtues' by which 'all one-sidedness, all exclusiveness, all restricted virtues, are annulled' (Hegel 1948: 246). To love 'is to feel one's self in the 'all' of life, with no restrictions, in the infinite' (Hegel 1948: 247). A life lived in love contrasts with a life under law for it has a 'much richer, more living, fullness that so poor a thing as a law is nothing for it at all' (Hegel 1948: 215).

When a crime has been committed, its underlying truth is that of violation, that a trespass has occurred. Viewed as an aspect of life and love, trespass goes beyond crime and punishment for in it there lies 'a destruction of nature' rather than an infraction of law. This cannot stand, for nature expresses life as love and unity so that violation creates 'as much destruction in what destroys as in what is destroyed' (Hegel 1948: 225). Love goes deeper than law and 'does not leave the judge to apportion its rights; it reconciles itself to its enemy with no regard to right whatever' (Hegel 1948: 216). To see the difference, consider how Hegel treats the command 'Thou shalt not kill'. As a Kantian universal maxim imposing a duty on every rational being, this should be contrasted with the command of Jesus, which 'sets the higher genius of reconcilability (a modification of love)' in place. Reconciliation after trespass acknowledges and restores wholeness. It involves a higher obligation that makes Kantian duty superfluous[3] because of 'the wealth of living relations with the individuals … with whom it comes into connection'. It gives a 'so much richer, more living, fullness' such that 'so poor a thing as a law is nothing for it at all' (Hegel 1948: 215). This contrast between abstract universal law (duty) and the concretely universal fullness of life and love challenges the retributive theory of punishment:

> An eye for an eye, a tooth for a tooth, say the laws. Retribution and its equivalence with crime is the sacred principle of all justice, the principle on which any political order must rest. But Jesus makes a general demand on his hearers to surrender their rights, to lift themselves above the whole sphere of justice or injustice by love, for in love there vanish not only rights but also the feeling of inequality and the hatred of enemies which this feeling's imperative demand for equality implies. (Hegel 1948: 218)

[3] 'In reconcilability the law loses its form, the concept is displaced by life; but what reconcilability thereby loses in respect of the universality … is only a seeming loss and a genuine infinite gain…' (Hegel 1948: 215).

In strict contrast with what he would later write in the PR, the law's retribution and punishment's 'equivalence with crime' does *not* reconcile the individual with his wrongdoing. Law can record and punish wrongdoing but finds no way to move beyond violation. When the law has done to the perpetrator 'just what he did himself, it then lets go, but it still withdraws to a threatening attitude; it has not lost its shape or been made friendly…' (Hegel 1948: 227). Law produces an impasse, an unproductive repetition, a 'bad infinity' without progression. A crime was committed and punished: bring on the next criminal – and repeat. A way forward must reach beyond this, to the qualitatively higher level of the fullness of life or love. This can bring about reconciliation beyond *and despite* the law. This, it will be said, sounds highly aspirational and we need to develop what a life lived in love means and how it relates to wrongdoing. I turn now to what Hegel says about the position of the person who violates another.

The Perpetrator: From Violation to Guilt

In serious violations, the reactions of both the perpetrator and the victim are at stake. The perpetrator has broken the law, but more deeply, has changed his relationship to life. This starts as a profound sense of unease at what he has done and which comes back to haunt him. His sense of himself is placed in question and he is forced to engage with what he has done. This may lead through anguish to the possibility of reconciliation. The perpetrator of a serious wrong may[4] experience it as a breach of universal order which profoundly affects his future. The idea of a 'fate' or destiny that does not measure wrongdoing in legal terms is important.[5] A killer destroys the fabric of his own life, turning fate as the promise of his own being, his trajectory through life and his sense of wholeness, against himself, making of it an 'enemy'. His transgression rebounds horribly so that the person slain turns from a fellow human being into a 'terrifying ghost which vindicates every branch of life and lets loose its Eumenides' (Hegel 1948: 229).[6] In killing his victim, the killer has undone himself. The proof lies in

[4] Hegel is describing a phenomenology of violation, guilt and reconciliation, a plausible account of a perpetrator's moral psychology. This does not commit him to claim that the process described must happen, only that it may, depending on the concrete experience of the perpetrator.

[5] Fate for Hegel stems from a number of sources and has different elements (Inwood 1992: 101–3). Fate happens to a person, but that person can also to a degree determine it. It is linked to an overarching ethical power whose workings are obscure but whose outcomes are concrete for the individual concerned. The individual acts on their fate in a way that can lead to inner growth and character formation. It aligns their development with what they are and can come to be, but this is in line with universal possibilities for them.

[6] The Furies, female spirits of justice and vengeance in Greek mythology. They are also referred to in PR (Hegel 2008: 106), but there they serve as a rhetorical embellishment to rational retribution. In SCF, spiritual turmoil in a deeply troubled conscience is really meant.

> the fact that the disembodied spirit of the injured life comes on the scene against the trespass, just as Banquo who came as a friend to Macbeth was not blotted out when he was murdered but immediately thereafter took his seat, not as a guest at the feast, but as an evil spirit. The trespasser intended to have to do with another's life, but he has only destroyed his own, for life is not different from life, since life dwells in the single Godhead. In his arrogance he has destroyed indeed, but only the friendliness of life; he has perverted life into an enemy. (Hegel 1948: 229)[7]

Hegel's language is allusive and literary, indeed Shakespearian, but what he is getting at is the sense of being undone that a troubled conscience experiences as it wrestles with guilt.[8] Such unease has a cause, however, and it presses towards resolution in the shape of reconciliation.

From Guilt to Reconciliation – Without Law

For the young Hegel, reconciliation has nothing to do with law. Law is no more than 'the lack of life, defective life appearing as a power', while the feeling of guilt at crossing the universal order goes deeper, becoming the place and beginning of redemption. Human life can 'heal its wounds again [as] the severed, hostile life … return[s] into itself again and annul[s] the bungling achievement of a trespass' (Hegel 1948: 230). This has nothing to do with law or punishment, for what the perpetrator feels is a profound sense of loss and yearning to put himself back to rights with the world. This is the rediscovery of the person's fate as a longing to rebalance life after its disruption through a process of grieving and redemption where the perpetrator may 'hold himself back [in order] to prolong his bad conscience and feeling of grief … until his longing for reunion [with life] springs from the deepest recesses of his soul' (Hegel 1948: 231–32). There can be a 'sensing of life … which finds itself again', and this reunion with life 'is love, and in love fate is reconciled' (Hegel 1948: 232).

The upshot is a move away from the division of the self and back to wholeness of the spirit. A sense of the universal in life is satisfied, 'since the trespasser has sensed as injured in himself the same life that he has injured' (Hegel 1948: 232). In properly grieving for what he has done, 'there is no longer anything hostile in the man, and the deed remains at most as a soulless carcass lying in the charnel-house of actualities, in memories' (Hegel 1948: 232). Hegel has developed here a metaphysics of violation, guilt and reconciliation which

[7] Compare Dostoyevsky's *Crime and Punishment* (1997: 334): 'Did I really kill the old woman? No, it was myself I killed! – it was myself I have irrevocably ruined.' See also the case of Anwar Congo discussed in Chapter 9.

[8] Compare Dostoyevsky again (1997: 74): 'He suffered cruelly from this conviction, that everything, even memory, even the most elementary prudence, was abandoning him. "Can this be the punishment already beginning? Indeed, indeed, it is!"' In modern theory of punishment, compare this with Herbert Morris's description of psychosomatic guilt as feeling 'rotten, depleted of energy, tense' (Morris 1976: 99): for discussion see Chapters 6 and 7.

centres moral experience on the inner ethical world of the perpetrator and not his relationship to political and legal processes. Law here sets form in the way of substance, establishing a block to be overcome. Love of self and the other, fate as moral engagement with what one has done, life as a wholeness that can be destroyed or repaired: these are the elements in Hegel's metaphysical language. They are bold and novel and speak to a modern concern that punishment does no good. They also speak against what Hegel would say in the later PR. It is important to underline that Hegel's reconciliation after violation and guilt is distinct from that achieved via an 'unfriendly' law, which serves to block it in favour of the repetition of violence (in punishment) in response to violence (in crime). Reconciliation after violation occurs 'with no regard to right whatever' (Hegel 1948: 216), for law threatens only to get in the way.

In its own terms, there are things lacking here. When Hegel writes of the guilt of the perpetrator and his reconciliation with the universal order, there is no real space given to what the perpetrator owes to his victim. It is true that the victim is present as the person in the universal order who has been violated, but attention then immediately switches to how this is self-violation for the perpetrator. There is solipsism where there needs to be a concrete relationship. The same is true regarding the broader context in which violation is experienced as guilt. At no point does Hegel's perpetrator reflect on his relationship to the broader social as opposed to the metaphysical world. Relational elements concerning the victim and societal engagement are lacking. Nonetheless Hegel's language is in large part the language of a modern moral psychology in which wrongdoing is felt and, to use a term that will feature in Part III, atoned for, leading the individual back to a sense of being at one with himself. As we will see, there is an important inflexion in 'atonement' to mean not so much what one does to expiate, but how one's goal is to be 'at one' again with oneself, one's life and one's relationships.[9] This is in line with the young Hegel's thought. I turn now to the nature of victimhood.

The Victim: Resistance, Submission and Reconciliation

In this section, I consider the experience of the victim with regard to the nature of forgiveness, reconciliation and law. Violation involves in its immediate setting the two sides of the perpetrator and the victim.[10] Regarding the latter, Hegel identifies two responses to violation. The victim may either bravely resist an attack ('courageous resistance') or may withdraw in its face and submit to its

[9] In Chapters 6–8, the idea of atonement in the work of Herbert Morris as a moral theorist and Hans Loewald as a psychoanalyst are compared. Moral theory and psychoanalysis represent the two sides of a fully developed moral psychology. Hegel's account is an important prototype, though he lacked appreciation of the psychoanalytical dimension.

[10] Beyond this, of course, it involves a broader social context and relationships.

consequences ('grieving submission'). Both responses display a certain nobility (a 'beauty of soul'), but both present their own problems. Hegel's discussion here is inconclusive and I try to develop it by thinking about the process whereby a victim grieves and comes to terms with victimhood. I conclude the section by returning to consideration of law in this approach and the particular case of 'righteous law-mindedness' and address an important criticism.

Courageous Resistance

This can be dealt with briefly. The victim of an unjust attack may bravely resist and 'arm and defend himself and his right'. In so committing himself, he 'clings to his right and defends it' and 'his [own] guilt, his fate, begins' (Hegel 1948: 233). On the face of it, acting courageously is better than submitting, for the would-be victim has stood up for himself. He has entered 'on the battlefield of might against might and ventures to oppose his adversary' thereby subjecting himself 'to fate', but also taking his fate into his own hands as a 'man of courage [who] engages with the sphere of right and might' (Hegel 1948: 233–34).

Hegel's account seems straightforward: better to have fought and lost than not to have fought at all, though better still to have won. But the starting assumption here is that the victim responded to a violation and that he might have prevailed. What if he were to lose the fight when he was wrongly attacked? Surely his failed resistance would then lead him to grief and injury at his (unjustified) loss? It may be a consolation that one resisted one's violation, albeit unsuccessfully, but that one resisted does not make the initial violation or the eventual outcome less violative. Where does it leave the victim when courageous resistance is insufficient to defeat a violative attack? In effect, he will be placed in the second position Hegel notes as a response to violation, that of 'grieving submission', though that, as we will now see, meets certain problems.

Grieving Submission

Grieving submission may be an outcome once courageous resistance fails, and one has to submit to defeat. Alternatively, it may be a pre-emptive choice in its own right. It is a psychologically interesting case where a person submits in the face of threatened violation and thereby safeguards his person, but at a cost. By surrendering, he 'escapes grief for loss, escapes handling by the other ..., escapes the necessity of engaging with the other' (Hegel 1948: 235). His fate is not determined by another's hand, but withdrawal leads nonetheless to grief not at defeat, but at having submitted. When attacked, the person 'withdraws himself ... and simply lets go into the other's hands a thing which in the moment of the attack he has alienated' (Hegel 1948: 235). He renders himself invulnerable as, in the manner of 'a sensitive plant, he withdraws into himself when touched' (Hegel 1948: 236). To be 'in another's power would no longer be the man himself' (Hegel 1948: 235), but his surrender pre-empts subjugation. Or does it? The price of being a shrinking violet is also a kind of annihilation for the victim renounces his commitments in a process of self-negation which 'drives him so far toward the renunciation of life that he must withdraw into the void altogether' (Hegel 1948: 235–36). In modern terms, he opts to 'suck it up' and in that lies grief in submission. It turns out that there is more than one way to lose your dignity.

The situation does not sound good for the victim but there is then a twist for it can turn morally in his favour. Since his surrender 'is his own will, his free choice', his 'fate is rooted in himself, [and] he can endure it, face it, because his griefs are … produced by himself.' He has indeed taken the moral high ground and 'lifted himself above fate entirely' for now it is life that 'has become untrue to him, not he to life' (Hegel 1948: 236). There is nobility in retreat, yet this still costs him for sufferance is at once both noble and ignoble. However you dress it up, the victim has still fled from his life so that his conduct combines 'the supreme wretchedest fate with elevation above all fate' (Hegel 1948: 236). The situation remains unhappy and unresolved, but hope is around the corner. Hegel now suggests the victim's self-abnegation is eventually the basis for reconciliation with the aggressor. A loving heart that has raised itself above the ties of right 'has nothing to forgive the offender, for it sacrificed its right' itself. To such a person, the offender can do no wrong for his heart is open to reconciliation and ready to 'reassume any vital relationship and to re-enter the ties of friendship and love' (Hegel 1948: 236). Yielding leaves 'no hostile feeling, no consciousness, no demand on another for the restoration of an infringed right ….' Self-abnegation reconciles the heart with 'one who hurts us [and makes] friendly just so much life as was hostile to it…' (Hegel 1948: 236). Grieving submission of this kind, Hegel claims, leaves the spirit in a position where reconciliation and the requital of grief become possible.

Can we accept this, or might we think that such reconciliation is at a serious cost to the victim who has surrendered, even if voluntarily? What Hegel is suggesting here is a form of unconditional forgiveness and this should not be discounted. We find an example, as he does, in Jesus and the beautiful soul experience of turning the other cheek (Hegel 1948: 236). This is a plausible moral scenario though it may not be the only possible response to grieving submission. Hegel's own account of its tribulations suggests that it will not correspond to the moral experience of all those who withdraw and accept defeat. The suffering of either the righteous resister who loses an unjust fight or the person who yields because he cannot bear the struggle would not seem to be cured by their surrender. To give up in the fight is not to give up the resentment that goes with retreat. Something may still need to happen to permit the victim to reconcile himself to the wretchedness of his fate or 'the void'. Life may have become untrue to the victim, but the victim still has to find a way of living. Without that, Hegel seems to abandon him to his unhappy fate.

Grieving Submission and Working Through

In Part II, I will argue that the injury caused by something like grieving submission cannot normally just be ignored in coming to terms with violation. It must rather be addressed and overcome through a psychological process that can lead either to forgiveness (in its different meanings) or at least to finding a better way to live with what happened. Such a process of integrating and working through violation is not simply yielding to the other. At its end, reflection on what happened in individual and universal terms may take victims towards reconciliation, but not before they have addressed hurt and loss. Hegel's position on grieving submission places too much weight on the victim and is unrealistic regarding an easy return to unity and wholeness. It leaves no space for the asymmetrical relationship between perpetrator and victim and the role of the perpetrator in initiating the problem. In this regard, his treatment of the perpetrator's guilt is also incomplete, as I noted earlier, in that he imagines his reconciliation without engagement with the victim or their representatives. That may happen but in general it ignores how violation establishes a violative relation between perpetrator and victim, which needs to be addressed.

An example of how this works is seen in Marian Partington's account of how she forgave Rose West, convicted with her husband Fred, for the cruel murder of her sister Lucy (Partington 2016). Her memoir of reconciliation affirms a metaphysics of love while showing how a process has to be worked through for a person to be open to forgiveness. Partington's route was complicated by the fact that Lucy's remains were hidden by the Wests and only discovered twenty-one years after her disappearance. She had to deal both with not knowing and then a horrendous discovery before anything could be retrieved for herself. She was faced with an ethical situation that was 'hardly possible to understand', that was 'sticky and staining', and involved 'trying to get the measure of it before one [could] let go' (Partington 2016: 2). Her way to reconcile drew upon the account of a medieval dream vision entitled *Pearl*[11] that she had read at university involving a father's grief for his dead daughter in four parts ('Crisis', 'Confession', 'Comprehension' and 'Transformation') (Partington 2016: 2–6). It depicted a process of active mourning through a metaphysics of love expressed in dream figures. The process also involved imaginary conversations with Lucy in which she worked out what she felt in her sister's guiding presence. She writes:

> ...words must be found. There must be something for all of us to learn from the profoundly shocking profanity of the murder of Lucy, my sister, before it becomes buried under the concrete of fear, prejudice, or even worse, indifference.... This speaking is about Lucy's truth, in her life and death. It is about trying to remain open to the pain, the guilt, the joy, the rage, the grief, the fear and what lies beyond. It is about my quest to find meaning. It is about living

[11] See Andrew and Waldron 2007 for the most recent published form.

> with the reality of violence, rape, torture and murder, trying to face up to it and trying to accept it. It is about poetry and transformation. The process is not always rational. It is about learning to follow my heart. It is a rite of passage. It is purgatorial. It is about time. The process is about 'Salvaging the Sacred' – the sacred in my sister, in myself and, ultimately, in all sentient beings. (Partington 2016: 9–10)

The process was complex. It involved recognising the universality of experience, in particular her own anger and potential for violence, and how she herself in other circumstances might have been a perpetrator. Partington eventually came to understand how West, 19 years old at the time of Lucy's disappearance, and herself the victim of rape and incestuous sexual abuse, was a human being like herself. She too had felt murderous rage relating both to her own child- and adulthood and the death of Lucy. Acknowledging these led her to see West's humanity as someone she should forgive and with whom she should seek to be reconciled. West's 'moral lens was utterly distorted', her 'traumatised, toxic patterns attract[ing] another violent abuser'. Partington came to recognise in West 'the complex cage of the fear, rage, shame, guilt and unresolved grief of her mind … a searing feeling of her isolation and shame' (Partington 2016: 138). Through this process, the possibility of forgiveness came to escape the 'barnacles of impossible piety' to become a '*for*-giving' to another which would allow her to be free. So doing Partington's own sorrow dissolved or at least changed into a new relationship with pain, which was also a feeling of being freed in herself (Partington 2016: 139).[12]

Partington's comments make it clear what may be needed and possible for reconciliation in the light of human universality. It shows how Hegel's simplistic understanding of self-withdrawal and being able to reconcile 'forthwith' is insufficient. Yet her metaphysical working through of grief to 'the sacred in my sister, in myself and, ultimately, in all sentient beings' points to Hegel's universal sense of love and life. Like him, it also points to a gulf between reconciliation and legal process. Unlike many victims, Partington felt that the criminal justice process had done well by her, but the trial, the conviction and the sentence could not really help her. Establishing the 'facts of the case' in the trial did not 'answer my need to know the truth of what happened to Lucy', a need, perhaps, for a moral truth that no facts could ever meet. She sees the process of trial and punishment as a repetition of the problem since it 'is mostly focused upon retribution, causing more pain' and not enlarging the human potential to heal. Healing was itself imprisoned by a process dealing in retribution, blame and punishment:

> There is a place that understands, deep within, that violence can only breed more violence and that this is where it must stop. It is not a place where justice means more pain, punishment and revenge. It is rooted in a strong instinct for this depth of pain not to happen to anyone else. The rawness of this wound

[12] Compare Partington's discussion of *for*-giving with my discussion of forgiving as giving to and giving up in Chapters 4 and 5.

> somehow strips away all that is unimportant. The deepest reality is laid bare.... It is a place that yearns for healing, which is willing to sacrifice the immediate response of revenge. (Partington 2016: 154)

Partington sought healing and reconciliation, which took her to a place that was ethically critical of an institutional practice based on law, blame and punishment. While Hegel's account of victimisation and reconciliation is insufficient because it lacks understanding of how a person works through violation, a developed account reflecting Partington's moral experience identifies what is lacking. Supplemented in this way, the similarity between the young Hegel's metaphysical theory and Partington's metaphysical practice confirms the importance of his prototypical moral psychology. While solipsistic in its conception and socially decontextualised, there is much in Hegel's metaphysical account of grief and reconciliation that reflects Partington's experience.

Righteous Law-Mindedness versus Reconciliation

In closing this section, I return to my initial comments about the difference between law and love. I consider a situation in which the young Hegel explores the danger of righteous law-mindedness and then consider a criticism of young Hegel's account of love in the modern social setting.

Righteous law-mindedness is a fanatical following of the law to the exclusion of all other considerations. This might be seen as a distortion of obedience to law, which should be tempered with wise discretion, mercy or judgement, but in terms of Hegel's position in SCF, it is probably better seen as the immanent logic of obeying the law. It occurs where law's satisfaction becomes a sanctimonious demand. It describes the pitfalls of surrendering to one's inner Kant. Hegel describes it as 'the righteous man's rage, a hating rigorous dutifulness, which must needs rage not over an injury to his individuality but over an injury to his intellectual conceptions, i.e., to the commands of duty' (Hegel 1948: 237).[13] The problem with this is that it accentuates the alienated part over the ethical whole and becomes a further block to reconciliation. Once we cling to legal judgement, we commit to an unchanging world of right and wrong in which we will all be judged and found wanting in perpetuity. The biblical

[13] Compare Inspector Javert in Victor Hugo's *Les Misérables*:

> Without being fully conscious of the fact, but still with a sense of his importance and achievement, he was at that moment the personification of justice, light, and truth in their sublime task of stamping out evil. Behind him and around him, extending into infinite space, were authority and reason, the conscience of the law, the sentence passed, the public condemnation and all the stars in the firmament. He was the guardian of order, the lightning of justice, the vengeance of society, the mailed fist of the absolute, and he was bathed in glory. (Hugo 1976: 267)

Poignantly, Javert eventually takes his own life when he realises the human folly of his righteous law-mindedness: see Hugo 1976: 1106–7.

command 'Judge not that ye be not judged' contrasts with taking legal right as the yardstick.

We should not take righteousness and love to be dependent on 'laws and ... commands, instead of regarding them as issuing from life.' To do so is to recognise 'a lord before whom you are impotent, who is stronger than you, a power who is not yourself ... an alien power over your deed.' It is to elevate 'into an absolute what is only a fragment of the whole of the human heart' (Hegel 1948: 237–38). If the law is a fragment of human nature, then so is 'the criminal'. Where law is elevated to the place of the whole the criminal can only ever be a criminal. Accordingly, the road to forgiveness and change is blocked:

> The punishment inflicted by law is merely just. The common character, the connection of crime and punishment, is only equality, not life. The same blows which the trespasser has dealt he experiences himself.... Of reconciliation, of a return to life, there thus can be no question so far as justice is concerned. Before the law the criminal is nothing but a criminal. (Hegel 1948: 238)

Law blocks change in favour of repetition and righteous law-mindedness takes this to its logical conclusion. Reconciliation in contrast goes the other way. It is 'not grounded in an alien law superior to the man', so that 'a return is possible to the original situation, to wholeness'. When that happens 'the deed still subsists, but only as something past, as a fragment, as a corpse'. The bad conscience in the deed disappears, for 'in love, life has found life once more'. Law plays no part in this since between 'sin and its forgiveness there is as little place for an alien thing as there is between sin and punishment'. Through reconciliation, life 'has severed itself from itself and united itself again' (Hegel 1948: 232). Law can only get in the way and while righteous law-mindedness looks like a pathology, it is in fact immanent to its concept.

An Objection: Love Diminished?

Finally, I consider Axel Honneth's comments in his *The Struggle for Recognition* (Honneth 1995) about the young Hegel. In this work, Honneth draws on Hegel's slightly later writings from his time in Jena (Hegel 1979) to plot a route away from what he sees as the narrow approach of the later PR. His interest is in identifying a 'recognition-theoretic' path which offers space for social concerns and questions of identity which are a part of concrete human individuality. Hegel's thought in the Jena period is depicted as moving beyond the early theological writings while holding onto the importance of love, though in a diminished form.

With regard to love, Hegel defines it in the Jena period as 'being oneself in another' (Hegel 1979: 110; quoted in Honneth 1995: 96), a definition which links it to close interpersonal rather than to universal relationships. Love operates in Hegel's *System of Ethical Life* as the basic human level at which men, women and children are capable of 'maturation of preliminary relations of mutual recognition that constitute a necessary precondition for every further development of identity' (Honneth 1995: 39). Love provides an indispensable self-confidence that is a precondition for legal and citizen relations, but Honneth notes that Hegel is keen here 'to work against the misconception to which he succumbed in his youth, when he was still trying to construe the affective nexus of a society as a whole in terms of quasi-erotic relationships of love' (Honneth 1995: 38). The love relationship, he writes, 'cannot be extended at will, beyond the social circle of primary relationships, to cover a larger number of partners to interaction' (Honneth 1995: 107).

The overextension of love to citizen relations is an issue which (as we shall see further) Hegel himself pondered in his discussion of modern society in SCF. There is however a way to deal with it, as Honneth also notes slightly earlier in his account. Love is marked by boundary dissolution between self and another and this takes a 'wide variety of forms, depending on the type of bond' (Honneth 1995: 105). It includes bonds of sexual union, between loving partners and with children, but also more broadly friendship, in an 'unselfconscious conversation or an utterly unforced moment together' (Honneth 1995: 105). If this is the case then love can appear differently in a variety of settings but still be love, with affects relevant to context. In the shape of identification with another, it can work its way, I shall argue in Chapter 7, into compassionate feelings for a stranger. Honneth's use of object relations psychology suggests how initial forms of love ramify differently in adult settings, creating 'a pattern of interaction whose mature reappearance in adult life is an indication of successful affectional bonds to other people' (Honneth 1995: 104). If love appears as part of a 'communicative structure that makes love a special relationship of mutual recognition' (Honneth 1995: 105) in a variety of settings, it should not be restricted to early and private relationships. We recognise the importance of 'being oneself in another' in a variety of settings. Psychoanalysis in a variety of veins recognises the importance of love relationships in both child- and adulthood.[14]

To be sure, Hegel's definition of love as 'being oneself in another' is narrower compared to that developed in the earlier SCF. There, it will be recalled, love is variously 'the complement of the virtues' by which 'all one-sidedness, all exclusiveness, all restricted virtues, are annulled' (Hegel 1948: 246). It is 'feel[ing] one's self in the 'all' of life, with no restrictions, in the infinite' (Hegel 1948: 247), a 'so much richer, more living, fullness that so poor a thing as a law is nothing for it at all' (Hegel 1948: 215). Love is cast much more widely than in sexual, familial or friendly relations, marking a generally metaphysical attitude to life and wholeness of being. His account

[14] As we will see in Part III, Freud himself wrote that love is the common thread in a wide range of relationships. While its nucleus 'naturally consists in sexual love with sexual union as its aim…, we do not separate from this … on the one hand, self-love, and on the other, love for parents and children, friendship and love for humanity in general…' (Freud 1985: 119).

of the guilty perpetrator and the grieving victim makes it clear that loving reconciliation is the key to moral development. Though his account is incomplete, it is clear that the parties to violation may be strangers. While Honneth is right to draw on object relations theory in psychoanalysis to pinpoint the importance of individual parent–child bonds, it is important to see these as setting a template for a much broader orientation to life, including, as it were, a life in crime.[15]

Law against Love: 'Mature' Hegel on Punishment as Legal Right

The young Hegel is concerned with the moral psychology of the perpetrator and victim organised around love and against law. He produces a moral language of violation ('trespass'), grief and reconciliation. In the PR in contrast, Hegel relates his thought centrally to law. The result might be thought to be a very different theory and it is. However, what really happens is that it reflects the earlier ideas in form while giving them a completely changed content. Here there is reconciliation but through punishment delivered by the state and its law rather than the working out of grief at violation. Here there is a metaphysical underpinning but in the form of the logical idea rather than with life or fate. Here there is a moral psychology justifying punishment in the name of reason and will rather than in terms of love and conscience.[16] If we give this the name moral psychology, it is a very different one, one that should attract Williams's 'peculiar' epithet (Chapter 1). Ethics are refashioned from those of a natural human response to become the object of a justice that is legal and political in form, a philosophy *of right*.

The PR has three main parts which I consider further. Starting with individual self-consciousness, Hegel's aim is to build a conception of moral life that incorporates the forms of modern law (property, contract, tort and crime – the sphere of 'Abstract Right'), to insist 'there is no alternative' to these (the sphere

[15] Honneth notes of the psychoanalyst Donald Winnicott that his account of child psychology yields 'far-reaching insights … into the connection between creativity and recognition', but these 'are of no further interest to us here' (Honneth 1995: 103). Yet such insights as to how a person might respond to the world, including where one human being violates another, are important to how a society deals with crime. Issues of creativity and recognition are indeed central to how people process violation as perpetrators or victims (see, for example, Chapters 5 and 9–11). Honneth supports a metapsychology dealing with love's centrality to human relations, where there is ample scope not to cut it off at the knees, but to see it as flowing through social and legal relations. If 'legal relations differ in just about every essential respect' (Honneth 1995: 107–8), this does not itself justify love's restriction without critical reflection on what law thinks it is doing.

[16] The contrast I draw between early and 'mature' Hegel can be seen in other aspects of his thought. One can for example chart the development of the Beautiful Soul as it moves from being a vital presence in his early writings to a failed and empty figure in the *Phenomenology* (a 'loser'), to an object of curiosity in the *Philosophy of Right*: see Norrie 2005: ch 10. So with reconciliation: in the early thought, humans are reconciled to each other; in *PR*, humans are the bearers of rational law which is reconciled to itself.

of 'Morality') and to provide a set of social arrangements which permit law and morality to operate ('Ethical Life'). In each of the three phases of the developing dialectic, crime and punishment play an important role while violation, grief and loving reconciliation are abandoned. I conclude by considering how the new legal and political model addresses social issues and whether it achieves legitimacy in modern society. Here, I consider Axel Honneth's account of punishment and recognition and a suggested wrong turn that Hegel took in preparing the ground for the PR.

Abstract Right

In PR's first part, the possibility of crime forces the rational subject to realise that the free will encounters other wills with which it can come into conflict. Right leads to the possibility of wrong and guilt takes the form of traducing a right that the rational subject would otherwise live by. The rational subject has offended against its own principle. Here guilt is treated formally, as a matter of reconciling abstract, universal, free self-consciousness or subjectivity with legal right. The injury 'which falls on the criminal … is … a right *posited in the criminal himself*, i.e. in his objectively existent will, in his action' (Hegel 2008: 102). Crime 'is to be annulled, not because it is the producing of an evil, but because it is an infringement of right as right' (Hegel 2008: 102). Responsibility is thus a matter of reconciling free subjectivity, abstracted from all psychological determinations, with a rational law of non-contradiction. Guilt has the effect of showing why law is necessary.

In this argument, the moral psychology that pervades SCF is abandoned. The subject of law is viewed as no more (and no less) than a rational entity. So strong is the force of this argument that what it means to be a victim becomes a non-question: 'The injury from the point of view of the particular will of the injured party … is only something negative. The positive existence of the injury consists solely in the particular will of the criminal' (Hegel 2008: 101). This is because the will of the criminal reveals the rationality of right and the need for law, and nothing else is at stake.[17] To be sure, in both SCF and PR, the demand of a universal metaphysics is referenced, but how different they are in their content. While the former invokes a restoration of loving relations in a vital life as a person's fate, the latter calls for the restoration of legal right, a claim that the young Hegel had previously disparaged.

Morality

Moving to the second part of PR, Hegel attends to a moral corollary of recasting punishment in terms of right. His target is the claim that the criminal has

[17] We might here recall Williams's comment that guilt is simply about respect for an abstract law without 'any special connection with victims' (Williams 1993: 219–22).

a moral conscience. It was of course the central assumption of non-alienated being in SCF that conscience could reflect authentically on action, operated at a deeper level than law, and would if need be, oppose it. If the central antagonism of SCF is the claim of moral conscience (as love, guilt and reconciliation) against law and legal punishment, this is inverted in PR where the validity of legal right is maintained against moral conscience. Whereas previously, the authenticity of a conscientious soul had been the guarantee of reconciliation, now moral conscience is discarded as dangerous to the precepts of law. What had been the source of moral beauty and friendly fate suffers a terrible reinvention, appearing now as 'momentary blindness, the goad of passion, intoxication, … the strength of sensual impulse' (Hegel 2008: 129). What is now important is 'to treat the criminal in accordance with the right and honour due to him as a human being … as essentially something universal' (Hegel 2008: 129), i.e. in terms of legal right. Life, Hegel is reported as saying, 'ceases to be necessary in face of the higher realm of freedom' (Hegel 2008: 125).

In this rationalistic mindset, any claim of moral conscience which goes against law represents a challenge rather than a precondition to reconciliation – for this can only mean reconciliation of right with right. Being human becomes being a cypher for this logical necessity, a claim of conscience that is no more than 'the highwater mark of subjectivity at the level of morality; … the form into which evil has blossomed in our present epoch' (Hegel 2008: 138). Note here that 'evil', abandoned in the first part of *PR* in favour of 'right as right', now returns but only in the shape of a moral conscience that would follow its own dictates against those of law. The moral conscience which animated ethical being in SCF must be crushed.

Ethical Life

All this prepares the ground for the third part of PR, which completes the picture by vindicating criminal justice as a form of public power. 'The task of knowing and actualizing what is right in particular cases without the subjective feeling of particular interest falls to a public authority – the court of law' (Hegel 2008: 208). The law court has become the crowning glory of the penal process, ethical life made concrete, but only, one might say, because ethical life in the young Hegel's terms has been obliterated. This is of course the very opposite to how law is viewed in SCF. If one were to summarise the vision of wrongdoing and punishment across the three parts of PR, at its core lies the idea of aligning the 'injured universal' with law and the state, via the abstract rational subject, crushing moral conscience in the process. Individual moral sensibility, generating the possibility of ethical reconciliation through guilt, is subsumed and denied by the rationalisation of individual right, the imposition of an official morality and the universalisation of the law court.

Abstract universality wins out over what I will call in Chapter 5 the concrete universality/singularity of human life and its attendant moral psychology.

The injured universal is an abstract universal, with punishment as the rational negation of the negation. Ethical life has become, in Honneth's words, 'a form of monologically self-developing Spirit and no longer constitutes a particularly demanding form of intersubjectivity' (Honneth 1995: 61). This produces its own moral grammar of guilt and punishment in a highly rationalised and abstract form but tells us nothing about the moral psychology of criminals, and even less about victims. What it does tell us about is the logic of being a citizen in a *Rechtsstaat*, under the formal governance of legal subjectivity, and subject to retributive punishment as the restoration of right. It confirms a rational necessity of which individual human subjects may be quite unaware (Norrie 1991: 78–81; Hegel 2008: 217), splitting ethical and rational subjectivity.

Hegel and the Social Question

The abstraction of right, the enforcement of morality and the imposition of universal necessity establish a philosophy of law geared to manage modern social life. There is repression here of human ethical possibility (as in the SCF) but also reflection on the modern social realities which the PR seeks to rationalise. These appear as 'social concerns' that are considered but not permitted to disturb its rational logic. They pick up concerns Hegel already aired in SCF, but these have greater bite given his growing awareness of the nature of modern capitalist political economy.

In 1798, Hegel was aware of the conflict between his metaphysics of love and the realities of modern life with its separation of people by commercial relations. In a fragment written before SCF, he commented of lovers that 'one who sees the other in possession of a property must sense in the other the separate individuality which has willed this possession', noting that 'even lovers cannot refrain from reflection on this aspect of their relations' (Hegel 1948: 308). In SCF, the ambivalence between love and property shows in his reflection on the difficulty of developing a loving community under modern social conditions. The 'love which a large group of people can feel for one another admits of only a certain degree of strength or depth'. Market society links 'many persons', 'depends on similarity of need, and … reveals itself in objects which can be common', but such 'similarity of mind is not love'. At best a 'common spirit delights … to be gay in unifying the group … in gladness and play' (Hegel 1948: 280), but the underlying problem is that separation is inscribed in modern property relations, their law and resulting social divisions. Wealth, he writes, 'betrays its opposition to love, to the whole', but this is because 'it is a right caught in a context of multiple rights' (Hegel 1948: 221). Of the gap between rich and poor, he writes that the biblical claim that a rich man may not enter Heaven 'is a litany pardonable only in sermons and rhymes, … without truth for us' for 'property has become too powerful for us to tolerate reflections on it, to find its abolition thinkable' (Hegel 1948: 221).

Twenty years later in PR, having aligned modern law and civil society with right and Spirit, Hegel returned to the problem of poverty and its effects on justice, this time with a fuller awareness of its significance. Wealth and 'the largest profits' produce, he now notes, a 'concentration of disproportionate wealth in a few hands' alongside the 'dependence and distress of the class tied to work'. This results in 'the creation of a *rabble of paupers*' while the 'important question of how poverty is to be abolished ... torments modern society' (Hegel 2008: 221). The situation promotes 'a consequent loss of the sense of right and wrong' (Hegel 2008: 221) since 'Against nature a human being can claim no right, but once society is established, poverty immediately takes the form of a wrong done to one class by another' (Hegel 2008: 221). Here, Hegel is the concerned liberal, accepting modern capitalist society but noting its underlying and unresolved problems, and concerned they may be unresolvable. Elsewhere in PR, dealing with how the state, the police and punishment should address resulting social disorder, he adopts a sterner attitude. Punishment, he observes, must be as weak or as strong as public order requires, and this 'is the justification for sometimes attaching the penalty of death to a theft of a few pence or a turnip, and at other times a light penalty to a theft of a hundred or more times that amount' (Hegel 2008: 208). Of the police in times of conflict, Hegel takes a similar position. 'Control is also necessary to diminish the danger of upheavals arising from clashing interests and to abbreviate the period in which their tension might be eased through the working of a necessity of which [the people] know nothing' (Hegel 2008: 217). Here universal Spirit performs a very concrete (and partisan) role.[18]

The problem is that modern social realities undermine the claims to justice of the retributive theory. They lead Hegel from broad social concern (how to deal with poverty), to recognition that social injustice challenges a just legal order (upends right and wrong), and then to undermine his own theory in the name of social defence (harsh punishment for minor crime). We could add that he turns his back on the experience of the poor (the working of an unknown necessity), but we have seen that this was always built into the theory. It may be said that legal retributivism does not achieve social justice because its purpose or rationale is to realise 'more basic conditions of political equality' (Ramsay 2016: 103), but so long as there is an intrinsic connection between social and legal justice it would be hard for any dialectical theorist to claim the one can be separated from the other.

A 'Recognition-Theoretic' Way Out?

Could things have been different for Hegel if as Honneth suggests he had not taken a false turn in writings in his Jena Period (after the SCF but before the PR)?

[18] I suggest that Hegel's account of the logic and the problems of punishment represents what Roy Bhaskar calls a 'TINA compromise formation' (Bhaskar 1993). That is, it is concerned with demonstrating that 'there is no alternative' to the rational explanation Hegel proposes, whereas in reality, the argument relies upon a series of buttressing sub-arguments (its compromise formation) to justify and maintain what is said.

Honneth discerns a link between crime and what he calls conditions of incomplete recognition in these writings. The 'criminal's inner motive … consists in the experience of not being recognised … in a satisfactory way' (Honneth 1995: 20). Honneth suggests Hegel may have had in mind concrete, social processes of recognition. The 'not-yet-recognised is apparently … related to the realisation of individual aspirations under conditions of equal rights and duties' (Honneth 1995: 54), without which a subject who has not been adequately recognised is 'disrespected', and crime becomes social protest and antagonism. One way this could happen would be that legal compulsion is framed in terms so abstract that 'the context-specific, individual motive for breaking the [law – AN] is not taken into consideration'. Law provides a 'false formalism' which disregards 'the particular circumstances of a concrete situation' (Honneth 1995: 54). A second way would see disrespect as 'linked to the exercise of legal coercion in the sense of an abstraction from the material conditions for the realisation of individuals' intentions' (Honneth 1995: 54). Recognition fails because the norms and relations 'are so abstractly constituted that the individual opportunities for the realisation of legally guaranteed freedoms are not taken into consideration' (Honneth 1995: 55).

For Honneth, it is important to note that the problem of formalism concerns not just the framing of the legal norms but their content which needs to be extended in favour 'of substantive equality of opportunity' (Honneth 1995: 55). This means that the issue of disrespect which leads to crime stems from the failure adequately to meet the social needs of those who then become criminals. Here, however, Honneth addresses the same social challenge confronted by Hegel previously. He follows TH Marshall's theory of citizenship, pointing to the historical movement in modern capitalist societies from the recognition of civil (property-based) rights (in the eighteenth century) to political (in the nineteenth) and then social rights in the twentieth. In this way, the formal sphere of law reaches out to more substantive needs and includes a broader range of people who are able to enjoy welfare rights, working, as it were, in a recognition-theoretic way.

Yet societies that moved in this direction in the mid-twentieth century extended social rights to an extent that was important but still left fundamental gaps, while developments from the 1980s onwards in the name of market-based, neoliberal political economy have seen these cut back. The challenge Honneth presses in Hegel's account of crime, disrespect and the failure to recognise was always, even in the heyday of post-war social democracy, a problem and criminal justice strategies from the 1970s have entrenched these. They include increasingly holding (falsely recognising) individuals as to blame to the exclusion of social problems, imposing a dangerousness label on subjects who are thereby both mis- and 'disrecognised',[19] and increasing modes of authoritarian regulation which fail to recognise subjects as citizens (Norrie 2017c: ch 2).

[19] 'Misrecognised' in the sense that the 'dangerous subject' is generally misperceived as a citizen who must behave dangerously; 'disrecognised' in that the outcome may be penal treatment unacceptable for normal citizens.

These all point to the continuing problem of disrespect and failure to recognise identified by Honneth, which Hegel had originally noted as the problem of justice. In his last sentence, Honneth raises a question he does not answer, whether the social reforms needed for recognition involve changes in socio-economic circumstances that 'are compatible with the conditions of a capitalist society' (Honneth 1995: 179).[20] This was exactly how Hegel left the issue of crime and poverty in the PR in 1821.

The Young Hegel as Ethical and Institutional Critic

In this final section, I consider how we should compare and contrast the young Hegel's theological writing with his later theory of the state.

Which Is the More Mature Way of Thinking?

Hegel's retributive theory in the PR is often seen as an outstanding rationalisation of the modern criminal justice system. It *is* a great intellectual achievement, but one that can be challenged in its own terms and according to its social setting. Consideration of the young Hegel's position also suggests a deeper line of criticism based on his metaphysics of love, grief and reconciliation. As a whole, we might see his trajectory as negotiating two horns of a dilemma. The journey from the early to the later philosophy (and pausing at his Jena period) is caught between an ethical completeness that cannot be made socially relevant and a social relevance based on ethical denial. Either Hegel runs with an understanding of how authentic moral subjects operate, or he builds an account of law and punishment appropriate to a world of private property, individual self-interest, wealth and poverty. The former cannot find its place in the latter because the latter systematically excludes the necessary metaphysical space.

Judged as a whole, Hegel's early-to-late oeuvre leaves more questions than answers, not least whether the label 'mature' is appropriate for his later retributive theory, given what it leaves out of the picture. Which achievement, we might ask, was the greater, the earlier or the later work? The PR is of course a huge intellectual edifice, SCF a briefer exploratory essay, but the latter offers

[20] Peter Ramsay suggests a similar way out of Hegel by expanding democratic rights through a 'democratic retributive abolitionist' position. The more liberal societies extend democratic rights, the less room they find for punishment. Recognising each person as a fellow citizen of equal value implies an immanent tendency to punishment's abolition. Ramsay also points out however that the modern tendency is to downgrade democratic participation and with that to promote penal populism and harsh punishment. Like Honneth, he places great weight on the social democratic capacity of the modern state to deliver citizen democracy (Ramsay 2016: 98–99). Paradoxically, what is in significant remission (expanded democratic rights) is that which should provide resolution, but, even if this problem could be addressed, a moral psychology of abolition must still be sought.

something different, a moral language of violation that can deepen our critique of law and punishment. From there, we can link Williams's call for critique of 'peculiar' thinking in liberalism and law to the ethical voice of grieving victims and guilty perpetrators. This opens the door to what is metaphysically important in our understanding of violation and wrongdoing and the suffering they bring. Hegel did not get it all right, missing much of the dialogic quality and the social context of a moral psychology of violation. He also of course wrote before we knew much about the workings of the human psyche and its metapsychology. Yet, his work is an early prototype of a perspective on violation that we ignore at our peril. The danger is that, under the aegis of the great philosophy, we continue with the 'tried and tested' methods of crime and punishment that constantly fail to translate a posited rational reconciliation into an ethically better or safer world.

Defenders of the PR and a liberal system of punishment more generally will reject the early theological writings with their radical account of love as unrealistic or impractical, a concern that the young Hegel had himself noted, and which Honneth repeats. The power of Hegel's argument in the PR is indeed precisely that it *excludes* direct ethical argument in favour of specifically political and legal considerations. Hegel's achievement is to have removed punishment from the sphere of moral affect and to have located it among rationalistic considerations of citizenship and law (c.f. Brudner 2009). It is true that we have seen in recent times how introducing moral considerations has had an inflationary effect on penal severity as part of a populist, ultimately antidemocratic, penal politics (Ramsay 2016). Similarly, a political system based upon *rechtsstaatlich* norms and practices should be respected and defended for the values it expresses.[21] These points are well taken but they miss the force of the young Hegel's position. His argument first and foremost challenges us to think about a real alternative to punishment as the way modern society deals with violation. There should be a better way that enables perpetrators to change their behaviour and victims to deal with their experience. Hegel's early arguments provide us with an initial focus on a radical alternative to law and punishment, one based on overcoming rather than repeating perpetually violation and its effects.

How Should We Use the Early Metaphysics of Love?

Second, Hegel's argument is targeted at moral redemption, not political power. One might imagine that the young Hegel would have conceded that his position was at once ethically realistic and socially and politically incomplete. It is ethically realistic in that it reflects seriously on what it means to violate

[21] See Norrie 2014: chs 2, 13. The political value of legal individualism is a theme I have considered elsewhere, exploring how law remains an ambivalent social form for supporting human freedom. Compare for example Norrie 2005: chs 5, 9, Norrie 2014 and 2017c: chs 2, 5.

or be violated and how human beings need to respond in order to come to terms with what has happened. It is politically incomplete in that it eschews those institutional forms that modern society has given over to dealing (inadequately) with violation. Rather than a weakness, this is its strength. It operates as an ethically real critique of existing institutional practices (an ERIC critique as described in Chapter 1), showing how they fail to deal with a basic human need. That these practices also fail to deliver what they say they will in their own terms (a valid legitimation of justice) only encourages the thought implanted by the young Hegel that there might be a better way of doing things. A starting point would be to address fundamental ethical needs arising out of violation for both perpetrators and victims.

Does this lead to an aporetic reading of modern punishment's diremption (c.f. Fine 2001)? If there is an irreconcilable gap between moral completeness and social, political and legal relevance, we could perhaps think of Hegel as a philosopher whose work lays bare the nature of criminal punishment in modern society, a thinker whose work can be read aporetically to identify the problems of criminal justice today. The horns of his dilemma are those of a modern criminal justice system which might like to do better but systematically struggles to identify what that could mean. Against that, it might be thought too generous to give modern criminal justice any benefit of the doubt. The system is essentially punitive and systematically lacking in attention to ethical relationships.[22] If society was serious about enabling victims to work through grief and criminals to process guilt with ultimate possibilities for reconciliation, the punitive form of the criminal justice system would have to be abandoned. Instead, the modern criminal justice system just repeats itself and fails even to begin to address the problem of violation.

I would not go quite that far. One final way of staying with Hegel is to consider what kind of critique we draw from his early *vis a vis* his later philosophy. The early account of guilt, grief and reconciliation stands as a thoroughgoing critique of his later work in the PR. It contributes to the possibility of an ethically real position from which to view violation today. Insofar as the penal system is punitive, fails to deal with those convicted in a way that helps address their issues, ignores victims and does not address the social problems which lead to crime, the young Hegel's ethical realism is the basis for an institutional critique of both the existing penal system and his own later efforts to rationalise it. Placing the early position in critical dialogue with the later establishes an ERIC (ethically real and institutionally critical) approach (see Chapter 1). Insofar as the penal system seeks to bring about change in its prison inmates, seeks to support victims, offers avenues

[22] I discuss this further below where I suggest that modern criminal justice systems possess a 'structure in dominance' that is punitive in the major and reconciliative in the minor key (Chapter 11). An interesting theoretical (see Chapter 8) and practical (Chapter 11) experiment is to reverse major and minor.

for reconciliation through restorative encounters, seeks to diminish its own punitiveness and so on, one can say that the existing system offers ways of bringing ethical critique into contact with institutional arrangements. The ERIC critique then turns positive, though remaining critical with regard generally to backsliding, or the need for change in the broader society. Insofar as the penal system is marked by a general punitiveness, the message of the young Hegel must be that enough is enough and abolishing what we do now should be taken seriously.

If the young Hegel could have written a memo to his older self, he might have said the following. Instead of thinking about crime and punishment, an ethically mature person should consider whether it would be possible for a modern institutional environment to deal properly with the moral reality of violation. If a theory takes us only to the eternal repetition of punishment, perhaps we should look elsewhere. While the young Hegel lacked the kind of full understanding of the metaphysical animal, the one that thinks and loves, developed here, he nonetheless points us in a very different direction for dealing with violation and its aftermath. He provides us with a critical basis for thinking beyond punishment and towards its abolition.

3

Guilt in Political Theory and Moral Psychology

> We have handed many of the responses [to wrongdoing] to a very special formation, the modern state, and we have principles governing what such a state can and should do [so that] our ideas … are … governed by a certain political theory of freedom, not by a moral refinement of the very conception of responsibility.
>
> Bernard Williams (1993: 66)

> Against nature a human being can claim no right, but once society is established, poverty immediately takes the form of a wrong done to one class by another.
>
> GWF Hegel (2008: 221)

> … making reparation … such an essential part of the ability to love… the primary condition for further happiness.
>
> Melanie Klein (1998: 342)

This chapter has two focal points, one specific and the other general. The specific focus is the moral guilt of perpetrators viewed as victims who victimise others in settings of structural social injustice. The observation is often repeated in normative political theory that those taken through the criminal justice systems of Western societies are in the main from the poorest and most socially disadvantaged groups. It is caught in the prefatory quote from Hegel, which links the previous chapter with the analysis here. Such people are often victims of systematic and structural violence and exclusion, which leads them to victimise others through criminal acts. Those whom they victimise are often themselves living in comparable social circumstances. Such perpetrators are therefore victims of the social system victimising others who are equally victims of that system. This poses a question for standard theories of punishment which focus on the justice of punishment. Such theories in one way or another contemplate the responsibility or the guilt of the accused. Where does guilt lie when perpetrators are themselves victims who victimise others?

The broader focus considers this question in relation to a deeper analysis of what it means to be guilty of committing a crime than is provided in normative political theory. The central issue there is the relationship between the guilt of an individual and their justified punishment by a political entity – a state, a polity, a sovereign and the law. This is in one sense understandable given that the punishment practices under investigation are normally conducted by such entities. There is however a danger, caught in the prefatory quote from Bernard Williams, of permitting the practical context to shape intellectual enquiry in a way that forecloses deeper questions. Two distinct elements that should be kept separate become fused. The first is that just described, of understanding the practices of a particular political and institutional form in terms that reflect the nature of such practices. This is what normative political theory seeks to do. The problem with such a mode of enquiry is that it may unconsciously extend its remit to absorb and obscure a second and different element in our understanding. This element concerns the underlying question of the moral psychology of guilt, which, it is wrongly assumed, should also be understood in terms of normative political theory. This second element considers the intrinsic moral psychology of violation for human beings, that is, for a metaphysical animal capable of thought and love.

In this chapter, a contrast is drawn between these approaches by juxtaposing two accounts of guilt as they concern the guilt of victims who victimise others. The first account is that of normative political theory. Here I look at modern classical formulations of the issue (Kant and Hegel) and then consider Antony Duff's approach (Duff 2001). I show how these accounts from normative political theory generate an impasse, while Duff begins some moves which, though constrained by the overall setting of liberal political theory, begin to take us towards an authentic moral psychology of guilt. The second account comes from moral psychology and begins to consider what guilt might look like from this deeper perspective. It takes up the work of two psychoanalytic thinkers, Melanie Klein (1998) and Jessica Benjamin (1988), to analyse what it means in moral psychology to talk about guilt for violation of another.

Guilt in this second view involves a moral and psychological state that perpetrators can experience, even if they are in social and political terms victims who victimise others. Moving from normative political theory to moral psychology helps us see that issues of guilt and justice have deeper foundations in human being than can be understood in terms of the relationship between a punishing authority and a responsible legal subject. Just at the point where a political and normative approach fails (guilt cannot be justified) is where we see the need for a deeper understanding of what guilt is that should be sustained. In this way, I develop a moral psychological account based on naturalistic premises of what guilt really is. As described in the two previous chapters, this involves an ethically real understanding of how the human animal, capable of thought and love, may respond to situations where it violates another.

Normative Political Theory: The Problem of Guilt in an Unjust World

In this section, I rehearse a well-known problem in the modern political theory of punishment, considering both its classical statement and one recent important recapitulation. Though I think it is a systematic problem underlying the development of the modern theory of punishment (Norrie 1991), my aim here is not fully to make the case, but to explore how the problem has been described in normative political theory. This then leads to thinking more deeply about the nature of guilt, and the relationship between normative theory and an underlying moral psychology.

The Classical Just Deserts Problem

Modern normative political theory in its foundational moments and its more recent forms entails a clash between a normative vision of why punishment is justified and a sociological account of how crime comes to be committed (Norrie 1991; Carvalho 2017). With regard to the former, the normative idea is of a world of individuals, owing obligations to a sovereign, who are responsible and may be punished for acts which breach the sovereign's laws. This idea may be stated in a variety of ways. Compare for example the difference between a contractarian approach such as provided by Hobbes or Rawls with a rationalist approach as developed by Kant or Hegel. My aim is not to rehearse the range of options, only to indicate a broad approach subject to a variety of formulations. With regard to the latter, crime is a social phenomenon and has its roots in ideologies, practices and conditions in society as a whole. Again, I do not aim to explore this broad claim in detail, but anyone who has studied criminology will understand that a different set of questions are deployed concerning the nature of criminogenesis in sociology than appears in the understanding of normative political theory. This difference in methods reflects a broad tension in our understanding of crime as either socially caused or conditioned or as a matter of responsibility and political obligation. The effect of the difference is felt within political theory itself, in a tension between what comes to be called 'the ideal' and 'the actual' (Norrie 1991: chs 2–5).

Classical philosophers of retributive punishment reflected on this tension as a disjunction between the model of guilt, responsibility or justice they fashioned and the social context and resulting moral psychology of crime on which they imposed it. Recognition emerged early of a split between an ideal theory of obligation and an understanding of the actual world in which the theory should be applied. Taking examples of 'honour killing' in his day (the soldier who kills in a dual, the mother who kills her illegitimate child), Kant wrote that so long as there is a conflict between a psychological sense of honour and the penal law, the civil constitution will remain 'barbarous and undeveloped'. It will be 'to blame for the fact that the motives of honour obeyed by the people are subjectively incompatible' with the objective law, 'so that public justice as dispensed by the state is *injustice* in the eyes of the people' (Kant 1991: 158). As we saw in the previous chapter, Hegel similarly wrote of poverty and its impact on crime. The built-in dynamic in modern society was towards impoverishment of those at the bottom of society so that poverty 'immediately takes the form of a wrong done to one class by another' (Hegel 2008: 221). There is a consequent 'loss of the sense of right and wrong' amongst the poor, who consequently become a 'penurious rabble' (Hegel 2008: 222). While he did not pursue the implications of this observation for his theory of punishment, nor did he find a way to reconcile them with it. They remained important but as marginal comments at the edge of his theory (Norrie 1991: ch 4).

Returning to Kant, the split between an ideal justice and the justice available in the actually existing world is acknowledged:

> In a world of moral principle governed by God, punishments would be categorically necessary (insofar as transgressions occur). But in a world governed by men, the necessity of punishments is only hypothetical, and that direct union of the concept of transgression with the idea of deserving punishment serves the ruler only as a prescription for what to do.... (Zweig 1967: 199)

And this stems from the antinomialism at the core of his philosophy, where he distinguishes the rational (the ideal) from the world of actual experience:

> If I promulgate a penal law against myself as a criminal, it is the pure rightful and legislative reason within me (*homo noumenon*) which subjects me as a person capable of crime, hence as one person (*homo phaenomenon*) along with all the others within the civil union, to the penal law. (Kant 1991: 158)

These problems were not resolved at the beginning of modern thinking about crime and punishment, and this remains the case today. If poverty becomes 'the form of a wrong done to one class by another' leading to the 'loss of a sense of right and wrong' (Hegel) or if socially accepted motives turn punishment into 'injustice in the eyes of the people' (Kant), then we have not only a gap between the ideal and the actual, but potentially a radical inversion in which the just becomes unjust, the guilty the innocent and the perpetrator (the poor, the socially dishonoured) the victim. This is a problem for normative political theory but also a problem in terms of how we think about guilt. If perpetrators become victims, what has become of *their* victims? How are we to deal morally with perpetrators as victims who victimise others? If perpetrators as victims are no longer guilty according to the categories of political theory, how are we to think about what they in fact did? Put slightly differently, if the question of guilt has been identified with the issue of political obligation, does the failure of a doctrine of political obligation necessarily entail a fundamental failure of our understanding of guilt? If the right to punish fails because guilt is cast in terms of a political relationship between state and subject, does that mean there is nothing more to say about guilt? There is an impasse here in normative political theory based on the idea of 'just' punishment concerning guilt.

Victims Who Victimise Today

A modern restatement of the problem by Antony Duff confirms its significance (Duff 2001; see also American Friends Service Committee [1971]). In his own terms, Duff offers a powerful argument for what a synthetic account of punishment in the modern liberal state should look like. He combines backward- and forward-looking rationales for punishment that may satisfy both retributivists and consequentialists, achieving this by virtue of an account of punishment as moral dialogue or communication. Punishment aims to communicate to offenders 'the censure they deserve for their crimes, and thus to bring them to repent their crimes, to reform themselves, and to reconcile themselves with those they have wronged' (Duff 2001: 129). This is a communicative enterprise between citizens in a liberal community, a form of 'secular penance, which … serves the aims of repentance, reform and reconciliation' (Duff 2001: 129). These moral achievements are made possible by the censure that lies in criminal punishment. Of particular note is Duff's claim that the aims of punishment relate to achieving moral change in a person (repentance, reform and reconciliation), while these achievements are set in the frame of moral dialogue in a political community. Duff's theory is about achieving moral–psychological outcomes in a way that vindicates modern state punishment, though he accepts that this leaves important matters unresolved, especially around how theory relates to actual practices of punishment. Making the same distinction as Kant and Hegel between the ideal and the actual, Duff notes that his account 'depends on an ideal(ised) conception of liberal political community', noting that 'we must ask how far our existing political societies come near to actualising such an ideal – and what the implications are if they do not' (Duff 2001: 130).

Duff lays out three related problems or perhaps three different angles on the same problem. These are: the problem of political obligation for those who reap none of the benefits of political citizenship; the problem of moral standing for those who judge where crimes reflect systematic or structural violence; and the problem of communication between parties in a moral community that is socially divided. With regard to the political obligation to obey the law, Duff observes that where we move beyond a situation of mere social disadvantage to one of 'serious, persisting, and systematic injustice', those who experience it 'are excluded – politically, materially, normatively – from the community whose law it is' (Duff 2001: 183), and thus from the obligation to obey the community's law. Such people's actions are not 'wrong qua criminal' (Duff 2001: 184) since they are not bound by the law in such circumstances. Duff describes here the perpetrator who is himself a victim and is therefore 'not bound to regard the law as a source of authoritative requirements' (Duff 2001: 184). The court, representing the wrongful community, no longer invokes a political obligation in the offender to obey the law. This leads to Duff's second point that the law and its officers in such a setting lack the moral standing to judge the offender: 'since the community in whose name [the court] speaks has so notably failed to treat him in accordance with its declared values, it can hardly claim the right to call him to account for his alleged failure to respect those values as embodied in the criminal law' (Duff 2001: 186).

Duff's third point then concerns the language of law. The criminal law must be what Duff calls a 'common law' that is one that is held in common by a political community. It cannot be viewed as an alien imposition but must be couched in normative terms that 'the citizens can understand and speak for themselves' (Duff 2001: 191). Here Duff's position is nuanced. He views the terms of the criminal law as sufficiently morally thick that citizens may recognise that genuine wrongs are encompassed in what law defines as crimes. He notes that most people 'are not psychopaths to whom the normative language on which the law draws is alien and inaccessible' (Duff 2001: 191), suggesting perhaps an obligation to obey based on a deeper moral grounding. Yet at the same time, he accepts that the language of the law will be inflected by the settings in which it is used. With regard to our 'perpetrator-victims':

> Suppose that they are politically, materially, and normatively excluded from many of the community's goods. Suppose too that the accents in which they are addressed ... by the law's officials ... are the accents not of respect but of contempt, not of authority but of mere power. They cannot then reasonably be expected to hear the language of the law as one that could be theirs.... They will rather, and reasonably, hear it as an alien voice that they might have to obey but that they could not make their own. (Duff 2001: 193)

In this situation, offenders will hear that language 'not as the voice of a community to which they belong and are treated as belonging, but as the voice of an alien and oppressive power; not as a voice that appeals to values that they share and are treated as sharing, but as a voice that seeks to coerce them into submission' (Duff 2001: 193). Duff acknowledges that his 'is not a comfortable position to take' but one that offers at best 'a highly qualified justification of criminal punishment as a necessary but – for the probably extensive time being – morally tainted enterprise about which our consciences should be far from clear' (Duff 2001: 200). How then to square the circle of legitimate punishment for the perpetrator-victim? Duff does suggest a way forward that brings out the nuance in his account:

> In other instances ... unjustly excluded offenders have still committed genuine wrongs, for which they must be called to account and punished. But their punishment must include some recognition of the wrongs they have suffered and of the morally flawed character of their punishment – which is still tainted by those wrongs. (Duff 2001: 200)

What does it mean though to commit a 'genuine' wrong, and who may call the perpetrator to account; on what basis will they do so? How does the criminal justice system deal with its own complicity in its commission without appearing hypocritical? The awkwardness of the situation is seen in the role Duff affords to the sentencer and probation officer. The sentencer should recognise her complicity 'in the regretful or apologetic tones' in which she passes sentence, while the probation officer's role is to persuade the convicted person to confront and repent their wrongs by persuading them to see 'that their punishment is still justified' while recognising 'the wrongs the offender has suffered at the hands of the community' (Duff 2001: 200). But how does it help the offender if the sentencer is regretful and apologetic, and how can the probation officer claim that punishment is still justified? Why should neither appear as 'an alien voice that [perpetrators] might have to obey but that they could not make their own'? Can the representative of an 'alien and oppressive power' apologise successfully while enforcing its rule? As Duff had indicated earlier in his argument, 'if the law lacks the standing to call the unjustly excluded to account, it lacks that standing in relation to *all* crimes, including the most serious *mala in se*' (Duff 2001: 184). So, in what sense is punishment 'still justified'? At this point, we could say that the political theory of punishment has run its course and has nothing more to say. The gulf between the ideal and the actual means that normative political theory lacks the ethical wherewithal to think through the justice of punishment where the perpetrator is a victim who victimises another.

Towards Moral Psychology

Of note in what Duff says is a split opening up between guilt as a category in normative political theory, and guilt as a reflex of something else, a deeper moral reaction to a 'genuine' wrong. This appears, however, as a 'patch' for the political theory that remains unconnected to its main lines of argument. What, however, if we took it not as an unintegrated supplement which enables a compromise formation[1] to operate, but as indicating an alternative starting point for thinking about the problem? Normative political theory with its ideal/actual split remains irredeemably holed, but from its wreck, two new things start to emerge.

The first stems directly from Duff's efforts to save the normative political theory from its difficulty. While a person is not answerable as a citizen to the political community that has excluded him, this is not to say that 'no one ... has the right to call him to account – no one to whom he is answerable.' Normally, he will still 'be answerable to his victim for the moral wrong he has done' and he may be 'answerable to the members of other communities to which he [genuinely] belongs, if he commits a wrong that properly concerns him' (Duff 2001: 188). Similarly, his conduct 'can still be judged and criticised by *other values and standards than those concerning its conformity to the law*' (Duff 2001: 184, emphasis added). In order to rescue the problem of justice in an unjust setting, Duff moves outside it to find underlying moral elements which hold the justification in place.

The second is not directly related to the problem but is also indicative of a move to something else. It concerns Duff's account of remorse, what I have

[1] The phrase references Roy Bhaskar's (1993) idea of the TINA compromise formation noted in Chapter 2 in Note 18.

termed guilt here. Duff contrasts first-person remorse with third-person shame. Shame is a response that stems from the reactions of others rather than coming from one's own 'authentically first-person judgment'. Such first-person judgement is remorse in which 'I judge and condemn my own conduct for myself' (Duff 2001: 117). In a morally dialogic view, the offender is an autonomous moral agent in a normative community in which we can 'appeal to him to judge his own conduct for himself in the light of values that he has made his own' (Duff 2001: 118). Remorse (or guilt) is a personal moral–psychological reaction to a wrong done even if one was oneself a victim and is the lynchpin for establishing the possibility of self-activated repentance, reform and reconciliation – the three 'R's of punishment (Duff 2001: 107). It operates beyond the penal relationship as a moral psychological quality in the wrongdoer.

The point about both these developments in Duff's account is their relationship not to a political community but to a different source, moral psychology. Neither requires a political or legal body to induce it. The sovereign, the court and the law are all the ancillary expressions of a political settlement which Duff seeks to vindicate, but his argument entails the (non-necessary) connection of two things. The first is the existence of a political entity (to be justified in terms of political normativity). The second is its alignment with a moral psychology that exists as an underlying human capability to feel remorse (guilt) or to recognise morality independently of legal wrong. Human beings are capable of 'authentically first-person judgment', and they can relate to other human beings in social settings. Both these basic claims operate separately from and regardless of the failings of a political community, its judges and its probation officers. They constitute the starting point for a way of speaking about moral issues such as guilt, responsibility and judgement, but they require development. They are the moral qualities that remain unexplored so long as the focus of enquiry is established by normative political theory. If we start instead with the development of a moral psychology, we will be in a position eventually to relate what is true in moral psychology to the social and legal field with its (unjustifiable) normative and political claims.

For a Moral Psychology of Guilt

What is the moral psychology that underpins our 'authentically first-person judgment' (Duff) in feelings of guilt or remorse, and how does it connect what we do with the social positions we take or the normative relations we form? A good starting point is to be found in the work of Melanie Klein on the human desire to repair in her 1937 essay, 'Love, Guilt and Reparation' (in Klein 1998). I use this as the basis for exploring how feelings of guilt (remorse) might be related to situations of perpetration. I do this by contrasting psychological states based on either mutual recognition or domination and submission. Crucial to guilt is the interaction in emotional lives between subject positions which know both sets of relations. For this part of the argument, I draw on the work of the feminist psychoanalyst, Jessica Benjamin (1988). My suggestion is that Benjamin's work on mutuality, domination and respect can build on Klein's view that guilt lies at the core of the human psyche. This moral psychology can be understood separately from the normative justification of political practices, though it is relevant to them.

Love, Guilt and Reparation: Klein

Melanie Klein's work provides some understanding of the basic psychic rationale for feelings of guilt and the desire to repair and reconcile in human life.[2] In the post-Freudian psychoanalytic world of which she was a part, emphasis was placed on very early phases in infant development, which were seen as central to the development of the child and the subsequent adult. Love, security and well-being were felt in the very first interactions between the mother and child, but in this earliest phase, feelings of love jostled with feelings of hate. The child who is not fed experiences extreme anger and 'phantasies' of destruction of the 'bad' mother. Love and hate in these early interactions 'are struggling together in the baby's mind', and this 'struggle to a certain extent persists throughout life' and 'profoundly influence[s] the course and the force of the emotional lives of grown-up children' (Klein 1998: 308–9).

How does this work? At the root of Klein's analysis is a dialectic of love and hate, guilt and reparation. Love and hate are the competing tendencies in the early child. When hate is expressed in phantasy as destruction of the 'bad' mother, this leads to anxiety in the infant that actual harm has been done to the one that is loved. That anxiety, located in the tension between feelings of love and hate, is the basic ground for emotions of fear and guilt. The child seeks to address its anxiety through phantasies of reparation, but it can never quite lose the initial feeling of guilt. Accordingly, guilt and the resulting need to repair are 'more deeply rooted than is usually supposed' (Klein 1998: 309), and they become a composite element integrated into the complex emotion of love. This is extremely important to Klein's understanding of certain altruistic instincts in the human being, both as an infant and as an adult. These instincts are not just 'given' to human nature; rather they stem from the necessary existential development of the love and hate, guilt and reparation complex in the infant:

> Side by side with the destructive impulses in the unconscious mind both of the child and of the adult, there exists a profound urge to make sacrifices, in order to help and to put right loved people who in phantasy have been harmed or

[2] Klein identified two psychological positions, the 'paranoid–schizoid' and the 'depressive'. Both will concern us in later chapters (Chapters 8, 11 and 12), as ways to understand different and opposed forms of guilt (as either persecutory and punitive or reparative). While both are important to understanding how guilt operates in the penal system, this chapter primarily explores guilt in its positive, reparative form.

> destroyed. In the depths of the mind, the urge to make people happy is linked up with a strong feeling of responsibility and concern for them, which manifests itself in genuine sympathy with other people and in the ability to understand them, as they are and as they feel. (Klein 1998: 311)

Crucial to this is the consideration or compassion that comes from putting oneself in the place of other people. In identifying with them, we access a capacity 'for identification with another person' which is a 'most important element in human relationships in general, and is also a condition for real and strong feelings of love' (Klein 1998: 311). What starts out in the parent–child bond extends ultimately to all our human relations, so that this 'making reparation is … a fundamental element in love and in all human relationships' (Klein 1998: 313). The resulting dynamic is one in which the child can transfer love beyond the mother and onto others in friendship and in broader social relationships based on compassion. A good basis for adult life is therefore given in the early emotional drama between parent and child. The love that commences there, mediated by the hate that is controlled by guilt and reparation, sets the dynamic complex in place on which later success or failure in human relations depends. The important thing to note in this dialectic of love and hate is that these are intertwined so that hate is a part of early emotional life, and care, compassion and reparation are not the product of an 'uncomplicated' love. Feelings of guilt and distress 'enter as a new element into the emotion of love' (Klein 1998: 311). Guilt and the desire to repair are accordingly emotions that are deeply engrained in the human psyche and linked to the early anguish about hating and harming (in phantasy) those we love.

With regard to our concerns in this chapter, Klein's emphasis on guilt as a fundamental element in the human psyche could be important for thinking about guilt or remorse as a mental instinct in the adult perpetrator. Reparation as a central element in moral psychology could also be important in terms of Duff's three 'R's – repentance, reform and reconciliation. However, the link is so far only a general one. We need to understand better the circumstances in which the feeling of guilt might be triggered, and with this, how the situation of both the perpetrator *and* the victim, and then the perpetrator who is also a victim, can be understood.

Love, Recognition and Separation: Benjamin

How do we get from the earliest emotional states to the mental organisation involved in being a person who could violate another? If Klein provides a foundation, I want to add to this the ideas of Jessica Benjamin and her work on feminist psychoanalysis. Klein and her followers such as Donald Winnicott developed the 'object relations' approach to psychoanalysis to analyse how early experiences in childhood establish an environment which affirms the child's place in the world. In this approach, psychoanalysis shifts from its Freudian focus on the psyche 'as a force field of drives and defences' to 'an inner drama of ego and objects', meaning by the latter 'the mental representation of others' (Benjamin 1988: 11–12).[3] How we as humans do that will establish what we feel about our actions and how we act in the world. The key here is the relationship between self and other. Becoming a human being involves entering into loving relations with other human beings, and it is the nature of these relations that indicates the possibility that a differentiated moral language will articulate the situations in which inter alia we might feel guilt, remorse and sentiments of reparation.

In Benjamin's account, the personality of the child evolves through a process of mutual recognition with others, most importantly in the earliest days, with those parent figures most closely involved in its care. Having an identity depends on being the kind of creature (a human animal) that can develop an identity, but it requires the process of identification and differentiation that good, loving parenting provides. A child grows in and through relationship with others, coming to see that 'I am the doer who does, I am the author of my own acts' (Benjamin 1988: 21). She does so by being with another person who recognises her acts, feelings, intentions, existence, independence and difference. At the core of recognition is the need for the differentiation of the child, but the paradox that the child's self-differentiation and assertion of itself is only possible through recognition by another. Autonomy emerges out of an ongoing relation to heteronomy. Recognition is reflexive, that is 'includes not only the other's confirming response, but also how we find ourselves in that response' (Benjamin 1988: 21), and this can only be helpful if it is the response of another who is herself independent. If she lacks independence, she cannot give recognition of independence to the child.

This involves mutual recognition (from parent to child and thence from child to parent) that can represent a sound basis for the development of the child and adult alike. Crucially, it can be contrasted with the ways in which mutual recognition may fail and, in its place, relations of domination and submission may emerge. Where things go badly, parents may dominate children, and vice versa. A balance is achieved where mutual recognition occurs in a respectful space where both parent and child may thrive. Whichever way it goes, Benjamin's emphasis is on the structure of relationships that follow from how the child develops in the child–parent bond. I will suggest that it is in these relationships and the crucial process of identification and separation that we find the intermediate level where love, hate and guilt in Klein come together with human interactions to create the perpetrator's experience of guilt and remorse.

[3] For her summary of the different currents in object relations, see Benjamin 1988: 247–8. More generally, see Greenberg and Mitchell 1983; Mitchell and Black 1995. For Winnicott's relationship to Klein's thought, see Winnicott 2018: chs 3, 16. For Winnicott and his relevance to political theory, see Nussbaum 2013. I discuss Nussbaum's more recent *Anger and Forgiveness* (Nussbaum 2016) in Chapter 4. I explore the importance of this shift for thinking about guilt and atonement further through the work of Hans Loewald (Loewald 1980) in Chapters 7 and 8.

Domination, Submission and 'Being With'

At the core of mutual recognition lies the possibility of an unresolved tension between self and other that takes the form of an openness to the other. Mutual recognition requires that in asserting myself, I recognise you as different from me, and vice versa. Thus, it holds open a space within me that is for you, and within you for me. What is at stake here is not only an understanding of the relationship between parent and child but something with much broader implications, in terms of the nature of adult and social relations in general.

Benjamin relates her exposition to Hegel's account of the relationship between the master and the slave. In this relationship, two self-consciousnesses recognise the need for each other. Only a self-consciousness has the capacity to recognise another self-consciousness. But at the same time, in Hegel's account, each self-consciousness sees the other as a threat to its autonomy and so these self-consciousnesses end up in conflict, as each seeks to assert its independence against the other. The result is a 'life and death struggle' in which one wins and the other loses. One becomes the master, the other the slave. But as a symmetrical relationship of mutual recognition becomes reshaped into an asymmetrical relationship of dominance and submission, the value of mutual recognition is lost. The master can no longer draw upon the recognition of the other who is now his slave, and the slave can no longer draw on the recognition of the master who has defeated him. Recognition of equals becomes transformed into an unequal relation in which one wins and dominates and the other loses and submits, but both lose out in the long run. The master in particular looks to have won but has lost the possibility of recognition from the one he has enslaved and ends up uncertain as to his true identity (Hegel 1977: 116–17).[4] This is plainly an unsatisfactory outcome. How could the struggle for recognition be handled better?

For Benjamin, sustaining mutual recognition is the means of achieving independence in a way that avoids the outcome of Hegel's dialectic. The experience of the early child–parent relationship provides a parallel situation but the possibly different result that mutual recognition persists. This is observed in an early phase of infantile development as the 'rapprochement' of the baby to the parent. Initially, the baby has a sense of omnipotence that its every demand ought to be met. This places it in conflict with the parent, and rapprochement is the struggle that then plays this out. The outcome is not predetermined but depends on the relationship between parent and child. One possibility is that the child wins, and the parent continues to accede to its every demand. This looks like a victory for the child, but it is the victory of Hegel's master over the slave. The parent has given in to the child and ceased to be an independent other who can then continue to give recognition. To

[4] Hegel portrays the slave as having 'a mind of his own' and becoming a self-will, but one that is still 'enmeshed in servitude' (Hegel 1977: 119).

win is ultimately to lose for the child, and the result is 'negation, emptiness, isolation' (Benjamin 1988: 35). A second possibility is that the parent insists successfully on their own position and is intolerant of the child's will. This looks like a victory for the parent, but the result is a child that is suppressed and adapts to its suppression, never gains real independence and becomes submissive and alienated.

In the first option, the child becomes the master, the parent the slave, in the second, the roles are reversed. In both, a relationship of dominance and submission takes over from one of mutual recognition. The third possibility then, beyond 'lose-lose', is that the relationship of recognition remains in place:

> In both [the first and second cases] the sense of omnipotence survives, projected onto the other or assumed by the self; in neither case can we say that the other is recognised, or … that the process of recognition has begun. The ideal 'resolution' of the paradox of recognition is for it to continue as a constant tension, but this is not envisaged by Hegel, nor is it given much place in psychoanalysis.… The decisive problem remains recognising the other. Establishing myself … means winning the recognition of the other, and this, in turn, means I must finally acknowledge the other as existing for himself and not just for me. (Benjamin 1988: 36)

This third situation preserves the appropriate tension in mutual recognition and refuses the turn to domination and submission. It involves a sense of 'being with' another which is predicated on an 'evolving awareness of difference, on a sense of intimacy felt as occurring between "the *two* of us"' (Benjamin 1988: 47).[5] Contrast this possibility of mutuality with that represented by asymmetrical relations of domination and submission. Who dominates or submits can be reversed between parent and child, but the underlying structure remains constant. The relationship remains one of 'doer and done-to' rather than, for example, one in which both parties may be said to be 'co-doers', but the situation is ongoing. When the tension involved in sustaining and balancing a relationship based on mutual recognition becomes difficult to sustain, the psyche may give it up in favour of polarity and conflict. As a result, oppositions 'can no longer be integrated [and] one side is devalued' (Benjamin 1988: 50). This is the terrain of domination and submission, resulting from a failure to sustain mutual recognition.

The overall point is that recognition or domination and submission are both possibilities and that human beings can move from one to the other. In contrast to Hegel, Benjamin notes that the 'basic structure of domination' is 'certainly one of the structures of the psyche, [but] it is not the only one. To

[5] Benjamin (1988: 48) elaborates: '"Being with" breaks down the oppositions between powerful and helpless, active and passive; it counteracts the tendency to objectify and deny recognition to those weaker or different – to the other. It forms the basis of compassion, [of] "co-feeling", the ability to share feelings and intentions without demanding control, to experience sameness without obliterating difference.'

see it as such is to leave no space for equality' (Benjamin 1988: 48). While mutuality is often confronted with 'evidence of the striving for omnipotent control, and the hostility to others', there are 'aspects of the self … that can oppose (and help to explain) these tendencies' (Benjamin 1988: 48). Such aspects concern the possibility of mutual recognition. There are two roads of travel, towards mutuality and equality or towards domination and submission. I would suggest both may be seen as ways of playing out the dynamic of love identified by Klein, *and then dealing with it*. If I have done something hateful towards another, I threaten a relationship of domination and submission, and fail to recognise or respect. I could however go the other way, recognising my failure and adjusting to it, and my guilt would be an enabling part of this.

Complex Love, Mutuality and Guilt

My suggestion is that Klein's underlying feeling of guilt and the desire to repair may be activated at the point of interaction between Benjamin's two states of mutuality and domination or submission. Both states are possible for most people in their interaction with others. A person might develop psychologically only in terms of mutuality of recognition, or only in terms of domination and submission. We could wish that the former state was true for all of us and the latter for none. For most people, the likelihood is that they operate between these two states. Different social and developmental settings will push people to different psychological positions. Insofar as we experience our relationships as involving positions of domination and submission, and act accordingly, these are likely nonetheless to jostle with the promise and demands of mutuality. It would be in the gap between the two experienced states that feelings of guilt and thoughts of reparation would be triggered among those who dominate. Where I have sought to dominate, I am aware that an alternative approach based on mutual recognition is available. The same would be true with those who experience grief or grievance at being made to submit or are victimised. Where I was forced to submit, I may feel a sense of violation that I should be treated in this way. To feel discomfited in either position is possible because the part of me grounded in the need and value of mutual recognition remains constitutive of my psychological formation – even as I dominate or submit.

It is true that I may fail to access this possibility of mutuality, either because I do not see what I am doing, or perhaps am only able to with hindsight. It is true also that I may sense that there is something to feel, but block it with psychological techniques (denial or splitting) which reinforce my sense of righteousness ('they deserve it'). The range of subject positions is broad, and I may never revert to the mutuality setting, or ever see that it applies, and then of course I will feel no guilt at violation for what I do. But if Klein and Benjamin are right, we should be cautious even in the case of repeated violative behaviours in ruling out the possibility of correction.[6] Insofar as I can self-correct, it is because I can access the possibility of understanding and mutuality in practices of recognition, established in early childhood, but of continuing significance in how adults navigate their lives. It is the tension caused by acting in relations of domination and submission while being aware of the possibility of mutual recognition that will drive a feeling of guilt for violation. The potential to view the one from the point of view of the other (from Benjamin) provides the point to instantiate the general sense of guilt and reparation (of which Klein writes). It provides the position from which we can articulate a moral grammar of violation as a natural feature of human experience.

I have drawn on Klein's template of love, guilt and reconciliation together with Benjamin's relational space of mutuality or domination to suggest how a moral psychology of guilt responds to conduct that violates another. The key point is that the possible mental attitude of domination and submission may coexist in the perpetrator's psyche with an alternative attitude of mutuality and recognition. If we start from the profound fusing of love and hate in Klein, leading to reactions of guilt and reparation, and then think of how love is expressed (or goes awry) in interpersonal relations in Benjamin, we can understand how feelings of guilt and reparation unfold in human interaction. Given the link between early childhood and adult experience (Klein) and with personal dramas of recognition (Benjamin), we have reason to posit this as the key to feelings of guilt and reparation in adult relations. What starts as a basic experience of infantile growth remains with us, generates our most basic moral feelings and feeds into how we relate practically to each other. Guilt as the experience of violating another stems from the internal conflict between the desire to achieve domination and a counter-experience of mutual respect and recognition. Here, we are not just in the realm of thought and speech. Guilt as remorse is a real feeling, something sickening, experienced in the body as well as the mind, leaving a person feeling 'rotten, depleted of energy, tense' (Morris 1976: 99).

It is that feeling that we should try to understand, and the moral psychology made possible by psychoanalytic thinking is an effort to do so. Relating expressible feeling to human psychological development, it develops Bernard Williams's claim that ethics should 'include our best understanding of our psychological life', in a way 'compatible with naturalistic explanation' (Williams 1995: 19–20). Of course, nothing in this simple sketch of the guilt-reparation complex suggests that the practical resolution of problems caused by treating another as an object of domination rather than a subject of recognition is straightforward. All it does is indicate what the logic of moral psychology underpinning the moral grammar of guilt and reparation might be and how moral feeling (Duff's 'authentically first-person judgment') that accompanies violation might be lodged at the core of human being.

[6] See Chapter 9 for a dramatic example of how denial may be overcome.

Beyond Political Theory

We have considered a problem in the political theory of punishment concerning the guilt of perpetrators who are victims and developed an account in naturalistic moral psychology of how guilt emerges as a moral feeling. The two approaches thus juxtaposed now need to be related. In light of naturalistic moral psychology, how should we regard the normative political theory approach?

The Impasse

A moral psychological approach can address questions of guilt in situations of injustice, but it cannot resolve the problem normative political theory faces. From a moral psychology point of view, perpetrators may be victims on the receiving end of social relations of domination. They may be poor, angry and excluded, but if they act to violate their victims, there still remains a psychological space for guilt grounded in experiences of love and mutual recognition. Most, though not all, have had such experiences, through parents, close family and so on giving rise to latent moral feelings that exist independently of any questions relating to the legitimacy of state punishment. Whether the perpetrator feels under a normative obligation to the state, recognises its authorities as having moral standing, or sees its language of law as common or alien, are different questions to those explored through a moral psychology of guilt. People may feel guilt without feeling that they should be legitimately called to account by a state authority.

In practice, of course, there may be overlap between a feeling of personal guilt and whether a person feels an authority can call him to account. It will often be the same violative conduct that is judged in the psyche and by the court. Two processes may become confused so that a person who has violated another mistakenly denies a sense of psychological guilt because he morally rejects the legal system that seeks to call him to account.[7] Alternatively, he might acknowledge his guilt in an institutional setting because he feels guilty in a psychological sense when he could have distinguished the one feeling from the other. In either case it would be possible for the perpetrator as social victim to think that in one domain (before the state authority, viewed with cause as illegitimate) they should not feel guilt, while in the other (the place of internal moral judgement) they should: 'I feel guilty, but not before you'. Analytically, there are two dimensions at play in situations of social injustice: what a person

[7] An example of how moral and legal guilt rub up against each other in a situation of political conflict is that of Patrick Magee, an IRA bomber (discussed in Chapter 4). Of his actions, he states: 'Someday I may be able to forgive myself. Although I still stand by my actions, because at the time we were trapped and there was no other way, I will always carry the burden that I harmed other human beings. But I'm not seeking forgiveness' (Cantacuzino 2015: 80). Morally, he seeks to forgive himself; before a British legal court, he does not.

owes morally to himself, his victim and his values, and what he owes to a court of law in a polity sitting in judgement over him. We cannot say either that injustice in judgement and punishment removes or cancels the perpetrator's moral guilt, or (per Duff) that such guilt compensates for injustice in the system that condemns him. What a person did is subject to his own moral judgement where reckoning is needed even if he rejects the court's authority, while the court's lack of authority is not cured because he feels personal guilt. Accordingly, the normative political theorist still faces the impasse discussed earlier where individual and social justice conflict.

But why *should* a perpetrator feel guilt if he acted to violate another in a socially unjust context? It is true that he might reflect on the social conditions that led him to violate another, but this would normally lead not to guilt denial but to weighing questions of responsibility in his own mind. Psychologically, he still acted to victimise another, and he cannot square this with an attitude of mutual recognition. He needs therefore to morally account for what he did, even if he also sees that what he did should be contextualised in what was done to him, as a victim of social conditions. He needs to take responsibility for his part even as he acknowledges the setting in which he acted.[8] The overall point is that we have two viewpoints that sit at different levels and do not conjoin, one as a matter of normative relations in a polity, the other as an issue of ethical and affective standpoint of the individual. The moral psychological position does not resolve the normative political theory impasse.

First Way Forward: Normative Political Theory and a Different Future

What if any are the ways forward? One way out of the impasse in normative political theory is unsuccessful, but it leads to a better position through the moral psychology approach. It involves considering how a normative political justification of punishment might apply justly in a reformed social setting. If social injustice issues undercut individual retributive justice, there would need to be structural social reform so that a polity is seen genuinely to wish to address them. Criminal responsibility would then begin to look less like blaming victims for social conditions for which they are not responsible. If past and present victimisation of perpetrators is actively addressed, their moral guilt can begin to be aligned with the blaming practices of the criminal justice system. Victimised perpetrators would begin to see they ought to feel guilty not just internally but in the external court of law too. A society that was demonstrating equality and mutual respect to its most disadvantaged could align its social messages with those concerning personal moral conduct, leading to a positive spiral of development. Guilt as an interpersonal psychological feeling and as a

[8] This is an example of what I call in Chapter 8 dealing with guilt by taking responsibility in a mature way.

societal practice could then align. Many years ago, Jeffrie Murphy[9] articulated this position well (but here the last sentence eventually becomes interesting):

> If we think that institutions of punishment are necessary and desirable, and if we are morally sensitive enough to want to be sure that we have the moral right to punish..., then we had better first make sure that we have restructured society in such a way that criminals genuinely do correspond to the only model that will render punishment possible – i.e. make sure that they are autonomous and that they do benefit in the requisite sense. Of course, if we did this then ... crime itself and the need to punish would radically decrease if not disappear entirely. (Murphy 1979: 110)

This reflects the normative political thinking we considered in the first section of this chapter. In its modern classical form, it will be recalled that Kant saw problems of bad social motives among people as stemming from a badly evolved arrangement of the 'civil constitution', while Hegel viewed poverty as the problem underlying challenges to the justice of punishment.[10] In Duff's modern argument similarly, problems of alienated judgement and unjust punishment are rooted in social injustice. If we were to take those away, his communicative theory works better. It is tempting to think therefore that the answer to the problem of justice for victims who victimise, or of doing justice in an unjust society, depends on radical social and economic reform, but is this all we should say?

'Jam Tomorrow, but Never Jam Today'

I will now raise two points against this argument which begin to steer us away from normative political theory and towards a moral psychological position. The first is that the deferral of just punishment to a future time obviously tells us nothing about justice in the present and what we should do for now. All that we know is that punishment is unjust under modern social conditions. Murphy's comment is from a 1973 paper, and we might think that under conditions of economic austerity things are no better today. Punishment meanwhile becomes more and more a feature of social life through increased use of the criminal law and particularly of imprisonment. Acknowledging the permanence of injustice means that writing and thinking about punishment becomes a melancholy science which can only repeat old themes before a seemingly inexorable reality. Debates about the usual philosophical suspects, retributivism, consequentialism, responsibility, freewill and determinism, continue without end, but these are all aspects of Williams's peculiar morality from which no one, it seems, can escape. The promise of a bright possible

9 I discuss Murphy's later work in Chapter 8.

10 On Hegel, see also the previous chapter. Axel Honneth's account discussed there of a different, materially grounded, theory of recognition from Hegel's Jena period, makes a similar point.

future begins to look hollow in the face of ongoing injustice, so that in truth the impasse continues.

A second point returns to Murphy's suggestion that radical social reform is necessary if we think that institutions of punishment are 'necessary and desirable'. There is something ironic in permitting the call for social justice to become a way of *maintaining* punishment. Should we think in this way? This is where his final sentence becomes interesting. If radical social reform were to occur, he suggests, the need for punishment might radically decrease or disappear. If that were so, why should he think punishment necessary and desirable? Perhaps we could permit him the 'necessary', but only in a practical sense, for the time being, for reasons of social protection, until punishment was no longer needed. If ex hypothesi it should disappear because it has become practically unnecessary, Murphy would surely not seek a moral reason for maintaining it. On this argument, which has a pedigree going back to Kant,[11] Murphy becomes an abolitionist. The underlying point here is that deferring just punishment to a time when no punishment would be needed represents a paradox that does not escape the normative political theorist's impasse. In the process, it raises an important question about the underlying ethical value of punishment, whether it is essential to human society, and whether there should be other ways of dealing with conflict between persons that lead to violation. We might say that this is a non-question since in an ideal state no such conflicts would occur, but on the moral psychological approach adopted here, human beings are complex and not saints. They are capable of acting in both 'doer–done to' and 'being with' ways, so even in the best possible of social worlds, it seems valid to consider what would take punishment's place.[12] This takes us to another way out of the impasse, one that follows a moral psychological route.

Second Way Forward: Moral Psychology and a Different Modality

The argument in what follows addresses the questions just raised: whether something could take the place of punishment, and what should happen in the present. Moral psychology has something to say here and I approach it

[11] And before him Plato. Kant claimed that 'it is quite reasonable to maintain, as Plato did, that in a perfect state no punishments at all would be necessary' (Kant 1993: 246).

[12] Peter Ramsay argues for a 'political' model of punishment that holds onto it as the deprivation of civil liberties and fines but sees it declining and abolishing itself in a radical democracy. There, people have reason to respond respectfully to each other both individually and in terms of social and political arrangements. Though his argument is Hegelian in inspiration, it aligns with the Kantian paradox. If there were to be no violation in a radical democracy then perhaps he would be right, but this would need to be argued for as part of a fuller theory about the nature of human behaviour. If we follow something like Klein's account of the complex nature of love (or other approaches concerning love's vicissitudes – see also Chapters 7 and 8), we might think that humans will always have to deal with conflict and violation, though this may be much less acute under better social arrangements. Ramsay argues for 'a vigorous reintegrative approach to punishment' (Ramsay 2016: 105–6) suggesting that a moral psychology lurks within such an idea.

by considering something Murphy says about autonomy. He writes that for punishment to be just, it would be necessary to provide a world where people really were autonomous in their decision-making (while noting the paradox that such people would not commit crimes). He confronts a common problem here in post-Kantian thought: that to be free or autonomous is to be rational and to be able to think and act aside from those conditions in nature or society which determine what we would otherwise do. I would say we can never be free in this way, and that thinking we can is indeed an example of Williams's peculiar morality at work (see Chapter 1). Importantly, seeing autonomy and freedom in such terms gives a false sense of what they might mean. The makings of an alternative approach are to be found in the moral psychology developed here.

Take the person who develops out of Klein's account of complex love and works through relationships based on Benjamin's mutual recognition. She is able to respect and love others and to maintain an attitude to them of 'being with' as a 'co-doer'. She can check herself against desires to dominate which lie at the heart of victimisation and alternatively resist efforts to make her submit to victimhood. She holds onto love and recognition as her ground and moral compass as she navigates the world, working with the psychological patterns she has developed to engage the social determinations she confronts. Her autonomy and freedom are not contra-causal but are rooted in her psychological being and social situation. They are rooted in her love-based psychological processes and how these sustain her in the world. She feels free and autonomous when she is able to act out of love and respect for herself and others.

This is also the basis on which a person addresses, and can be supported in addressing, violative behaviour by herself or by another to her. To violate another is to fail to recognise or respect them as worthy of mutual regard, and the moral aim of any person who does this is to work through her psychological roots in loving self- and other-identification where she can 'be with' others. It follows that any process aimed at dealing with violation should be designed to support a person coming to terms in this way with what she has done. Something similar is true with victims who have been forced to submit to another's violation and need to recover their sense of self as worthy of love and mutuality. A *substantive* freedom and autonomy in a moral psychological sense of being able to express love and recognition of self and other is the aim of the process.

The Individual and the Social

This begins to answer the question of a different modality to that of punishment and it also addresses the question of what we do now. It suggests that issues of violation need not be deferred until society is radically restructured, a prospect that seems in any case far distant. It can be addressed now, though not by way of punishment. As regards dealing with violation now, it remains impossible to deny the significance of social and cultural practices which make violation and victimisation a part of the modern world. To radically restructure, as Murphy suggested, remains a necessity. However, in the absence of this, people who violate, or are violated by, others still need *in the present* to address and understand what they have done, and how (and why) they might not do it anymore. It is therefore necessary in the present to find ways of addressing violative behaviour, even if we know that an individual's motivations cannot be completely separated from their social context. Acts of violation as either perpetrator or victim sit with people and need to be addressed by them, even if it is true that perpetrators acted in circumstances not of their making.

One way of dealing with this is to argue that addressing behaviour that violates another should both identify internal psychological processes and link these to their social environment. This would show how both the psychological and the sociological contribute to violative action. For example, if a man has behavioural issues around his female partner that lead him to be violent, it would be important to address how he characteristically thinks about personal relationships, women and the family, and how he has been brought up to make certain assumptions about gender. He may need to address internal painful experience in his own past relating to how a parent dominated and refused to respect him, setting up repetitive patterns of domination in his adult life (Wilson 2021a). In addition, he may consider how his assumptions are supported by images of men and women on social and other media. A social culture that encourages 'doer–done to' relations in terms of a range of ideologies concerning winners and losers, class or racial superiority, or masculine values will also encourage behaviours that violate and victimise.[13] In modern societies, such a social culture comes with both an economic structure that is unjust and exploitative and with psychological self-understandings affecting individual relations which need to be addressed.

Punishment as a 'Doer–Done To' Relationship

Thinking in this way takes us away from the penal with its roots in a legal psychology of responsibility, blame and punishment in favour of ways of addressing violation in moral psychological terms. There is a further fundamental reason why addressing violation does not track the route of punishment. This argument will be developed as the book progresses, but it is also reflected in the argument of this chapter, so I raise it here. It starts with why human beings might want to dominate and force others to submit and then comes to punishment as a form of domination.

[13] Examples of how a social setting and a psyche come together to produce violation abound in the testimony of victims in The Forgiveness Project, some of which are discussed in Chapter 5. Here some victims come to see how their personal violation reflects a broader set of social practices which also need to be addressed.

The issue arises from the possibility of another kind of psychological reaction to that based on love and recognition that we have just discussed. This is a negative reaction that is closely associated with punishment. As we have noted, Klein offers an account of love that is complex, in which anger and hate are connected to produce a psyche anxious to repair relationships it thinks it may have damaged. In Klein, two basic positions ground human development, one which holds to love, the other which through anger and hatred wishes to destroy and persecute.[14] Complex love emerges out of the desire to develop a reparative commitment in reaction to this negative force. In this other mindset, human beings behave in a way that is rageful and punitive towards others. They seek to dismiss and to punish the other in a 'doer–done to' way. People generally grow out of such an approach, but they can fall back into it in times of anxiety. This underlying possibility explains why domination and submission are a real possibility in the human psyche alongside the potential for mutuality and recognition.

How does this argument relate to punishment as a social practice? I argue below (Chapters 8 and 11) that the modern penal system is based on two fundamental elements, a restorative (mutual and recognitive) and a punitive (dominative and submissive) approach to violation, but the dominant mode is the latter. A system based on punishment and imprisonment is designed to be punitive and controlling, to return pain for pain and to require submission. Punishment in a penal system that has as its apex the modern industrial and security prison involves responding to hurt with hurt, violation with violation. Its effect is to enforce its domination through the pain of the penal instrument, especially the prison sentence. Of course, punishment comes wrapped up with other elements, for example, a philosophy of just deserts (Kant and Hegel) or of penal communication (Duff), and these morally elevated ideas obscure the fact that punishment is itself a matter of domination, and violation, of another. Similarly, there are elements of care and reform in the penal system and a desire to make life better for prisoners, an element of 'love' in the penal system (Bennett 2019). Yet these are secondary to and shaped and limited by the overall punitive nature of the process. There is at the core of the modern penal system an effort to dominate and control and to establish a 'doer–done to' relationship by means of a disciplinary regime.

From this point of view, there is a reason why punishment is inimical to the kind of moral psychology advanced here and why it should be abolished. For the moral psychologist, the aim is to reinstate relationships based on love (Klein) in moral states of mutuality and recognition (Benjamin) and to resist relations of domination and submission. Yet through the central form of punishment, involving its apex institution (the prison), the penal system is itself based on the psychological relation that is to be opposed, that of domination

[14] The two positions identified by Klein are termed by her the 'paranoid–schizoid' and the 'depressive'. I deal with this in depth in Chapters 7, 8 and 11.

and submission. It is hard to see how a person who is to be punished for violating another will be encouraged to see the wrong in 'doer–done to' relations of domination and forced submission when that is precisely what he receives in return for his own act of violation. Punishment in its essence repeats the cycle of 'doer–done to' relations. This is the central reason, I will argue in Chapters 11 and 12, why a moral psychological view should aim for an abolitionist outcome with regard to punishment.

Moral Psychology as Ethical Critique

In this final section, I consider the implications of juxtaposing two very different approaches to guilt, one based in normative political philosophy, the other being developed out of psychoanalytic theory.

The Impasse of Just Deserts Theory

There is a parallel between this and the previous chapter. Writing of the young Hegel in contrast with his later systematic philosophy brings out the difference between a metaphysics of love and violation and its political and legal institutionalisations in terms of crime and punishment. Two contrasting vocabularies emerge: of violation, grief and reconciliation on the one hand, and of law, responsibility and reason on the other. The former reaches into the moral experience of perpetrating, or being subjected to, violation and generates an ethically real ground for thinking critically about the latter. It provides an ethically real and institutionally critical (ERIC) basis for evaluating the nature and the limits of the later legal and political theory.

Something similar has informed the discussion of this chapter. Here we started with a problem in normative political theory concerning the victim of social injustice who victimises another, raising the question of how punishment delivers just deserts in an unjust society. This is a problem that we partially canvassed in the previous chapter, for the older Hegel was one of the first to note it, though he found no way of resolving it. Here, we put together Kant and Hegel and considered a modern theorist, Duff, and the way he deals with it. Normative political theory circles around the problem of just deserts in an unjust society and still finds no way of resolving it. To the extent that it has an answer, it invokes a world where just deserts would be possible – but unnecessary. The paradox is that where punishment is needed, it is unjustified, but where it is justified, it is unneeded.

This is the impasse or the aporia of modern just deserts theory which underlies every discussion of criminal justice. Of course, it is possible to identify a range of consequentialist functions that punishment can be claimed to deliver (protection, security and deterrence), but once the question of justice raises its head, sooner or later normative political theory runs up against its impasse. We also found, however, in probing this problem that the very idea of crime and punishment was called into question. Punishment began to look not like a universal institutional foundation to be retained for all times, but one that is conditional on particular negative social settings. If people are truly rational and autonomous and are given a 'good go' at social life, punishment should wither away; who would wish to retain it save as a curiosity of the past, like the steam-driven engine?

Taking the Moral Psychology Route

The focal point of the chapter has been on guilt which is something that normative political theory views in terms of blame, responsibility, freedom and punishment. To these, I have opposed the guilt terms of a moral psychology which identifies in human nature a love that develops intertwined with hate, producing a complex love committed to repair imagined damage to another. I then fed this Kleinian position into an account of human relations which sees them as pursuing either mutual recognition and respect or seeking to dominate and submit (Benjamin).[15] Complex love must negotiate the difficult world of 'doer–done to' versus 'doing together' or 'being with' others, while guilt is the point of psychological disturbance, of feeling, as Morris puts it, 'rotten, depleted of energy, tense' (Morris 1976: 99). That occurs when human beings that are psychologically grounded in complex, reparative love appreciate they have disrespected another by victimising or violating her.

Taking the moral psychological route is not a way of curing the normative political impasse, since unequal and unjust social and political relations are not repaired even if individual guilt is a reparative emotion. There does exist a route from one to the other since the desire to repair individual harm eventually identifies its social roots, but in modern societies, this is the road we seem destined not to take. This leaves two distinct levels of the social and of the individual which need to be combined, but they exist as a matter of social reality rather than as a simple theoretical impasse. What the moral psychology of guilt points to in the meantime is a functioning concept of moral guilt even where guilt's political and normative justification has failed. The two must be kept separate for the one is not a compensation for the lack of the other, but the question of moral guilt still calls for attention, however imperfectly, now and not in a future that will not happen any time soon.

Prisons for example are sites, I suggest, where both social injustice *and* torturous psychological guilt are played out. The moral psychological route suggests things that should be done, carefully and with a broader social

[15] In Chapters 7 and 8, I develop a second metapsychological route to guilt through Freud and the work of Hans Loewald, which focuses on the idea of atonement ('at-one-ment'). This and the fact that Loewald develops the core idea of a psychological structure with a flexible understanding of what it means to be responsible make his account attractive. I offer the two routes, this prototype here and the later approach, as parallel attempts to engage metapsychologically with guilt after violation.

viewpoint in mind, for those who have seriously violated others. At the same time, the need to address violation and the grief it causes points to the conclusion that punishment is an unhelpful approach that should be abolished. Few will learn to abandon 'doer–done to' relations by being further submitted to them in a prison cell. Addressing violation involves efforts to recognise the mutuality rather than the otherness in a perpetrator as a basis for understanding how disrespect works by domination and making another submit, and thereby starting to change behaviour. Punishment is in its essence not designed to do this.

This chapter, like the previous, represents a prototype ERIC ('ethically real, institutionally critical') argument, identifying the ethically naturalistic basis for critique of institutional ways of dealing with violation. With young Hegel, we looked at a metaphysical philosophical argument for love and fate which we contrasted with the normative political theory of his later work. Here, we have developed the critical position in a different way, through a metapsychological enquiry into how the human animal emerges out of fundamental emotions to deploy a complex love and to choose between respect and domination. As I indicated in Chapter 1, my aim is to build up a picture of the metaphysical animal as a whole, which includes the capacity to think in deep ethical terms about its condition and actions, and the grounding of that capacity in its naturalistic species development. The unifying point for both is (complex) love, which drives human development both metaphysically and metapsychologically. These are the two basic dimensions of the metaphysical animal that thinks and loves.

Part II

Moral Psychology, Law and the Metaphysics of Forgiveness

Introduction to Part II: Towards Synthesis

Part I left a question and invited a development. The question was, if the two prototypes of a moral psychological approach followed an ethical, metaphysical route (Chapter 2) and then a metapsychological (Chapter 3) one, how were these related? The answer provided at the start of Chapter 4 is that the relationship is synthetic with the metaphysical expressing at its own level the metapsychological and the latter being its ground. The topical or substantive development is from the moral psychology of *guilt* (Chapters 2 and 3) to that of *forgiveness and reconciliation* (Chapters 4 and 5). Developing our understanding of the nature of moral psychology would at the same time take us beyond perpetrators' guilt to a broader understanding of what is at stake with violation.

Martha Nussbaum's *Anger and Forgiveness* (2016) plays an important role in Chapter 4. For synthesis, a deep grasp of human ontology must include both the metaphysical understanding expressed in our moral psychology and how it is made possible by our metapsychology. We are animals that think and love, and it is in our nature for these elements to work together. Nussbaum's book appeared when I was working through these ideas and her past commitment to both ethics and psychoanalysis suggested it would support my argument. In *Anger and Forgiveness*, however, she discards her main metapsychological argument in favour of a simpler ethical commitment to unconditional love and compassion. Since I wanted to conjoin metapsychology and ethical metaphysics, her argument became a helpful foil rather than a direct support (though foils are supportive too). Chapter 4 begins with an argument for retaining and synthesising the two 'metas' which make up the metaphysical animal. I compare and contrast my position on the importance of metapsychology with Nussbaum's discarding of it.

With regard to the moral language of forgiveness, Nussbaum was also an interlocutor. Here there is something in common and something with which to disagree. She too opposes the approach of normative political theory with its emphasis on forgiveness as an exchange process, what she calls 'transactional forgiveness'. This essentially makes forgiveness an extension of guilt in an exchange relation linked to crime and punishment. She wants to go beyond 'the whole forgiveness idea' (Nussbaum 2016: 85) in favour of directly changing the social world as a response to violation. I argue this throws out the baby of valid *moral-psychological* exchange (transactions) with the bathwater of recriminatory blaming practices. There is a deeper kind of forgiveness that is based on a 'mature' moral psychology rather than the law's 'primitive' one, and which is necessary if those who have been violated, and their violators, are to move forward.

Chapter 5 presses the argument in favour of the metaphysics of forgiving by linking a phenomenology of love, forgiveness and reconciliation. It draws upon the work of *The Forgiveness Project* to contrast the nature of an ethically mature moral psychology of forgiveness with what Bernard Williams (1995: 202) called a *moralised* account. The latter permits the terms of modern law and exchange to shape and limit what a naturalistically developed moral psychology can achieve. My aim is a moral psychology with an adequate metaphysics of forgiveness, which the chapter seeks to provide. Jeffrie Murphy once criticised accounts of forgiveness of this kind as involving 'obscurity and mystery for their own sake', requiring 'leaps into special realms' (Murphy and Hampton 1988: 30). Chapter 5 suggests we need such 'special realms' to understand our moral experience and supports such 'leaps'. The contrast between its two main sections then provides the basis for an ethically real and institutionally critical (ERIC) analysis of mainstream forgiveness in theory and practice.

4

Love, Guilt and Forgiveness

> ... whether I can let go of the need to blame ... sometimes I can and sometimes I can't ...
>
> Jo Berry (Cantacuzino 2015: 79)

> Someday I may be able to forgive myself.... But I'm not seeking forgiveness.
>
> Patrick Magee (Cantacuzino 2015: 80)

As human beings, we are metaphysical animals who think and love, yet we are also, as we know only too well, members of a species capable of violating each other often very badly. In daily life, we use ethical language to reflect on what we do and who we are. Our moral sentiments enable us to express a sense of responsibility and, where appropriate, guilt and other moral feelings for our roles and actions in the world. In this chapter, we will consider how this language extends to an understanding of forgiveness as a central term in our moral psychology. Such a language is possible because humans are animals with the capacity to express themselves in ethical terms, as members of a species with particular moral and psychological attributes. Taken at its fullest, moral psychology concerns both the ethical and psychological dimensions of human ontology and how these are conjoined. This book argues that the underlying basis for this to happen is love, in both its ethical and psychological dimensions, which is central to what humans are.

This chapter has two main objects, one general, and the other specific. First, it takes the idea that the human animal exists at two levels, the specifically ethical (the metaphysical) and the metapsychological and makes the case that both are necessary for an account of how humans deal with violation. My argument is that it is only if we see human being as mind and body, as thought and feeling, as the animal that thinks and loves that we will be able to understand violation. Only from such a synthetic perspective will we be able to know how violation should be dealt with in terms of human nature. I presented in Part I two prototypes of such an argument with regard to love and guilt. One of these (on the young Hegel) took a specifically ethical and metaphysical route, while the other (on Klein and Benjamin) was metapsychological in its approach. These two approaches now need to be synthesised, as they are in human ontology, to establish a complete account of our moral psychology as ethical, metaphysical and metapsychological beings. This does not yet occur with the prototype arguments of the previous chapters.[1]

The second main object is to take this overall understanding and to address some arguments recently developed by Martha Nussbaum in her *Anger and Forgiveness* (Nussbaum 2016) concerning guilt and forgiveness and the nature of psychoanalysis. Nussbaum's approach has some similarity to my own, but in fact challenges what I am trying to do. She too places love at the centre of her argument and she has written previously about the importance of psychoanalytic metapsychology for moral and political argument (Nussbaum 2004, 2014). *Anger and Forgiveness*, however, is a recent statement on crime and punishment where she rejects her earlier position. Partly as a consequence of this, she rejects the moral importance of guilt and forgiveness, preferring instead to see the anger violation causes as a means of committing directly to social reform through what she calls 'the Transition'. She sidelines directly moral transactions around guilt and forgiveness between perpetrators and victims in favour of socially and politically eudaimonic action. While I do not deny that social change is extremely important, I argue that morally engaged transactions and social transitions should both be part of eudaimonic change.

This chapter has three main sections. I begin the next section by arguing for the conjoined nature of metaphysical and metapsychological experience in the moral psychology of the human animal. I argue that the nature of love leads to analysis of their relation and combination and that this is central to understanding one kind of moral experience, guilt. In the second section, I move to consider Nussbaum's discussion of guilt and forgiveness and with it, her rejection of psychoanalysis. This leads me into a discussion of her account of the biblical parable of the prodigal son and the role of forgiveness in it. I argue from this for the moral importance of forgiveness in reconciliation.

In a third section, I then take a 'case study' of guilt, forgiveness and reconciliation in action, considering the moral dialogue between Jo Berry and Patrick Magee (Cantacuzino 2015). Berry's father was a Conservative politician killed by the Irish Republican Army in Brighton in 1984 in an attempt on the British Prime Minister Margaret Thatcher's life. Magee was one of the bombers. Since his release from prison, Berry and Magee have conducted a sustained dialogue aimed at forgiveness and reconciliation important both to perpetrator and victim in moving forward. This is, however, a complex process that occurs in a social and political setting and one that limits the possibilities for individual as well as social change. Both individual and social change are necessary for reconciliation, but neither is finally possible without the other. As we will see, this point is illustrated in the hesitations evident in the two brief quotes at the head of this chapter. I emphasise against Nussbaum the irreducible value of moral

[1] Though the link between metapsychology and metaphysics is immanent in Benjamin's discussion in particular in Chapter 3.

engagement alongside social commitments to change (transition), and that an ethical critique of law and punishment[2] requires us to understand the difference between legal and moral transactions (engagements) around violation. To use Nussbaum's word, transitions require the latter kind of transaction.

Guilt and Love: Combining Ethics and Psychology

I aim in this section to make good my claim for the necessary combination of metaphysical and metapsychological elements in how we understand guilt in moral psychology. The argument has three elements. First, I go back to my initial thinking about guilt and love in discussing a problem in Hannah Arendt's *Eichmann in Jerusalem* (Arendt 1964; Norrie 2017c) and how it might be solved with the help of Karl Jaspers and Primo Levi. This was one of two encounters that got me thinking about how criminal justice should be understood in relation to love. I mentioned one of these at the end of Chapter 1; I start this section with the other. Second, I argue that love must be understood as combining both metaphysical and metapsychological elements. Third, I then explain why I think guilt should be understood in a similar way.

The Importance of Metaphysical Guilt: Arendt, Jaspers and Levi

If we dig deep enough into legal and political theory, we find an understanding of guilt that might initially be denied but which is necessarily ethical and metaphysical in its nature. I came to this conclusion from considering Karl Jaspers's account of metaphysical guilt in his discussion of German war guilt (Jaspers 2000)[3] and Primo Levi's moral experience of living in and after Auschwitz (Levi 2013). I approached Jaspers through a philosophical dialogue I worked out between him and Hannah Arendt in her *Eichmann in Jerusalem* (Arendt 1964). I argued that Jaspers provided the necessary ethical basis for an answer to a problem Arendt encountered, one that was supported by Levi's experience of life in a concentration camp (Norrie 2017c: chs 7, 10).

Arendt's Problem and Jaspers's Solution

Put briefly, Arendt had asked how a court of law could validly punish Adolf Eichmann who lacked a moral outlook with which it could engage. The problem with Eichmann and others like him was that they were 'neither perverted nor sadistic' but were rather 'terribly and terrifyingly normal', representing a 'new type of criminal [who] commits his crime under circumstances that

[2] That is, an ethically real institutionally critical (ERIC) approach as described in Chapter 1.

[3] For Jaspers, 'metaphysical guilt' has a specific meaning in a fourfold typology of political, legal, moral and metaphysical guilt. He found the first three of these lacking in adequate depth for dealing with German war guilt (see Norrie 2017c: ch 7). As its name suggests, I see metaphysical guilt as reflecting a form of metaphysical thinking, in the same way as I presented the young Hegel's work l in Chapter 2.

make it well-nigh impossible for him to know or to feel that he is doing wrong' (Arendt 1964: 276). As a result, Eichmann could not be punished for normal ethical reasons, only killed because no one 'can be expected to share the earth with you' (Arendt 1964: 128). I felt there was something compelling yet counterintuitive here, suggesting as it did that the worse a defendant's behaviour, the less it could be validly judged. It spoke cogently perhaps to the limits of legal judgement before a deeply immoral actor but the suggestion that Eichmann could not be held morally to account seemed wrong. How could one address this problem?

I turned here to what was expressed by Jaspers as a sense of metaphysical guilt. Jaspers used this idea to explore why it might be that ordinary Germans who were not exposed to criminal charges or a sense of their own moral failings might still be judged guilty for what had been done in their name. He wrote 'Somewhere among men the unconditional prevails – the capacity to live only together or not at all' (Jaspers 2000: 26). Metaphysical guilt involved 'the lack of absolute solidarity with the human being as such – an indelible claim beyond morally meaningful duty' (Jaspers 2000: 65). While the meaning of metaphysical guilt was not entirely clear (Norrie 2017c: 134–40), it provided an underlying ethical ground that countered what Arendt saw as Eichmann's lack of a sense of guilt. If he felt he had done no wrong, there was a deep metaphysical sense in which he had. A court addressing Eichmann's denial could reach for this underlying form of guilt to respond to him.

Levi's Experience

The argument however led to another question. If a deeper ethical sense of guilt could be identified in something like Jaspers's terms, why should we trust it? Jaspers himself worried that it would be dismissed as just the 'crazy idea of some philosopher' (Jaspers 2000: 68). Alternatively, could it be seen as an ontological facet of human being, triggered in a particular context? To answer this question, I drew on Primo Levi's thoughts and experience as a concentration camp survivor in *The Drowned and the Saved* (Levi 2013). Levi wrote that in the camp, 'Almost everybody feels guilty of having omitted to offer help' as a basic failure to meet the 'demand for solidarity, for a human word, advice, even only a listening ear [that] was permanent and universal but rarely satisfied' (Levi 2013: 82). Inmates felt shame for the misdeeds of others 'in which they felt involved, because they sense that what had happened around them … was irrevocable' and could never be cleansed (Levi 2013: 92). The failure to help in the presence of such deeds 'introduced into the world of existing things' (Levi 2013: 75) was the source of the survivor's guilt. Such guilt no doubt affected the person in a psychologically traumatising way, but Levi understood and expressed it in metaphysical and ethical terms.

Levi's practical moral experience of guilt in the camp (failed solidarity, irrevocable evil introduced into the world) came remarkably close, I argued, to Jaspers's philosophical reflections on metaphysical guilt (Norrie 2017c: ch 10).

Comparing Jaspers and Levi, we can see the same idea of a universal solidarity that has been breached as a deep, non-actual, human sense of guilt emerging from the experience of a particular reality. Levi gives us reason to see metaphysical guilt, as expressed by Jaspers and as he directly experienced it himself, as a part of human ontology and not just the 'crazy idea of some philosopher'.

Love as Metaphysics and Metapsychology

Thus far, the argument explains how metaphysical guilt grounds ethical relations and is reflected in human experience. I have not yet explained why I relate this to love. Before doing so, I turn to love's general nature and then to its relation to guilt. Love is the general ground, guilt the particular experience.[4] Love, I argue, is both metaphysical and metapsychological in its nature.

Two Approaches to Love

One way of thinking about love is philosophical and metaphysical and here I draw on Roy Bhaskar's philosophy of what he called metaReality (Bhaskar 2012, 2016: ch 7), which accounts for love as an ethical force with both conditional and unconditional forms. In its conditional form, it relates to specific settings that shape it, for example as sexual love, love of a parent for a child or 'civic' love. In its unconditional form, it reflects forms of love that are universal in their terms. Such love can be represented, Bhaskar suggests, as moving outwards in a series of increasing circles, from a person's love of self to love of another, to love of all other human beings, to love of the species and to love of other species. From there love proceeds to its broadest form as 'the source or sustaining power in creation itself, most customarily known as god' (Bhaskar 2012: 181).

This is, in Bhaskar's thought, a kind of dialectical process of mutual entailment of unconditional love that moves from who we are individually to the broadest expression of our place in the universe, and the universe in us. We are all part of a huge work of being and creation, which is customarily, but not necessarily, spoken of in terms of god. It is a philosophical way of speaking about love as a universal phenomenon familiar from a range of world religions, but equally requiring no particular religious commitment. Others will describe and understand it differently, but something like this route is familiar to most of us as part of our everyday human speculation about ourselves and our place in the universe.

[4] Love can be discussed both as a key emotion and motivation and more deeply, as ontologically constitutive of human being. Both are important but the deeper sense, pursued here, is more fundamental. It is not only psychologically but also sociologically constitutive as Christian Smith (2015) argues. Love for him is the latent category that emerges from enquiry into human flourishing, destructive tendencies and the erosion of trust in modern societies. For discussion, see Norrie 2017a.

A second approach to love is different. It is through Freudian metapsychology, and here I draw on different psychoanalytical sources. Generally, love is seen as a libidinous drive together with emotional relations of identification, care and reciprocity that 'get us going' as creatures in the world. It lies behind the human desire to live and be and to develop a sense of oneself. Human love is also generalisable in this conception in that it is only made possible through the love of others which educates each of us in being ourselves. Sigmund Freud spoke of libido, the life force, love and Eros. In the previous chapter, I drew on Melanie Klein (1998) and Jessica Benjamin (1988) on complex love and loving recognition. In Chapters 7 and 8, I will draw on Hans Loewald (1980) and Jonathan Lear (1990, 1998, 2015) to talk of how love and identification in human metapsychology leads to a sense of wholeness. Lear writes of Freud as identifying 'a basic developmental force in nature … which he called love'. Romantic love is only one manifestation 'of a far-reaching psychological force' which 'permeates the animate world and tends towards the development of ever higher and more complex unities' (Lear 1988: 12).

From these rather different psychoanalytic positions, the argument is that human being is about love and how it develops. There is the psychological idea that a person can love themselves because they are loved by others, go on to love others in turn and extend their love outwards to the world. Love in metapsychology, as Freud developed it,[5] is central to human nature. This is the second, metapsychological route to love, but it might be thought to be very different from the idea of metaphysical love sketched previously. Can these two routes be combined?

Ethical Expression and Psychological Ground

It might be thought that these are not just distinct ways of thinking about love but that they are split and divergent. I suggest to the contrary that love can be understood as both grounded in the libidinous, psychological and relational powers of the human animal and, by virtue of that grounding, involving a metaphysical relationship to the world. That relationship can be expressed in the terms of universal love such as those set out earlier. Such terms will vary in how they are linked to particular settings, but they will generally involve understanding what is owed to another and to the world in terms of appropriate feelings and actions. It is in other words true of human beings that they are both an animal species and one that is capable of developing their psychological experience in metaphysical terms. We are creatures with animal needs that include the ability to speculate on the nature of the universe and our place in it. Our being generates the question: how is it possible that the human animal can think as it does save as it develops with the capacities so to think? Given our

[5] As Lear elaborates, Freud's understanding of love grew unevenly and incompletely but found its proper location in his later structural account of the psyche: Lear 1998: ch 6; 2015. Loewald (1980) presses the case for developing this element in Freud's thought: see Chapter 7.

human experience as thinking and feeling beings, it seems impossible not to see an intrinsic link between our human metapsychology and our metaphysical powers. It follows therefore that we should think that the two approaches, of psychoanalysis and philosophy, should be combined.

Let us look at it from the point of view of the psychoanalyst regarding philosophy and then the other way around. For psychoanalysis, the attitude to metaphysical thinking explored here might initially be thought alien. Freud was famously negative in his view of religion as a form of metaphysical thought, encouraging a tradition of dismissing it in psychoanalysis. Against this, Jonathan Lear suggests that religious thinking might involve something Freud did believe in, 'that love is a force permeating nature' (Lear 1990: 221). What religion and other kinds of metaphysical thinking do is transpose to a metaphysical realm what is otherwise viewed as central to human psychology. That can be seen as an illusion and dangerous (Freud 1927), but it should be recalled that Freud also took a different view. He wrote for example that 'the "Eros" of the philosopher Plato coincides exactly with the love-force, the libido of psychoanalysis' and he continued that 'when the apostle Paul … praises love above all else he certainly understands it in the same wider sense' (Freud 1985: 119–20). Religious metaphysics in Paul look as if they express something relevant to metapsychological experience.

Lear has also suggested that psychoanalysis is one sided and wrongly dismissive of religious metaphysics, ignoring 'basic experiences of trust, oneness, and belonging' organised in 'highly integrated functions' of the psyche (Lear 2017: 204). Once Freud begins to open the door to the overall significance of love in human nature, it is hard to deny forms of experience that express it metaphysically where these represent meaningful accounts of reasons to act in moral ('highly integrated') ways. There is more to metaphysical thinking than an illusion or wish fulfilment, though of course that is a risk. Psychoanalytical and metaphysical understanding as described here appear as ways of speaking about love in different but connected registers. As Freud himself said, bringing together love in its metapsychological and metaphysical forms is 'an entirely justifiable piece of unification' (Freud 1985: 119).

As regards the relationship the other way around, different philosophies will take different views. My background is in critical realist philosophy and from that point of view, it is important to recognise both the metaphysical dimension of human life and that humans are constituted naturalistically as biological, psychological and social beings. Psychoanalysis should be understood as an important science in its own right (Bhaskar 1979; Collier 1994) that explores the intrapsychic dimension of human social being (Bhaskar 1993). At the same time, human beings are capable of profound metaphysical experience (Bhaskar 2012). These are two sides of the one experience for human beings. Bhaskar's metaphysical account of love's universality holds that such experience is central to the nature of human being, but this is not incompatible with seeing us as the physiological and psychological creatures we are. Our physiological, moral and psychological species being makes a metaphysics of love possible (Norrie 2020). Humans operate at the level of both body and mind so that for them, as Lear says of Freud, the mystery is how 'the flesh' becomes changed into 'the word' (Lear 1990: xii). Yet this is not entirely a mystery for we know it to happen with each and every one of us, as our human experience of growing from infancy into being an animal that thinks and loves. The crucially important addition to this commonplace yet amazing development is to note that when we use words deeply, we speak often enough of our metaphysical experience.[6] A 'Bhaskarian lover', one might say, started out life as a Freudian animal that could grow in a particular way and is grounded in such growth.

Guilt as Metaphysics and Metapsychology

Thus far, I have outlined why it is important to identify a form of ethical guilt that expresses itself in metaphysical terms and explored how love operates to combine metapsychology and metaphysics in human experience. This is a preparation for now arguing that the metaphysical language of guilt stems from love and also involves both levels.

Two Approaches to Guilt

The metaphysical link of guilt to love can be brought out as follows: Consider the closeness of what Jaspers (and Levi) say on solidarity and guilt and what Bhaskar says on unconditional love. If we can talk with Bhaskar about a metaphysics of love as entailing inter alia love for humankind, we are already operating with something like a concept of universal solidarity in line with Jaspers. If that solidarity were denied by an act or by being present at an act (as in survivor guilt), this generates per Jaspers a sense of metaphysical guilt. To have an unconditional relationship, an 'absolute solidarity', with the other of the kind Jaspers (in philosophy) and Levi (out of thoughtful experience) describe is just to have a loving relationship with the other, one that is grounded in a sense of universal love. The failure to act in light of that relationship is marked by guilt that one has not done so. Metaphysical guilt in Jaspers's sense follows on a failure to act in accordance with unconditional love for (a sense of universal solidarity with) the other. The metaphysical solidarity in guilt (Jaspers, Levi) expresses a metaphysics of love in the name of solidarity.

What about a metapsychological link between guilt and love? Chapter 3 provides a path through Melanie Klein's argument that the relationship between love and guilt emerges complexly in the developing infant and remains with

[6] This 'mystery' is in fact a case of what critical realists call emergence, that is a situation in which a higher level of reality emerges from a lower one on which it is dependent for its possibility, but from which it differs in its essential modes of operation (Collier 1994: 107–34; Hartwig 2007: 166).

it as it grows into adult life (Klein 1998). In this early position, the infant feels intense anger when things are not going well. Hungry, uncomfortable and desperate, it rages against the parent figure but then turns from anger to fear and anxiety that it may have damaged the one it loves. This sets up anxiety and a desire to repair that carries through its life and which lies at the heart of the feeling of guilt. Using the work of Jessica Benjamin (1988), my further suggestion was that the tension between respectful and dominating behaviour is the proximate basis for thinking about guilt and responsibility. Guilt is, then, the feeling of tension and anxiety which emerges from complex love and the desire to repair (Klein), which experiences the difference between recognition, respect and mutuality on the one hand and wishing to dominate and make submit on the other. Later on in this work, we will examine another account of the relationship between love and guilt drawing on the work of Hans Loewald (1980) and Jonathan Lear (1990), but the Klein–Benjamin argument makes the point sufficiently for our purposes here. Guilt is embodied and felt psychologically in the time it is thought and expressed philosophically.

Combining the Two Kinds of Guilt

If metaphysical guilt involves love and can be understood in the terms of metapsychology, then it seems we can tie together both experiences as we did already with love. If the capacity to express love in metaphysical terms is an emergent property of human metapsychology, then guilt will similarly appear as a form of ethical expression grounded in psychological development. Another way of linking the two would be to note that guilt is both reflected on and felt. It is something we think about in moral and philosophical terms but also something we feel 'in our hearts' or 'in our guts'. It keeps us awake at night as a feeling of being troubled and ill at ease. It may haunt our dreams and bring physical pain. As the philosopher Herbert Morris describes it, it may make us feel 'rotten, depleted of energy, tense' (Morris 1976: 99). As we see in Chapter 9, guilt may make us vomit or dissolve in tears and mucus. Such physiological symptoms and disturbances of our unconscious being tell us that guilt is metapsychologically present and metaphysically reflective in its form. We need to understand how it can exist at these different levels if we are to grasp its moral psychology.

When Jaspers wrote of guilt, he expressed it in philosophical, metaphysical terms, but I do not imagine it existed for him only as a philosophical notion. Jaspers, who lived in Germany through the Nazi period and had a Jewish wife, did not intend it should only be experienced in the library or the study, but in the body and the soul. It can both be thought of and felt, and these are two sides of the same guilty coin. We use the term 'psychosomatic' pejoratively to suggest that someone is not really sick, but guilt suggests that the word might be used also to confirm why Freud called love a 'justified unification'. The 'psycho' and the 'somatic' are two things conjoined, not one thing reduced to another. The philosophical and the psychological experience of guilt can and should be connected because the former is a way of making cognitive sense of the lived *and felt* experience of the latter. Mind and body come together to produce a moral psychology of guilt; metapsychology is the ground that makes metaphysics possible. Thus humans become a metaphysical animal.

Love, Guilt and Forgiveness in Martha Nussbaum

If we turn now from my general objective in synthesising the metaphysical and the metapsychological to the specific focus on Martha Nussbaum, there are two specific reasons for considering her recent *Anger and Forgiveness* (Nussbaum 2016). The first concerns the trajectory of her thought and the problem this poses for mine. While her earlier work (Nussbaum 2004, 2014) drew on psychoanalytic theory and love,[7] *Anger and Forgiveness* starts from love but discards the psychoanalytic aspect. Given my argument earlier, it should be clear why I engage here with her rejection of psychoanalytic argument. The second reason follows on in that disengaging from psychoanalysis leads Nussbaum to reject the moral significance of concepts like guilt and forgiveness. Whereas I see these forms of moral engagement as important to understanding how to deal with violation, Nussbaum thinks that guilt and forgiveness are backward-looking and law-focused categories that (with one exception) get in the way of eudaimonic change.

I would say this may happen, but this depends on guilt and forgiveness taking particular forms associated with law, crime and punishment. There are however strong reasons rooted in moral psychology why moving forward without addressing past guilt and with a view to forgiveness is problematic. Moral engagement over what happened is central to moving forward but that does not necessarily mean being punitive. For her, guilt and forgiveness (even unconditional forgiveness) are related to legal notions of punishment or 'payback' which she rejects as repeating the past. Anger at violation should not be addressed as such but quickly channelled into commitments to make change for the better (what she calls 'the Transition'). Guilt and forgiveness get in the way and psychoanalysis underpins their backward, narcissistic, self-absorbed quality. The goal of social change, given impetus by loving compassion, is sufficient after initial anger at violation. I argue to the contrary that moral engagement grounded in love does real transitional work alongside commitments to social change. Importantly, such moral transactions are not the same as the punitive penal measures which Nussbaum and I would both criticise. She misses the sui generis importance of moral engagement around guilt and forgiveness which remain central to change and are not to be assimilated with legal transactions based on punishment and 'payback'.[8]

[7] On difficulties with Nussbaum's approach in this earlier work, see Wilson 2020.

[8] For a similar criticism of Nussbaum's position, see also Allais (2021).

Guilt without Metapsychology

While it is good to be angry with oneself or another as a force for future moral improvement, anger is often associated with what Nussbaum calls payback, a punitive reaction related to guilt. It is 'a negative emotion directed at oneself on the basis of a wrongful act' (Nussbaum 2016: 128). Influenced previously by psychoanalysis, Nussbaum saw guilt as a 'major creative force in the moral life, because it leads to reparative activity' (Nussbaum 2016: 129).[9] Now she sees it as narcissistic and opts to cut out what she sees as backward-looking guilt in favour of forward-looking love:

> I now think I was too influenced by the strongly Kantian views of certain psychoanalysts, and that what I said about guilt is highly problematic. We don't need self-inflicted pain to correct ourselves and help others. And we do not need the fear of the torments our own conscience will inflict, as a motive to pursue our ideals. A positive love of others, combined with compassion at their predicaments, seems a sufficient motive for moral conduct.... Indeed, if one can only pursue morality by lacerating oneself, one's devotion to morality is surely very incomplete ... love of [others] and a desire to do better by them, seems more productive than guilt, which is all about oneself and not about them. (Nussbaum 2016: 130–31)

The psychoanalytic view should be set aside in favour of a simpler account based on human love and compassion. Looking back should be replaced by 'forward looking thoughts of welfare, and from anger into compassionate hope' (Nussbaum 2016: 31) through the 'Transition' (capitalised in her text), a loving focus on improving the lot of the other that has been harmed.

Like Nussbaum I think guilt may be narcissistic, but we should be careful about what this means. We need to distinguish narcissism as a developmental deformation of the psyche, or as a moral description of selfishness and self-absorption, from something rather different, a psychological condition relating to early human development based on love (Freud 1984; Lear 1998: ch 6). The Kleinian analysis described in Chapter 3 is grounded in a primary narcissistic condition of omnipotent feeling, and this may be said to find its echo in worldly practices of blaming the other and harsh self-punishment. Yet from that early phase narcissism is turned into the positive and productive desire to repair after the phantasy one has harmed another. This is what happens when things go well developmentally for loving, balanced, 'good enough' individuals. Guilt in a self-absorbed, narcissistic vein, resulting from neurosis or other psychological or cultural condition, is also possible but as a pathology of development. It should also be remembered that *rejection* of guilt may reflect narcissism, a denial of one's acts in the world, a sense one is always right or someone else is to blame. Nussbaum's no-nonsense 'Transition', demanding that others who have been violated do not dwell on their reaction, could

[9] Here she follows Melanie Klein as I did in Chapter 3.

itself be interpreted in this way – as an inability to see that others, perpetrators or victims, could genuinely be suffering and that guilt is real.

Such narcissism is prevalent today and perhaps even a qualification for high office. The point is that guilt may be narcissistic in a negative sense, but the concept of narcissism goes wider in terms of its meaning and implications. To seek to work through violation, and this is true for the perpetrator as well as the victim, could be negatively narcissistic but it could also be positive and developmental. From there, a desire for change to the self and the other becomes possible, and it can also lead to a desire for social change. The human psyche can turn primary narcissism into a desire to repair, a relationship of positive respect for the other and a world in which respect for others becomes generalised. While guilt and compassion are closely entwined, guilt is *pace* Nussbaum more than just a trigger to compassion. It is a feeling in its own right, part of our moral psychology as a felt experience and ethical process. To reduce, downgrade or remove it from the picture is to short-circuit important moral and psychological activity. The forms of metaphysical guilt that Jaspers and Levi described earlier involved valid moral emotions that had to be engaged with. Though Nussbaum is right that guilt can take unproductive forms, it nonetheless provides an important link to a complex panoply of moral terms by which humans navigate the world and a way into change that can then take different social forms.

What of 'the strongly Kantian views of certain psychoanalysts' to which Nussbaum refers? These go unnamed but suffice it to say that there are good grounds for accepting that Freud himself held such a view (in his *Civilisation and Its Discontents* [Freud 1985]). However, I will argue below that it was not his only view or the better one to be derived from his work. The 'strongly Kantian view' generates what I will call in Chapters 7 and 8 an understanding of primitive guilt, to be contrasted with a mature view that is in line with the Kleinian–Benjaminian view discussed in Chapter 3. It is a view of guilt based on love, not anger, fear or hate. This is what is lost if the psychoanalytic view previously supported by Nussbaum is abandoned. If we cut out this psychoanalytical dimension, we will fail to appreciate why people need to deal with violation and why they need to dwell in the past not for itself (which would involve a primitive view of guilt and forgiveness) but in order to move forward through mature development of the self. We will fail to appreciate the moral value of guilt apart from its role in legal payback or status correction. Yes, these are forms of a primitive moral psychology engaged in magical thinking and narcissistic error (Nussbaum 2016: 38), but we should not ignore the role of a mature moral psychology in making sense of our experience of violation.

'The Whole Forgiveness Idea'

Discussing Nussbaum is helpful because it pushes the discussion beyond guilt to forgiveness. Here the same issue comes up, concerning the moral value of forgiveness, and again I argue that it involves an important moral engagement. Nussbaum writes of what she calls 'transactional forgiveness' (Nussbaum 2016: 57–74) which it turns out covers forgiveness in its main forms. She wishes to argue for a simpler compassionate and love-based relation as in her discussion of the parable of the prodigal son. To understand how said son fits in, I need first to say something about how guilt and forgiveness feature in Nussbaum's argument.

I mentioned earlier the notion of 'the Transition' in Nussbaum's argument. This is the moment when a person who has done or witnessed wrong moves from a sense of anger (self-anger in the case of the wrongdoer) at the shock of the wrong to feel that the situation needs to be made better for the victim. The Transition is a forward-looking moment that is ameliorative, consequentialist and eudaimonic. It is contrasted with the typically backward-looking way in which many people and the law think of crime and punishment. There the philosophy of retributivism emphasises suffering inflicted for a past harm in the irrational anticipation that putting someone down (a correction of relative status) or 'paying them back' will somehow make the world a better place.[10] She sees this view as deriving from 'deep-rooted but misleading ideas of cosmic balance' (Nussbaum 2016: 5) and is generally against a range of ideas that are seemingly not related to forward-based change, but which wish to linger on the past and the wrong done.

Forgiveness tunes into the same issues as guilt and blame about pay back and status. To forgive is already to declare there is something to forgive, which means looking backwards, not forwards. It comes in both conditional and unconditional forms, but both are caught up in matters of blame and guilt. Conditional or 'transactional' forgiveness is bad because it says I will only give up my anger towards you if you will apologise, change or submit to me. It is a way of putting someone down and contains, she says, elements of 'aggressiveness, control, and joylessness' (Nussbaum 2016: 58). At first sight, unconditional forgiveness looks better, though it also contains a sense of put down: 'the minute one sets oneself up as morally superior to another, the minute one in effect asserts that payback was a legitimate aim – but one that I graciously waive', one's thought is 'about the past, and it gives us nothing concrete with which to go forward' (Nussbaum 2016: 77). If unconditional forgiveness is accompanied by love, it *may* look forward: here Nussbaum cites the case of the families of victims of the Charleston shootings in the United States. Their acts of love and unconditional forgiveness perhaps reflect the possibility of Transition, but such forgiveness still offers no concrete way forward.

It is the Transitional path to change that should be engaged and forgiveness provides even at its best no real help. The only thing that works is love, which is the key to unconditional forgiveness moving beyond payback limits. There needs to be a qualitative moral jump *beyond* 'the whole forgiveness idea' (Nussbaum

10 Of course, a modern political theorist such as Antony Duff (2001) argues that retributivism has both backward- and forward-facing functions.

2016: 85) to a position of unconditional love as the way to 'the Transition'. Of course, forgiveness may be a form of controlling behaviour designed to rub someone's nose in what they did, but it seems to me that this is only one possible use to which it is put. The crucial question remains how people who have been violated deal with their real grief and if possible, move beyond it in a way that is true to their moral experience. This is not in terms of a need for payback or degradation of a perpetrator but in terms of working through violation. Getting beyond forgiveness involves, I argue, going through it.

The Prodigal Son, Love and Forgiveness

I want to lend support to 'the whole forgiveness idea' in both its conditional and unconditional forms because I think it points beyond itself and towards change. It can have the kind of negative, locked in quality Nussbaum criticises, but it does not have to. From a moral psychological point of view, the language of forgiveness is important in dealing with grief and mourning. It has a deep resonance in the human psyche where a person has been violated and I think we can see this even in the case Nussbaum discusses as her example of unconditional love beyond it. This is the parable of the prodigal son with which she illustrates how loving change needs no forgiveness[11] in line with 'the Transition':

> But when [the younger son] was yet a great way off, his father saw him, and he was seized by a surge of emotion …, and he ran, and fell on his neck, and kissed him. And the son said unto him, Father, I have sinned against heaven, and before thee, and am no more worthy to be called thy son. But the father said to his servants, Bring forth the best robe, … And bring hither the fatted calf, and kill it; and let us eat, and be merry: For this my son was dead, and is alive again; he was lost, and is found. And they began to be merry. (Nussbaum 2016: 79–80)

Nussbaum suggests that the father's reaction cannot be seen as involving forgiveness at all. He sees the son coming from a distance and cannot know what the son will say or do. 'He just sees that the son he has believed dead is actually alive, and he is seized by a violent surge of strong emotion … a type of intense love'. Even after the son has spoken, the father 'does not acknowledge the issue of contrition at all' (Nussbaum 2016: 80), but goes ahead with the celebration. This is neither conditional forgiveness based on repentance nor unconditional forgiveness, for there is no forgiveness at all: 'This father is taken over by love…. This story concerns the depths and the unconditionality of parental love…. This father … does not pause to calculate and decide: he just runs to him and kisses him. He has no thought for wrongs done to himself; his only thought is that his son is alive' (Nussbaum 2016: 81).

[11] This goes, Nussbaum says, against the grain of much of Christianity. For a powerful argument concerning the role of forgiveness in Christian thought that seeks to transcend the distinction between conditional and unconditional forgiveness, while basing itself on unconditional love, see Volf 2005, 2006.

This is beguiling but the question is whether there is something in the language of forgiveness that makes a valid moral demand. While a term like forgiveness might be diminished by notions of payback or status correction, it remains central to our moral psychology. To get to a better social world, we need to learn moral lessons from the past and deal with them. That involves a moral language that can engage with the past without getting stuck in it. A significant part of this concerns the moral responsibilities that lurk there, and it is only through discussing these that we find the way to a better future. Nussbaum senses this, though does not see the implication for her argument when she says of the father that he

> might still, at some later time, talk to the son about his life's course. Unconditional love is fully compatible with guidance; indeed, since the father wishes well to this son, he is almost certain to give him advice so that his life will go better henceforth. The direction of his emotion is Transitional: his love points to a future, and that future will almost certainly contain advice. The initial impulse toward the son, however, does not come from advice or calculation. (Nussbaum 2016: 81)

As the son of a loved father and the father of loved sons, it has not always been my experience that the giving of advice by a father enables the son's life to 'go better henceforth'. Above all else, psychoanalysis surely has something to tell us about this. Still, one might say that it is a parental obligation from love to tell a child (and, as appropriate, vice versa!) not just that something is not going well but, where relevant, that there is a wrong and a responsibility to be addressed in order to move forward. This does not undermine unconditional love: the parent still loves the child whatever he has done even if the child ignores effort at moral dialogue. With the prodigal son, we might hypothesise that the father's immediate relief at regaining his son prioritises a warm welcome over a 'postmortem' as to why he left, but the father–son relation is owed a reckoning. Nussbaum knows this but cannot know it given her theory of forgiveness: 'guidance' and 'advice' are euphemisms. Love must however link the future to the past, so that the father's 'advice' must be morally engaged with its rights and wrongs. He would not give what he owes his son otherwise. In sum, the past and its wrongs and the future with its changes are intimately connected to moral agents. Pace the 1970s film *Love Story*, love does *not* mean never having to say you're sorry, though if an apology becomes repetitive, something is probably going wrong.

Nor is Nussbaum correct to link the demand for acknowledgement of wrongdoing to an assumption of superiority. There could be this, but the contrary can also be argued: that wronging another puts the wrongdoer into a position of superiority that the apology redresses. Nor is it obviously narcissistic to wish, for example, that a serious violation of bodily integrity be recognised for what it is by the one who did it. The larger suggestion behind these thoughts is that getting to a better future involves dealing morally with actual relations in the past. A moral language of guilt and forgiveness ought not to be thrown away in favour of an abstractly expressed universal ethic of love which discounts moral engagements over violation in favour of feeding directly into eudaimonic Transition. Nussbaum's target here is to break away from responses to violation that are repetitive and lock people into the past. Payback for wrongdoing repeats pain, status correction repeats inferiority. These are both linked to certain kinds of (what I have called primitive) guilt and forgiveness, but not to them *tout court*. The idea of a universal ethic of love is of course crucial but it is crucial because it ties in with the account of guilt I developed in the first section of this chapter, one in which human love is expressed metaphysically and metapsychologically in concepts like guilt (and forgiveness) which are mature in their form.[12]

Violation, Moral Engagement and Reconciliation

In this final section, I consider a morally dialogic relationship between a perpetrator and a victim to explore how moral transactions operate and why they are important. In the following 'case study', however, it is initially unclear whether what is said supports my position or Nussbaum's, that forgiveness gets in the way.

The Victim: Through Forgiveness to Reconciliation

As stated at the beginning of the chapter, Jo Berry is the daughter of a British Conservative politician Member of Parliament killed by a bomb blast in 1984 while Patrick Magee was one of the Irish Republican Army unit that planted it. He was caught and imprisoned in 1986 and then released under the Northern Ireland Good Friday Agreement of 1998. Their dialogue shows, I believe, how it matters to address the moral rights and wrongs of the past in order to move forward. Guilt and forgiveness are at stake though not in the terms of control, status correction or payback. I start however by considering a statement by Berry in three parts in which it is not clear that what is said favours my view over Nussbaum's. In this first part, Berry begins by declaring her ambivalence about forgiving Magee:

> An inner shift is required to hear the story of the enemy. For me the question is always about whether I can let go of the need to blame, and open my heart enough to hear Patrick's story and understand his motivations. The truth is that

[12] Of course, Nussbaum's position is not the only one that derives from ethics of universal love per se. Another approach is to deploy such ethics to think through why concepts of guilt and forgiveness are important in what Michael DeValve (2015) calls a criminology of love. DeValve draws on the major religious traditions to articulate an ethics of love and care which can then be applied to transform existing criminal justice practices. Such work is attractive but it establishes an ethical 'ought' which it directly relates to a current reality. Linking metaphysics to metapsychology takes a deeper route to understanding why the human animal is capable of acting in better (and worse) ways with regard to violation.

> sometimes I can and sometimes I can't. It's a journey and it's a choice, which means it's not all sorted and put away.... (Berry in Cantacuzino 2015: 79)

Here the question is whether Berry can give up blame in favour of letting go, that is, forgiving him. She goes on, however, to question whether forgiveness is what is required: 'In those early years I probably used the word "forgiveness" too liberally.... Now I don't talk about forgiveness. To say "I forgive you" is almost condescending – it locks you into an "us and them" scenario, keeping me right and you wrong.... But I can experience empathy, and in that moment there is no judgement' (Berry in Cantacuzino 2015: 79).

This position of course reflects Nussbaum's argument discussed earlier. Moving on, Berry takes a position that could be said either to return to the importance of forgiveness or its irrelevance:

> Sometimes when I've met with Patrick, I've had such a clear understanding of his life that there's nothing to forgive. I wanted to meet Patrick to put a face to the enemy and see him as a real human being.... I feel I've been recovering some of the humanity I lost when that bomb went off.... I've realised that no matter which side of the conflict you're on, had we all lived each other's lives, we could all have done what the other did.... I could easily have made the same choices Patrick made. (Berry in Cantacuzino 2015: 79–80)

We cannot tell here whether 'there's nothing to forgive' means that Berry has successfully forgiven Magee or that she refuses to use the language of forgiveness. Whichever, there are elements in these passages which support both my argument that forgiveness is morally important in producing change and Nussbaum's, that forgiveness is a block to it. On one side, Berry speaks of recovering her humanity by putting herself in Magee's place. There is a link between the empathic moral sense that 'we could all have done what the other did' and understanding that personal violation was in fact impersonal and part of a universal logic. That we are all the same reflects the metaphysical experience we explored with regard to guilt, though now it is on the side of forgiveness, what Berry describes as letting go. Moral engagement through dialogue involving forgiveness is a means of effecting change. On the other side, however, forgiveness looks 'almost condescending' and recreating division. She wants to get beyond it to a deeper level that is about empathy and placing oneself in the position of the other. Loving herself again is ultimately about being able to love the other unconditionally even when the other was the perpetrator. Forgiveness may get in the way.

In Berry's testimony, the lines on forgiveness and blame seem at best ambivalent, perhaps even to back Nussbaum's view that forgiveness blocks change. How should we interpret them? For me, the question in this passage as a whole is how one gets beyond blame and anger, and whether one does so except by passing through these states to forgiveness. There is a process of moral dialogue in play that moves from anger and blame to forgiveness and then to compassion and empathy. The outcome of the process is that blame and anger may be given up in favour of empathy and compassion. Forgiveness is a necessary step in that process rather than an end state in its own right. To not go through a process of forgiveness would be to remain with anger and blame, but to rest in a state of perpetual forgiveness would be to stay with the violation and not get beyond it. This accounts for the importance and also the ambivalence around forgiveness: that it is a necessary staging post in change, but not an end in itself.

Putting this in metaphysical terms, we start with a violation leading to a victim's need to feel anger and to want to blame, and we end with a sense of a universal human bond and solidarity that generates empathy and compassion through a shared humanity. Both sides, a feeling of having been violated by another *and* a sense of universal solidarity with that other, are necessarily in play. Moving forward involves using the moral dialogue triggered by the former to get to the empathy of the latter by means of a process of working through moral dialogue about what happened. The intermediate step between violation which sets people apart and compassion which brings them together is filled with moral conversations around blame, guilt, responsibility, apology and forgiveness. In this passage, I suggest, Berry expresses both the need for blame, the hope for forgiveness and the possibility of empathy with the scales tipping, but not yet tipped, in favour of a final position. Whether that is the eventual result depends on many things, including, as I shall argue in what follows, the overall setting in which the moral dialogue occurs. What the example shows, however, is the vital role that moral forgiveness plays in getting from acts of violation to a universal sense of solidarity expressed in terms of empathy and compassion.

The Perpetrator and Forgiveness

This point takes me to the relationship between Berry and Pat Magee. The difficulty and poignancy in their situation might not be that Berry's forgiveness would be condescending but rather that it is not ultimately possible because the dialogue with Magee can only go so far. Here is what Magee says for his part:

> *Someday I may be able to forgive myself.* Although I still stand by my actions, because at the time we were trapped and there was no other way, I will always carry the burden that I harmed other human beings. *But I'm not seeking forgiveness.* If Jo could just understand why someone like me could get involved in the armed struggle, then something has been achieved.... *Between Jo and me, the big issue is the use of violence. I can't claim to have renounced violence, though I don't believe I'm a violent person* and have spoken out against it many times.... No matter what we can achieve as two human beings meeting after a terrible event, the loss remains and forgiveness can't embrace that loss. The hope lies in the fact that we are prepared to carry on. The dialogue has continued. It's rare to meet someone as gracious and open as Jo. She's come a long way in her journey to understanding; in fact, she's come more than halfway to meet me. That's a very humbling experience. (Magee in Cantacuzino 2015: 80, emphasis added)

There is a contradiction in his words that is not about him so much as his situation. 'Someday I may be able to forgive myself.... But I'm not seeking forgiveness'. Guilt for harming other human beings is offset by a refusal to accept what was done as wrong. The need to be forgiven is countered by the political claim that his acts were justified, so there is nothing he should be forgiven for. Though not a violent person, he has not renounced violence. Analytical philosophers will contest Magee's logic, but it is possible psychologically to hold onto contradictory moral claims, though at the cost of unresolved tension. Magee resists the moral language of guilt and forgiveness and its compassionate release because of the political context in which he operated. He maintains the right to have waged guerrilla war against Britain, and Berry understands why he might, but he still suffers remorse for the deaths he caused. Political justification and what we could call 'metaphysical regret'[13] are juxtaposed and unresolved. In broader terms, we might say there is a tension between the messy social and political realm of moral engagement about the actual past and the underlying metaphysical level of guilt and responsibility. At the level of the political here and now, Magee may resist, but guilt and the need for forgiveness linked to universal metaphysical experience persist.

Unresolvable Dialogue and Reconciliation

When Berry lost her father, it 'felt as if a part of me died in that bomb' but she held on to 'a small hope that something positive would come out of the trauma' (Cantacuzino 2015: 79). Her conversations with Magee are about her recovering her humanity as he recovers his. What is at stake is reconciliation with another and with the past that can move through moral engagement around blame and forgiveness to a universal understanding of human being. Magee's position is unresolved and maybe unresolvable in that he is caught between an historical denial and a metaphysical need. This in turn stalls the dialogue for Berry since she is faced with a man who cannot show the repentance that might take her through and beyond forgiveness. If Magee cannot ask for forgiveness, Berry cannot give him it, even if she wanted to. To be asked for forgiveness and to be able to give it might help further to overcome the desire to blame. Giving it to Magee might help her give up her anger and deepen recovery of her humanity,[14] but the moral reconciliation cannot be completed. If Magee were to ask for forgiveness, would that not change the moral landscape for both people? Without it, it is surely understandable that Berry should continue to pause between a desire to blame and a desire to empathise. An unconditional request for forgiveness might not make a

[13] Drawing on Bernard Williams's (1981) account of 'agent regret'. See also Cantacuzino (2022: 211–18).

[14] In Chapter 5, I argue that there are two sides to forgiveness. The more obvious one is that it involves giving absolution to a perpetrator; the second is that it entails the victim giving up her sense of grief and violation.

difference, but on the other hand, it might. Magee's conflicted position, I suggest, withholds completing the moral conversation that would enable a fuller reconciliation.

What this suggests is that the compassion and unconditional love that lead to reconciliation may be blocked where blame and forgiveness cannot be worked through. Perhaps in conclusion, we should turn the focus around to the social and political world which turns people of such goodwill into the violator and the violated and then keeps them apart. 'People of good will' sounds like a terrible cliché, but it is nonetheless true of Berry and Magee. The underlying problem is that they live in a part of the world which still needs to resolve deep-seated social and political conflicts. This makes ordinary people its victims, both at the time of conflict and afterwards, producing difficult and unresolved moral dialogues like theirs. That human beings can show an extraordinary capacity for honesty, love and grace in such situations is testimony both to the moral power of the human metaphysical animal and the deep-seated social and political difficulties in the way of reconciliation. The example shows two things. The first is that even if social transitions are difficult and obstructed, there is no way beyond moral engagement about the past for change to occur. The second is that these two things are intrinsically connected. The social situation is capable of blocking the individual engagement, just as the individual engagement may assist the social transition.

Transitions, Moral Engagement and Law's Ethical Critique

I began this chapter by developing an argument for the synthesis of philosophical metaphysics and human metapsychology, thereby unifying the approaches developed in the two previous chapters. The human animal has the capacity to think and act according to ethical premises and that capacity is grounded in its animal nature, which includes its metapsychology. The metaphysical animal is precisely a creature that is able to think and to love, where these two elements are inherently connected as human mind and body.

With regard to developing an account of guilt and forgiveness, I sought to show how a metapsychological grounding is the condition for feeling guilt and seeking forgiveness. Like Nussbaum, my interlocutor here, I suggest we think about violation in terms of its ethical foundations in a flourishing humanity reconciled. Unlike Nussbaum, I believe our loving being is expressed through our moral psychology, including our moral experience of guilt and forgiveness, and this rests on our capacity to feel the need to address the past. Humans express this 'psychosomatically' in both their feelings of grief and pain after violation, whether of guilt or victimhood, and in their metaphysical language of universal love and compassion. These are two sides of the same coin. The young Hegel (see Chapter 2) was right to see the importance of love, grief and grieving as the basis for reconciliation. To start from moral psychology, its language and engagements is to embrace the mediations of love that we express as moral feeling and thought. But there is a level underlying these ethical processes that is also important. We do not step straight into an overarching ethical design without working through our moral agency as individuated and loved, respected and respecting, persons in the world (Benjamin). Equally the moral language of responsibility, guilt and forgiveness is a language for us because it aligns, in the Kleinian account, with the basic psychological propensity to repair what has been violated (see Chapter 3). A psychoanalytic understanding proceeds immanently to a metaphysical account of respect and attention for the other.

For Nussbaum, like Bernard Williams before her, the law's retributive language is used by justice institutions to govern. For Nussbaum criminal justice degrades and adds further violation to those convicted of violation by payback and status degradation. She has a point but her solution is over-inclusive. She bypasses both legally punitive transactions and a morally engaged psychology, which she conflates, in favour of solutions based directly on unconditional love and eudaimonic change ('the Transition'). My position to the contrary is that we should seek to understand how human beings as metaphysical animals can express reparative feelings through a moral language different to that of legal payback. Between legal transactions with their 'peculiar' moral form (Williams) and transitions as the need for social change, there lies an immanent path of moral and psychological experience which cannot be reduced to one or the other.

For Nussbaum, the road to human flourishing is a forward-looking enterprise, and in this she is surely right. The question however is where this leaves our moral language of guilt and forgiveness. Since we are moral beings who develop over the course of our lives, it seems that one of the ways we move to a better future is by coming to terms with the past. That requires appropriate moral reckoning and a language of what was done by one to another, and how both sides now feel about it. Forwards and backwards: there is a philosophical as well as a metapsychological argument that the past, the present and the future are deeply interconnected (Bhaskar 1993: 140–44; Norrie 2010: 33–34). Jo Berry and Patrick Magee's commitment to taking the moral past into the present as a means of looking to the future indicates the artificiality of shutting one off from the other. We need to look back and make sense of what happened, without remaining stuck in the past. Their experience also shows that the past may indeed block or limit the present and the future, but it does not show that their dialogue in the present lacks intrinsic value. Overall, it shows how development at individual and social levels are both necessary for reconciliation.

That this moral psychology may also be transmuted into legal forms that narrow and thwart moral outcomes (payback in Nussbaum, 'peculiarity' in Williams) cannot deny its basic validity. If we do not reduce serious moral engagement to the level of legal transactions, Nussbaum's overly demanding strictures against guilt and forgiveness may be reconfigured as a criticism of the gap between ethically real experience and its institutional expression (leading to what I have called an ERIC critique). Investigating that gap requires us not to ditch but to defend a naturalistic moral language, a moral psychology of guilt and forgiveness, in order to see its critical relation to institutional settings and social transitions. That language cannot deny psychoanalysis because it is its essential ground, that which necessarily conjoins the metaphysical and the metapsychological for the animal that thinks and loves.

5

Law and the Metaphysics of Forgiveness

> You can't play games around murder – there's a kind of vulnerability and transparency that occurs and you have to become a better person to get through. You can't stay around in the fog. You need to soar, to go higher.
>
> Wilma Derksen (Cantacuzino 2015: 117)

> I knew it would be a meaningful gift, but it became a gift to myself as well.... Forgiveness is really nothing more than an act of self-healing and self-empowerment.
>
> Eva Kor (Cantacuzino 2015: 37)

> I find myself drawn, when reflecting upon forgiveness, to the idea of transcendence, to grace, and ... the mystery that lies at the heart of forgiveness .... The concept of grace, something that makes for the good that transcends what is within our will's compass, allows for grasping this mystery.
>
> Herbert Morris (1988: 16–19)

Candace Derksen was kidnapped and murdered in Winnipeg in 1984 at the age of thirteen. The man believed to be the killer was convicted only in 2011 but released in 2017 after an appeal and retrial.[1] Wilma Derksen and her husband made the decision to forgive the perpetrator before his identity was known, explaining their position in the first quotation above. What was the emotional thought process behind this? For Derksen, grief around such violation demanded complete truthfulness about what had happened to her daughter, what the implications were for her own life and how she felt about the perpetrator. Such truthfulness concerned what it meant to love one's child, oneself and one's family and, beyond these, one's community, those who do well by us, and those who do us harm. This is truth that is not factual or abstract but truth that gets 'to the heart of the matter' in terms of what is thought, felt and done. It concerns what matters in the heart. Not everyone who is victimised and violated will follow Derksen but those who do articulate how they relate to others in the most honest and loving way they can. If this is a possible position to take in the face of violation, what does that tell us about forgiveness, human nature and moral psychology?

[1] For a report, see Bernhardt 2017.

I argued in the previous chapter that the metapsychology of love makes possible a moral psychology and metaphysics for dealing with guilt and forgiveness. Human metapsychology makes our ethics and metaphysics possible because we are animals who think and love. In this chapter, I continue the discussion in relation to forgiveness. My argument is organised around two concerns. The first is to think through its moral psychology and ethical reality. I do this by identifying five forms of love which inform the human power to forgive. Drawing on the work of *The Forgiveness Project* (Cantacuzino 2015), in which Wilma Derksen is a participant, I consider the experience of victims in dealing with forgiveness and how this relates to reconciliation.[2] Considering what people who have been victimised and violated say and do, I analyse what it means ethically to forgive in relation to the capacity to love.

The experience of victims shows us how love operates phenomenologically in our moral psychology. Three things stem from this. The first, as the prefatory quotation from Eva Kor illustrates, is that forgiveness involves both a 'giving to' and a 'giving up' so that it aids both the perpetrator and the victim of violation. The second is that there is something mysterious and gracious in forgiveness that is central to how it operates, and this is reflected in the quote from Herbert Morris. Third, the examples we explore show that this is a theory that may be put into practice here and now. Victims who forgive engage with forgiveness and seek to reconcile as a real and practical activity, rather than what might be thought by some to be idle or fanciful wish-fulfilment.

The second concern relates to the relationship between the moral psychology of forgiveness and law. It concerns how an ethically real moral psychology of forgiveness and reconciliation relates to the normative political theory that is expressed in the institutional framework of criminal justice. There is a contrast between an understanding of forgiveness which I describe as based on 'dispositive humility' and the kind of exchange relation between apology and forgiveness understood to be at the heart of forgiveness in legal settings. Identifying this contrast develops the theoretical approach to criminal justice described in Chapter 1, one that is 'ethically real and institutionally critical' (an ERIC critique). A moral psychology that is developed independently of legal understandings of criminal justice offers an independent position from which to examine those understandings and analyse their problems.

The chapter has two main sections. In the first, I consider the ethics of forgiveness grounded in an ontology of love that I draw from the philosophy of Roy Bhaskar and the practice of *The Forgiveness Project*. In the second, I consider the relationship between an ethics of forgiveness based on dispositive humility and forgiveness as envisaged in the institutional framework of criminal justice.

[2] See also the more recent Cantacuzino (2022).

Love Actually: The Ethical Reality of Forgiveness

My overall argument is for understanding the human being as a metaphysical animal that thinks and loves. This generates the possibility of a moral psychology and language of guilt, responsibility, forgiveness and reconciliation. It identifies how moral transactions among victims and perpetrators may engage their different experiences so that they may continue or change their lives. There are two roads to understanding these moral processes, one through metapsychology and the other through metaphysical ethical experience. Love operates in both so that the former grounds the latter and the latter articulates what we think and feel. Love is the basis of feeling, while thought, language and action are the means of expressing it. How, then do we express our loving feelings with regard to the experience of violation and the practice of forgiving? In the previous chapter, I drew on Roy Bhaskar's philosophy of metaReality and his account of love and I return here to explore and relate it to the experience of people involved in *The Forgiveness Project*.

Five Forms of the Metaphysics of Love

As we already saw in Chapter 4, Bhaskar describes love as forming a series of circles moving out from the individual and into the world:

> Although love is consistent with many different forms of action, and can be expressed in an infinity of number of ways, there are various conventional categorisations – which range from erotic, romantic, familial, civic, through to ethical and spiritual modalities. I prefer to think in terms of five radiating circles of love. When you are in one circle this will almost inevitably take you into other circles. These circles are the circle of love for yourself; for another human being; for the totality of other human beings; for the totality of other beings in creation; and for the source or sustaining power in creation itself, most customarily known as god. (Bhaskar 2012: 181)

Just such an account of love with its 'five radiating circles' is central to understanding the moral psychology of forgiveness. Personal accounts from *The Forgiveness Project* show how it is possible to identify love as the underlying ethical dimension in situations of violation, which is then expressed in practice. My account of the circles of love varies a little from Bhaskar's, but is consistent with his overall design. I will move from (1) love of self to (2) love of the other, and then I add (3) love of the relationship between self and other. These lead to two further universalisations of loving experience: (4) love of self and other in a wider community setting (Bhaskar's 'totality of other human beings') and (5) love of self and other in their concrete universality and singularity.[3] I

[3] Save for the fifth form, explained in what follows, these ways of expressing love are self-explanatory. The idea of the 'concrete universal/ singular' is explained below. While not mentioned in Bhaskar's account of circles of love, it is a concept that he discussed elsewhere (Bhaskar 1993; Norrie 2010: 113–14). Bhaskar's fourth form of love, for the totality of other

will now link these five forms of love to the moral experience of participants in *The Forgiveness Project* (Cantacuzino 2015).

Love of Self

In 1993, Ginn Fourie's daughter Lyndi was shot dead in South Africa by members of the armed wing of the Pan Africanist Congress. She writes 'I have come to understand forgiveness as a process which involves the principled decision to give up your justifiable right to revenge. Because to accept violation is a devaluation of the self' (Cantacuzino 2015: 55). Another South African experience is that of Linda Biehl, whose daughter was stabbed to death in 1993 by four youths. She says 'I can't look at myself as a victim – it diminishes me as a person….' (Cantacuzino 2015: 134). There may be an element of simple self-protection in these situations. Wilma Derksen, who expressed herself similarly (as discussed earlier), wrote of the need to protect her surviving family against the destructive forces that would be unleashed if they did not forgive their daughter's killer. But to see any of these cases as only about self-protection, or about a selfish desire to shut oneself off from violation, would be to miss their deep moral significance. Linda Biehl is not prepared for the devaluation of the self that would follow accepting the role of victim both for herself and her daughter. Instead, both Fourie and Biehl see the way of maintaining their humanity as involving forgiveness and reconciliation with those who killed their daughters. These are examples of victims 'going higher', as Derksen put it, because they love themselves, and from that love, there is then generated a love of the other.

It turns out that forgiveness is something that the forgiver does out of love both for herself and for the perpetrator. Here is Jean Paul Samputu from Rwanda, whose father and others in his family were killed by Hutu members of his village: 'During this retreat I heard a voice telling me that even if you become a Christian it's not enough; you need to forgive the man who killed your father because you cannot love again if you still have hatred in your heart. And that voice was telling me forgiveness is for you, not for the offender' (Cantacuzino 2015: 160). This issue of love of self is an important moral aspect of forgiveness, where the usual understanding is that forgiveness goes from the victim to the perpetrator. As I argued in Chapter 4, and return to in what follows, we can consider forgiveness as involving both a 'giving to' the perpetrator and a 'giving up' of grief by a victim. This is because a basic element of any loving engagement starts from the love of one's self. While experiencing violation, there is a desire not to be defined by it and to remain above it.

beings in creation, is not drawn on here when speaking about forgiveness where one human violates another. Another form of love not mentioned by Bhaskar here (though it was central to his worldview) is love of nature and the natural world. A broader conception of love including both love of other species and of the planet is possible and would expand the discussion of what humans owe to others, and therefore how forgiveness might operate more broadly.

Love of Other

A second form of love is love of the other, that is the perpetrator, or as in the first case here, their familial representatives. Bud Welch's daughter Julie was killed in the 1995 Oklahoma bombing in the USA by Timothy McVeigh. Starting out hating McVeigh, Welch eventually travelled to meet his father and sister: 'When I got ready to leave, I shook Bill's hand, then extended it to Jennifer, but she just grabbed me and threw her arms around me. She was the same sort of age as Julie but felt so much taller. I don't know which one of us started crying first' (Cantacuzino 2015: 49). Similarly, here is Grace Idowu, whose son David (14) was stabbed to death in a London park in 2008, on meeting his sixteen-year-old killer: 'When I arrived in the room, Elijah was crying bitterly with his head held low. I'd been told he'd been crying all morning.... I broke down; it was the first time I'd cried in front of other people. When I recovered myself, I told him, "I'm not crying for David, I'm crying for you. What have you done with your life?"' (Cantacuzino 2015: 110). And Linda Biehl of her daughter's killers: 'I've grown fond of these young men. They're like my own kids. It may sound strange, but I tend to think there's a little bit of Amy's spirit in them' (Cantacuzino 2015: 133).

In these comments, one sees the victim create a loving connection to the perpetrator through the idea that the violation engulfs everyone connected with it. Whether as perpetrator, victim, or family of either, the violative act sweeps up all those involved in a kind of joint fate. Anger and grief affect everyone brought together by the act, leading to a strong sense of identification. Welch tells the McVeighs that 'the three of us are in this for the rest of our lives' (Cantacuzino 2015: 49) in a feeling of empathy that extends out from the victim and her family to the perpetrator and his, who are all caught by the violation. Welch connects his feelings for his daughter to his experience of McVeigh's sister. In Grace Idowu's case, she puts herself in the position of a son who is the killer of her own son grieving for the moral damage he has done to himself. Biehl identifies with the spirit of her daughter's killers. The moral ruin that follows violation touches all concerned so that to love oneself and to love the victim may extend to the possibility of loving the perpetrator. The perpetrator is also his own victim, brought down by the violative act.

Love of the Relationship between Self and Other

This leads then to commitment to the relationship between the parties. We have already seen Bud Welch's comment to the McVeighs that 'the three of us are in this for the rest of our lives'. He went on to say to Jennifer McVeigh that he did not 'want your brother to die and I'll do everything to prevent it.' As he walked away, he realised that 'until that moment I had walked alone' but now 'I had found someone who was a bigger victim of the Oklahoma bombing than I was, because while I can ... say wonderful things about Julie, if Bill McVeigh meets a stranger he probably doesn't even say he had a son (Cantacuzino 2015: 49). The sense of relational oneness is also powerfully expressed by Cathy Harrington, whose daughter was murdered by Eric Copple, on meeting Copple's mother: 'I was absolutely terrified but when I saw her coming towards me I knew I needed to [meet her]. She was trembling – more terrified than me. I was stunned by how similar we looked, and thought, "Oh my God. I'm her!" Then we just embraced and there was such relief and compassion in that embrace' (Cantacuzino 2015: 165).

This is not just the love of the other, though it is that too. It is the love of and investment in *the relationship* between the self and the other, the recognition of the importance of that relationship for oneself. The bond with the perpetrator and his family becomes something sustaining and in need of maintenance. Linda Biehl sets it philosophically in the South African context in terms of a restorative justice underpinned by a sense of connection: 'I have come to believe passionately in restorative justice, [in] "ubuntu": to choose to forgive rather than demand retribution, a belief that "my humanity is inextricably caught up in yours"' (Cantacuzino 2015: 134).[4] That sense of a common fate and humanity, a relational bond that grounds a common future, assumes a significance in its own right, beyond the moral experiences of love for self and love for the other. It migrates around the relationship between families. When Ginn Fourie visited the community of her daughter's killer, she declined to use the bedding provided so as not to inconvenience the killer's sister. The sister was however disconcerted as she had 'wanted to sleep in the sweat of the woman who forgave her brother' (Benjamin 2018: 241).

Love of Self, Other and the Wider Community

Why should such a bond stop between two families? The sense of the relationality of love is extended further in moving from the relationship between individuals to a more universal understanding of how the experience of violation affects a wider group. Ginn Fourie visits the killer's community, and she initiates a dialogue around racism with the man who killed her daughter. In his village, she feels 'able to apologise to his people for the shame

[4] This is not to deny that an idea such as Ubuntu can be instrumentalised for social and political ends so that a conception of loving humanity is limited, channelled, perverted or abandoned. How loving ethics of forgiveness plays out in an historical context is a different question from how it makes primary moral sense for a victim in the face of a perpetrator (c.f. Norrie 2017c: ch 9). Richard Wilson sees the political effect when he writes that Ubuntu 'should be recognised for what it is: an ideological concept with multiple meanings … the Africanist wrapping used to sell a reconciliatory version of human rights talk to black South Africans' (Wilson 2001: 14). Compare this with Drucilla Cornell who writes that it 'points us to a new humanism [based on] solidarity' but agrees that it is subject to different political inflections (Cornell 2014: 179–80). From my point of view, I would expect to find a tension between an ethically real understanding of Ubuntu and a political practice expressing it. This would be the basis for (an ERIC) critique of a particular institutional reality which seeks to shape and subsume an ethical practice.

and humiliation which my ancestors had brought on them through slavery, colonialism and apartheid. Vulnerable feelings, when expressed to other people, have the potential to establish lasting bonds' (Cantacuzino 2015: 56). In a very different context, an English woman, Jayne Stewart, writes of the relationship between the sexual abuse visited on her by her father and its broader implications:

> when I am aware that this most private of oppressions between father and daughter is also part of a much bigger picture and that all these issues relate not only to sexual abuse but also to all of the abuses that we perpetrate in the world, I feel less alone and more inspired to create something meaningful from my traumatic experiences that will also be healing for the world. (Cantacuzino 2015: 45)

What we see here is a contextualisation of the relationship between the perpetrator and the victim, which reflects the systematic and structural problems of society. To understand the ruin in violation is to become committed to removing the conditions that engender it because they were its underlying cause. If not addressed, they will trigger further violations like it. The experience of love violated and the need for change to stop violation becomes generalised in light of underlying structural causes. In this way, individual moral commitment against one violation becomes aligned with the need for social change to stop further violations of the same kind.

Love of Self and Other in Their Concrete Universality/Singularity

My meaning here is less obvious, but it denotes the metaphysical deepening of forgiveness. If love travels outwards from the individual to the other and through their several relationalities, it also moves inwards to a deeper understanding of the self and its relationships. By concrete universality/ singularity, I mean how each human being is ontologically a unique person emergent from a particular set of circumstances, and therefore a *concrete singular*. There is intrinsic value in the unique experience of each individual life. To have such a life is also to live in a world where every other individual has the same unique experience. To be a concrete singular is therefore to share a universality with every other person, to be a *concrete universal*. To be such is to be valued for one's singularity and in one's universality, as a concrete universal/ singular (Norrie 2010: 113–14, 218–19). This provides the universal metaphysical basis for valuing each person as unique in their difference and as essentially, humanly, the same.

A practical extension of this is the idea that in different circumstances, we could have turned out to be the other because we share an essential commonality. Concrete difference and universal experience are both valuable as two sides of the same human coin. In the following comments, universal identification in the mode of the concrete universal/singular lends itself to deep identification with the life experience of the other in the form of intrinsic metaphysical self-expression. Love ramifies outwards but also deepens inwards as those who have experienced violation reflect on the implications of human universality in relation to concrete differences. There are two aspects to this, the capacity to identify with the other as basically like oneself and the capacity to explore the depth of the metaphysical experience stemming from the connection.

Identification with the Other's Concrete Difference

In England, Madeleine Black regrets the earlier lives of the two teenagers who violently raped and abused her at 13, for they had started out just like her:

> Most of my life, I hated the men who raped me and wished them a slow, painful death. However …, something happened that I never set out to do and that was I chose to forgive them. I used to think they were evil, but I started to understand that they didn't come into this world that way. They were born just like me as an innocent baby, and then I wondered how they knew to be so violent and cruel to another human at such a young age. It made me think they couldn't have had the best of lives and had witnessed or experienced violence themselves. (Cantacuzino 2015: 66)

There is grace in such understanding of the perpetrator as basically like the victim, both originally innocent in their being. I would say however that there is still a critical dialogue to be had between two people who are not symmetrically positioned in terms of their actions. In Chapter 4, I quoted Jo Berry's view that she has 'realised that no matter which side of the conflict you're on, had we all lived each other's lives, we could all have done what the other did…. I could easily have made the same choices Patrick made' (Cantacuzino 2015: 80). Similarly, Marian Partington says of the serial killer Rose West that her story 'seems to be about the impoverishment of a soul that knew no other way to live than through terrible cruelty. A life deprived of truth, beauty or love. I imagine that the deviant ignorance that fed her sadistic, egotistical crimes was rooted in her ruined, crooked childhood.' She wonders: 'Will she ever know the sacredness of life?' (Cantacuzino 2015: 152). These are moments of metaphysical identification with the other in their otherness, in their concrete singularity, but this is possible because a fundamental similarity in human potential is shared.[5]

Metaphysical Depth and Concrete Universality/Singularity

Marian Partington argues that forgiving Rose West 'seems to be the most imaginative way of becoming free and offering freedom…. In this way I can use my life to transform the cycle of violence.' In so doing, she has sometimes 'experienced the sacredness of my own life and the inter-connectedness of all our lives. In this place forgiveness is spontaneous…. I feel I'm honouring Lucy by lining myself up for forgiveness' (Cantacuzino 2015: 153). This is surely what

[5] Such metaphysical identification has its counterpart in the kind of metapsychological identification I discuss in Chapters 6 and 7 which operate as its deeper ground.

it means 'to soar, to go higher' as Derksen put it: to find the unique value and gift in every individual life, its 'sacred' and universal quality revealed through engaging with violation.

While Partington was influenced by Buddhist meditation, Jean Paul Samputu comes from the Christian tradition: '…I heard a voice telling me that even if you become a Christian it's not enough; you need to forgive the man who killed your father because you cannot love again if you still have hatred in your heart' (Cantacuzino 2015: 160). Samputu's reference to his religious conviction perhaps suggests that it is that conviction that drives his spiritual views. Wilma Derksen similarly approached the murder of her daughter as a Mennonite. It would be wrong however to think that these reactions of forgiveness simply reflect a pre-existing religious commitment. The expression of love for self and other that sometimes takes a religious form ('most customarily known as god' – Bhaskar) can be as much engendered by the experience of violation as led by pre-existing religious belief. Here for example is Madeleine Black's account of a strange moral projection that accompanied her dealing with victimisation:

> During the event I became aware of a young Tibetan monk in burgundy robes … by my right-hand side. I was also aware that I had floated out of my body and was on top of the wardrobe watching what was happening … The monk was praying next to my body and telling me I was going to be OK. He covered up my naked body … and calmed me down. (Cantacuzino 2015: 63)

In a later period when she had found stability in her life, she describes the ongoing mystical experience that expressed her love for herself as a valuable human being:

> When my eldest daughter was nearly 13, I started to have lots of flashbacks. I had nightmares for about three years… and I could feel the presence of the young men in the room … But the monk was always beside me too. (Cantacuzino 2015: 65)

These are moments of experiencing the universal in the self by means of psychological projection, one's own unique value given symbolic expression. The monk is a symbol of self-love and care, but given a spiritual, mystical representation which reflects a metaphysical understanding of the value of what it is to be human.[6] Experiencing the self as concrete universal/singular in situations of extreme violation opens the door to this kind of deep, universal reflection. I think it is as much the reaction within one's moral psychology (one's metapsychology) that generates the quasi-religious projection as any pre-existing religious stance dictating the moral psychology.

[6] The forty accounts collected in Cantacuzino 2015 are drawn from people from a variety of religious backgrounds (Buddhist, Christian, Jewish or Muslim) as well, so far as one can tell, from those without any formal religious conviction. Insofar as there are varied religious experiences as well as none, this reflects Bhaskar's statement of the fifth form of love as generally available, though given a conventional name: 'the source or sustaining power in creation itself, most customarily known as god' (Bhaskar 2012: 181).

Giving To and Giving Up

Having identified the five ways in which love informs the experience of forgiveness, I finish this section with two points about how forgiving works. The first starts with a caution that leads to a question. The caution is not to be reductive. It would be wrong to think of forgiveness as being 'just like love' in some 'normal' sense of how people in loving relationships are with each other. We speak here of a particular moral and psychological relationship between a victim and a perpetrator, or their families, after violation and grief. It is built on loss, ruin and tragedy. If being in love with another is hard, how immeasurably harder and qualitatively different it must be to achieve loving identification with a perpetrator. The relationship is never chosen and without an analysis like the one mentioned earlier, it would seem just strange to think in terms of love.[7] Yet there can be, and needs to be for these victims of violation, a 'soaring or a going higher', a deep identification with the other which I argue happens in the light of the universal human condition of concrete universality/singularity.

The caution leads then to a question. How could this experience of moral repair through forgiveness happen if it is only something that the victim *gives to* the perpetrator? How does this work to change the position of the one who has been violated? Forgiveness might reasonably be thought of as a gift going only in one direction and in a sense this is clear. Despite the potential for identification and commonality, the starting point is asymmetrical. It would make no sense to think that a perpetrator should in normal circumstances forgive her victim. Even if we said that the perpetrator had herself been the victim in an earlier round of wrongdoing, there would still be a violation by a perpetrator of a victim at a particular point. There would be two acts of violation where perpetrator and victim simply exchanged places. Similarly in a situation of trading blows, both actors would operate as perpetrators or victims simultaneously. In the moment of violation, there is a 'doer' and a 'done to', so one to forgive, the other to be forgiven.[8] Despite this difference, at another level, forgiveness is directionally bivalent, revealing the underlying symmetry in an initially asymmetrical relationship. It is this underlying symmetry which makes reconciliation between the two sides possible and it works because forgiveness operates on both the perpetrator and the victim.

That this is so is seen in the word itself, which may be both subject and object focused. Forgiving means both a 'giving to' (I forgive you for what you have

[7] It is easy to seem glib here and I find Jeffrie Murphy's persistent scepticism about what he calls the 'uncritical boosterism' around forgiveness (Murphy 2012: ch 1) an important reminder. However, it is equally possible to be glibly dismissive of the real examples of forgiveness seen earlier.

[8] On the asymmetrical relationship between forgiver and forgiven, see Griswold 2007: 47–59. In Murphy and Hampton's (1988) dialogue, Murphy focuses primarily on what it is to forgive, Hampton on what it means to be forgiven. Cantacuzino (2022) describes the moral and psychological connection between the two.

done) and a 'giving up' (I give up my grief at having been violated). Forgiving in this latter subjective sense is like 'forgoing' or 'forswearing' (both forms of doing without), that is, it is a form of forbearing (another such word) in relation to the self's, the victim's, violation, not the other, the perpetrator's, act. The word itself reflects an ambivalence: *for*giving as giving up, for*giving* as giving to. That a love of self (our first form of love, as mentioned earlier) is reflected in forgiveness confirms the moral centrality of 'giving up' to what happens. Here are two further illustrations from *The Forgiveness Project* of how this works to add to those of Linda Biehl, Ginn Fourie and Wilma Derksen. First Anne Marie Hagan, whose father had been axed to death by a thirty-year-old man with mental ill health, writes that 'I could never have imagined that in [forgiving him] I would set myself free. Finally I was able to let go of all the pain and torment that had held me captive, realising I had been my own jailer.... I felt joy again; the numbness was gone....' (Cantacuzino 2015: 72). Or, consider Eva Kor, who as a young child in Auschwitz had been used in twins' experiments by Josef Mengele, her twin sister dying prematurely as a result:

> As I [read my letter of forgiveness at Auschwitz in 1995], I felt a burden of pain was lifted from me. I was no longer in the grip of hate; I was finally free. The day I forgave the Nazis, privately I forgave my parents whom I hated all my life for not having saved me.... And then I forgave myself for hating my parents. Forgiveness is really nothing more than an act of self-healing and self-empowerment. (Cantacuzino 2015: 37)[9]

Forgiving as freeing oneself and absolving the other lies behind the possibility of moral–psychological connection between victim and perpetrator. There is however a proviso to this. To forgive in the sense of 'giving up' is not to 'abandon' the past and what happened, nor to 'surrender' one's position to the other. What is being given up is the complex set of unhappy emotions based around unresolved grief so that one lives better with what happened, protecting oneself against such emotions through a variety of responses to grief and mourning (integrating, distancing, compartmentalising, working through and beyond). Forgiving in this sense is not the same as forgetting, and it is a work in progress.

A final illustration capturing questions of giving to and giving up as well as the necessary nature of dialogue and the possibility that the process is ongoing concerns a young woman in Rotherham, England (*Guardian*, 1 April 2017). Sammy Woodhouse was sexually groomed and abused as a fourteen-year-old and had a child by her abuser at fifteen. Now in her early thirties, she runs a campaigning group for victims of abuse, which targets both abuse and how the criminal justice system deals with it. Such forms of dialogue have allowed her

[9] Kor was criticised for forgiving the Nazis publicly by others of their victims, who felt she had no right to forgive on behalf of others. Her response was to say that she only forgave for herself and that she believed that none of those who suffered would wish her to carry the burden of that suffering throughout her own life.

to move forward: 'I don't want to constantly live in my past. I've come forward, I've reported them [the professionals who let her down]. I'm one of the success stories, if you can call it that.' Of her abuser, she says:

> I feel different things about him. If I was to hate him, that's going to damage my son, and also it's going to damage me, because carrying hate and anger around is not healthy. I can't go back and change things. Have I forgiven him? Probably, yes. Not because I think it's right, what he did, but I need to move forward.

She adds that neither she nor her son will ever have contact with the abuser. These comments reflect Woodhouse's ambivalence about what to do and why she is doing it, but the link is clear between accusing (the authorities, the perpetrator), acting (reporting what happened, running the campaign group) and forgiving (giving to the perpetrator and giving up for herself and her son). Forgiveness as giving up is about escaping the cycle of anger in order to build a loving and emotionally healthy life. This is a case where moral blame and personal change for a better future are interlinked, but this is also a case of activating the subjective side of forgiving, the giving up of anger as forgiveness which is also, to an extent, the giving of forgiveness to the perpetrator. If forgiveness has two sides, as it does here, we can see why moral transactions around guilt and forgiveness are an exact means of retrieving humanity. On one side, it releases the perpetrator from the claim that he is a violator; on the other, it releases the victim from the grief of having been violated. These transactions are complicated because forgiveness as an aspect of moral psychology is itself complicated. To be able to forgive (give up) must in most cases be made so much easier by a successfully achieved forgiving (giving to), or it may be vice versa. Transitioning to a better future without anger and grief and where empathy and compassion are possible is then an outcome of the ethically forgiving transaction.

Eventually, a victim forgiving in the double sense (giving to and giving up) may help a perpetrator forgive herself – again to forgive but not forget, to hold at a distance. It is when both meet on the higher level of a universal solidarity that the relationship works best but often it seems to be a way of surviving better on a day-to-day basis. However well it works, giving to and giving up, and how one may lead to the other, inform the relationship between victim and perpetrator. This moves it away from the asymmetry of 'doer' and 'done to' and towards a symmetrical matching of moral psychologies around grief, the universality of human experience and reconciliation.

Forgiveness as Psychological Process

The second point is one of caution and follows on from the preceding. We are talking here of a psychological process that is often ongoing and rarely complete, and one which works differently for different people. People work towards forgiveness, through their psychological or emotional reactions. They do not get there by an 'easy' act of metaphysical reflection, and of course, sometimes they do not get there at all. The same Cathy Harrington, who felt a powerful bond of identity with the mother of the young man who killed her daughter dreads the thought of meeting the perpetrator himself:

> I'm not [at forgiveness] yet, and the thing that terrifies me most is the thought that one day I may need to meet Eric Copple. I've been in the dark for many years; it's getting clearer now. Lots of things in life are senseless. There's so much we can't explain, but we need to be able to love the questions. (Cantacuzino 2015: 165)

In the previous chapter, we saw how Jo Berry's position is one of seeking to forgive, but not always being able to give up anger and blame. A dialogue may become blocked for a variety of reasons, some concerning the people involved, and sometimes their situation (as with Berry and Patrick Magee). Anger in its different forms needs more analysis than I can give it here.[10] That victims can spend their lives with the trauma of violation is the moral truth that sits alongside possibilities of love and forgiveness. The process is difficult, cannot be forced, and may not be embarked upon at all.

Difficulties of psychological process are seen in the case in Australia of Kelly Connor who in 1971 at seventeen hit and killed an elderly woman, driving her car at 45 mph in a 35 mph limit. In this case, the police out of kindness turned a blind eye to the fact she had been speeding. Perpetrators can not only benefit from forgiveness, they need in its wake to forgive themselves. Connor's ongoing problem has been to forgive herself: 'I still almost choke to say I forgive myself and sometimes I can't integrate it into my life, but I've reconciled that that's how it has to be. The moment I've fixed forgiveness, it's no longer real. It has to be changing and constantly challenging. What I forgive myself for today, I don't know it will apply tomorrow' (Cantacuzino 2015: 141–42). Forgiveness of oneself or another may never be the last word on the harm caused. It is how the moral experience is held and handled that reveals the process at work. What would it mean for Kelly Connor to be able to forgive herself? It could not mean that she ceased to be the person who killed the lady, a responsibility she will always carry. To be able to forgive herself would represent a readjustment in relation to the guilt she carries. Where she ends up and how much she can give up her guilt is a work in progress.

Similarly, if a victim refuses to forgive, no judgement or demand can be attached such as 'you ought to forgive'. This is at least so in relation to the kinds of severe victimisation described in *The Forgiveness Project*. With lesser forms, Griswold (2007: 70) may be right that it shows praiseworthy character to forgive where a wrongdoer has apologised or shown remorse, but the general

[10] I explore how anger is a complex part of human moral psychology in Chapters 7, 8 and 12. I argue that it may be both vindictive (wanting to strike back) and vindicative (seeking to affirm what is right and what is wrong). Victims may of course stay with the former, whereas the latter is an avenue that can eventually lead to the desire to forgive and reconciliation.

point could be put in Kant's terms as between categorical and hypothetical imperatives. The former command us morally that we ought to do something, whereas the latter say 'if you want to achieve X, then you ought to do Y'. 'You ought to forgive' involves a categorical imperative, while 'if you want to get through this sense of violation, it may help you to think how you might forgive the perpetrator' would be hypothetical. The psychological possibility of forgiving generates a hypothetical reason why it might be good to forgive.

Forgiveness as Ethical Reality and Institutional Practice

In this section, I pick up the idea of demarcating an ethically realist account of forgiveness in the terms developed in the previous section from a legal account, in order to set up their difference and how the ethical account can be the basis for a critical analysis (ERIC) of a legal account.

Two Accounts of Forgiveness

Here are two different accounts of forgiveness, one developed in criminal justice theory, the other from *The Forgiveness Project,* reflecting its sui generis ethical (moral and psychological) experience. From the latter point of view, Marina Cantacuzino rejects the idea that forgiveness is linked to ideals of self-abnegation or heroic endurance in favour of an 'up-down-backwards-forwards-inside-outside-on-off quality it has in reality' (Cantacuzino 2015: 9). While decidedly messy rather than noble or holy, she nonetheless writes that forgiveness is as mysterious as love, with a tragic aspect and incorporating the double meaning of forgiveness (giving up and to) discussed earlier:

> the only thing I know for sure is that the act of forgiving is fluid and active and can change from day to day, hour to hour, depending on how you feel ... or what triggers your encounter.... Forgiveness may unfold like a mysterious discovery, or it may be a totally conscious decision, something you line yourself up for having exhausted all other options. It may have a strong degree of pardoning attached to it, or it may just be a sense that you have released something poisonous or let go of something heavy.... It requires a broad ... understanding that life is morally complicated, that people behave in despicable ways and that some things can never be explained. (Cantacuzino 2015: 2)

A process likened to the mystery of love is not simply about human messiness. Something much deeper is at stake, as the contributors to *The Forgiveness Project* make clear. I think Cantacuzino is right to reject the sense of saintliness that some would attach to forgiving, which overlooks its practical day-to-day quality for those non-holy, ordinary people who do it. Setting them up as acting in extraordinary ways is perhaps a way of marginalising their experience. Still, the connection to mystery and love is central to this way of experiencing forgiveness. We have discussed love quite a lot earlier in this section, we should also consider more the aspect of mystery.

Compare this with Antony Duff's account in the criminal justice literature as to how forgiveness is causally related to apology:

> Apologies for wrongdoing ... express ... not just regret at the harm that I caused but remorse for the wrong that I did, my repudiation of that wrong..., and my implicit commitment to strive to avoid doing such wrong in future... They thus also seek forgiveness from and reconciliation with the person whom I wronged and to whom I now apologize ... [The wrong] created a flaw, if not a rupture, in the relationship [that] can be removed or remedied only by an apology made by the wrongdoer and accepted in a spirit of forgiveness by the victim. (Duff 2001: 94)

Here forgiveness is sequential and takes the set form of an exchange of apology for its acceptance 'in a spirit of forgiveness'. Duff adds that the apology for a serious wrong is only sufficient if accompanied by 'forceful expressions of apology' which show the wrongdoer 'takes his wrongdoing seriously, by undertaking [a] burdensome task for the victim' (Duff 2001: 96). Duff is speaking here in the specific context of a criminal process involving mediation within the bounds of law, so involving something burdensome and forceful to reflect the need for punishment. The underlying model is however broadly used, as Martha Nussbaum indicates, calling it the classic account of conditional or 'transactional forgiveness' (Nussbaum 2016: 58). In its canonical form, it involves 'a change of heart on the part of the victim, who gives up anger and resentment in response to the offender's confession and contrition' (Nussbaum 2016: 63).[11]

For participants in *The Forgiveness Project*, forgiveness does not have to follow apology and the victim's 'spirit of forgiveness' may lead as much as it follows. Nussbaum speaks of the victim 'giving up' her anger in the classical model, but this is something she does in a kind of exchange relation: a *do ut des* ('I give that you give'). It is the exchange of one thing for another to set a relationship to rights and move on. Where in this would we find the connection to an experience that is as 'mysterious as love'?

Forgiveness as Exchange Relation

The conflict between an ethical account of forgiveness and one that is shaped by modern criminal justice practices has been explored in a debate between Jeffrie Murphy and Herbert Morris. Murphy's argument reflects his endorsement of a retributive theory of punishment and is aligned with criminal justice thinking. A violation has attacked a sense of self-worth and self-respect

[11] The recent set of essays by Warmke, Nelkin and McKenna (2021) reflects a similar framing in which there is wrongdoing, a holding of blameworthiness and the moral standing to forgive. This generates a paradigm 'in which a victim ... forgives the wrongdoer for a ... wrong done' under conditions that make the forgiveness valid for both victim and wrongdoer (Warmke, Nelkin and McKenna 2021: 18).

(Murphy and Hampton 1988: 16), and it is appropriate to desire to pay back the perpetrator. Murphy calls this desire 'retributive hatred' (Murphy and Hampton 1988: 90), but this righteous moral emotion may be countered by other moral reasons a perpetrator may introduce, for example by seeking to make amends, showing contrition, or by apology (Murphy and Hampton 1988: 24–30). The perpetrator thereby separates himself from his own prior act, perhaps even condemning it, and places himself on the side of the person he had victimised. There is then a logic based on moral reasons why a victim might decide to forgive a perpetrator. In the absence of such reasons, a victim who forgave might do so prematurely and might reveal an absence of a sense of her own personal self-worth.

The argument identifies a moral dialogue and exchange whereby a perpetrator indicates a change in his moral position, which can lead to a change in the victim's position in favour of forgiveness. We could speak here of a *do ut des* exchange of moral reasons for shifting one's position. From the point of view of legal justice, there is something compelling in this proposal. The *do ut des* of apology and forgiveness looks a lot like the logic of a contractual exchange or that of a punishment for a crime. Underlying these would be the model of the economic exchange of commodities (Pashukanis 1978). It takes the form of a recompense or an exchange of equivalents. In making it, however, Murphy identified and sidelined arguments that take a different turn. One of these is that we should forgive not because the perpetrator has shown remorse but because we are all creatures who will wrong others and, in our turn, need to be forgiven (Murphy and Hampton 1988: 30). In other circumstances, we might all have done this thing. The human condition suggests we should cultivate humility and the disposition to forgive those who are ultimately no different from ourselves. If we speak about perpetrators and victims, we should do so cautiously lest these terms become permanent categories around which we organise all our experience.

Such a broad account of forgiveness reflects what occurs in *The Forgiveness Project*. It exists independently of the kind of moral exchange Murphy identifies, operating regardless of *do ut des*. Based on personal humility, it may not indicate a lack of self-worth but the contrary. Thoughts like this provoke discomfort for Murphy, who warns that they take us 'into a religious dimension that transcends or suspends the ordinarily ethical'. Worse, they occupy a place of 'obscurity and mystery for their own sake', involving 'leaps into special realms' (Murphy and Hampton 1988: 30). Recall that Cantacuzino also noted the mysterious quality of forgiveness, but from a different and very positive perspective: for her this is how forgiveness is. Murphy does row back from his assessment and gives the argument for humility its due, concluding that its main problem is just that it fits badly with legal processes: 'The arena of resentment and forgiveness is individual and personal in a way that legal guilt and responsibility are not' (Murphy and Hampton 1988: 33). The ethical argument that forgiveness as humility 'leaps into special realms' is thus not eventually defeated, only seen as inapplicable in a criminal justice framework. Precisely so, but it leaves the question of what constitutes an ethically true account of forgiveness unresolved and unresolvable in the terms of law. The latter has its own particular and peculiar objectives: when it talks of forgiveness it shapes this to meet the legal setting. Murphy's *do ut des* exchange for reasons imposes a particular format that is not inevitable. From the point of view of the 'leap into special realms', it lacks humility and establishes set categories of perpetrator and victim as the subject and object of forgiveness in perpetuity.

Dispositive humility on the other hand is not especially obscure. It reflects the idea of love in relation to human concrete universality/ singularity discussed in the previous section, for it depends on the possibility of the universal experience of being responsible for doing something that violates another. Pace Murphy, it does not assume a necessarily religious dimension, though it may be taken up in different religious traditions, or none. A belief in common humanity would serve as well. It may appear religious because there is a universal identification underneath humility and a disposition to forgive that goes beyond the 'ordinarily' ethical. (For 'ordinarily' could we substitute Williams's 'peculiar' here?) Though it does not deny that moral engagement in the form of contrition or apology can come from the person in the position of perpetrator, it indicates that forgiveness can be unilateral and without moral engagement or could occur through moral transactions initiated by the victim. It could be about a desire to give up the pain of violation as a sign of moral strength rather than weakness rather than a desire to give absolution. People may go beyond the 'ordinarily ethical' (in legal terms) because their *ordinary* ethical experience requires it.

Forgiveness as Dispositive Humility

This intuition informs Morris's response to Murphy. He suggests that Murphy's exchange of moral reasons may be a part of the picture, but there is a deeper ethical level to forgiveness. Moral reasons 'may till the soil and sow the seed, as it were, so that forgiveness may more probably burst into bloom', but 'there is something beyond these actions, the sun and the rain if you will, that must cooperate for forgiveness to come about' (Morris 1988: 17–18). The metaphorical language is significant, I think, for Morris is reaching to explain something that is not easy to express in standard moral terms. His important point however is that forgiveness is ultimately not based on an idea of exchange at all. 'Finally,' he says, 'I find myself drawn, when reflecting upon forgiveness, to the idea of transcendence, to grace, and … the mystery that lies at the heart of forgiveness' (Morris 1988: 16). That word 'mystery' reappears, linking Morris to Cantacuzino and *The Forgiveness Project*, but also reflecting on the issue of universal identification (concrete universality/ singularity) in the moral experience of forgiveness. Note also that Morris brings out the question of 'grace' at the heart of the mystery of forgiveness.

For Morris, as for participants in *The Forgiveness Project*, forgiveness is a complex process involving identification with the concrete universality of another, recognising common humanity as the basis for giving up the sense of violation. It involves an ethical agency that is eventually in oneself as well as connected to events or the actions of others. It leaves the victim not just in the position of having cancelled a moral debt, but potentially in a qualitatively new situation, even with the person forgiven. Between the 'tilling and sowing' and the 'sun and the rain', there may or may not be a connection (the metaphor begins to break down). Cantacuzino's messiness comes into play. You may behave well having victimised me, but I may choose not to forgive you; you may behave badly having victimised me, and I may choose to forgive you. Forgiveness takes us to a deeper level than our particular identities shaken and stirred by events. In the end, there is a human choice to see and act one way or another, and with or without a certain grace. In the light of a grace that we could designate either as human or divine, our actual, personal identities become what Morris refers to as 'contingent' connections in the following quote. Forgiveness

> is a virtue that benefits both the giver and the receiver, liberating both.... [It] embodies a generosity of spirit and is made possible only through our overcoming contingent connection with and investment in ourselves. It is, in this respect, close to the divine, involving as it does some detachment from self in circumstances where the pull runs deep in precisely the opposite direction.... The concept of grace, something that makes for the good that transcends what is within our will's compass, allows for grasping this mystery. (Morris 1988: 19)

Forgiveness involves something that is 'mysterious' and like the love that is available in a 'non-special' way to the human as a metaphysical animal. It is Wilma Derksen's 'vulnerability and transparency' that makes you 'a better person to get through', to 'soar, to go higher' (Cantacuzino 2015: 117). It moves beyond the *do ut des* of 'ordinary' (read legal or peculiar) exchange, connecting metaphysical ethical experience to forgiveness practices.

Rational Exchange or Dispositive Humility

What is the relationship between a forgiveness practice based on *do ut des* exchange and one based on dispositive humility? To identify the ethical importance of humility from universal identification as against the exchange of moral reasons is not to discount the latter, but to think about how *two different understandings of an ethical practice* sit in relation to each other and interact.[12] We should talk here of a complex relationship between on the one hand reasons in a

[12] This is the main difference between my position and Nussbaum's, as discussed in Chapter 4.

moral economy of exchange and on the other a graceful, ethical decision.[13] The ethical work of forgiveness exists in its own terms as the real experience of dealing with grief at violation and this may come into contact with processes adopting a *do ut des* logic of exchange. A simple way of highlighting the difference would be to ask the question, how is a victim of violation likely to experience a criminal justice system run along the lines of a moral economy of exchange? How does he relate the ethically 'individual and personal' to the way in which 'legal guilt and responsibility are not' (Murphy and Hampton 1988: 33)? The question has two levels. The first concerns how the system deals with victims empirically, on a day-to-day basis, often with inadequate resources, and generally with its main focus elsewhere, that is on perpetrators. The second involves the moral logic of the criminal justice system if it were working according to its own best image of itself. How could such a system, with its overall logic of crime and punishment, accommodate the need of violated victims to grieve and forgive?

The need for a moral grammar different from that of the law is articulated by Marian Partington, whose description of forgiveness in the wake of the murder of her sister Lucy, is as follows:

> The 'facts of the case' and the way that they were manipulated during the trial were only small aspects of the truth that was sought. More than this, there was a need for understanding of the intricate context of human relationships within our society. Ultimately, there is a need for meaning, resolution and healing. The later trial and the sentence did not answer my need to know the truth of what happened to Lucy. Human justice is mostly focused on retribution, causing more pain. Our human potential is not enlarged by this punitive process. Healing is imprisoned. (Partington 2012: 52)

When Partington speaks of 'the truth of what happened to Lucy', I take her to mean two things. One is that the trial process did not elicit the facts of what had become of Lucy – how she had been picked up, held, violated and killed. The other is the deeper sense of the moral truth of her death: with what heart did Lucy meet the dreadful fate bestowed on her by the Wests, and what can be said morally for them? Beyond that, there is the quest for truth that animates Partington's own journey. How did grief at her loss affect her, how much did she share with Rose West in terms of potential for murderous rage and what can she do to return love and goodness to the world after so ruinous an event? Criminal justice appears in this account unable to achieve what a moral psychology based on love and forgiveness should seek, but there are still Partington's 'small aspects' and I wonder what these might be.

[13] Jacques Derrida, who is unpopular with normative political theorists, got much of this right:

> It is important to analyse at its base the tension … between, *on the one side*, the idea which is also a demand for the *unconditional*, the gracious, infinite, aneconomic forgiveness granted *to the guilty as guilty*, without counterpart, even to those who do not repent or ask forgiveness, and *on the other side*…, a conditional forgiveness proportionate to the recognition of the fault, to repentance….' (Derrida 2001: 34–35)

Law and the Moral Psychology of Victims

There are two things I would like to explore. One is that the forensic 'facts of the case' do in fact remain crucial to the experience of the victim. Victims need to know what happened to those they have loved and lost as part of the process of mourning. We see this in Partington's case where finding Lucy's remains many years after her disappearance was traumatic but ultimately morally enabling. We see it also in Chapter 10 where we consider the moral experience of women searching the Atacama desert in Chile for the lost bodies of their disappeared loved ones. To find even a part of the physical body may assist in mourning. Another example concerns the retrieval of murdered victims disappeared by the South African police whose location was disclosed by the work of the Truth and Reconciliation Commission (Boraine 2000). The forensic facts matter. However, this last example makes the point that it is not criminal justice practices per se that are important but processes geared towards establishing the factual truth of what happened, which may take different forms. Nonetheless, one would have to say that a factual forensic process is a central part of a criminal justice process, and this is important for victims.

A second point concerns how this forensic process feeds into the broader criminal process of conviction and punishment. The process leads of course to a finding of guilt where appropriate but this leaves victims and perpetrators to deal with the fallout from often serious violation. Perpetrators are sent to prison and victims must grieve and mourn, and never the twain shall meet. But there is still an important nuance here for it may be rightly said that a criminal process aids victims by *vindicating* their experience in a public forum. It is hard to watch the struggle of victims to 'have their day in court' or to have their story heard and believed and not to realise that the public acknowledgment of what happened, if done sensitively, can be very important as a matter not of retributive payback but of having the truth heard. This is an issue that I take up in my final chapter, but the main line of argument there concerns how a criminal trial occupies a space in which conflicting moral aspects are at play. I call these elements in Chapter 12 the 'vindictive', the 'vindicative' and the 'validatory'.

In brief, *being vindictive* involves seeking to punish, to be punitive to hurt for a hurt done, Nussbaum's payback. *Being vindicative* involves upholding a sense of what is right and wrong for individuals and a community, and the public moral condemnation of the wrong. (This is of course often open to contestation, but nevertheless it works successfully in many cases.) *Being validatory* is a term I use to recognise the whole moral experience of those involved in a crime: the perpetrator, the victim, the broader community as well as the question of coming to terms with violation and finding ways to go on after it. Whereas being vindictive, as its name suggests, leads to a primitive, punitive form of moral experience (as I explain in Chapters 7, 8, 11 and 12), the third with its holistic, compassionate and reconciliative commitments reflects a kind of mature ethical judgement that would be in line with the kind of dispositive humility described in this chapter.

But here is the point: the second, vindicative form of justice sits between the vindictive and the validatory. It upholds the victim's sense of having been wronged but this can be linked to two different approaches. It could be accompanied either by a standard punitive process or it could be the basis for a more ethically supportive outcome which would assist the victim (and the perpetrator, and the broader community) in moving forward. In the modern criminal justice system, it is primarily the former, punitive (vindictive) outcome that will ensue. The latter would entail a process that was reparative and reconciliatory rather than punitive. Accordingly, the vindicative moment in criminal justice can be pushed either forward in the direction of the validatory or backward in the direction of the vindictive. Though it is compatible with both, the existing system's dominant punitive commitment means that the vindicative moment is generally coupled with, and falls back into, a vindictive outcome (Norrie 2023). In the latter case, vindication will not thrive and grow, but will rather become subsumed and perish in an unproductive repetition of punishment. The vindicative–vindictive combination leaves perpetrators, victims and communities alike still to deal with the consequences of violation despite the law's authoritative moral pronouncements, and these become hollowed out by their association with a punitive mindset.

Moral Psychology, Love and Forgiveness, and Law

This chapter has considered how love is actualised in moral relationships between victims and perpetrators. What is at stake is a metaphysics, and with that a metapsychology, of love generating a moral psychology and language of guilt, forgiveness and reconciliation which allows victims and perpetrators to come to terms with violation and grief. This is not a programmatic understanding of how the two *ought* to be configured according to a normative political or legal theory. It accounts naturalistically for the heterogeneous nature of individual engagements where sometimes a perpetrator asks for forgiveness and sometimes a victim provides it. Sometimes, a victim forgives alone, without even identifying the perpetrator; sometimes, equally, a victim resolutely refuses to forgive. Processes of forgiveness may never take off, may get stuck, need further completion or be blocked. Underlying this is a moral psychology of grief and grieving, for victims and often also for perpetrators, where reconciliation depends on finding a higher and a common ground. Importantly, *The Forgiveness Project* show how this works in practice for ordinary people and not what sceptics or cynics might characterise as 'holy fools' or 'heroes of self-abnegation' whose very virtue is a reason why they should be marginalised. Forgiveness is a practical moral necessity and a hypothetical imperative; mostly it is a real possibility for ordinary human beings.

Modern criminal justice systems often appear to deal in moral terms with wrongdoing and to restore a rightful balance to human relations. This is the stuff of television drama in which a human and flawed criminal detective negotiates an inhuman and flawed criminal justice system to uncover a crime and restore the world's order. A malefactor gets her comeuppance, and the viewer is assured that a flawed system can produce a kind of reconciliation. The victim has been vindicated, the perpetrator is sent to jail and the moral order, however imperfect, is restored. A simple mystery focused on finding 'who did it' has been solved according to a reassuring metaphysic. It is amazing how much this narrative occupies our airwaves, suggesting our fascination and our need for the story that is told. In some ways, the storyline reflects at least roughly the understanding of criminal justice that legal theorists have promoted for 200 years: that the criminal justice system gives offenders their just deserts (Kant) and restores right to individual and society (Hegel). Left at the margin of these stories are two issues. The first is that criminal violation is a social phenomenon linked to poverty, the inculcated desire for wealth and the objectification of sexual relations. Kant's false motives among the people (Chapter 3) are manifest and manifold, though kept at a distance by the storyline (Norrie 2023). Once we consider the experience of victimhood in terms of loving relations that extend from love of self to love of others placed in the same position as ourselves, with the different stops in between, an ethically more serious commitment to reconciliation and social change working through the experience of violation becomes possible.

The second follows the first. Law reconfigures social tendencies for violation as a relationship between responsible and guilty individuals committing crimes and being punished for them (Norrie 2000, 2014). In line with this, the victim's relation to violation is fashioned either as a desire to punish or as an exchange relation of remorse and apology for forgiveness. With regard to the exchange relation, moral experience is given a particular cast as it is tailored to fit the legal model, and this model becomes the way in which we understand human psychology and relations. This is a form of moral*ised* rather than moral psychology (Williams) whereby an underlying ethical reality is shaped according to the norms and forms of law and political and legal theory. My aim in this and the preceding chapter has been to resist this reshaping by developing an ethically realistic account of forgiveness and reconciliation that is independent of institutional shaping. Forgiveness in moral psychology is more complex, developmental, reconciliative and social, whereas in law it is primarily individualistic and retributive in the sense of completing a moral economy based on *do ut des* exchange and punishment. My aim is for a metaphysics of forgiveness linking love to metapsychology and a moral language able to deal with violation and grief, and then to contrast that with what the more limited legal model offers in an ERIC (ethically real, institutionally critical) critique.

Part III

Guilt and the Animal that Thinks and Loves

Introduction to Part III: Synthesis and Atonement

The metaphysical animal that thinks and loves possesses an ethical sensibility which expresses an underlying metapsychological condition. These three chapters provide a fuller case for a moral psychology that unifies metaphysical and metapsychological elements in a naturalistic moral psychology of guilt. They expand the remit of moral philosophy to include psychoanalytic concerns and develop an ethically real and institutionally critical (ERIC) account of retributive punishment. They begin with a metaphysics of guilt that goes beyond modern morality's 'peculiar' (Williams) practice and thence move to develop an underlying and parallel metapsychology. The result is a developed moral psychology at both levels which include *two* kinds of guilt, one that is 'primitive', the other 'mature'. The former is shown to be linked to law and retributive philosophy and the latter operates as its ERIC, its ethically real institutionally critical alternative. From this a different, mature, retributivism becomes possible.

I begin (Chapter 6) with the critical philosophical analyses of Bernard Williams and Herbert Morris. Williams suggests we might push the 'peculiar' forms of modern moral philosophy in the direction of a psychoanalytically informed moral psychology. Morris argues that we should go beyond them to see how guilt combines psychological identification with another, involving emotional and potentially physiological pain and anxiety. He identifies 'atonement' as a need to be 'at one' again with oneself and others after an act of violation. These approaches take modern moral philosophy to the edge of its conventional limits and beyond. They suggest how these might be transcended in the direction of psychoanalysis. I argue, following Jonathan Lear (2015), that what is at stake is the modern post-Freudian renewal of the Socratic understanding of philosophy: knowing ourselves involves psychoanalytical or metapsychological understanding, here with regard to guilt after violation. This is the properly extended domain of modern moral philosophy.

The stage is now set to investigate the metapsychology of guilt in depth (Chapter 7). I identify two theories of guilt in Freud. The first in the comparatively late *Civilization and Its Discontents* (1929) reasserts his earlier, more mechanical, understanding of how human drives need to be repressed. Guilt stems from the internalisation of anger and fear which keep basic instincts under control. The second can be developed from Freud's later structural theory of how the human force of love develops through early close relationships to create ego and super-ego forms in the psyche. Following Hans Loewald, the psychology of self-formation makes loving identification with others the root of responsibility, guilt and atonement. The super-ego is indeed an 'atonement structure' making guilt a positive and productive desire to be 'at one' again with oneself and others (Loewald 1980). If the earlier ('Kantian') theory identifies a primitive guilt based on fear and anger, the later ('Aristotelian') theory finds a mature guilt in line with Morris's metaphysical account of identification and atonement.

Chapter 8 begins by recapitulating the primitive and mature kinds of guilt in Freud and then supports the case for their twin existence by relating them to Melanie Klein's account of infantile life where guilt is either primitive and persecutory or mature and restorative. Here, I take the two consolidated accounts and consider them as different practical ways for organising guilt in law and society. I argue both that legal guilt as understood in existing retributive theory is essentially primitive and punitive in its form and that an alternative approach based on a mature retributivism is possible. The elaboration of a mature conception of retributive guilt as atoning, reparative and reconciliative constitutes an ERIC critique, the ethically real basis for a critique of law's existing institutional practice.

6

Guilt Beyond Philosophy's Limit

> ... the other psychological forces (such as love perhaps) that make blame possible.
>
> Bernard Williams (1995: 16)

> ... feeling guilty we ... felt rotten, depleted of energy, and tense.
>
> Herbert Morris (1976: 99)

> This need to make amends ... at the core of guilt ... is atonement, being at one with.
>
> Herbert Morris (1976: 100)

Introducing a set of his later essays, Jeffrie Murphy noted that he started to question his commitment to retributive philosophy in the light of the thought, amongst others, of Sigmund Freud (Murphy 2012: xii). Murphy followed here in the footsteps of others disenchanted with or ambivalent about the modern philosophical debate around punishment. His essays on guilt and shame pursue a critical if ambivalent line that reflects the work of earlier sceptics like Bernard Williams (Williams 1993, 1995, 2011) and Herbert Morris (1976, 1987, 1988). Behind them, Freudian metapsychology also lurks, raising two questions. First, what exactly is the sceptical and disenchanted line in the philosophy of punishment and, since it is not well established, how might it be developed? Second, since this is where I think it might lead, how might psychoanalytic thinking, that is, Freud's metapsychology, be related to scepticism in the philosophy of punishment? And as a rider to that, what exactly does it say about those issues of guilt, blame and responsibility which are central to retributivism? This chapter together with the next two considers these questions.

My main target here however is the first question and I consider the work of Williams and Morris in some depth. My argument is that their dissatisfaction with orthodox legal and philosophical theory leads them to the brink of metaphysical and metapsychological positions which not only challenge the mainstream but also question the nature and limits of philosophy itself. Morris's work is particularly important here, but I begin with Williams's general criticism of the 'peculiar' nature of liberal normative theory and where this takes him. I introduced Williams in Chapter 1, and as developed here, he sets the stage for Morris's rich account of moral identification, atonement and what I will call 'quantum guilt'.[1] All three concepts challenge the standard legal and moral conception of guilt, taking us into first a metaphysical and then metapsychological understanding of our terms. In Williams and Morris, modern normative philosophy is brought to an awareness of its limits and the brink of a new and better understanding of itself. This transcends the standard modern political and legal accounts and aligns itself with an older Greek view expressed in the Socratic injunction to know oneself. This ancient view is however given a radical modern twist in the argument that 'knowing oneself' entails a psychoanalytic alongside a philosophical understanding of what it means to be human (Lear 2015: ch 1).

In line with previous chapters, I argue that the metaphysical animal capable of thought and love is at its heart a metapsychological being and philosophical understanding must come to terms with this. A philosophy adequate to human guilt must understand how 'the animal that thinks and loves' combines metaphysical thought and metapsychological process. This chapter takes us to the point of seeing why this is so by engaging with Williams and Morris as they confront modern philosophy's limits. They begin to see that an adequate moral philosophy, one that combines philosophy and psychoanalysis, ethics and psychology, is both possible and necessary if we are to understand the human experience of violation. The first two quotations at the head of this chapter show Morris and Williams reaching towards metapsychology, while the third identifies a key concept that will occupy us over this and the next two chapters, and indeed the rest of the book. 'Atonement' however will be given a particular meaning in line with the word's constituent parts, as 'at-one-ment', being at one.

In the next section, I develop Williams's criticism of modern normative political theory as a 'peculiar' intellectual practice. Williams's approach leads him to two critiques: one is a political critique of actually existing moral forms, and the other is less clear but involves a push to find a better ethical and ontological basis for understanding moral life, one that links a naturalistic psychology to moral feelings and their expression. I see this latter critique as building a bridgehead between philosophy and psychoanalysis, and a way of drawing them together into an expanded understanding of how philosophy should deal with violation. In the following section, we see how Morris offers a parallel approach through reflection on the limits of legal guilt through concepts of identification, atonement and 'quantum guilt'. Being ethically critical in the ways Williams and Morris are takes modern moral philosophy to its limit and beyond, to the brink of an underlying psychological terrain that it should embrace but which it usually seeks to keep at a distance. This expanded conception of philosophy is developed in the third and final section.

[1] I am indebted for this term to Amanda Wilson (2021a).

Two Critiques of Modern Guilt

In this section, I outline Williams's two critiques of the modern idea of guilt. His account of modern moral philosophy, as expressing a 'peculiar' understanding (Williams 2011: ch 10), led him to both a political and an ethical critique of modern morality. With regard to the former, I wish to bring out the way that his account of modern morality's peculiarity links with his understanding of law, and how morality's limits, its peculiarities, reflect its connection to modern legal institutions. This is Williams's first, political, critique. With regard to the latter, these political limits at the same time point to ethical possibilities that lie beyond morality in its 'peculiar' form, possibilities that he summed up by invoking the idea of a naturalistic moral psychology. Such possibilities should reflect broadly and more truly on the nature of moral experience than does what we might call 'actually existing morality', morality in its 'peculiar' form, as endorsed in modern liberal political and legal thought. Here Williams focused on the, to him, strange idea that guilt involved 'voluntary' action. This is Williams's second, ethical, critique. I begin though with the first critique, which situates the problem that the second critique then engages.

A Political Critique: Against Conflation

For Williams, concepts like blame, guilt and responsibility are systematically limited and impoverished by their connection to modern political and legal institutions. They are given their specific form and shape by the liberal state. Writing of modern morality as a 'peculiar' institution in *Ethics and the Limits of Philosophy* (2011), Williams noted that it served the function of rendering modern society workable. Focusing on the nature of obligation, he noted that it secured reliability in social matters, for people could reasonably expect others to behave in certain ways. However, it bought social functionality at a price. Williams saw blame as central to crime and punishment, but as involving the fiction that people were free to act otherwise than they did. Agents were treated as though relevant ethical considerations established by state and law were the reasons on which they acted. The system had the function of integrating citizens into the fiction of a universal, deliberative community, and this was an achievement of the morality system. Since it was fiction, however, he questioned whether the system could survive with a clear understanding of how it worked.

A key but problematic concept was that of 'the voluntary'. Linking acts unproblematically to a person and her character, the focus was not on freedom in a critical sense, and whether, for example, a person might really have had the ability to have chosen otherwise. Ignoring the importance of character or society, the blame system narrowly focused on the conditions of the particular act. It was able to function in this way because it did not operate alone, being linked to other practices of encouragement and discouragement to keep to the law, but this additional institutional support for concepts of the voluntary was ignored within the conceptual understanding of the morality system itself. There was always a pressure in the system 'to require a voluntariness that will be total and will cut through character and psychological or social determination', allocating blame on what is claimed to be 'the ultimately fair basis of the agent's own contribution' (Williams 2011: 216). Williams however did not see this as ultimately fair at all, for it ignored the additional contextual information essential to ground an ethics that could address how and why people really act, and how, in light of that, they might be persuaded morally to behave in ways non-violative of others. Most people know that blaming and punishing people as voluntary actors is ineffectual in controlling crime, but we are stuck with the morality system and blame because we can see no alternative. If we did away with it, we would be left with forms of persuasion indistinguishable in spirit 'from force and constraint' (Williams 2011: 216), which would be as bad or worse. We stick therefore with the devil we know, believing it keeps us honest, when in reality it only works because of ancillary social institutions which hold its language in place.

In the following passage, already encountered in Chapter 1, Williams speaks of overemphasis on 'the voluntary'. This results from the modern conflation of a particular view of morality and the particular institutional setting of the liberal state. The outcome is an impoverished moral theory for morality has been conflated with politics:

> We have handed many of the responses to a very special formation, the modern state, and we have principles governing what such a state can and should do. An important ideal that helps shape those principles is that an individual should, so far as possible, have control over his or her life, in relation to the power of the state.... To the extent that our ideas about legal responsibility are shaped by that ideal, they are governed by a certain political theory of freedom in the modern state, not by a moral refinement of the very conception of responsibility.... We deceive ourselves if we suppose that public practices of ascribing responsibility can be derived from an antecedent notion of moral responsibility, or that the idea of the voluntary is uniquely important to responsibility. (Williams 1993: 66–67)

This is Williams's political critique of modern guilt. The weakness of modern orthodox liberal theory resides not just in its intrinsic limitations but in the fact that its concepts conflate a political aim and setting with a genuine philosophical elaboration. It is because of the unwarranted fusion of morality, law and politics that we can say that one of Williams's targets is the historical and political critique of modern moral and legal forms. From this position, the move is to a critical understanding of the nature of modern liberalism and how it shapes the social order for good and ill.[2] The second target in light of these

[2] This is in essence the direction already taken by critical legal theory in relation to criminal law. The result is a political and historical critique of the structure, function and form of the law. See e.g. Norrie 2000, 2014; Ramsay 2009; Farmer 2016; Lacey 2016; Carvalho 2017. For discussion of the one-sided nature of this critique, since it omits the ethical direction developed in what follows, see Norrie 2017b. As explained in Chapter 1, my focus here is more on the ethical and does not pursue the road already taken of political and historical critique.

limitations is to sketch an ethical alternative in the form of a critique of what he calls moral*ised* psychology, that is a version of moral psychology which is itself shaped by 'peculiar' moral preoccupations. In its place, he proposed an ethical approach that could more openly and honestly reflect the true nature of human ethical being. What he argued for was 'a reflective and nonmythical understanding of our ethical practices. It is certain that the practices of blame, and more generally the style of people's negative ethical reactions to others, will change. The morality system, in my view, can no longer help them to do so in a desirable way' (Williams 2011: 215).

He was no doubt overly optimistic about the possibilities for change in modern blaming practices, but not wrong about the need for an alternative. What, then, was to take the place of peculiar ways of thinking in the morality system?

An Ethical Critique: The Internalised Other

Williams's second critique was *ethical* in its form, going to the deeper moral psychology underlying such terms, which Williams glimpsed, but did not fully pursue. Important here was his emphasis on going to theorists of morality beyond the mainstream, who had something different to offer. Amongst those that Williams noted as providing a better account of morality was Freud though he did not elaborate very much.[3] Williams's second critique did however point to a different road of travel for modern morality. He spoke of a 'naturalistic account of morality', a term that, he conceded, was not 'at all perspicuous' (Altham and Harrison 1995: 203), but which related moral phenomena to human psychology: 'A truthful ethical life is, and always has been, one that can include our best understanding of our psychological life, and we know that such an understanding is compatible with naturalistic explanation' (Williams 1995: 19–20).

This was the point of distinguishing a moral*ised* from a moral psychology. In the former, a given political or legal theory dominated and shaped ab initio the understanding of morality which was then read into human psychology. It shaped psychological concepts, so that the resulting account copied the political theory it was supposed to develop. Modern morality's emphasis on voluntary control of action thus appears to represent the basis for an understanding of how human moral psychology works, but in reality, it imposes a particular political and legal understanding onto psychology so that it is moralised rather than moral per se. A non-moralised psychology would relate to the open psychological question of how humans act, and how their moral categories emerge from behaviours and settings, understood and investigated naturalistically: 'A non-moralized, or less moralized, psychology uses the categories

[3] Eventually Williams found a different and lesser direction through Nietzsche. On the significance of Williams's opening of philosophy both to a limited Nietzschean critique and to psychoanalysis, see Lear 2003, 2004.

of meaning, reasons, and value, but leaves it open, or even problematical, in what way moral reasons and ethical values fit with other motives and desires, how far they express those other motives, and how far they are in conflict with them' (Altham and Harrison 1995: 202).

Williams's examples of a naturalistic moral psychology that does not prefigure the end from the beginning are various. They include Hume and Nietzsche, but also writers such as Thucydides, Diderot, Stendhal and the ancient tragedians, who have a 'powerful understanding of human motivation, in particular of relations between ethical and non-ethical motivations' (Altham and Harrison 1995: 204). But, in this discussion, the first example Williams gives of a modern who had such an understanding is Freud, and we can see how this works in Williams's *Shame and Necessity* (1993) in two ways.

The book contrasts modern guilt and shame, but also involves an underlying comparison of the ancient Greek and the modern standpoint. Shame predominated in the Greek world in a way it does not in the modern but it is not so much a question of Greek shame versus modern guilt as of how the Greeks declined to separate the two (Williams 1993: 91). The modern approach does separate them, creating an account of guilt that is individual and voluntaristic. Shame's quality is that it is more contextual, permitting understanding of failing or inadequacy and what it means in an actor's and other people's lives. Modern guilt follows the 'peculiar' moral approach, simply affirming one has done wrong, without a broader understanding. 'Shame can understand guilt', says Williams, 'but guilt cannot understand itself' (Williams 1993: 93). At this point, Williams invokes 'psychological materials' (Williams 1993: 93), naturalistic elements for a moral psychology, to illuminate shame and guilt. Here, we can identify psychoanalytic ideas in Williams's argument, though Freud's name goes unmentioned:

> Even if shame and its motivations always involve … the gaze of another,… for many of its operations the *imagined gaze of an imagined other* will do…. What I have called the *internalised other* … is conceived as one whose reactions I would respect…. The *internalised other* is indeed abstracted and generalised and idealised, but he is potentially somebody rather than nobody, and somebody other than me. He can provide the focus of real social expectations, of how I shall live if I act in one way rather than another…. The world … is represented … by *an internalised other*…. (Williams 1993: 82–85, emphasis added)

This idea of an imagined or internalised other that is in-me-and-not-me involves intrapsychic identification with another. It is taken from psychoanalysis, where, to quote Freud, it 'is known … as the earliest expression of an emotional tie with another person', one that 'endeavours to mould a person's own ego after the fashion of the one that has been taken as a model' (Freud 1985: 134–35). In *Shame and Necessity*, Williams reaches for moral psychology to explain the ethical quality of shame as it emerges from encounters central to psychic development.

That is his first encounter with moral psychology, but there is a second, in an addendum entitled 'Mechanisms of Shame and Guilt', a four-page endnote that was not integrated into the book. Here, Williams proposes a moral psychology of guilt alongside that of shame, complete with its own particular internalised figure, that of a '*victim* or an *enforcer*' (Williams 1993: 219). In line with the protocols of moral psychology, this cannot simply be stipulated or derived as a necessary moral form, but must be traced back to the conditions of psychic development understood in a naturalistic manner:

> In the case of guilt, this condition can be met by supposing that, at the most primitive level, the attitude of the internalised figure is anger, while the reaction of the subject is fear.... From this primitive basis, it is possible, by what is sometimes called 'bootstrapping', to develop the model to allow for reactions that are progressively more structured by social, ethical, or moral notions. So mere fear at mere anger becomes fear of recrimination.... (Williams 1993: 219)

As we shall see, the strong echo here is to Freud's *Civilization and Its Discontents* (Freud 1985), where fear and anger of the father or another authority figure represents the basis of guilt. But Williams was only sketching possible links in these four pages, indicating the bridgehead to moral psychology rather than developing it systematically. Note also two things: that these thoughts are contained in an addendum and not the main body of the work; and that he was drawn to psychoanalytic ideas without having a settled view as to what they were. In the passage I have just quoted, guilt is a fearful or angry result of identification with a victim or enforcer, which evolves into ethically elaborated notions. Elsewhere, however, Williams wrote of the psychoanalytic grounds of moral psychology in quite different terms:

> As soon as we look at blame not as a uniquely appropriate expression of truly moral judgement, and not, on the other hand, simply as an instrument of social control, but see it as part of a concrete ethical life, we shall be helped to understand the other psychological forces (*such as love, perhaps*) that are needed to make blame possible as a manifestation of the ethical dispositions. (Williams 1995: 16, emphasis added)

The passage comes out of the blue in an essay on free will, but significant here is the emphasis not on fear and anger, but *on love*, a very different basis for feelings of guilt, though one that is well developed (as we shall see) in the psychoanalytic literature. We will pursue the difference between these two approaches – fear and anger, love – in the next chapter. This is, then, what we get from Williams: bridgeheads to the political critique of modern morality as socially functional and historically shaped but intellectually shallow, and to the idea of a moral psychology that would underpin ethical experience, and that would be naturalistically truthful to what it means to be human in a way that the modern 'peculiar' institution, with its moralised psychology, cannot be. As for what the nature of the moral psychology of guilt should be, this is clearly only a start, but what it shows is Williams confronting the limits of modern moral theory and looking for a way beyond them through a naturalistic moral psychology.

Pursuing the line of this second critique, I now turn to Herbert Morris's analysis of guilt, which provides a deeper and more substantive account of what a moral psychology of guilt might look like. Key here, as we shall see, is Morris's account of identification, and from that his understanding of what he calls atonement (and something he, wrongly in my view, calls 'nonmoral guilt'). In the next section, I argue that Morris's account finds him developing further, more sophisticated, arguments of a psychoanalytic kind for understanding human moral psychology and moving beyond the extant limits of legal and political theory.

Atonement, Guilt and Identification: Towards an Adequate Moral Psychology

In 1976, Herbert Morris published a book of essays called *On Guilt and Innocence*, which he followed later with an essay called 'Nonmoral Guilt' (in 1987). From the former, we get two ideas which link guilt to love and psychoanalysis: ideas of atonement and what I call 'quantum' guilt. In the latter, Morris develops the idea of identification. This work echoes initial themes in Williams but goes beyond them. Compare Williams's account of the internalised authority figure discussed earlier with this passage from Morris about guilt: 'Because they have defined themselves in a manner that reveals identification with others, the actions of those others are granted power over them.... Individuals may in these circumstances believe themselves guilty' (Morris 1987: 240).

Atonement, identification and quantum guilt push us to the brink of a psychoanalytic understanding. They show that legal guilt points to broader moral and psychological commitments once the limits of its 'peculiar' moral preoccupations are explored. In this section, I consider Morris's view of atonement, identification and quantum guilt seriatim. Through these, we find the door opened both to human moral experience as that of the metaphysical animal and to the claim that this is grounded in a sense of human metapsychology.

Guilt and Atonement

Morris's 1976 book is subtitled 'Essays in Legal Philosophy and Moral Psychology', so his use of the term 'moral psychology' predates Williams.[4] Morris notes that philosophers have written exhaustively on punishment and responsibility, but that their focus is limited to questions of the justification of punishment and the ascription of responsibility. Little attention has been paid to 'concepts of guilt and guilt feelings, and ... to the rich assortment of related

[4] In *Shame and Necessity* (1993: 198, note 35), Williams acknowledges Morris's work.

concepts such as remorse, repentance, contrition, forgiveness and shame' (Morris 1976: viii). The 'complex world of moral feelings, a world so central to our lives, so deep in significance for us, so vividly and thoroughly displayed in literature' has attracted little attention from philosophers. He urged that a 'better grasp of guilt and related concepts will mean a more informed judgment of the merits of our common moral and legal practices' (Morris 1976: viii). Today I would say that not much has changed, with Morris's own contribution remaining at the margin of discussion (but see Murphy 2012; Wilson 2021a).

The division implicit in his book's subtitle ('between legal philosophy and moral psychology') suggests closeness to Williams's critical distinction between naturalistic moral psychology and morality as a 'peculiar' institution. In a short initial essay, 'Guilt and Shame', he writes that, in contrast to shame, guilt 'finds a natural role within the law' (Morris 1976: 63), and this because law maintains 'a certain balanced distribution of freedom … by ordering relationships among individuals through rules that set up a system of reciprocal rights and duties' (Morris 1976: 63). Though he does not mention the term, this is Williams's realm of 'the voluntary', the space of a moral*ised* psychology under the rubric of legal form, which here Morris contrasts with shame. But this short piece is only a starting point and in later essays, Morris will move beyond its terms.

Restoring Wholeness

In 'Guilt and Shame', Morris accepts that law in its form and nature is the home of modern guilt, but in the next essay, 'Guilt and Suffering', he begins to dismantle the certainties around this claim. Guilt becomes more personal and more metaphysical, and more at odds with how he described it previously. Here, guilt is not just legal but is instead psychic *and* somatic: it means feeling bad, 'rotten, depleted of energy, tense' (Morris 1976: 99), and this psychological feeling is related to ethical reasons. The core idea is of real emotional pain that comes from separating oneself off by an act of violation from union with a valued other. Such union, best exemplified in love, provides a feeling of wholeness or completeness, while guilt leaves wholeness broken and undone:

> In seeing oneself as cut off from others one feels a sense of incompleteness, as a lover who loses a loved one may feel that a part of him has been taken away or torn from him. The person feels that peculiar pain and uneasiness when feeling guilty of cutting off a part of himself.… In cutting oneself off from others one comes to see oneself as being cut off, not whole, as if one had destroyed what one loved and thus also destroyed a part of oneself. This image of cutting off and being cut off, not whole, finds support in our view of the guilty person as not being able to function as a whole person could and does, not being able to enjoy life fully.… (Morris 1976: 99–100)

Guilt weighs on a person who has brought such feelings on himself. The emotional pain of the broken self presses to restore wholeness, to return to being *at one* with oneself and others:

> To feel relieved of guilt is to feel again that one is joined together with others and with oneself, to no longer be divided within and at war with ourselves and others. This need to make amends, to mend what has been damaged, and to be at one again with others and oneself is at the core of guilt. If it is successful, *it is atonement, being at one with*. (Morris 1976: 100, emphasis added)

To atone is to return one's guilty self to a state of wholeness, to restore the lost connections, to be back to being 'at one'. This is the original early modern meaning of atonement and it involves moral, emotional, psychic and somatic pain (feeling 'rotten, depleted of energy, tense') both in coming to acknowledge one's brokenness and then in seeking to address it. It is the pain of self-anger and shame in the face of the other at what one has done; it is a consequence of acknowledging to oneself that one was in the wrong. It is what makes genuine confession or contrition so hard, just as the release they eventually bring is genuinely felt as a lifted weight.

Embodied Feeling

As I have stressed, Morris suggests a link between the psychic and the somatic. Moral contrition is a matter of pain, of feeling rotten, depleted and tense. Emotional pain is felt as *embodied*, pointing to the kind of connection that Williams-style moral psychology would expect to find as it builds up from psychic states that are rooted in natural human conditions. This thinking is very much in line with psychoanalysis.[5] Important too is the critical line that Morris draws between *this* account of guilt and guilt in law. The pain 'we suffer when feeling guilty and the pain involved in the expression of those feelings differs from pain that is inflicted with the significance for us of punishment' (Morris 1976: 104).

The essence of legal punishment lies in deprivation with a meaning that is communicated to the person who is to be punished. It is deliberately inflicted pain for wrongdoing, but it is not delivered with a restorative purpose to produce a sense of *individual* psychological wholeness. It may be viewed as restoring a 'certain disrupted rule-established equilibrium of benefits and burdens', but this system value of completeness in 'impersonal, reciprocal legal situations' (Morris 1976: 104) is very different from the wholeness that the moral psychology of individual human guilt seeks. In this latter setting, the value of punishment to the requital of moral and psychological guilt is 'non-existent, insignificant, or positively perverse'. If we think of guilt and atonement in a context akin to 'where a friendship or love relationship based on affection, respect, and trust has been damaged' (Morris 1976: 105), punishment in its form and content is very different. Ethical guilt and the restoration of wholeness are different from and at odds with the functioning of an inculpatory legal process and punishment:

[5] Consider here Jonathan Lear's wonderful summary of Freud as setting out to solve 'the mystery of the flesh made word' (Lear 1990: xii; cf Norrie 2020), that is, how biological drives are transmuted into psychological states.

> While punishment might be seen as restoring a rule-established equilibrium of benefits and burdens by taking from the wrongdoer benefits not permitted him, it is never by itself restorative of relationships that are defined by feelings and commitments. Something must come in these relationships from the injured party if ever there is to be restoration – forgiveness. But something of course must also come from the guilty party, [in terms of] restorative responses. (Morris 1976: 105–6)

Most importantly, punitive pain is objectively imposed rather than subjectively expressed; a legal system passes sentence principally according to a tariff without regard for the perpetrator's psychology. Morris to the contrary is focused on the subjective experience of guilt in the territory sketched by Williams of a naturalistic moral psychology that would grasp ethical feelings that violation invokes. Guilt is here linked to forgiveness and reconciliation.

The value of his account here is his linking of guilt as metaphysical experience to the subjective moral feelings of a person and a body. With regard to the former, compare some of Morris's comments previously discussed to the young Hegel's discussion in Chapter 2. With regard to the latter, note Morris's psychological route to guilt is through *love* rather than *anger*. In this way, he not only distinguishes guilt in a moral–legal sense (Williams's 'peculiar' institution) from a deeper ethical (metaphysical) experience in line with moral psychology, he also develops the latter substantively in ways that link moral experience to the emotional feeling of love (not fear and anger). This brings the ethical, the psychic and the somatic together around the idea of love, taking philosophical guilt and reparation to the threshold of psychological embodiment, and in contrast to the logic of guilt in the law. With the further concepts of identification and quantum guilt, Morris steps over it.

'Nonmoral' Guilt as Identification

Morris's account invites a question. He notes the desire to restore wholeness that lies at the root of guilt and he links this to an account of love. To feel guilt, we have seen, is to be like 'a lover who loses a loved one may feel', that 'a part of him has been taken away …, as if one had destroyed what one loved and thus also destroyed a part of oneself' (Morris 1976: 99). This seems a reaction fit for people already emotionally close to each other, whereas a suitable account of guilt for which one should atone must include the situation of violating a stranger. We need to understand how such a person may feel guilty, for while we may talk of loving a stranger, this may be thought to overstretch the workings of love. We need more 'psychological material' to explain how the moral psychology of guilt and love works with regard to violating a stranger.

Nonmoral Guilt

This brings me to Morris's account of identification, intriguingly entitled 'Nonmoral Guilt' (Morris 1987), which provides the start of an answer. In addressing this, we will however ask whether his title is apposite. The contrast here is with 'moral guilt', but the opposition is question-begging, for the contrast is drawn by comparing guilt of a legal kind with a broader sense of guilt (called here nonmoral), but which is in reality a conception which simply transcends legal guilt and is fundamentally moral in its own right. The title 'Nonmoral guilt' indeed emphasises precisely Williams's point that there is a particularly modern way of speaking about guilt which aligns it with the law and which sequesters the general by virtue of the particular. Moral guilt in this sense is none other than Williams's 'peculiar' guilt, based on voluntary control of agency,[6] and which contrasts with the broader metaphysical sense Morris explores, but calls, inaccurately, nonmoral. Such a broader sense Morris had developed in his 1976 book; in the 1987 essay, he draws on it to cover situations where a person may feel guilt without having acted in a legally culpable way. Nonmoral guilt occurs, for example, when someone has been the unwitting beneficiary from bad outcomes for others, or complicit in a distanced way with a bad action, for example, committed by one's country, or historically, by an earlier generation. Because of his use of the idea of identification, Morris considers such feelings of nonmoral guilt to be morally appropriate. In this, he is right.[7]

Identification

Why should one feel guilt when one has not acted or is distanced from others' actions? 'Nonmoral guilt' in Morris's terms, that is guilt not based on moral culpability from control of one's voluntary actions, exists because *one nonetheless identifies with another*, and this is through a psychological mechanism that links guilt and love through connection to others: 'Feeling guilty, then, would both mark one's attachment to principles of fairness and justice and manifest one's solidarity with others. *While nonmoral, it would derive from a moral posture toward others.* One's feelings would track the scope of one's identificatory ties with the less fortunate, those before whom one feels guilty…' (Morris 1987: 237, emphasis added).

The italicised sentence indicates the terminological problem (a guilt that is both moral and nonmoral) but the key idea here points to a deep ontological connection between the self and another. It is not just a simple sympathy with others from imagining their experience nor is it based on a direct connection with the other. It involves rather an underlying inter- and intrapsychic reality of identification, whereby one enters into the experience of the other with whom one identifies:

[6] 'Moral guilt' involves culpable responsibility for wrongdoing, involving 'the intentional transgression of prohibition … by a definite voluntary act' (Morris 1987: 220).

[7] Murphy (2012: 98) calls Morris's choice of terminology 'unfortunate' for allowing a Kantian ethic of voluntary wrongdoing 'to gobble up the entire domain of morality'. Unfortunate, but also perhaps affirmative of the hegemony of the form in modern moral thinking.

> An identification with others, then, may be operative that is not limited to particular aims or dispositions that have led to evil.... One's identification with another implies, for example, that we suffer when they do, just as we are pleased when they are. We imagine their feelings, thereby 'entering into' them. We have the feelings we imagine them to be having as contrasted with our merely responding in an appropriate way, say with sympathy, to the feelings we imagine them to be having.... (Morris 1987: 239)

Importantly, this entering into the mind and experience of the other does not mean we become the other. We retain our own identity at the same time as we identify with that person. This is exactly Williams's imagined or internalised other who is in-me-and-not-me, but whereas Williams deployed the idea to think of the voice that speaks 'to me', Morris uses it to explain why a person might feel for or identify with the violation or suffering of another and therefore might feel guilt for what has happened to her, though one did nothing oneself. The guilty subject speaks out. Where, for example, a parent has been a perpetrator,

> Identification would have us imagine what our own reactions would be were we the wrongdoer.... [T]he process of identification, once operative, carries a psychological momentum so that, in identifying with the person engaged in wrongdoing, one imagines how one would oneself feel.... [These] feelings connected with identificatory processes are often perfectly normal, and it is their total absence that may occasion concern.... Because they have defined themselves in a manner that reveals identification with others, the actions of those others are granted a power over them.... Individuals may in these circumstances believe themselves guilty. (Morris 1987: 239–40)

To identify with another is to have a sense of wholeness and solidarity with, to 'enter into', another; and the entering into another is also the taking of the other into oneself.[8] The move of identification is both inward–outward and outward–inward, and this is because the initial idea is of the self that is linked to the other by love, connection, wholeness and solidarity. In this way, Morris combines his earlier account of guilt as the fracturing of wholeness leading to atonement ('at-one-ment') (Morris, 1976: 100) with an understanding of the mechanism by which the fracturing is experienced (identification). This internalisation of the distanced other explains why a moral agent may feel guilt for violating a stranger.

Morris has brought us here to the realm not just of identification but of 'identificatory processes' so he has taken us right into Williams's 'psychological materials'. We are on the brink of changing our understanding of how moral thinking works. We started with a discussion of guilt which required us to see how a legal conception leads us to explore guilt's metaphysical character. Underlying this we now see a new domain, that of metapsychology, in

[8] Identification in Morris's examples can be with both a perpetrator and her guilt, and with a victim and her violation.

which a naturalistic understanding of how the human animal feels and enters into another reveals how guilt works. This leads us in turn to think differently about philosophy as entailing both metaphysical and linked metapsychological claims which underpin it. Morris's analysis of atonement, (so-called) non-moral guilt and identification flesh out the implication of Williams's claim that the best account of philosophy will be one that is in line with a naturalistic understanding of human psychology.

Quantum Guilt

Finally, the term quantum guilt is not Morris's but it denotes a kind of guilt that indicates how a repeated cycle of violent conduct followed by an apology indicates a deeper problem in a person than is seen with single acts of violation (Wilson 2021a). What is at stake is the problem of repetition.

Beyond Repetition

The fact that violations keep repeating, and the repeater continues to feel bad, suggests a meaning of guilt that goes beyond individual acts. It involves a quantum shift in the way we see guilt operating in the human psyche:

> What is most troubling about guilt is its focus on some specific past wrong and the righting of it. Thinking in terms of guilt alone too easily locks one into an endless round of hurt done, hurt felt, hurt made up for. All the while one must wonder, 'is not there something more to be said, something more to be done, something more to be achieved?' (Morris 1976: 108–9)

It is a common criticism of guilt that it lives in the past, taking events that have happened too seriously, and not looking forward. Morris suggests to the contrary that it may not take the past seriously enough. He takes the example of a man in an abusive relationship. If he violates his partner but feels guilt and remorse and expresses contrition, his victim may feel able to forgive him. If, however, he continues with violative acts while repeatedly experiencing guilt, remorse and contrition, the pair become locked in 'an endless round of hurt done, hurt felt, hurt made up for' (Morris 1976: 108). In violent relationships, a victim comes to see that even the most contrite apology is not enough, for the act will be repeated. Something more is going on in the man's psyche that should be addressed. Something interferes 'repeatedly with the love he has for the woman and interferes, too, with the love he would like to be able to have for himself. He is constantly racked by feelings of guilt' (Morris 1976: 109). Such guilt is not just for the acts done, but for being the sort of person that consistently carries out such acts. This, says Morris, is 'a guilt pushed out of mind, but a guilt that nevertheless explains'. Should it be faced, and its 'manifold connections with self-defeating patterns of feelings and conduct understood, the man, seeing things for what they are, might be able to relinquish them' (Morris 1976: 110).

Three Kinds of Restoration

In this situation, and others like it, guilt moves qualitatively beyond acts to psychic structure, and it pushes us to see that guilt at its deeper levels is about more than acts. At play here is a question that hinges on the idea of 'restoration'. Morris links the word to the legal restoration of rights, but there is more to it than that. Why someone repeats actions damaging to themselves and others may signal 'a concern with fundamental change rather than restoration' (Morris 1976: 109), but is 'fundamental change' not also concerned with restoration? The term may have three different meanings. First, it may concern restoring the legal and political relationship between a criminal and society and the balance between benefits and burdens a crime disturbed. That is the stock legal meaning to which Morris adverts. It can also mean something different in moral–psychological terms: restoring a relationship between a violator and a victim, on the violator's side through guilt, remorse and contrition; on the victim's side through coming to terms, forgiveness and reconciliation. This is atonement on both sides as discussed previously. The third form is the deep and qualitative change in a person brought about by the realisation that guilt has a quantum aspect involving fundamental change. Here guilt about who one is may relate to past unresolved guilt, 'a guilt pushed out of mind' but one that 'nevertheless explains' (Morris 1976: 109). Stating more fully Morris's point above: 'If this guilt can be faced and its manifold connections with self-defeating patterns of feelings and conduct understood, the man, seeing things for what they are, might be able to relinquish them; and with this change he may bring about a transformation in his attitudes' (Morris 1976: 109–10).

Such change is also a restoration for it is linked to the love which 'conditioned our earliest feelings of guilt'. Quantum guilt thus leads us back to love and its own kind of restoration: of an earlier, more 'grace-ful', way of being, before a person's life was deflected by traumatic or violent events. At stake in quantum guilt is a kind of moral rebirth linked to a change in one's basic psychological orientation. The old mental ways control one's being and fix one in a repetitive way of life where one is not in control. In metaphysical language, Morris writes that such a person lives in 'the dominion of death', which can only be countered by a renewal of love in how one starts to live now. Here, the road is clear: from a peculiar morality of the will to a metaphysics of love, and from there to a search for its psychic grounds, that is, the road is from law to metaphysics to metapsychology. Ending his essay with a long quote from John Wisdom's *Philosophy and Psychoanalysis* (1969), Morris shows the road forward: 'Love for others and for ourselves conditioned our earliest feelings of guilt; love for ourselves and love from others can help release us from its crushing effects' (Morris 1976: 110).

Guilt in the Individual and the Social

Two questions might be asked of quantum guilt. The first would be whether it is not too specific to a particular kind of person, one with an unfortunate past that not all who violate others share. It ought not to be regarded as a general form of guilt central to our discussion. There is some truth in this, but if we step back from the specific psychological situation of one repeating a violent past, we can ask how much the violation of others is generally linked to unresolved feelings of anger or other negative emotional states that are situationally capable of repetition. Repeating psychological patterns has a broader reference in the ways in which social situations more generally recycle violative conduct. Here the quantum patterning of violation spreads from individual situations into the broader social context.

This leads to a second question concerning where the focus of guilt should be located: in the individual or the social? A potential weakness in quantum guilt is that anger may be personally acted out but is nonetheless heavily linked to social contexts. Surely it is there that critical discussion should be focused, seeing individual acts of violation as part of a bigger picture. This is especially brought out in discussions of how a society needs to change its core assumptions if it is to move beyond violation. If we take Morris's case of the abusive relationship, we need to be aware of how much male and female behaviours are socially inculcated through ideas of 'hegemonic masculinity' and misogyny, or in the structural divide between the 'public' and the 'private' spheres. These may also be exacerbated by structural problems of poverty and race. Violation is much more social than individual in its form, so does a concept like quantum guilt takes us in the wrong direction?

It is true that cultural ideas provide the settings and scripts which encourage action and make it crucial to address them at their own level. That does not mean however that one should lose sight of the individual in the social just as the alternative of blaming the (culpable) individual in isolation from the social is equally unacceptable. The victims who victimise others discussed in Chapter 3 act out social roles, but they do so through their individual emotional reactions. Anger may very well be in response to social conditions but it is often also individually channelled, expressed and directed. Violation may link individual agency and social setting but this is indeed what quantum guilt in its extended form is getting at. It involves concern for a past that is always already social: one's relationships with parents and other important life figures, the role of schools and social groups, dominant cultural images, and social and political ideologies. Violation is always socially embedded and one can certainly speak of social responsibility and indeed social guilt,[9] but within these lies a question of what an individual did and why they did it, and why they might continue to do it. The complexity and structural mediation of

[9] Morris's account of nonmoral guilt deals with social guilt that is generalised to feelings for the plight of the other, beyond any possible moral obligation. In a further essay on 'shared guilt', Morris draws, as I did in Chapter 4's discussion of Hannah Arendt, on Karl Jaspers's argument for metaphysical guilt. Here he identifies a line where guilt at lack of agency melds into something else, a shame at having turned one's back in impotence on human solidarity (Morris 1976: 132–35).

individual agency lies behind the claims that guilt has a quantum form, one which implicates both actor and setting.

Extending Philosophy to Metapsychology

Williams's work provided a bold if incomplete challenge to existing political and legal theory by insisting on its 'peculiar' moral focus, which had more to do with social and political organisation than with human moral experience. Motivated by his own challenge, he focused on the limits of the voluntary, the importance of community and history, and then the possibility that a naturalistic moral psychology would be one that engaged with the 'psychological materials' in depth, whether these concerned anger or fear or love. Morris's work proceeds with a series of interrogations of what it might mean to think about the 'restorative' purposes of law and legal concepts and how reflection takes us to deeper meanings of restoration in terms of atonement, identification and 'quantum guilt'. Here, profound reflection on the metaphysics of guilt opens up the field and leaves in question what law and punishment can achieve. Law may be counter-productive with regard to what needs to be restored if violation is to be addressed. It fails to see how legal guilt misses out on atonement, (what he called) 'nonmoral' identification and the spread and depth of guilt in its quantum form. More broadly, Williams and Morris together open the door by immanent critique to the potential of psychological theory to explore how it is that human beings come to violate each other and what it could mean to address such behaviours in terms that make moral and psychological sense.

This chapter has however started rather than ended an investigative process. It has taken two unusual thinkers of modern legal and political theory and shown how their work takes us to the brink of a new terrain, one in which normative political and legal theory yields before critical argument and opens up to the deeper ground of metapsychology. The chapter has prosecuted Williams's case outlined in Chapter 1 that a 'truthful ethical life is ... one that can include our best understanding of our psychological life' in line with 'naturalistic explanation' (Williams 1995: 19–20). It has not however identified what such an understanding would entail. Some clues have been given: it would involve thinking further about ideas like atonement, identification and quantum guilt (from Morris); but these need to be systematically understood and presented in psychological as well as ethical terms and that is the work of the next two chapters. For the present, I would like to conclude by making good my claim that what is at stake here is not just a way of taking questions of guilt in the specific area of the moral psychology of violation but a more general way of understanding philosophy. Why should a philosopher who accepts philosophy's existing commitments be persuaded that these should be recast to include human metapsychology of a broadly Freudian kind?

An initial reason would be to claim that following Williams and Morris should persuade us that when it comes at least to guilt and violation, we need to examine more closely how such issues take us beyond what is normally accounted as the bounds of the discipline. Concepts like guilt, anger, love, atonement, nonmoral and quantum guilt occupy a border territory between philosophy and metapsychology where, once we see their relevance, it just makes no sense to hang back. The spirit of truthful enquiry should push us on, realising that we must incorporate what we might otherwise see as from another discipline as being part of the overall philosophical picture, and requiring us to move beyond how philosophy is traditionally understood. A further, more compelling, reason is provided by Jonathan Lear, who argues that the move into psychoanalysis with its attendant metapsychology is a way of developing philosophical enquiry *according to philosophical criteria*. In accepting Williams's invitation to moral psychology and naturalistic enquiry, we are extending philosophy appropriately, not moving perchance to include another field.

Let us pursue the argument more fully. If we connect metapsychology and philosophy around guilt, is it a question of admitting a non-philosophical supplement or is the psychoanalytical element part of a fuller, more rounded, philosophy? Lear is a philosopher of the ancient Greeks (Lear 1988) and a psychoanalyst who has developed an original interpretation of Freudian psychoanalysis (Lear 1990), which he links to Plato and Aristotle (Lear 1998, 2015, 2017). Drawing on the psychoanalytic work of Hans Loewald (Loewald 1980),[10] he develops an account of Freud that emphasises the importance of his later structural theory of mind. Important there is an understanding of how the force known severally as love, Eros, the life drive, or libido evolves as it is 'enformed' through relations with others. As in Morris's philosophical approach, guilt, identification and atonement play a central role, and from this work, we can see how an expansion of philosophy to include 'psychological materials' becomes philosophically necessary. Lear's distinctive philosophical contribution is to align an interpretation of Freud with the Greeks. He seeks to engage the 'rational' and 'non-rational' sides of the psyche, in order to follow the Socratic injunction to know, and to be true to, oneself as the basis for a flourishing, eudaimonic, life (Lear 2015: ch 1).

This is philosophy's own authentic project, common to both the ancient and the modern thinker. In the first book of his *Nicomachean Ethics*, Aristotle raises the *philosophical* question of the relationship between the rational and the non-rational parts of the psyche (Aristotle 1984). However, he possessed a weak conception of that relationship, which modern psychoanalysis in effect seeks to develop through its account of the conscious, the unconscious and their relationship. Psychoanalysis, Lear argues, is a modern discipline rooted in an ancient philosophical quest:

[10] This is discussed in detail in Chapter 7.

> Philosophy has long considered human life to be distinctive (and valuable) in virtue of its capacity for self-conscious awareness.... From the time of Plato and Aristotle ... one of reason's central tasks has been taken to be the thoughtful, self-conscious integration of the human psyche. The point is not merely that psychoanalysis provides insight into how such integration might be achieved – far beyond anything Plato or Aristotle imagined – it is that psychoanalytic activity itself *is the very exercise of self-conscious, thoughtful integration of the psyche*.... Psychoanalysis gives us unparalleled access to the microcosm of reason's working at the interface of (what Aristotle called) the rational and non-rational parts of the soul. (Lear 2015: 212, emphasis added)

Psychoanalysis is no more nor less than the modern continuance of the ancient quest for the rational achievement of a eudaimonic state of being. In Freudian terms, it becomes the engagement between the conscious and the unconscious mind in a process that is different from what is often assumed. The move is not one of Kantian withdrawal from the senses in order to critically reflect on natural impulses. More than rational judgement of the passions, emotions and inclinations, it involves coming to terms with that which is uncomfortably and ongoingly a part of one's thought process.[11] Nor is it a question, as it is in Aristotle's *practical* ethics, of refinement of and training in virtuous practices; rather it involves acknowledgement of, and reasonable engagement with, a part of the psyche that has its own unconscious reasons. The aim is for the rational and non-rational sides of the human psyche to be constructively engaged in a way that permits a person to act with a degree of unity of the self, hence, in Socrates's terms, to be confident that one knows and is true to oneself. This permits one to be self-reflective in action, and, on that basis, to be in the best position to flourish as a person. Freud 'simply', one might say, helps us pursue Socrates's injunction that we should before all else know ourselves. The key value in psychoanalysis is truthfulness about the self, in terms of what we know of ourselves and how we act: 'In this way, psychoanalysis can be seen as an attempt to resume the ancient project of an ethics and politics grounded in and explained by a robust conception of human flourishing. This is the project the ancient Greek philosophers could not themselves complete' (Lear 2015: 17).

Other names for psychoanalytic activity are thus 'truthfulness, rationality, freedom and *eudaimonia*' (Lear 2017: 47). This is Lear's argument for expanding the bounds of philosophy to include metapsychology.

[11] Murphy beautifully illustrates the difference between Kant and Freud when he writes: 'Freud and other psychoanalysts talk brilliantly about the infantile origins of our loves, but surely one of our missions – as autonomous and rational human beings – is to attempt to transcend the limitations imposed by those origins, not to surrender to them' (2012: 239). Between transcendence and surrender, there is however a third option: living and knowing engagement with that which remains a part of us. The contrast in approaches is seen in Murphy himself when he reflects on his own shame as to how he treated his father as a child (Murphy 2012: ch 5). Why should he do so had he truly *transcended* his own childish mental state as an autonomous and rational Kantian being? When he owns these long-past sentiments, he is at his most human.

Taking this back to our main topic, Lear's claim to Socratic truthfulness through psychoanalysis picks up Williams's aspiration for a truthful ethical life which must include understanding as best we can our psychological life in a naturalistic manner. The further question then would be how this incorporation of psychoanalysis within philosophy relates to the understanding of guilt as we have developed it here, in terms of atonement, 'nonmoral' and quantum guilt. In delving into the psychoanalytic understanding of guilt, I believe we can hope to deepen our grasp on how it functions as a human response, and this would have an important bearing on how we should deal with our responses to violation. This would be a *philosophical* enquiry enabling us to act with greater self-awareness and freedom with emancipatory and eudaimonic consequences for our institutional practices. In that spirit, we now leave our critical philosophical companions Williams and Morris behind and delve more deeply into the 'psychological materials'.

7

Two Accounts of Guilt in Freud

> … an agency within … like a garrison in a conquered city.
>
> Sigmund Freud (1985: 316)

> … an atonement structure, a structure of reconciliation … a supreme achievement.
>
> Hans Loewald (1980: 393)

In the previous chapter, I considered the sceptical and disenchanted view of the theory of punishment explored in different ways by Bernard Williams and Herbert Morris and indicated how their thinking led them beyond standard criminal justice ideas of blame, responsibility and punishment to a broader, more metaphysical, understanding of a concept like guilt. This in turn led to a deeper linking of guilt to psychological mechanisms in the human mind concerning, in Morris's account, atonement, identification and love.

I also identified further questions to address which ensue from the previous argument. These concern what philosophy learns about the nature of human moral psychology once it crosses over into a psychoanalytic approach to punishment, and what such an approach might say about guilt, blame and responsibility. My focus in this chapter is on Freud's understanding of guilt in his *Civilization and Its Discontents* (Freud 1985), where the obvious reading is not the most helpful. This relates guilt to fear of paternal anger and turns the superego into an internal policeman monitoring the psyche for bad instincts. A different reading, however, consistent with Freud's developing thought, is possible. This reading relates to how humans develop as rational, autonomous, loving beings in relation with each other, as animals who think and love. Such creatures are capable of acting on metaphysical thought and experience. The two quotes at the head of this chapter both describe the superego but have very different conceptions of it. The first is from Freud himself, but the second, from Hans Loewald, involves a different version on the basis of Freud's thought. I will suggest that this second view illuminates and underpins the moral concerns of thinkers like Williams and especially Morris. Guilt for Morris, as we saw, is based on responsibility and a wish to atone (to be 'at one' again) for wrongdoing, and this is very close to Hans Loewald's view of the superego.

This is the kind of reading which might appeal to Jeffrie Murphy as a Kantian scholar troubled by where such thinking takes him (Murphy 2012). Freud's basic problem for Murphy lies with the view of the superego in the first quotation because guilt is imposed and mechanistic. There is no relationship between guilt and a person's real sense of moral responsibility. If we think that guilt stems from internalizing a parental authority figure ('like a garrison in a conquered city'), we may agree with Murphy 'that the development of a moral sense or conscience (a superego)' only 'involves the internalization of parental commands perceived as authoritative' (Murphy 2012: 96). This however provides only a *causal* reading of guilt which cannot account for the person thinking in an authentically critical way, for example, by contemplating her moral responsibility in relation to an act. It is hard to discern a genuine subjective sense of being troubled by guilt in this account. This is a fair criticism of Freud as he is normally, and reasonably, taken to think on the face of the most prominent argument in *Civilization and Its Discontents*, his key text. But there is a different way of constructing the metapsychology of guilt in line with Freud which pursues a more promising strand in his complex and conflicted oeuvre. This starts from the idea of a psyche developing out of love and into thought and a range of authentic moral experiences based on identification and atonement: based, indeed, on the idea of a metaphysical animal that thinks and loves.

This chapter has three sections. I start the first by identifying two approaches to guilt to be found in Freud's *Civilization and Its Discontents*, and then go on to develop the second approach in line with Loewald's view of Freud. The first approach involves the internalisation of external authority figures who act to repress a dangerous subjectivity. The second approach emphasises the development of love and the life force in the development of the ego and superego. This reveals a metapsychological basis for moral concepts like guilt, atonement and responsibility that see these possible ethical states as integral and existentially important to the human animal. In the second section, I identify two accounts of guilt, one in relation to the harsh superego and the other one in relation to its benign form. The latter is shown to align with Morris's account of guilt involving responsibility, identification with others and the need to atone (to be at one again) for wrongdoing. In the third section, I summarise the argument of this and the previous chapter to show how metaphysical thought and metapsychological development come together.

Freud's Two Routes to Guilt

From Williams and Morris, we have the idea that the intrapsychic reality of the guilty person involves a relationship with another. This could be the angry internal voice that makes us feel bad (the victim or enforcer in Williams) or it could be the feeling of entering into another in order to identify with her pain, which then becomes our pain (Morris). Though superficially having similar kinds of expression as painful feeling, these approaches involve different kinds of psychic interiority. Williams's internal other is angry, and guilt comes from fear of that anger. It will however be recalled that elsewhere, Williams thought that *love* might be at the heart of the psychological reaction that leads to guilt, and love is much more the key to Morris's account of identificatory guilt. The person identifies with the other by seeing or placing herself in the other's mind and feeling either as she might feel as a victim or as a perpetrator. Identificatory guilt is feeling emotional and somatic pain ('rotten, depleted of energy, tense' (Morris 1976: 99)), and such pain is related to the breach in wholeness that is a loss of emotional unity in oneself and with others. Identificatory guilt involves the loss of wholeness that comes from love of self in relation to the other, and it results in psychosomatic pain.

In this section, I consider how these two conflicting routes to guilt (anger and fear versus identificatory love) reflect differences in psychoanalysis itself, and especially in Freud's work. I begin with Freud's predominantly anger- and fear-based approach in *Civilization and Its Discontents* but note a subsidiary and conflicting love-based approach there.[1] Underlying the difference is an unresolved conflict between understanding the psyche in terms of either the instincts and hedonic pleasure or eudaimonic happiness involving a loving and flourishing life. This, as we shall see, takes us to Loewald's account of Freud.[2]

Primary Route: From Repression, Anger and Fear

The difference between love and a combination of anger and fear as the ground of guilt is important because it reveals two roads down which a psychoanalytic understanding of guilt might travel. In Freud's *Civilization and Its Discontents*, it appears that fear and anger are key to guilt, but this is not necessarily the

[1] Any serious account of Freud on guilt will have to reflect the conflicts in his work. John Deigh (1996) takes his analysis from what Freud says in *Civilization and Its Discontents* and then acknowledges that the account there is hard to square with Freud's general position. Accordingly, he finds a 'Nietzschean' account of superego formation and thence guilt in *Civilization*, which compares with the 'standard' account elsewhere. The difference concerns the role of the Oedipus complex in creating the superego, which is unimportant in *Civilization* but central elsewhere. (It appears once, in discussing the story of the band of brothers who kill their father, but not in relation to the superego.) As we shall see, it is central to Hans Loewald's account, in a more extended, less sex/gender focused, version than Deigh describes. Deigh is not wrong to find a different account in *Civilization* than elsewhere; the question is how that difference is to be explained. I argue that the underlying conflict is between an earlier stimulus satisfaction, pleasure-based, account, and a later structural theory, grounded in love and ego formation. Deigh notes the difference between earlier and later Freud but does not build on it. In my view, the 'Nietzschean' account Deigh describes is descriptively valid but leaves Freud in a cul de sac with regard to a plausible ethics of guilt, which is available in the terms developed here.

[2] As per Lear: '[On] a familiar reading of Freud's *Civilization and Its Discontents*, the world is not a place that is conducive to human happiness. And … the aim of civilization … is to keep us in line…. This reception has become boilerplate; one of the joys of Loewald's writings is that he offers a different choice of inheritance' (Lear 2017: 193).

case. Nonetheless, if we consider Freud's account in the text where he most clearly set it out, guilt results from aggression, fear and anger. In the following passage, for example, Freud identifies two sources of guilt. One involves fear at the angry response of an authority figure and the other involves an angry resentment at having to suppress one's desires, which gets turned back onto oneself (introjected) as the development of a harsh superego:

> Thus we know of two origins of the sense of guilt: one arising from fear of an authority, and the other, later on, arising from fear of the superego. The first insists upon a renunciation of instinctual satisfactions; the second, as well as doing this, presses for punishment, since the continuance of the forbidden wishes cannot be concealed from the superego. (Freud 1985: 319)

The two sources, external and internal, are connected and the internalisation of fear at anger results in 'the severity of the superego [and] the demands of conscience'. The internal form indeed 'is simply a continuation of the severity of the external authority, to which it has succeeded and which it has in part replaced' (Freud 1985: 319). In this bleak analysis, human beings are forced by nature to repress their instincts in order that society might be possible. Civilization is a necessary but an uncomfortable place to be. Aggressiveness is at the core of human agency and it becomes its own means of self-control. It is internalised through the superego, 'which now, in the form of "conscience", is ready to put into action against the ego the same harsh aggressiveness that the ego would have liked to satisfy upon other, extraneous individuals.' This is then the basis for 'the sense of guilt [which] expresses itself as a need for punishment' (Freud 1985: 315–16). The individual achieves a sense of guilt by identification with the anger of authority figures which he internalises:

> A considerable amount of aggressiveness must be developed in the child against the authority which prevents him from having his first, but none the less his most important, satisfactions ...; but he is obliged to renounce the satisfaction of this revengeful aggressiveness. He finds his way out of this economically difficult situation with the help of familiar mechanisms. *By means of identification* he takes the un-attackable authority into himself. The authority now turns into his superego and enters into possession of all the aggressiveness which a child would have liked to exercise against it.... (Freud 1985: 12, 322, emphasis added)

I have laboured Freud's account of the anger-fear nexus here to show both its centrality to his thought and that it bears little obvious resemblance to the view in the previous chapter expressed by Morris as to how identificatory connection with another works. We can see how it connects with Williams's comments about fear and anger linked to internal voices of the enforcer or the victim, but it is nothing like the identificatory connection described by Morris. For Morris, identification is related to love and wholeness, not fear, aggression and resentment at authority. The identificatory impulse in Morris seeks to find wholeness again, to work through pain that a breach of unity between self and other has brought. For him, anger at self may ensue, but it is not based on introjected fear or resentment, but on the failure to act as a whole person. So, on the face of it, Freudian metapsychology is unlikely to provide the route to an understanding of the psychology of guilt that can take us to Morris or to Williams when he talks of love. Identification can thus be linked either with love and wholeness or with the internal voice of fear and anger, but in Freud, it is the latter, not the former, connection that is to the fore. Is there another way forward in Freud's thought?

Secondary Route: From Loving Identification

There is a secondary route to guilt in *Civilization and Its Discontents*, which does involve love and loving identification. This involves a reconstruction of the argument based on some of its elements, and a link to a broader change in Freud's position as his work developed. We may approach this through the interpretation of Freud developed by Loewald and Lear, whose accounts centre on love, a theme that is explicit, but unevenly developed in Freud's later structural theory of ego formation (Loewald 1980; Lear 1990, 1998: ch 6).

Love and Ego Formation

In his introduction to Freud's thought, Lear suggests (as we saw in the previous chapter) that there was an ancient Greek agenda implicit in his work related to themes of self-knowledge and human flourishing, but which he was unable fully to develop. This was because he adopted, and failed to distinguish, two contradictory approaches to metapsychology, one resting on the significance of hedonic *pleasure* and the other on the importance of eudaimonic *happiness* (Lear 2015: 197–99). The latter takes Freud towards Aristotle, but the former remains dominant in his work. The importance of pleasure as a hedonic experience rested on a modern 'scientific' understanding of human behaviour, which emphasised the importance of instinctual forces including sexual and aggressive impulses. These sought satisfaction and had to be repressed or sublimated if civilization was to be possible. This was a mechanistic, scientistic, nineteenth-century model of human behaviour, emphasising the pursuit of pleasure, understood as the satisfaction of impulses, desires and instincts. It was quite distinct from a model that could be linked to the kind of Aristotelian approach which emphasises love and eudaimonic happiness, based on the engagement of the rational and the non-rational sides of the psyche. It is the instinct-based, pleasure-seeking, approach that underpins the account of guilt rooted in fear and anger that we have just described as to the fore in *Civilization and Its Discontents*.

Yet the approach that could develop the eudaimonic account is *also* present in Freud's thinking, developed in his later structural account of how the ego and the superego emerge from the earliest, protean, period in a child's life, where an undifferentiated love between a mother and a child begins the human journey to become an individual person. Freud named this earliest phase of human life as 'primary narcissism', but the term does not have its modern reference to an overdeveloped self-regard.[3] The basic argument is from *The Ego and the Id* (Freud 1984), in which the ego and the superego represent important differentiations in an unformed life or love drive in the evolving structure of the psyche. These enable the individual to develop as an autonomous self- and other-related being. Key to this development is the 'enforming' of the initially formless libido as both an ego and then, within the ego, a further differentiation that is the superego. This is a process wherein the child identifies with parental figures in order to take them in as 'ego-ideals', and to refashion them as building blocks in its own self-identity. In this structural theory of the mind, loving identification with parental (and other) figures permits the child to grow as an autonomous being in its own right. In this approach, identification is not to do with a voice of aggression, fear or anger but is instead the 'earliest expression of an emotional tie with another person', moulding 'a person's own ego after the fashion of the one that has been taken as a model' (Freud 1985: 12, 134–5). How does this relate to guilt?

Love, Ego Formation and Guilt

There are general indications of the importance of the eudaimonic line in *Civilization and Its Discontents* alongside the predominant instinct-based themes that we have described earlier. The first section of the work is indeed given over to an account of the development of the ego out of a field of undifferentiated love. Here the infant begins with a basic life force or libido, an inchoate and primal love for life, which is unseparated from the parent in the phase of primary narcissism. The ego then begins to form out of basic interactions between an infant and parent once their separation has begun. As the initial unity begins to dissolve, loving interaction with parental figures begins to fill the necessarily developing gap with the formation of an ego. This produces an infant's own internal forms of being and as a result a sense of what is external to it:

> An infant at the breast does not as yet distinguish his ego from the external world as the source of the sensations flowing in upon him. He gradually learns to do so, in response to various promptings … In this way there is for the first time set over against the ego an 'object', in the form of something which exists 'outside' … One comes to learn a procedure by which … one can differentiate between what is internal – what belongs to the ego – and what is external – what emanates from the outer world … In this way, then, the ego detaches itself from the external world. Or, to put it more correctly, originally the ego includes everything, later it separates off an external world from itself. (Freud 1985: 254–55)

Frustratingly, Freud does not pursue this theme into an understanding of guilt which remains stubbornly linked to aggression, fear and anger as we have

[3] A point noted by Murphy (2012: 111, note 27) in the punishment literature.

described. There is, however, a point in *Civilization and Its Discontents*, where he finds himself at a loss and reaches for love as an explanation of guilt. It is the point where Freud revisits the story of the 'band of brothers' who in the earliest time killed their father. This is the 'phylogenetic' story of early human life, involving an extension of what Freud said in *Totem and Taboo* (Freud 1990) about the origins of humankind. It concerns the fact that 'man's sense of guilt springs from the Oedipus complex and was acquired at the killing of the father by the brothers banded together' (Freud 1985: 12, 324). This story of the origins of guilt is problematic for its speculative and mythic quality, but it is important for how Freud depicts the relationship between guilt and love. In the original relationship, sexual rivalry, aggression and hatred lead the sons to kill the father. This leads to a question in terms of Freud's account of guilt. If the sons have deployed murderous aggression towards the father, then they have not internalised the prohibition against killing nor have they introjected their aggression to stop them from so doing. The internalisation of guilt has not taken root: why then should the sons feel guilty for their father's murder?

Freud initially negotiates this question by suggesting there is a difference between feeling remorse and feeling guilt, but he acknowledges that remorse, like guilt, presupposes the existence of a conscience.[4] In the end, he asks: where does remorse come from if neither it nor conscience had been internalised as fear and anger before the deed? His response is to turn at this tricky point *to love*, because, it now turns out, guilt might not only be about the internalised control of the harsh superego. Rather, it 'was the result of the primordial ambivalence of feeling towards the father. His sons hated him, *but they loved him, too*' (Freud 1985: 12, 325, emphasis added). After their hatred had been satisfied by their aggression, '*their love came to the fore* in their remorse for the deed' (Freud, 1985: 12, 325, emphasis added). It was their love that 'set up the superego by identification with the father; it gave that agency the father's power' (Freud 1985: 12, 325). In this alternative explanation of guilt, we see 'the part *played by love* in the origin of conscience and the fatal inevitability of the sense of guilt' (Freud 1985: 12, 325). But this is a different route to guilt, the route of love, or Eros, rather than fear and aggression. Now Freud builds love into his account of guilt. The sense of guilt now becomes 'an expression of the conflict due to ambivalence, of the eternal struggle between Eros and the instinct of destruction or death' (Freud 1985: 12, 325). But where did love come from in psychoanalytic terms if it was not presaged in the account of the control of the instincts through guilt?

If we wish to base our theory of guilt on the 'part played by love', we must follow Freud's concession away from the hedonic instinctual approach

[4] Deigh (1996) seeks to reconcile a fear- and anger-based approach with a love-based one by portraying guilt in terms of infraction of an authority's rule, while remorse is linked to feelings of love. The underlying problem here is how to introduce the love-based approach to rescue the phylogenetic story, given the overall setting of guilt in *Civilization*, on what Deigh calls 'Nietzschean' lines.

and take up the eudaimonistic approach anticipated in the first chapter of *Civilization and Its Discontents*. This will take us into a discussion of psychic structure that can relate ideas of love, atonement, identification and guilt in psychoanalysis to those we saw in Morris's ethical account in Chapter 6. In making this connection, we shall see, the superego plays an important, but not a nasty, part.

Guilt, Atonement and the Superego

In this section, I want to put together Freud's later, unevenly developed, structural theory of love and ego formation, converting primary, unformed, love into ego and superego formation, with an account of guilt as based on loving identification with another. I begin by focussing on the role of the superego in the alternative anger-based approach and then turn to how it may be developed in line with loving identification, in the work of Loewald.

Guilt and the Harsh Superego

The anger- and fear-based approach to guilt that we have already rehearsed owes its provenance to the pleasure-based account of human instincts. Pleasure is about instinct satisfaction, and since the instincts are of various kinds and include sex and aggression, repression and their sublimation loom large in this model.[5] Human beings in this view are ill-equipped to coexist and need civilization to control aggression. That is the main story of *Civilization and Its Discontents*, and it enlists the superego as the internal figure that represses and controls. Conscience is the introjection of the 'same harsh aggressiveness that the ego would have liked to satisfy upon other, extraneous individuals' (Freud 1985: 315), and it takes the form of a special agency that acts like an occupying power over the mind:

> The tension between the harsh superego and the ego that is subjected to it, is called by us the sense of guilt; it expresses itself as a need for punishment. Civilization, therefore, obtains mastery over the individual's dangerous desire for aggression … by setting up an agency within him to watch over it, like a garrison in a conquered city. (Freud 1985: 315–16)

The militaristic metaphor is telling, for the superego is a harsh form of judgement reflecting society's internalised anger and the aggression and resentment felt by the individual against repression. This grim image of an alien authority, it should be noted, is complemented by the following passage, from another

[5] Such an approach enlists non-sexual love as a means of converting aggression into peaceableness, but that is not at all the same as building emotional reactions on the basis of a primary love and the enformed structures that organise it for ego development. Down the pleasure and instinct route, sexual love demands satisfaction, while non-sexual love operates to dilute and sublimate sexual and other aggressive demands. See Freud 1985: 274–326 for discussion.

text,[6] which links the hostile superego to the philosophy of Kant: 'The superego – the conscience at work in the ego – may then become harsh, cruel and inexorable against the ego which is in its charge. Kant's Categorical Imperative is thus the direct heir of the Oedipus complex' (Freud 1984: 422).

Why the Oedipus complex should be introduced here, and whether this is a necessary representation of Kant is not the point. The main thing here is that Freud follows through on the repression of the instincts in the pleasure-based approach by establishing the superego as a harsh and aggressive entity policing the ego. This raises the question of whether another approach to the superego is possible from within Freud's metapsychology, one more reflective of a eudaimonic approach: of, say, an Aristotle as opposed to a Kant.

Guilt and the Benign Superego

As we have seen, the alternative structural approach to ego formation in Freud is based on how early inchoate feelings of love in the mother–child union evolve. As the primary undifferentiated emotional state is nurtured by parental and other figures interacting with the child, they draw out its latent potential to develop its own identity. From a sense of undifferentiated unity, the child starts to become a self in its own right, one that is at once worthy of love, self-loving and capable of loving others. For the child, parental figures' existence as individuated loving selves becomes the first identification by which it 'takes in' another to establish its own individuated being. It forms itself by learning from others, so that a sense of its own identity, autonomy and self-worth becomes possible, paradoxically, through reliance on those who love and care for it. In the process, an ego is formed out of the early, inchoate, undifferentiated, loving environment (primary narcissism). We saw earlier how in the first chapter of *Civilization and Its Discontents*, Freud described this process, but he did not pursue it in his account of guilt. How to connect the two?

We can construct an answer to this question through Loewald's account of the relationship between the ego and the superego, which draws, first, on what Freud called 'ego ideals'; and second, through his account of the superego as an *atonement structure* (Loewald 1980: ch 23).[7] In both situations, which I will explore further, the underlying relationship is based upon identification between the ego and the other, as this is developed into the making of the superego. But the superego on this account has a very different mien than the harshness in the alternative approach described earlier. In the eudaimonic or love-based approach, the superego provides coherence and oversight of ego activity in a way that allows the person to flourish. It emerges as a special

[6] This quotation comes from the 1924 essay 'The Economic Problem of Masochism' (Freud 1984).

[7] This connects with our discussion of atonement as the goal of guilt in Morris's moral psychology in Chapter 6. For discussion of Loewald's work, see Mitchell 1998; Lear 1998; Chodorow 2003; Nields 2003; Whitebook 2004, 2017: ch 5.

agency of the ego, coming out of the resolution of the Oedipus complex, which is given a different, more positive, role than in the instincts-based approach.[8]

The Oedipus complex is generally understood to involve a child coming to terms with issues of sexual identity associated with its parents. More than this, however, it is an account of how a child gains a more complex and coherent sense of its own autonomy. The superego's formation is a sexual phase that involves father and mother identifications, but it is also the phase in which is formed a 'precipitate in the ego, consisting of these two identifications in some way united with each other', giving rise to a special agency that 'confronts the other contents of the ego as an ego ideal or superego' (Freud 1984: 11, 373). The superego is generally a means of organising the self at a higher level than the ego, producing a measure of overall coherence by means of a supervening element within the ego itself, able to organise ego activity. It involves the development of a higher general level of self-organisation in a family structure, leading to a 'childhood florescence of ambivalence towards the important people in one's life' (Lear 2015: 180), alongside but distinct from questions of gender or sexual desire.[9] The result is that the formation of the superego equips the individual with a sense of responsibility and, with that, a potential sensibility for guilt. Let us see how this works in relation to, first, the nature of 'ego ideals' and, second, the idea of the superego as an 'atonement structure'.

Responsibility, Guilt and Ego Ideals

For Loewald, the development of a superego integrates the different identifications that the child takes in from the parent and other figures, and it does so in order to form a sense of personal responsibility:

> Responsibility to oneself, within the context of authoritative norms consciously and unconsciously accepted or assimilated from parental and societal sources, is the essence of superego as internal agency.... It involves appropriating or owning up to one's needs and impulses as one's own, impulses and desires we appear to have been born with or that seem to have taken shape in interaction with parents during infancy.... [So doing] we begin to develop a sense of self-identity [which] means to experience ourselves as agents, notwithstanding the fact that we were born without our informed consent and did not pick our parents. (Loewald 1980: 392)

It should be noted that this sense of responsibility has a double, and contradictory, characteristic. On the one hand, it appears to the person as her own, that is, as something that is existentially constitutive of who she is. On the other hand,

[8] Thus, the two accounts of the superego, as harsh and as benign, are both linked with the Oedipus complex, but the account based on harshness indicates that the Oedipus complex is unresolved and perhaps unresolvable, whereas the love-based approach sees it as capable of at least an acceptable equilibrium.

[9] For this reason, superego formation, like the ego formation that precedes it, 'implies an abandonment of sexual aims, a desexualisation' (Freud 1984: 11, 369).

it is only possible because it stems from an early social context, primarily from parent figures, which makes the sense of self possible. For that eventually to survive and flourish, such figures must eventually be put in their place, and that is the role of the Oedipal struggle. From the beginning, self-development involves a social process where an individual absorbs models for ego development ('ego ideals') taken from its immediate environment. Such ideals, which we 'appear to have been born with', are synthesised out of our latent biological potential and social guidance. They become the source of a sense of individual responsibility, and from that, of the possibility of guilt (c.f. Murphy 2012: 292).

The term 'ego ideal' was not used consistently by Freud, but one thing it referenced was ideas of what was admirable in parents (and other significant figures in childhood) that the child absorbed as the basis for creating its own sense as to how it should behave. In childhood, before the superego is formed, it is not possible to differentiate parental direction and childish initiative, so a sense of personal guilt based on individual responsibility cannot exist. Once the superego is formed, such ego ideals become part of the child's self-organisation, which it identifies as such and avows as its own. This then becomes the basis for tension between what the child owns and aspires to be and what it is or does. This can lead to a negative reaction in the 'form of tension between ego and superego. We have a sense of guilt concerning past or present thoughts, feelings and deeds, but only inasmuch as they represent a nonfulfillment of the inner image of ourselves, of the internal ideal we have not reached' (Loewald 1980: 273–74).

The idea of a tension between the ego and superego is, of course, also present in Freud's account of the harsh superego in *Civilization and Its Discontents*. In Loewald's development of responsibility and guilt from Freud's theory of ego and superego formation, it is not the internalised angry voice of the external authority figure that informs the superego, but the internal tension brought about by not behaving as one would like to at one's best, according to one's developed ego ideals.[10] This is one aspect of a guilt that a person would feel for doing a wrong act – not as external repression absorbed to deal with anger, but as something having an ethical ground in loving admiration of the good qualities of parents. This is the feeling that one has done badly according to parental standards with which one has identified, taken in, and then set for oneself.

The Superego as Atonement Structure

This account of the absorption and adoption of ego ideals does not yet get to the heart of guilt in Loewald's terms. The guilty tension between what we

[10] In his *New Introductory Lectures on Psychoanalysis* of 1933, Freud observed that his account of the superego seems 'to have picked out only the parents' strictness and severity …, whereas their loving care seems not to have been taken over and maintained' (Freud 1964: 62). To address this, he there identifies three functions of the superego which chime more with the argument here: self-observation, conscience and maintaining the ideal models drawn from parents, educators and teachers.

should like to do and what we do is one thing, and the more or less coherent, benign, superego is the means for experiencing this. But more than this, the superego is for Loewald in its very existence what he calls an 'atonement structure'. The deeper point is that a sense of guilt is embedded in the very process of forming a superego because doing so involves separating off from those people one has until then loved and accepted as part of oneself. This is the true aftermath of resolving the Oedipus complex. Creating a superego – being a self-reliant individual – is an urgent requirement for psychological development but it is one that one cannot help but feel bad about. Take the father in Freud's phylogenetic story whom the sons both love and hate. Loving and hating the father are perfectly understandable in terms of the Oedipal drama, since love reflects identification with him, while hate represents the need to break from him. A son's hostility to the father is part of the quest to become himself, but it reflects the conflict between the 'quest for emancipation and self-responsibility [and] his desire for identification and becoming one with his father' (Loewald 1980: 391). One loves the father, but out of love for one's developing sense of self, one must also resent him – and then feel bad about such resentment.

This is not just a matter of fathers and sons. One can speak more generally of 'the parent' here, for the same is true of any parental figure, and for the girl as well as the boy. The parent is a constitutive part of the child's psychic being, but the child has to make such a psychic being its own. It must actively suppress the parental identification and, so doing, address that part of its own being that to that point the parent had co-constituted. The Oedipal struggle is to negate the parent insofar as the parent has until then been constitutive of the child. The child's aim is to create a clearer, demarcated, sense of its self, developing its interiority and subjectivity by forcing the parent more completely outside it. By creating a distance between the parent and its own emerging sense of self, it may be free to be itself. The parent must be sidelined, but that hurtful act disturbs the child:

> In an important sense, by evolving our own autonomy, our own superego …, we are killing our parents. We are usurping their power, their competence, their responsibility for us, and we are abnegating them, rejecting them as libidinal objects. In short we destroy them in regard to some of their qualities hitherto most vital to us. Parents resist as well as promote such destruction no less ambivalently than children carry it out. (Loewald 1980: 390)

The freedom sought as necessary for selfhood is accordingly measured against remorse at the manner of its achievement, the internal death of the parent in the previously fused child–parent entity. This is the basis of the guilt that accompanies the creation of the superego, and hardwires the superego thereafter to a residual need to atone: 'Without the guilty deed of parricide there is no autonomous self … no individual self worthy of that name, no advanced internal organisation of psychic life, [so that] guilt and atonement are crucial motivational elements of the self' (Loewald 1980: 393).

This is why guilt is more than just an occupying enemy garrison imposed on the psyche, or too much of a dose of Kant. It is rather rooted in the valid experience of the well-developed psyche: 'Guilt then is not a troublesome affect that we might hope to eliminate in some fashion, but one of the driving forces in the organisation of the self. The self, in its autonomy, is an atonement structure, a structure of reconciliation, and as such a supreme achievement' (Loewald 1980: 393–94).

At the core of Freudian psychoanalysis in its later structural phase is the theory of identification between parent and child. The growth of personhood occurs through the taking in of models drawn from those who offer loving identification to the child. From the earliest world of the unformed libido, the primary narcissistic state evolves through the creation of an ego and ego ideals into the more complex self-organisation of the superego. The latter is achieved by virtue of a struggle over identification for self-identity, autonomy and emancipation with those loving figures who have nurtured the child. This is a battle as the child resets its psychological relations and establishes a more coherent and sophisticated sense of itself. It abandons central arrangements of its psychic life up to that point, in exchange for a qualitative enrichment of its independent powers. Eventually, a renegotiated relationship with parents will usually emerge, but the struggle leaves its mark. It had involved denial of love given and taken, a seeming rejection of an emotional debt owed. Its residue is accordingly an underlying and constitutive desire to repair the bad feeling it has caused, and this we call guilt.

But this is not to say that we are all stuck with the kind of harsh superego that Freud linked to Kant and his categorical imperative. In writing of the superego as a necessary development for human emancipation which is at the same time linked to a sense of guilt, Loewald makes rather the 'Aristotelian' point we encountered in Chapter 6, in the philosophy developed by Morris: that guilt is deeply connected in the mature human psyche with atonement, which means 'literally and in many contexts … to cause or to become *at one*, to reconcile, to bring to concord or harmony' (Loewald 1980: 390). In this deep sense of how a self becomes itself, guilt is at its source connected to a desire to make or restore wholeness. Guilt as atonement is not the requital of deserved punishment but the desire to be at one again after conflict, to be in a state of 'at-one-ment'. Because this state is constitutive of who we are in our mature self-formation, it is something we carry through into our subsequent relationships and actions as we move forward in our lives. In this, it is no doubt guided by those ego ideals that we discussed previously, which are in turn sustained by an underlying desire for wholeness.

Guilt and the Undone Self: 'Feeling Rotten'

If processes of identification and the results of the Oedipal process might engrain the psyche with guilt and the need to atone, there is a final element I would like to propose. The experience of guilt is not just related to how one treated the loved parent, it is also concerned with a resulting displacement and disturbance in the child as it sets the parent at a distance. This fundamentally disturbs its sense of self as it has existed to that point. Through identification, the parent has been a constitutive part of the child's evolving ego, so that the Oedipal struggle involves both negating the parent-in-the-child and, as part and parcel, the child's own internal (parent-and-child) psychological set-up to that point. This involves at the least unsettling of the child's existing sense of self in the time before it can reconstitute itself by resetting parent–child boundaries. Adolescence is notoriously a time of fraught emotional reactions. This suggests both a sense of feeling bad (guilty) about repudiating those one loves and in addition an internal sense of being psychologically displaced. Ejecting the parents leaves the child internally stripped out before a new, more sophisticated, sense of self comes into being. To feeling bad for the internal rejection of the loved other is added the bad feeling that is the turbulence brought about by displacement in the child's own being.

Talk of the Oedipal drama and of 'killing' the parent puts the point of rejection and negation dramatically. Of course, there may be times when the child imagines it would like to 'kill' the parent (and vice versa), and the metaphor makes the point that this is a profound shift in the nature of their relationship. In reality, of course, parricide is generally part of a psychic, not factual, reality (Loewald 1980: 393), and the result is usually not the actual death of the parent, but rather the evolution of the parent–child relation to one where there is 'some sort of balance, equality, or transcending conciliation', albeit one that 'remains vulnerable' (Loewald 1980: 395). But the experience of love and rejection, of destabilisation and reconfiguration, is formative, and it gives a psychological basis for the existence of guilt as the sense of both feeling bad about another *and* of feeling bad within oneself. This leads to the kind of psychosomatic feeling suggested by Morris in relation to doing something bad or violative of another. One feels 'rotten, depleted of energy, tense' (Morris 1976: 99) in such a situation and this might describe both the underlying ground state in the Oedipal drama and how one feels at any subsequent actual violation of another. Similar feelings are invoked in both, and the initial Oedipal setting becomes the emotional prototype for what may follow. The psychological sense of being undone by a guilt feeling, either for something done or imagined to a parent or in subsequent guilt-inducing situations, leads one to feel rotten about oneself.

Prospective Identification and Stranger Violation

The argument is that the period of Oedipal struggle leaves the psyche with both the means to measure ego ideals against actual performance (responsibility) and an imprint or template in terms of guilt as the desire to be at one again after an act violative of another (feeling bad about the other and within oneself). Yet, there is plainly a jump in the argument from guilt at 'killing' a parent and, let us say, the violation of another beyond the family setting, especially if this is a real rather than an imagined event. Why should one feel guilty in relation to a violation perpetrated on a stranger? In particular, why is guilt carried forward at all, and why does it apply to someone who is not close to us?

As regards carrying guilt forward, the psychic stages a person passes through leave their mark. While we might think the Oedipal stage to be one that once passed is in the past, Freud insisted that formative psychic experiences live on in different settings. Loewald makes the point beautifully, quoting from lines of Ariel in Shakespeare's *The Tempest*: nothing fades 'but doth suffer a sea-change into something rich and strange' (Loewald 1980: 394). As regards guilt for violation of a stranger, people do indeed feel guilty in connection with acts they have done that are not related to close others. The question for the theory then becomes: how do we get from guilt in the resolution of personal identity with parental figures to guilt for the violation of another, who may be a stranger? The guilt of parricide is after all a very particular drama in the formation of the coherent and autonomous ego. The question is whether it has relevance for thinking not only about the guilt of the metaphoric parricide but also, for example, for the harm in killing another human being who may be a complete stranger. Actual homicides really do happen, and perpetrators are capable of feeling bad for what they have done. How could that be where the connection between the perpetrator and the victim may involve no prior identificatory relationship?

I suggest that the way to think beyond metaphoric parricide to guilt in real 'stranger violation' cases is in terms of a 'prospective' or 'anticipatory' identification. To violate seriously any other human being is to wrong a figure who has been a potential object of love and identification. It is to threaten or destroy a person who has been a source of identification for others, and who might have been a figure who the violator could under other circumstances have identified with. Identificatory possibilities extend broadly, indeed, to all members of the human species. Every person is a potential source of identification: we are all some parent's child, some child's possible parent, or other close relation.[11] Every human being is constituted by love, identification, and ego formation; we are all the same in this regard. Symbolically to kill the Oedipal object of one's identificatory love is to repudiate in psychic reality a part of oneself. To violate another in reality is to threaten or put an end to a source of identificatory love for others who are just like us in a relevant human sense. Imagined parricide of a loved figure is close to home, but its benevolent upshot can be a development of a further, more balanced, relationship with that figure. Actual violation combines a more distant relation with another human being with a form of destruction that is real and may be complete. Serious violations

[11] This is the source of the idea of a metaphysical guilt that extends universally and is picked up by world religions (Morris 1987: 240). I suggest it lies at the root of Karl Jaspers's account of German war guilt as involving a metaphysical dimension (Jaspers 2000), as discussed in Chapter 1 (and see more generally Norrie 2017a: ch 6).

lead to real damage that may not be reversible and no one survives her own homicide. To violate another is to threaten to destroy a figure with whom one could have identified, who had the possibility of loving identification for others, and who in relevant human ways is just like the one who violates.

To illustrate the point, just such a moral psychological logic is to be found in Dostoyevsky's *Crime and Punishment*, where the author describes Raskolnikov's grief at killing the old woman. In this account, Raskolnikov experiences both the sense of a punishment that comes back to him through prospective identification with the victim, and the way in which his existential being is displaced. With regard to identification, he asks: 'Did I really kill the old woman? No, it was myself I killed! – it was myself I have irrevocably ruined!' (Dostoyevsky 1997: 334). This is identificatory guilt for killing the old woman to whom emotionally he was in an everyday sense a stranger.

With regard to his own emotional displacement, Raskolnikov 'suffered cruelly from this conviction, that everything, even memory, even the most elementary prudence, was abandoning him'. He asks: 'Can this be the punishment already beginning? Indeed, indeed, it is!' (Dostoyevsky 1997: 74).[12] This is his own sense of being undone, of 'feeling rotten', that partners identificatory guilt. These are the two different grounds for bad feeling that can be deduced from the account of atonement, guilt and superego formation around the idea of identification. They may exist in the case of the real stranger-violator just as much as in the psychic reality of metaphoric parricide. They are underpinned by an anticipatory or prospective identification – that this was a person just like oneself, with whom one could under other circumstances have identified. They constitute the basis for a moral experience of guilt and reconciliation that can be identified metapsychologically as the ground state for the philosophical and ethical practices discussed in Chapters 2, 4 and 5 and which Chapter 6's philosophical rebels, Williams and Morris, could have pursued.

Linking the Metapsychology and Metaphysics of Guilt

We began this discussion in Chapter 6 with Bernard Williams and the bridgehead he offered to two critiques of guilt. The first was the political critique of guilt as a core part of the 'peculiar', institutionally fused, form of morality shaped by the modern liberal state. Because the modern discourse of guilt is aligned to particular political purposes, it is essentially limited. The second critique involved the demand for a naturalistic moral psychology that could deepen moral theory and help to understand what a term such as 'guilt' might truly mean once we move beyond its modern 'peculiar' appearance. This suggests how the limitations of the modern discourse of guilt may be overcome.

[12] Compare Raskolnikov with the case of the killer Anwar Congo in the film *The Act of Killing*, discussed in Chapter 10, where Congo asks if his sense of profound disturbance is his own acts coming back to him.

We pursued this second line through Morris's thoughtful account of guilt, atonement and identification. Taking these together, we identified an account of guilt that went beyond moral guilt in its 'peculiar' form, to a deeper sense of the relationship between wholeness, love, atonement ('at-one-ment') and identification. In Morris, these terms are inflected by the kind of moral psychology argued for here but nonetheless lack grounding at the deepest level, that of Williams's 'psychological materials' – those metapsychological mechanisms linked to the idea of identification explored here.

The claim to take moral psychology to its deeper metapsychological level raises important questions about what we should find there. We noted that Williams was ambivalent between anger and love, though it is anger that comes to the fore in his admittedly limited sally into psychoanalytical theory. This suggests a very different approach to that which comes from Morris, for there atonement is related to wholeness and love, and identification is related to fellowship with another into whose being one enters. Anger could not be Morris's first port of call. Anger is of course surely possible, but it would not be a direct expression of punitive desire. Rather it would be what the guilty person feels for having failed in relation to love, wholeness and the other with whom one identifies. It would be an extension of the rottenness and tension Morris identifies, not because of an internalised, redirected, anger at breach of a norm.

Here we confronted a possible impasse, in that Freud's metapsychology of guilt clearly focuses on aggression, fear and anger, and not on love. We noted, however, that such an approach was not inevitable if we pursued Freud's thought, picking up the point from Loewald and Lear that there was an unreconciled conflict in Freud between the earlier pleasure- and instinct-based theory and the later structural, emancipatory account based on love's enformation. The latter leads psychoanalysis down the route to eudaimonic happiness, truth and self-knowledge and the relationship between the rational and the non-rational self. Lear's remarkable contribution is to show how Freud follows in this line and produces in his metapsychology a potentially richer answer to the original questions posed by the ancient Greeks.[13] Williams perhaps sensed this possibility in some of his broader statements about Freud and moral psychology, but his 'psychological materials' in *Shame and Necessity* did not move in such a direction.

Finally, we reached beyond Lear to his mentor in metapsychology, Loewald, whose account of responsibility and the superego as an atonement structure provides both an immediate link to Morris's metaphysics of guilt and locates the source of such feeling in the formation of the latent potential

[13] Aristotle's answer to the question of knowledge of the non-rational self is limited (see Lear 2015: 26–27, notes 14 and 23); accordingly, since the person cannot properly unify herself, one could think this explains why Aristotle's account of the development of the virtues rests on the importance of education and training rather than their self-development and reflective adoption by a person.

to think and love of every individual human psyche. Guilt most fundamentally relates to the creation of a self, organised around ego ideals and a superego. It is concerned with how a person handles identification with parental figures (the creation of ego ideals), and, especially, ambivalence to those one loves and holds within, but must push out in order to be oneself. This is the creation of the superego for its benefits in terms of self-organisation, but which also sets in place its underlying quality as an atonement structure. Desiring a wholeness that has been given up remains a residual ethical reflex for post-Oedipal encounters. It underpins the reaction to our wrongful, violative acts and makes us want to correct them. Just as parents enter into the developing child's psyche, and that psyche experiences guilt at discarding an identification at its heart, so the post-Oedipal child and adult enter into loving relations with others through a variety of relationships that can be close or distant. The unity these bring, if broken, triggers a desire to atone, to be back 'at one', embedded in the enformed psyche. Such unity may be with those who are strangers to us, but are in important human ways like us, so that identification for guilt may be with regard to relationships that are anticipatory or prospective.

This point about strangers links Loewald's metapsychology with Morris's metaphysics. The unity that comes from 'entering into' the life of the other qua stranger lies in the experience of prospective identification, by means of which a broad, even universal, form of identification with other members of the human species is possible. Such relationships are based on universal identification with other human beings, on feelings of universal solidarity, which bring us to the point where we see the metaphysical and metapsychological dimensions of our human animal nature converge. We can tie the metapsychological argument for prospective identification together with Morris's metaphysical account of identificatory, 'nonmoral' guilt,[14] for he too argues for just such a universal form:

> Now, if we accept the legitimacy of identificatory ties … can we not also find it acceptable that individuals establish those identificatory ties with others and that they may do this without irrationality? We might not ourselves make such commitments; but others reveal through their emotional responses that they have. Some even reveal, as much religious thought makes evident, a scope of identification that embraces the human race. I do not myself presently see that such a position is open to challenge. (Morris 1987: 240)

Nor do I. What is needed for an adequate moral psychology is that we relate Morris's moral intuition to an adequate account of psychic development, grounded in the 'psychological material'. There is a route to do this through Freud, Lear and Loewald, Williams and Morris having brought existing philosophy to its limit. Through these writers, we can see how guilt

[14] As explained in Chapter 6, this term is wrongly named by Morris.

as prospective identification is rooted in guilt and atonement ('at-one-ment') located in human moral psychology as both metaphysics and metapsychology. Human metapsychology grounds ethical metaphysics without diminishing its importance to the human being as a metaphysical animal. In this way, we place a proper appreciation of the importance of ethical concepts like guilt on the table and reinvigorate the Aristotelian eudaimonic impulse by interpreting what we might call the 'rational' (the moral) and the 'non-rational' (the nonmoral) sides of guilt. We thereby expand the bounds of philosophy as we pursue the ancient philosophical injunction to know ourselves – in modern, Freudian, terms as animals who think and love and can take their moral responsibilities seriously.

8

Primitive and Mature Retributivism

> punishment [to] extinguish guilt … does not work … and more … is needed.
>
> Hans Loewald (1980: 391)

> … the slippery slope of retributive thinking … [is] to endorse cruelty and inhumanity…
>
> Jeffrie Murphy (2012: 88–89)

In the last two chapters, I developed a moral psychology of guilt adequate to the experience of a metaphysical animal, one whose nature makes it capable of thought and love. Chapter 6 finds that there are some central elements in the ethical and philosophical experience of guilt such as atonement, identification and the sense of human wholeness which push us towards human metapsychology. Chapter 7 argues that Freud's dominant view of guilt as based on anger and fear produced a primitive conception while his later structural theory links love and ego formation to a mature account of guilt and thence to the ethical and philosophical account. Metapsychology with a mature conception of guilt completes metaphysics for the human animal that thinks and loves. In this chapter, I want to now consider what this mature kind of moral psychology contributes to an understanding of modern criminal justice practice.

While I recognise that theories of deterrence, incapacitation and rehabilitation are all relevant to punishment practices (Norrie 2014: ch 12), I take the retributive theory of punishment to be central to justifying *morally* legal concepts like blame, responsibility and punishment. How does the moral psychology developed here engage with it? I suggest that we have to consider how both primitive and mature forms of guilt play an active part in penal practice today. I suggest that Freud's earlier primitive model of guilt, though superficial and inadequate, operates as a particular way of understanding how punishment should work in the modern criminal justice system. Antiquated and shallow in its assumptions, and overthrown (at least implicitly) in Freud's later structural work, the requital of anger model remains central to modern penal practice.

If it seems odd that an inadequate theoretical model might animate modern criminal justice practice, politically powerful talk confirms the problem. The then United Kingdom Home Secretary stated in 2019 that she wanted criminals 'to literally feel terror at the thought of committing offences', a view consistent with her past support for capital punishment.[1] This of course has flavours of deterrence and incapacitation in it, but there is also anger at bad people for doing bad things and a desire for requital. Though political rhetoric, it pretty much sums up the purported aim of the modern punishment model that hopes both to deter people and to give them their just deserts. Of course, many just deserts theorists are appalled at this kind of view and argue that censure and requital should be accompanied by penal parsimony, but the major premise of both those who wish to be more and those who wish to be less punitive is that punishment is *deserved*.

The weaknesses of this approach are reflected in Murphy's words quoted above about the slippery slope of retributivism which starts out nicely liberal but ends up supporting cruelty and inhumanity. Freud was never fully able to shake off the primitive guilt of *Civilization and Its Discontents* and it seems that western criminal justice systems have not been able to in their own way either. Of course, there are many reasons for this relating to the social, political and cultural setting of criminal justice thinking, and how law and order rhetoric mobilises popular support (Simon 2007; Wacquant 2009; Carvalho and Chamberlen 2018; Reeves 2019; Norrie 2024). The point I want to make in this chapter is that the rhetoric rests upon a specific and inadequate moral psychology with which a more sophisticated model can be compared. What in Freud represented an early and inadequate theory of psychological development has been preserved as a morally primitive, punitive, theoretical practice in modern criminal justice systems.

The chapter has three main sections. In the first, I return to primitive and mature guilt in Freud. Here the argument recapitulates but also develops what was said in Chapter 7. In the second section, I introduce a further element in the shape of Melanie Klein with the aim of deepening and consolidating the argument. Klein, it will be recalled from Chapter 3, also developed two accounts of guilt in examining the moral development of infants, in either the 'paranoid–schizoid' or the 'depressive' positions she identified. If these can also be characterised as primitive and mature, then her account dovetails with Freud's to offer a coherent metapsychology of two competing kinds of guilt at both the infant and child stages of human development. Both writers, it should be noted, argued that what is developed in early mental life is relevant to and ongoing in the adult setting. In the final section, I suggest that a critical understanding of criminal justice rests on seeing how *both* primitive and

[1] See Priti Patel:

> I do actually think … where we have seen murderers, rapists and people who have committed the most abhorrent crimes in society, go into prison and then are released from prison to go out into the community to then re-offend … again and again. I think that's appalling. And actually on that basis alone I would actually support the reintroduction of capital punishment to serve as a deterrent. (Patel per BBC 2019)

An alternative view would be that the revolving door of crime and punishment shows that the existing model does not work, while the death penalty masks this.

mature guilt relate to the modern criminal justice system via retributive theory. I suggest that the different forms of guilt allow us to identify the basis for a new *mature* retributivism based on an adequate metaphysical and metapsychological understanding.[2] This not only leads to a qualitatively better account of retributive theory, but it also places in question the need for such a theory to involve punishment. A mature retributivism, one that is in line with treating human beings as the metaphysical animals they are, suggests the abolition of punishment as both a psychological and ethical necessity.

Primitive and Mature Guilt in Freud

In this section, I revisit the two accounts of guilt in Freud established in Chapter 7: one that is there on its face and the other which can be developed from his later structural theory following the development begun by Hans Loewald and pursued by Jonathan Lear. There is a degree of recapitulation here, but I hope this is helpful in terms of focusing the argument on two kinds of retributive theory. It generates a view of a mature guilt that is developmentally and ethically progressive, alongside an early form that is punitive, persecutory and ethically regressive.

Two Freuds

Martha Nussbaum has recently written about how she gave up her previous commitment to the psychoanalytic view of guilt (see above, Chapter 4). She came to see it as self-centred, self-lacerating and narcissistic, and as echoing a harsh, retributive, Kantian style of ethics (Nussbaum 2016: 127–35). Leaving to one side whether this is a complete account of Kantian ethics,[3] this is a one-sided view of what psychoanalysis can offer, for it misses the progressive ethical view of guilt developed in Chapter 6. However, as we have already seen, some of Freud's statements on the subject suggest that she has a point: 'The superego – the conscience at work in the ego – may then become harsh, cruel and inexorable against the ego which is in its charge. Kant's Categorical Imperative is thus the direct heir of the Oedipus complex' (Freud 1984: 422).

This is a prominent line in Freud and is properly subject to Nussbaum's strictures. In *Civilization and Its Discontents*, it can be said to be the dominant approach. However, the case can also be made for the conflicted nature of Freud's thought, and for an alternative approach implicit in his metapsychology, especially as it evolved in his later structural writings. From this approach, we find a different way of thinking about guilt, in what I call its mature form. Here, guilt is creative, developmental and ethically progressive,

[2] As I make clear in what follows, this involves a radical reworking of the idea, though one that is perfectly valid. It is not another attempt to reinvent the punitive wheel.

[3] I explore the Kantian position in the theory of punishment more fully later in this chapter.

warranting the label 'eudaimonistic' for its future-oriented commitment to human betterment.[4] It is a love-related version of guilt which contrasts with the anger and fear version foregrounded in *Civilization and Its Discontents.* This different account, developed in Chapter 7, is as consistent with Freud's metapsychology as the other, 'Kantian', account. If we call the first persecutory account Freud's 'Kantian' moment, we can call the second his mature account, and see it as the opening up of an 'Aristotelian' moment in Freud.

Early Guilt: 'Kantian' and Persecutory

'Kantian' persecutory guilt runs through Freud's *Civilization and Its Discontents.* Summarising from the previous chapter, two quotations indicate the nature of the argument:

> Thus we know of two origins of the sense of guilt: one arising from fear of an authority, and the other, later on, arising from fear of the superego. The first insists upon a renunciation of instinctual satisfactions; the second, as well as doing this, presses for punishment ... We have also learned how the severity of the superego – the demands of conscience – is to be understood. It is simply a continuation of the severity of the external authority, to which it has succeeded and which it has in part replaced. (Freud 1985: 319)

The second quote:

> The tension between the harsh superego and the ego that is subjected to it, is called by us the sense of guilt; it expresses itself as a need for punishment. Civilization, therefore, obtains mastery over the individual's dangerous desire for aggression ... by setting up an agency within him to watch over it, like a garrison in a conquered city. (Freud 1985: 316–17)

In this account, guilt emerges from fear of the anger of authority figures, and as these are brought back into the psyche, fear of the person's own superego. The latter acts like 'a garrison in a conquered city', while the demands of conscience represent a continuation of the anger of external authority, once it is introjected into the psyche. Overall, the need for the 'civilizatory' (i.e. the punitive) authority of the superego stems from the forcefulness and the danger of instinctual satisfactions, especially of an aggressive and sexual kind, which civilization, external authority figures and the strict superego keep in check. We

[4] Martha Nussbaum also writes of a response to violation in terms of the eudaimonic, involving eudaimonic anger (Nussbaum 2016: 16). This could be related, as I do, to eudaimonic guilt, but she does not develop such an account. Anger for her is a quick reaction which should translate into a desire for social change rather than addressing guilt. Guilt, she says, would be the 'wrong motive' while 'positive love and compassion' are the right ones (Nussbaum 2016: 131). I argue that there is a mature kind of eudaimonic guilt, and associated anger, which is necessarily embedded in love and compassion, and is of the 'right' motivational kind alongside commitments to social change. This is why moral transactions around guilt and forgiveness are so important: see Chapter 4.

can see here why Freud might have compared the superego to the categorical imperative since both could be said to involve an external command system, which is internally endorsed.

We can also see why Nussbaum might have objected to its self-centred narcissism: there is no regard here for the other, it is all about the ego's self-absorption. Freud's model of human conduct, social life, and moral psychology here is bleak, primitive and persecutory. The human condition here is one of domination by base instincts and fears, where guilt's facial expression is a snarl. Freud describes man as a wolf in *Civilization and Its Discontents* (Freud 1985: 302), and we can see why. There is no development of a consolidated ethical subjectivity in this account, but rather psychic states playing the role of ethical censors, emerging to control animal instincts. All that stands between humans and their viciousness is fear and its internal mental representative, the superego: the garrison over the conquered city, the categorical imperative imposed upon animal passions. Small wonder that Nussbaum should distance herself from this 'Kantian' Freud, but another Freudian view beckons.

Mature Guilt: 'Aristotelian' and Reparative

While Freud's main argument in *Civilization and Its Discontents* is as we have described it, another view is also present. Loewald emphasised the importance of love and the life instinct (libido) in the later Freud's structural theory, and Lear developed this view, as we saw in Chapter 7, linking it to ancient Greek philosophy. From this position, it is possible to create another account of guilt as complex, morally creative and psychologically developmental, that is, as eudaimonistic, and therefore 'Aristotelian', in its nature. This approach comes from Freud's later, structural, metapsychology of ego and superego development, as the process whereby the human psyche becomes 'enformed'.

In the earliest stage of human life, the infant operates in a state of primary narcissism or what can be called 'ideal egoism',[5] which is a protean and inchoate state of love for life – an undifferentiated state of being between a mother and a baby in which the baby's life instinct, what Freud called libido or Eros, first appears. The process of psychic development is one in which the child interacts with parent figures to differentiate itself as an individual with an identity by creating an ego. Later, the ego evolves by creating a further, self-reflective, element or 'precipitate', which Freud called the superego (Freud 1984: 367–79). Out of this evolution, we get the development of possibilities for self-reflection and a sense of responsibility, a conscience, the possibility of feelings of guilt and a desire to repair wrongs. Importantly, all these developments are relational, that is they are emergent from social situations of love

[5] To simplify, 'ideal egoism' refers to the earliest stage of the narcissistic libido, which is distinguished from the later situation where the ego has taken on ego ideals from parent and other figures: see Loewald 1980: 46–47, 268–69.

and solidarity with other human beings – primarily, but not exclusively, parent figures. The process of *individual* self-development is always at the same time a *relational* and a *social* process. This begins in childhood and remains significant throughout life.

Elements for an Account of Mature Guilt

Three elements from Loewald's elucidation of Freud's structural theory are identified here: the sense of responsibility, the sense of guilt and the desire to repair.

A Sense of Responsibility

This basic element of human moral psychology is located in the evolution of the child as it develops its sense of autonomy as an ego and superego out of and away from parental relationships. It identifies with how a parent relates to it and builds from this a sense of how it could be a self (an ego) in its own right, with self-agency and overall reflexive powers (as a superego):

> Responsibility to oneself, within the context of authoritative norms consciously and unconsciously accepted or assimilated from parental and societal sources, is the essence of superego as internal agency … It involves appropriating or owning up to one's needs and impulses as one's own, impulses and desires we appear to have been born with or that seem to have taken shape in interaction with parents during infancy … [So doing] we begin to develop a sense of self-identity [which] means to experience ourselves as agents, notwithstanding the fact that we were born without our informed consent and did not pick our parents. (Loewald 1980: 392)

If one can feel responsible for what one has done, this implies both an ego that acts and an element in it, a superego, reflecting on those actions, establishing an agent capable of self-reflexivity. This is the basis for a sense of responsibility, which with the capacity to think holistically about the self over time, generates the idea of quantum guilt described in ethical terms in Chapter 6.

The Possibility of Guilt

Out of this comes the monitoring of potential tensions in the psyche between the things one does and the things one would do if acting according to the best, or ideal, commitments one has developed. The tension between the ego's acts (as ego) and the ego's ideals (as evolved from parental and other social figures and collected in a self-reflexive superego) can leave one feeling bad and angry about what one has done. Such a tense, negative, anxious, feeling is guilt, a 'form of tension between ego and superego' (Loewald 1980: 273) – and this is of course Morris's description of feeling 'rotten, depleted of energy, tense' (Morris 1976: 99). For Loewald, we 'have a sense of guilt concerning past or present thoughts, feelings and deeds, but only inasmuch as they represent a nonfulfillment of the inner image of ourselves, of the internal ideal we have not reached' (Loewald 1980: 273–74). Pace Nussbaum, this is not a question of beating oneself up for the narcissistic pleasure of it. Nor is it grounded in an unreflective fear of parent figures. Rather it is a concerned self-reflection and criticism that lead a developed subject in the direction of their ideals in relations with others.

Of course, identifying this mature source of ethical guilt in the human psyche does not exclude the possibility of other, less mature, forms of guilt related to anxiety, dominant parents or negative narcissistic forms of psychological development. These are all possible vicissitudes in human growth, but they represent the ways in which things can go awry rather than the necessary foundations on which human psychology is constructed. Against the 'Kantian' Freud, eudaimonistic, 'Aristotelian' guilt is not the screaming anger of the superego keeping one in line; it is the evolving self, seeking to act well according to its achieved sense of its own best lights. Against the primitive, angry and fear-driven animal that acts in persecutory and self-persecutory ways, guilt is here constructive, related to one's ideals, aimed at addressing how one has acted and with a view to putting things right.

A Desire to Repair

There are two aspects to this. First, responsibility and guilt are accompanied by a desire to restore or repair wrongs, that is, to act responsibly to lay to rest psychic conflicts arising from negative behaviours. This is a desire to be at one with oneself that incorporates the holistic sense of one's identity across time (the possibility of quantum guilt). This is the corollary of guilt anxiety at breaching one's ideals, but it is supported by something else: a second, deep-seated, atonement reaction of the superego stemming from the process of its own formation.

For the latter, the superego emerges out of the resolution of the so-called Oedipal struggle.[6] The psychological control parents have of the pre-Oedipal child comes because they dwell inside its psyche. The Oedipal struggle is the effort by the child to take control of itself to become a person in its own right. A successful struggle, 'kicking out' or 'killing' the parent inside, generates the possibility of a more coherent and self-reliant self (with a superego). Yet this necessary achievement leaves the child with residual bad feeling – guilt – about what it has done. It absolutely needed to wrest control of its own psyche, but in so doing, it also rejected the internal loving parent that was fused with it. Normally, of course, this struggle leads to a new modus vivendi over time, but the rejection of the old emotional order leaves a deep sense that the child has betrayed a deep loving relationship. This is the basis for a deep-seated, residual, desire to repair. As we saw in Chapter 7, Loewald wrote of 'guilt and atonement [as] crucial motivational elements of the self'. Guilt was 'not

[6] This is commonly understood to relate to issues of sexual identification, but it has a broader implication with regard to superego formation: see Chapter 7.

a troublesome affect that we might hope to eliminate in some fashion, but one of the driving forces in [its] organisation….' The self in its autonomy is indeed 'an atonement structure, a structure of reconciliation, and as such a supreme achievement' (Loewald 1980: 390–94). Here we encountered an original meaning of a term. 'To atone' as an active verb means to pay or make good, generally, 'for one's sins'; but in its original sense, it is to find a way once again to be whole, to be 'at one', and here, as we saw, metapsychology and metaphysics coincide (Morris 1976: 100; Loewald 1980: 390). The superego has an inbuilt tendency to wish relations with others to be restored to wholeness, and this works alongside the desire to address tensions around its ego ideals.[7]

It should be clear that this 'Aristotelian' account of a guilt that repairs is very different from the persecutory kind we identified previously. The 'Kantian' anger and fear model operates with a simplistic account of instincts and their control. While the superego is invoked there, it can only be a primitive, rudimentary version of the mature superego that Loewald draws out of superego formation and resolution of the Oedipal complex. When Freud 'equates the sense of guilt with need for punishment, he takes too superficial a view on the matter,' appearing to 'ignore his own deeper insight that more than repression is involved in superego development' (Loewald 1980: 390). It is hoped that 'punishment will extinguish guilt, but it does not work for any length of time and more punishment is needed' (Loewald 1980: 391).[8] The 'Kantian' superego is the voice of angry authority figures, introjected, and with the volume turned up, but it has no progressive value for the subject.

Anger may also be present in the mature, reparative, model, but it takes the form of a tension within the psyche resulting from frustration at failing to live up to one's best ways of dealing with things. The subject's mature development establishes moral action as the outcome of a complex, structural, psychic evolution which takes a person from the earliest phase of the basic life drive (primary narcissism) to ego formation, the creation of ego ideals and the Oedipal struggle to create the 'Aristotelian', self- and other-respecting, superego. All these are complex – individual, social and relational – processes out of which guilt and the desire to repair emerge as ethical possibilities. The resulting human being is able to think and act creatively in relation to wrongs it may have done or that it observes in the world.[9] 'Bearing the burden of guilt' makes it possible to master it but 'not in the hasty form of repression and punishment, but by achieving a reconciliation of conflicting strivings' by means of an 'affect [that is] borne for a time' and where '[t]hought and feeling … are "delayed action"' (Loewald 1980: 391). The reparative model of guilt is complex, evolved, emergent, mature and creative, contrasting in most ways with

[7] The wish to restore wholeness has both backward and forward aspects. The desire to get back to an early childhood state is present but regressive; the desire to look forward and to find wholeness in mature relations takes an early form of being and puts it to progressive uses.

[8] A comparison with the repetitiveness of state punishment is to the point here.

[9] This is what Morris in ethical terms refers to as 'nonmoral' guilt: see Chapter 6.

an earlier form of guilt in which the person is less complete and subject to basic instincts and controls. These are two very clearly demarcated ways of thinking about guilt and anger in Freud.[10] If we turn now to consider Melanie Klein's account of guilt at the earlier infantile stage, we will see a remarkable parallel to the early and mature forms we have identified in Freud.

Persecutory and Reparative Guilt in Klein

Here I pick up the discussion in Chapter 3 of Melanie Klein's work. She pioneered a move grounded in Freud's thinking but pushing it in two directions. The first was to take psychoanalysis to the earliest time in an infant's life, where Klein found, earlier than Freud, the rudiments of ego and superego formation. According to Hanna Segal, where Freud 'discovered the child still dynamic in the adult', Klein 'discovered the infant in the child and the adult' (Klein 1998: ix). The second was to identify two successive 'positions' in an infant's early development, evolving stages that remained part of the child and adult throughout its life. An infant developed from the earlier 'paranoid–schizoid' position into the later 'depressive' position, but there could also be regression, and though these positions were most obvious in the behaviour of disturbed children and adults, they represented general forms of human psychology, which could be observed both in individual behaviour and in social practices. These two positions provide parallel accounts of primitive and mature guilt in Klein to those just described in Freud, but at an earlier stage of development. After describing them, I will explore how Klein's two positions can be related to primitive and mature guilt in the Freud–Loewald approach. I will then finish this section by considering how punishment is likely to work on people whose psyches operate in paranoid–schizoid or reparative ways.

Klein's Two Positions[11]

A person's development involves a process of psychological integration that deals with basic human anxieties about being loved and having that love secured. In Klein's 'paranoid–schizoid' phase, the infant has no clear sense of itself, or anything else, as a whole. Profound emotions of fear, anger and love jostle as the infant first experiences the world and reacts to an environment on which it depends. The first object it experiences is the breast, which can be either giving (the so-called good breast) or withholding (the 'bad breast'). While the former is a source of nurture, warmth and security, the

[10] Mature guilt, and any associated anger, are about ethically valid self- and other-criticism and the desire to repair, and they lead to a sense of responsibility to address personal violation or violation in the world at large. This is akin to the 'eudaimonistic anger' Nussbaum identifies but does not pursue in relation to guilt in her account (Nussbaum 2016: 16).

[11] See Reeves (2019) and Reeves, Norrie and Carvalho (2019) for fuller discussion of Klein's work and its implications for punishment and law.

latter generates perplexity, anxiety and anger. Perceptions of the good and the bad remain unconnected in the infant mind, which deals only in 'part objects', and this is reflected in a psyche that perceives the world as split into either fearful and angry (bad) or loving and nurturing (good) forms. The world is seen as either all good or all bad: when good, it is very good, and when bad, very bad. Without any overall connection being made between good and bad parts, badness cannot be seen as a temporary experience in an overall good setting, anxiety is overwhelming and anger when it comes is all-consuming rage and aggression. Herein lies the root of a persecutory anger that responds instinctually in a destructive way to objects that are perceived as all bad. This is Klein's initial, paranoid–schizoid, position.

The 'depressive' position, which supervenes on this, also involves anxiety, but of a different kind. Gradually the infant sees that part objects it had perceived as all good or all bad are really one object that sometimes appears as good (for example gratifying) and sometimes bad (for example frustrating). It begins to see a whole object, and to understand, in a sufficiently reassuring environment, that the objects that surround it, the mother's body, the mother and the father, are all capable of acting in ways that gratify – while sometimes they may frustrate. As these objects come to be seen as whole objects, there is a growing sense in the infant that it too could be whole and could love those who surround it in their own differentiated wholeness.

This position is an advance in developmental terms on the paranoid–schizoid position, but it brings its own emotional difficulties, which leads Klein to call it the 'depressive' position. It involves a new kind of anxiety related to the earlier persecutory forms of anger and rage against part objects. These now jostle in the infant with feelings of love for what it is coming to see as whole objects. Those whom the infant is coming to love as whole objects, and which give it a sense of its own wholeness, are the same objects at which it had directed its anger and rage. In a situation where the rageful phantasy to destroy is indistinguishable from the imagined outcome, the infant may imagine it has destroyed the whole object it is now coming to love. This generates a troubling anxiety about destroying what one loves, and in turn an anxious desire to repair the harm one thinks one has done. Developing and then becoming embedded in the infant's psyche, there emerges an urge to repair that which one loves and imagines having harmed, and this becomes generalised in the infant's worldly interactions.

As with Freud, these two positions generate a sense of guilt, either of an early and primitive or a more mature form. I will now consider these, starting first with mature guilt and working back to its earlier form.

Mature Guilt: The Wish to Repair

From early infantile experiences, there comes an anxious desire to restore loved objects, and this is the basis for a sense of guilt and remorse:

> The feeling that the harm done to the loved object is caused by the subject's aggressive impulses I take to be the essence of guilt.... The urge to undo or repair this harm results from the feeling that the subject has caused it, i.e. from guilt. The reparative tendency can, therefore, be considered as a consequence of the sense of guilt.[12]

Love is developing, but there is also hate from the earlier paranoid–schizoid position, and the anxiety that the hate might have been efficacious against loved objects produces a reparative default position. This becomes a formative experience in the human psyche. Since the early emotional states are retained in later life, this reparative desire becomes an important aspect of the grown adult in social settings. The infant is the parent to both the child and the adult as it comes to terms with its loving commitments and its fears for what it may have done. A wish to make things better, because one has wished them to be worse, stems from the depressive position, interacting with the paranoid–schizoid position it comes to supersede.

This wish lies at the heart of mature adult relationships. The anxiety operating in this position becomes what we know as moral states of guilt and remorse and lies at the root of the development of a conscience. In the depressive position, the infant's primary aim is to make good the whole object, of which it now understands itself to be a part. While it feels 'strong conflicts between aggressive impulses and feelings of love', the latter lead to 'feelings of guilt and ... wishes to make good' (Klein 1998: 310). The depressive position thus lies behind 'the urge to make people happy', a 'strong feeling of responsibility and concern for them' and a 'genuine sympathy with other people ... as they are and as they feel' (Klein 1998: 311). This generates a sense of 'conscience in the true sense of the word' and the means whereby 'a moral and ethical attitude are activated' (Klein 1998: 252). It raises the interesting question as to how this mature instinct for conscience and reparation, embedded at an earlier stage in human life, fits with Freud and Loewald's arguments concerning responsibility, guilt and atonement in the later Oedipal phase. We will return to that question further, once we have considered more fully the second, more primitive, account of guilt in Klein.

Early Guilt: Persecutory Anger

If the later, depressive, position is the source of a more developed, rounded, orientation to loved objects, and thence of a mature ethical guilt with its desire to make good, the earlier paranoid–schizoid position, which it seeks to

[12] See Klein 1997: 36; see also Klein 1998: 270:

> The ego comes to a realization of its love for a good object, a whole object and in addition a real object. Together with an overwhelming feeling of guilt towards it. Full identification with the [loved] object ... goes hand in hand with anxiety for it (of its disintegration), with guilt and remorse, with a sense of responsibility for preserving it intact against persecutors ... These emotions, whether conscious or unconscious, are in my view among the essential and fundamental elements of the feelings we call love.

overcome, leaves its trace on guilt through the forms of anger and rage that are its stock in trade. These direct their attention to what are seen as all-bad others, figures split off from any redeeming features, who are only worthy of outright, and potentially ferocious, condemnation. In this position, the primary aim of the immature infantile ego is to defend itself by going on the attack. Through Manichean splitting, it angrily blames and persecutes an all-bad other, while preserving an absolute sense of its own goodness.

The persecutory attitude in its hostility holds the all-bad other irredeemably guilty and worthy only of recrimination. Importantly, this attitude may also be turned back on the infant itself. In her clinical work, Klein had noticed how fiercely punitive young children could be in their play, and how this attitude was turned back on the child itself as a form of stringent guilt. Writing before she had identified the paranoid–schizoid position, Klein described an early feeling of guilt that was engendered by the nascent superego in what she called its 'sadistic' phase. In this phase, a sense of guilt emerges in the infant that stems from the prohibitions of parents and fear of them, but it is augmented many times over by the sadistic imagination of the infant itself. Such infants develop 'fantastic ideas of *what the parent might do to them*: kill them, cook them, castrate them and so on' (Klein 1998: 179). In this way, early sadistic impulses in the infant ensure that a persecutory form of guilt emerges such that 'the Biblical precept "an eye for an eye" is at work' in the infant's psyche (Klein 1998: 179).[13] Thus an early sadistic instinct, magnified inside the very young infant, becomes the basis for a rudimentary, but very aggressive, superego dishing out a persecutory sense of self- as well as other-guilt.

Just as with Freud in the Loewaldian development, we thus find two kinds of guilt in Klein's work, the one based on anger and persecution, the other on love and a desire to repair. Klein's account traces these back to the earlier stages of infantile development, and her work raises the question as to how we relate guilt found at this stage to how it develops into the later Oedipal stage.

Klein and Freud–Loewald Compared

Comparing Klein and Freud–Loewald on primitive and mature guilt, I argue that Klein's rudimentary forms may be seen as parallelling those found in later childhood by Freud in his Loewaldian development. They could be seen as prototypes of the latter.

Early Persecutory Guilt

Comparing Klein with Freud, her view of primitive, persecutory guilt starts from Freud's view in *Civilization and Its Discontents*. Her account is based on

[13] That the superego promotes an 'excessive violence in this early stage would thus be accounted for by the fact that it is an offshoot of very intense destructive instincts, and … very large quantities of aggressive ones' (Klein 1998: 250). In this setting, the limit form of the *lex talionis* might appear as an ethical advance on a more general destruction!

his understanding of self-directed aggression deployed to control aggressive instincts (Klein 1998: 250). What she does is to push back the beginnings of this process to the earlier period of infant life, where the aggression is all the infant's. Nonetheless, the idea of persecutory guilt founded in aggression and anxiety is present in both thinkers (see e.g. Klein 1997: 2). Klein's paranoid–schizoid position with its account of persecutory anger and rage at all-bad, non-whole, others may be seen as an early fit with Freud's 'Kantian' side.

Comparing Freud with Klein, Freud's 'Kantian' subject of introjected anger, dealing with fear of the father's wrath, and deploying this to control basic instinctual desires, is equally not really a whole person. It is a split subject with uncontrolled instincts, which need external 'civilizatory' controls to be internalised in order to live in the world. In both accounts of early guilt, the subject is submitted to the rule of an anger or aggression which starts within, and which it never rises above.

Similarly, love is lacking in both earlier positions. Klein's model of persecutory anger and guilt is seen as present at an earlier, infantile stage than in Freud, but both retain the sense of a split, anger- and fear-related guilt that is superseded by a later, more complex, ethically progressive, holistic form. Klein's persecutory guilt, based on infantile fantasy, might be seen as the early mapping of what become the more complex forms of persecution, incorporating the internalisation of fear of the father, in Freud's harsh superego. Klein deals with the infant in the child, Freud with the child evolving towards adulthood. Both, however, develop an account of early persecutory anger and guilt in contrast to a later, more mature, love-based, form.

Mature Reparative Guilt

Klein's mature, reparative guilt in the depressive position comes much earlier than that found in the Freud–Loewald account. Comparing the two approaches, the discussion is complicated by Klein's identification in early infantile life of a rudimentary superego, albeit one that has less space for the enformed structure of id, ego and superego in Freud. The latter suggests that the way in which libido or the life drive (Eros) develops through ego and superego formation leads to feelings of guilt, responsibility and the desire to atone (to be 'at one'). The ego develops a sense of its own autonomy and responsibility, incorporates ego ideals, and then, through the resolution of the Oedipus complex, evolves a superego with an inbuilt desire to restore wholeness. Klein's account of mature guilt in contrast emphasises the earlier stage of the depressive position at which an infant becomes able to perceive both others and itself as whole objects. Yet in this infant period, love and anger are mediated by the early form of psychic organisation that is the depressive position; hence Klein's argument is that the foundation of the superego occurs at this early stage.[14]

[14] 'Gradually … as the infant … establishes within himself complete and uninjured objects, essential developments in the superego organization take place' (Klein 1997: 74).

We are talking here of developments that are relevant for the early phases of infancy, but it seems these rudimentary forms of mature guilt and the superego in Klein may be interpreted to form the basis for later, more sophisticated, yet essentially homologous, developments in Freud's structural theory. While mature guilt in Freud–Loewald evolves at a later stage in the child's life, we can see a similar pattern evolving and might see Klein's infantile form of mature guilt as an early protype of that found in the Freud–Loewald approach.

That we might see the Kleinian and Freudian forms of guilt, either in persecutory or in reparative mode, as building on each other is supported by the view that, once experienced, a basic mental structure is seldom discarded. It is rather taken up and finds its place in a more advanced form of psychic organisation. Klein thinks that the reparative tendency in the depressive position continues into adult life, while Loewald's argument makes the same claim for the superego as an atonement structure. These look like similar moves at different stages, with the earlier reparatory move being taken up and renewed at a higher level in the later atonement structure. More broadly, we can see how Klein's reparative instinct aligns with Loewald's account of responsibility and atonement: how anxiety around doing harm to loved objects could be reset as anxiety around the conflict between ego action and ego ideals; and how the early Kleinian foundations of the ego and superego in the development of a whole subject facing whole objects could develop into Loewald's account of atonement as a holistic, restorative desire to be 'at-one' with oneself and one's world.

Persecutory Blame in Practice

I finish this section by exploring the nature and effects of persecutory self- and other-guilt in what Klein initially called the sadistic phase and what she would later call the paranoid–schizoid position. Towards the end of her career, Klein returned to this idea of persecutory guilt, considering the effect of blaming a person whose mental life is governed by paranoid–schizoid thinking. I then consider how this may be relevant to thinking about criminal punishment today.

Punishment and the Immature Psyche

In Klein, the depressive position supersedes the paranoid–schizoid position, but it does not abolish it. It may re-emerge, for example in situations of social disruption, stress and heightened anxiety. Blame that is targeted on a mind in the paranoid–schizoid position does not trigger a desire to repair or a sense of responsibility, as in the depressive position, but the perception in the immature psyche that it is, indeed, being persecuted. This person cannot bear a guilt and blame that is 'premature' (Klein 1997: 194), and cannot therefore desire to restore a wholeness that does not yet exist. Instead, there is further disintegration in one who is not yet capable of holding blame. While guilt for the person in whom depressive sentiments are strong represents an opportunity to do better in outward relation to others, the paranoid–schizoid mind can only be led to further internal breakdown.

The reason for this stems from the different kinds of anxiety in the two positions, and what they focus on. Directed at oneself, persecutory anxiety in the paranoid–schizoid position 'relates predominantly to the annihilation of the ego, while depressive anxiety is predominantly related to the harm done to internal and external loved objects by the subject's destructive impulses' (Klein 1997: 34). Persecutory blame as the imposition of guilt is not only savage and Manichean, it is also morally counter-productive for those on whom it is imposed. The person who is already inclined to self-persecution is pushed towards further disintegration. Angry recrimination against the person who cannot handle it, because that person operates at the level of angry reaction, simply undermines their ability to develop towards a whole response to what they have done. In line with their paranoid–schizoid tendency, their response becomes only angrier.

Punishment and the Maturing Psyche

Persecutory guilt is outright, recriminatory, blame directed at an 'all bad' person. If it is destructive for the person who already feels persecuted, how would it affect the person who is able to think reparatively about their guilt?

One response might be to shut down the desire to repair in the broadly depressive and reparative mind. If I am inclined to change by doing better in relation to the wrongs I have done, but I experience blame as outright condemnation for my unchangeable badness, this is likely to undermine my sense of myself as a person who is able to repair things in the world. I *thought* I was a person who could respond as one able to repair harm I may have done. If I am addressed as an inherently bad person, for whom persecutory blame is the only valid response, I may come to think that is after all what I am. Alternately, persecutory blame may provoke resistance and indignation at the calumnies directed at me, so that I feel further and wholesale resentment against a world that could only see me in this way, pushing me to become the 'animal' 'they' always thought I was. In other words, punishing and blaming the person who is capable of developing in a restorative way as if this is impossible may be counter-productive, pushing him back into the paranoid–schizoid position out of which he was developing.

The Logic of Criminal Punishment

Comparing reparative and persecutory guilt and blame, we can see how these have different ethical consequences and logics, and that they could lead to different reactions and outcomes. I make these points, albeit briefly, because they have implications for how punishment is utilised in society today. Klein's early and mature forms of guilt are not just infantile manoeuvres, they have effects on individuals throughout their lives and in adult social settings. They matter when we think about how punishment and blame in the modern social world might take on a persecutory or a reparative form. Is a modern response to violation persecutory, exclusionary, condemnatory and lacking in possibility of re-inclusion? Or is it restorative, offering the opportunity for repair or retrieving wholeness in perpetrators and victims?

It is all too easy to see the enclosed, regimented, overcrowded and security-focused world of prisons as essentially dehumanising. Together with the ramped-up political rhetoric of 'lock them up and throw away the key', focused on offenders that are regarded as beyond redemption, both medium and message are essentially persecutory. The idea that fear of punishment should 'literally' terrorise human beings[15] regarded as being without value promotes this logic, but with what effect on the psyches of those whose minds hover between the paranoid–schizoid and the reparative? Here is an illustration of where this logic eventually leads, taken from the prison memoir of Jimmy Boyle, a Scottish life prisoner of the 1960s. It shows how a violent prison setting could activate exactly the kind of paranoid–schizoid worldview of which Klein wrote:

> I decided that I would now live by my laws, not giving one fuck for society or the laws of society … [T]he media were labelling me 'Animal', 'Maniac' and lots of other names. From now on I would totally reject everything and everyone and label them the 'Dangerous Majority' and the 'Perpetuators of Fascism' … From now on the world could go to fuck. I hated everyone and distrusted everyone. They made it plain that they felt the same about me, so we all knew where we stood. (Boyle 2016: 177–78)

The idea that the penal system only encourages repetition of violation is given support by analysing how a fear and anger model directed at people who know only fear and anger works in practice. Jimmy Boyle's autobiography is analysed at length in Chapter 11 and though his reaction was dramatic and extreme, it brings out in its extremity the underlying persecutory logic of the modern prison system and where it leads.[16] Of course, not every punishment is like this nor is it even the case that every prison is. Yet insofar as the penal system holds onto the modern prison as its ultimate form of punishment, and political practice insists that ever harder punishments can address effectively the problem of crime, then persecutory action and reaction will be the repetitive and reductive outcome.

If these thoughts are uncomfortably relevant to a modern penal system, this is not to deny that more mature elements of restorative practice are present in it. Again, I will return in Chapter 11 to the issue of how modern prisons may operate through examining one remarkable effort to take penal experience in a different direction. I mention it here to balance the earlier comments and show how Klein's second position may also be relevant to analysing penal experience. Though something of a 'failed' experiment, the Special Unit run

[15] See text in Note 1.

[16] A similar memoir from the same prison experience is Collins 1997.

at Glasgow's Barlinnie prison (1973–1994) juxtaposed an overall persecutory environment (the prison as a whole) with one pocket of reparative practice (the Unit). The nurturing effect of the Special Unit was remarkable on prisoners who had become too violent (like Jimmy Boyle) for the system to contain. If the overall institutional setting of high-security prisons triggered a paranoid–schizoid cycle of violence, living in the Unit encouraged more mature responses. In this environment, creative human interactions led prisoners like Boyle to develop thoughtful and caring, indeed loving, relationships.

I will suggest later that the prison system can be seen as persecutory in the major key and restorative in the minor, or that these two strands are contained in a system governed by an overall 'structure in dominance' that is persecutory.[17] How we characterise punishment relates to the nature of the psychological experience in giving and receiving it. The suggestion one may take from Klein is that a punitive mechanism aimed to exchange pain for pain cannot be received productively by either those with underdeveloped moral psychological capacities or by those who are disposed to act more reparatively. Alternative ways of dealing with people who violate others, even in the heart of the penal system, might do better in promoting change in the direction of wholeness and atonement. But this raises an interesting question: if punishment is essentially retributive in its form, is it necessarily morally primitive in how it operates or is it capable of achieving outcomes which encourage mature moral reactions?

Towards Mature Retributivism

It is permanently fashionable to be sceptical of the claims of Freud and Klein about guilt, to believe that what they had to say depends on imaginative projections that are scientifically ungrounded. Indeed scepticism extends to the entire psychoanalytical enterprise, so it may seem unpromising to consider links between these accounts of guilt and the way that a society thinks about forms of penal practice. Yet, it is plain that modern punishment expresses forms of hostile affect which portray the offender as 'the other', an all-bad, evil, perpetrator who should be shunned and may be treated as a general enemy of humanity. As pointed out (note 1), a recent UK Home Secretary stated that she wanted criminals 'to literally feel terror at the thought of committing offences', a view that is consistent with her past support for capital punishment. And why not? If a person is only capable of repeat offending in the same very bad way, what else could one do but execute them?[18] These thoughts of terror and of the irredeemable offender might be cast in either Kleinian or Freudian terms, but whichever, it would be the primitive, persecutory form of guilt that

[17] On the idea of two keys present in the history of the western penal system, see also Norrie (2019b), discussing the work of Didier Fassin (2018).

[18] This is the logic behind arguments for the death sentence in the US state of Texas: Deambrogio 2023.

was reflected. It would be a person who is all-bad, who can only be restrained from base instincts by angry and fearful punishment, and who, when that runs out, can only be put to death.

Politicians come and go, and others take a more mature view, emphasising for example the need to support young people to stop them offending, to deal with the conditions of crime, to understand why ordinary people commit serious crimes, to identify with offenders. Different historical periods approach these questions with different mindsets. The underlying point is how different social and political viewpoints express different affective perspectives. The affect revealed in comments about fear and terror, and their ability to conjure a socially hostile solidarity, or the more welfare-oriented, holistic views expressed elsewhere replicate at the socio-political level the two approaches to guilt and punishment described by Klein and Freud (Norrie 2024). If some politicians, together with the sections of society they seek to represent, get caught up in persecutory fantasies, we have to eventually wonder why these are so compelling, and why they resonate in the human psyche. Every time someone feels either anger at, or compassion for, an offender, a question is raised about the psychological tripwires (persecutory *or* mature) that have been engaged. Political ideologies work because they have psychological traction, so the investigation of the grounds of human affect is important, as is how these become integrated into social practices like punishment.

Is Retributive Guilt Necessarily Primitive?

The views of politicians inevitably feed into their policies, so primitive or mature thinking around guilt will shape criminal law and criminal justice. For example, sentencing strategies are an obvious target. There is, however, a deeper question as to the law's internal connection to psychological approaches to guilt. How does law itself reflect these different emotions which are part of the public imagination? Is law simply a neutral form which may be more or less coloured by social, political and psychological emotion, or is it more directly implicated in primitive or mature kinds of affect?

My starting point is to note that law is a social form which proclaims itself ethically neutral as between different affective approaches. The claim to neutrality derives from the nature of legal responsibility. In law, we find an abstract and universal legal subject, a responsible individual enjoying freedom and identity with every other individual, homo juridicus, in modern political discourse (Norrie 2014). Such legal abstraction or formalism is attractive in that it suggests a formal equality within a political and legal system. It does however possess the structural tendency to hide, finesse or manage substantive social and economic differences between individuals which lurk behind the legal form. In this way, abstract legal form endorses substantive social and ethical positions, though it does so by appearing to say nothing about them.

Its substantive commitments are hidden by its formal appearance, and these are revealed only in situations of disruption. From this position, we could ask how abstract legal subjectivity operates in relation to the primitive, persecutory and the mature, restorative accounts of guilt we have examined here. I suggest that when it comes to justifying punishment in ethical terms, the legal form reflects primitive persecutory themes by virtue of its abstract character, but that the same abstract character indicates the possibility of its opening up towards mature, restorative approaches. When it does so, however, it begins to look like a rather different proposition.

Murphy's Law

The obvious place to examine this issue is the abstract theory of punishment known as retributivism, which grounds much that is done within the criminal justice system and here I find Jeffrie Murphy to be a helpful interlocutor. Murphy's work over forty plus years reflected an ambivalence about retributivism as the central ethical rationale for justifying punishment. Starting with a deep ambivalence to retributive theory and recognising its role in obscuring underlying issues of social inequality and exploitation (Murphy 1979), he became the defender of a theory of retributive hatred as a justified response to wrongdoing (Murphy and Hampton 1988). More recently, he argued for the need to balance claims to justice in punishment against compassion for a fellow human being (Murphy 2012). More specifically, he has argued we cannot know the depths of a person's character, and therefore cannot condemn that person as irretrievably bad, and that when we judge another, our own unpleasant resentments may come into play. Murphy's work describes a parabola that led him in mid-career to endorse a primitive, persecutory anger-based approach, while at its beginning and end, he was aware of the difficulties in so doing from a social and a mature moral psychological standpoint.

From Murphy's point of view is law in effect tied to a primitive and persecutory standpoint? His answer to this question is linked to his concern that punishment reflects a nastiness in human affect. He is fond of quoting Nietzsche's aphorism that in condemning others for their monstrosity, there is a danger that we become what we condemn.[19] There is a slippery psychological slope in condemnation that leads from the judging of a bad act to the judgement that the person is bad and then to move on to further persecutory condemnation. From a legal finding of guilt, we move easily to persecutory judgements like '"you have a vicious character" or "you have a hardened, abandoned, and malignant heart" or "you are evil and rotten to the core," and then on to "you are scum" and "you deserve whatever cruel indignity I choose to inflict on

[19] The nastiness is already in us and brought out by condemnation of others: 'Whoever fights monsters should see to it that in the process he does not become a monster' (Nietzsche 2000: 279).

you'" (Murphy 2012: 88–89). Is this, then, the hidden truth of legal or retributive punishment, that within it the high principles of just punishment disclose something nasty and persecutory?

While Murphy thinks this is a danger with punishment, he sees it not as an intrinsic feature of the practice but rather as something to be aware of and guarded against in punishing. The link between punishment and resentment is not 'a logical transition', but rather one that he fears 'is psychologically a rather common and in some ways compelling one, one that may tempt us to endorse cruelty and inhumanity' (Murphy 2012: 88–89). Such a slide would be to precisely the kind of persecutory account of blame described by Klein in terms of the guilt of the all-bad person, who is worthy only of hatred and destruction. The position Murphy takes is that the slide to persecution is not compelling to retributive, and therefore to legal, theory. Is he right to argue that it is caused only by unfortunate psychological side commitments, or is there an intrinsic connection between persecutory punishment and the form retributive theory takes?

An Historical and Structural Logic

Like Murphy, I do not think that the retributive form of legal punishment is in itself inextricably tied to persecutory punishment. The link is not 'logical'. Nonetheless there is a link that enables us to say that modern punishment is essentially of this kind and that legal and retributive theory supports it. There is a missing element in Murphy's thinking which is provided by the *historical and structural logic* that underpins modern legal form and links it to the play of a persecutory psychological mindset. Paradoxically, in an early essay, Murphy (1979) saw this. He pointed to the need to hold together a social and economic analysis of the conditions of crime and the retributive justification of punishment. In a world premised on social exploitation, violence is structural and the role of retributive law is *through its abstraction* to present a different image and practice, one premised on individual responsibility at a remove from the social forces which give what people do shape and meaning. This works well enough most of the time to legitimate punishment, while calling attention to it presses the need for radical social reform. Without that, the law's abstract individualist conception of justice, expressed through the retributive theory of punishment, aligns with the underlying structural violence, obscures the social explanation of that violence and constitutes a form of injustice.

How does this observation about retributive punishment's contested legitimacy relate to the question of how legal retributive punishment and persecutory practice are intrinsically linked? An answer to this question may be approached by thinking about the following problem. We have said, with the early Murphy, that the socially causative, structural conditions of crime have been obscured. If that is the case, what explanation may be given why a person did something that was very bad? Where the obvious social explanation has been embargoed, the only compelling alternative would be that there was something intrinsically wicked about that person that made her act in that way. The result of excluding a social explanation would be to think that the more appalling an act, the more we have to focus on this person and what was going on inside her. The more we go down this route, the more we are forced to Murphy's slippery slope from a bad act to a bad person, to a greater punishment and eventually to the death penalty.

Hence the attribution of individual wickedness and a persecutory logic of punishment may not be directly connected to legal retributivism's responsible subject, but in terms of a causal, functional, explanation, the linking of act to individual character is compelling if a social explanation has been excluded. Where else can one look? To condemn the act is logically not the same as condemning the actor, but the retributive attribution of responsibility for bad acts to individuals apart from their social context carries as its corollary the attribution of bad qualities to the actor. Hence, either a split, persecutory, sense of a person as all bad (early guilt in Klein), or a fear-based, punitive, view that violent natural instincts in an individual must be deterred (early guilt in Freud), or both, is invoked by the abstract subject of law as this is reflected *historically* in the responsible subject of retributive philosophy. Murphy's slide follows an historical logic under modern social conditions of structural inequality. Abstract legal form comes to entail an early account of guilt despite its seeming neutrality where a structurally violent setting is excluded. This is not logical in formal terms, but it is logical in a historical context.

Could Retributive Guilt Find Maturity?

If legal retributive philosophy is linked to primitive psychological guilt because of its historical and structural shaping, would it be possible to link it instead with mature guilt as described earlier? To answer this question, I return to Murphy's concerns about punishment. Alongside his worry that retributivism expresses hidden resentment against others, he argues that compassion for the perpetrator must recognise that he too is human, a view that Murphy links with an ethic of Christian love. He also argues that since we cannot access the deep moral character of another person, we cannot properly judge his inherent badness. This is a view Murphy takes from Kant, where it represents the compassionate underside of Kant's otherwise self-righteous stance on the justification of punishment (Murphy 2012: 41). Compassion for another and the limits of human knowledge both tell against the sort of problematic condemnation that comes with primitive persecutory judgement. The problem with both these objections is that while they react fairly to the persecutory impulse, they do not go far enough. Yes, we are all human beings, and yes, we cannot know or judge the inner workings of another's heart and mind, but these provide a caution against persecutory punishment, not an alternative to it. Eventually, Murphy will say that he reluctantly remains a retributivist, but this is having his cake and eating it.[20] Could we perhaps find another way forward premised on ideas of common humanity and our deep moral character?

The route missed by playing the antinomial game with Kant, setting compassion and human vulnerability off against categorical punitiveness, is the possibility that people who commit violative acts might be, or become, mature moral–psychological subjects capable of identification with another and wishing to atone through reconciliation. Such people could contemplate and grieve for what they have done and try to restore relations for their victims and themselves. Where compassion is simply paired with punishment, there is no conception yet of the potential for mature guilt as a psychic mechanism in actors who have done bad things. To think in these terms could lead to a different, mature retributivism in which the abstract rebalancing of right and wrong by a state and its law is replaced by a real, concrete, human form of restoration. Under classical retributivism, punishment acts as the rational restoration of the moral order that has been undermined by the crime. The abstract proportioning of punishment to crime through the *lex talionis* (Kant 1991: 155) or the exchange of equivalents (Hegel 2008: 96–108) reflects this rebalancing of the moral order. It is carried out by the state, directed at the criminal and presented as the criminal's own act returning to himself. None of this has to touch the actual moral experience of violation either for the perpetrator or the victim and so it easily becomes seen under modern social conditions as the vindicated allocation of a just amount of pain, without a further progressive outcome either for the criminal, the victim or society as a whole.

Could it be otherwise? Let us assume I am in the position of a perpetrator who has committed a violent and angry act against a victim. What morally could I do about it?[21] From the point of view of a moral and psychological working through, I need to accept that I have violated another who is, in the ways that matter, just like me. As I analyse what I did, I come to realise that my victim was a whole person worthy of dignity, and not the all-bad other I felt no need to respect in the heat of anger. I move in Klein's terms from a persecutory attitude to a troubled, depressive position and begin to think of how I might address my violation for myself, my victim and society at large. Alternatively,

[20] Murphy (2012: 42) unfairly disparages his own valid doubts when he describes them as leading to 'some sentimental orgy of love and self-doubt'.

[21] This is linked to the work of Nicola Lacey and Hanna Pickard on the possibility of a form of responsibility without blame, based on forgiveness, and against what they call affective blaming: Lacey and Pickard (2013, 2015); see Lacey (2024) for a helpful summary. It seems that ideas of mature blame, guilt and retributivism are in line with their project. Affective blaming looks similar to early, persecutory, blaming in my terms. The kind of responsibility Lacey and Pickard seek, with its close link to forgiveness, is connected to the acceptance of wrongdoing, from which forgiveness may flow (Lacey 2024: 5), and this is precisely what a mature guilty subject pushes towards. The idea of 'responsibility without blame' makes sense where it is primitive blame that is resisted, though I would say a form of mature personal and dialogic blame remains possible. I wonder if the terminology of 'punishment as forgiveness' is more problematic in that it seems to blend the primitive and the mature in a way that might prove contradictory (Lacey 2024).

in the Freud–Loewald reading, I come to realise that in violating another, I acted against my ego ideals which I had blocked unreflectively when I acted. I realise that in violating another who is human just like me, I placed myself at odds with my sense of the world in which I too could be whole. I want to cease feeling 'rotten' (Morris 1976: 99), again to be at one with myself: I want to atone (Morris 1976: 100; Loewald 1980: 393–94). This kind of mature making amends could represent the real foundation for a different kind of retributive theory, one in which past and future actions are combined in reflection of the mature, guilty, subject. That subject wishes to make amends for past acts and to make things better in the future for herself and the other.

Retributivism: What's in a Word?

Why should we call this moral–psychological desire to atone, meaning to take steps to be at one, a form of mature *retributivism*? I confess a degree of provocation here to existing theory but also see a perfectly valid argument. A link between *retributivism* as a modern secular philosophy of punishment and *retribution* as a visitation of harsh punishment to which the word 'divine' is easily added can be made but is not compelling. Kant's philosophy was a means of reworking Christian religion as rational thought. Recalling his concern to render modern and practical the Old Testament Lex Talionis ('an eye for an eye, a tooth for a tooth'), it is not surprising that divine retribution should be reformulated as retributivist philosophy and rooted in the responsibility of abstract rational subjects. I suggest however that Kant's move is not necessary and that the term should be retrieved from this narrow and inessential meaning. It may be pressed in the different direction of mature moral psychology stressing repair and atonement (at-one-ment). Essentialising the term around blame, punishment and just deserts does language an injustice. Didier Fassin recently pointed out that the Latin *retribuere*, which is linked in ancient Rome to 'dividing among tribes', came in the Middle Ages to bifurcate its meaning between a fair compensation for what work merits and an adequate punitive requital for God's wrath. The former points towards recompense and restitution, the latter punishment for wrongdoing (Fassin 2018: 47).

We can go further if we return to the original derivation. Originally, the Roman polity was organised around its tribes, starting with three and expanding to thirty five as the city grew. They were a means of organising politics and voting, taxation and the army, while belonging to a tribe was a requirement of citizenship (Momigliano and Cornell 2014). *Tributum* as tribute, a term derived from *tribus* (tribe), was eventually linked to conquest and taxing subject peoples across the empire, and was bitterly resented, but in Rome's earlier times, it was an extraordinary tax levied on the body of citizens which might later be repaid (Burton 2014). Similarly, the phrase *suum cuique tribuere*, which is found in both Cicero and Justinian, means to give to each his own and is a basic principle of ethical and legal justice. It reflects earlier Greek usage in Plato and

Aristotle (Gamper 2021: 13–15).[22] Of modern words in English which share the Latin root, most have a variety of positive or at least neutral connotations: to pay tribute, to contribute, distribute and attribute. It is only with 'retribution' and 'retributivism' that a specific meaning of being punitive has been seized on by Christian, enlightenment and Victorian philosophy from a variety of uses that might otherwise be associated with the original Latin 'giving back'. The much broader ethical *suum cuique tribuere* with its Greek as well as Latin references reflects much more ideas of individual wholeness, giving a person what she needs, or perhaps a distributive, restorative or reparative commitment. *Retribuere* could be readily associated with the phrase and its broader meaning and this is the domain of what I have called a mature retributivism.

If understood in this broader sense, retributivism also offers a direct challenge to what might otherwise seem the morally essential notion of just deserts, an uncontestable ethical datum which might be rejected, but which will still remain an essential part of the discourse. Retributivism does not have to be this way. A deeper form in line with a mature moral psychology of repair and wholeness is an equally valid use of the term, as well as one that is in substantive ethical terms deeper and better. Placed in the historical context of a modern state, where formal freedom and abstract equality hide social and economic inequality and structural violence, retributivism becomes aligned with a set of primitive and persecutory goals centred on punishment and the industrial or maximum-security prison. The wrongdoer's requital is with the rational law (Kant, Hegel) rather than with an actual human victim or one's own humanity (save to be an abstractly rational being). It is served by an allocation of punitive pain which abstractly matches the level of wrong in the crime. Retributivism as a genuine giving back at the human level is lost as the philosophy aligns with retribution in a punitive sense, whether categorical or divine. Mature retributivism thus offers and operates as an ERIC critique of its narrow punitive form.

From Mature Retributivism to Abolition

Looking forward, we can see here the ontological starting point for a critique of modern punishment that argues for its abolition. I took the argument of the two previous chapters for a moral psychology of guilt which could identify primitive and mature responses to violation and considered how in practice these could be related to the theory of punishment. I developed in particular the possibility of a mature retributive theory which could free it from the persecutory practices with which it is otherwise associated. I should note that I will say more about how law aligns with primitive or mature retributivism further (in Chapter 12). For the moment, however, I have made the case for a

[22] For example Plato in *Republic* (434 b and e): 'this doing one's own work ... is justice ... the having and doing of one's own would be accepted as justice' (Plato 1997: 1065).

mature retributivism that is consistent with the moral and psychological experience of grief at violation and how it might be repaired and atoned. That is, I have established how a naturalistic argument for a different kind of mature retributivism is possible based upon what it means to be a metaphysical animal capable of thought and love.

We should then however identify and address an impasse that is on one side social and political and on the other moral. At the start of this chapter, I indicated that a mature retributivism would consider whether it still remained a theory of punishment, or whether treating human beings according to their nature in moral psychological terms would suggest punishment's abolition. In moral terms, a mature mode of atonement is clearly within the natural powers of human beings as they are. This chapter, building on the two previous, develops a naturalistic metapsychology of guilt which confirms and grounds the metaphysical experience of violation and reconciliation explored in Chapters 2, 4 and 5. Socially and politically, however, there are strong reasons why the social and political setting of criminal justice in a world of structural violence and with its institutional form of the modern prison make it impossible for a mature approach to violation to be achieved. The present system is structurally weighted in favour of persecutory punishment by virtue of its social location in a class society, its top-down institutional organisation, and its primary setting of the prison. We can thus see both the human possibility of a mature retributive response to violation and diagnose the problem of the present social system as its inhibition.

This theoretical and practical impasse does not however defeat the moral psychology. Rather, it identifies a valid ethical ground from which to interrogate and criticise the institutional reality. It constitutes an ERIC critique. The practical conclusion to draw is that we should redirect our energies away from the prison and find other ways of dealing with violation. What this and the previous chapters in this part have done is to build an account of human being as involving metaphysical possibilities grounded in metapsychological qualities. These point to the human ability to deal with violation in mature ways based on identification and atonement (at-one-ment). While many questions remain unanswered, it is a start to distinguish different kinds of retributive theory, where a mature retributivism in line with naturalistic human being provides a different approach to the primitive forms we otherwise assume to be natural. Mature retributivism represents the positive naturalistic core to a position otherwise designated by a negative, that of abolition. It is abolition's rational theoretical ground regardless of any practical considerations.

Part IV

Three Case Studies

Denial, Mourning, Freedom and Reconciliation

Introduction to Part IV: Towards Abolition

The moral psychology of criminal justice suggests an understanding of the human being as a metaphysical animal that thinks and loves, at two levels. The first is that of an ethical being constituted by the capacity for metaphysical expression and reflection. The second involves metapsychological being, where embodied human nature grounds and enables such expression. The book so far has built this argument around guilt and forgiveness. A synthetic, two-level understanding of guilt was developed in Part III. The following chapters develop further the moral psychology to consider questions of denial, mourning and melancholia, freedom and reconciliation. They do so through three 'case studies' where the experience of violation for perpetrators and victims generates further moral-psychological concepts.

While the moral psychology of guilt is central to moving beyond violation, we must also understand denial as a moral-psychological phenomenon at two levels. Denial may be the ethical form which discloses an underlying metapsychology of what Freud called disavowal. In Chapter 9, I consider Stanley Cohen's investigation of these terms in his pathbreaking *States of Denial* (2001). Of note is Cohen's ambivalent support for a Freudian metapsychology of denial and I address his main concerns. I do so in order to address Joshua Oppenheimer's film *The Act of Killing* (2014), concerning guilt and denial among perpetrators of the Indonesian genocide (1965–66). These men are treated as celebrities in their homeland calling to mind Hannah Arendt's concept of the 'banality of evil' (Arendt 1964). Yet in such an unpromising situation, the film's ingenious (I would say quasi-psychoanalytic) method brings out feelings of guilt which are expressed both metaphysically and metapsychologically in a way that gives real meaning to the idea of 'transitional justice'.

In Chapter 10, I return to victims as they face their violation. In Chapters 4 and 5, we considered the moral metaphysics of forgiveness (both a 'giving to' and 'giving up'). In now exploring Freud's ideas of mourning and melancholia, we consider how, as with guilt, such a metaphysics is rooted in the metapsychology of violation. Here, the case study is of Patricio Guzmán's film, *Nostalgia for the Light* (2010), about the aftermath of the Pinochet dictatorship in Chile (1973–90). I focus on two women who seek to come to terms with the murder of family members by searching the desert for remains and a third who reflects on what she has lost by never knowing her 'disappeared' parents. Their moral thinking and engagement with the state express the need to come to terms with their experience in ethical and metaphysical terms. In a film that is itself an act of mourning, they address their loss and resist the state's melancholic conclusion that their searches are worthless. The struggle to retrieve their loved ones' remains and recover what was lost is both metaphysical and metapsychological.

Chapter 11 focuses on metaphysical questions of freedom and reconciliation and how these are grounded in metapsychological issues. The case study this time is different: not a film, but Jimmy Boyle's autobiographical *A Sense of Freedom* (2016). A Scottish life prisoner, Boyle describes a moral phenomenology (a metaphysics) of both freedom and reconciliation in his life, his time in mainstream prisons and his move to the Special Unit at Barlinnie prison, Glasgow. Based on principles for developing mature moral-psychological and democratic relations between prisoners and staff, the Unit enabled people like Boyle to change. The resulting metaphysics of violence and its transcendence Boyle describes is grounded in his own metapsychology, as a person capable of developing the ability to express love. This chapter reflects earlier discussions of freedom and reconciliation in the young Hegel, complex victimhood, atonement and punitive versus restorative approaches (Chapters 2, 3, 6–8). It leads our moral psychology to a latent or immanent abolitionist position, one that is 'deep' or 'tendential' in its nature. Boyle's book thus operates as an ethically real and institutionally critical (ERIC) account of the prison.

9

Denying Guilt and Taking Responsibility

On Joshua Oppenheimer's *The Act of Killing*

> Only psychoanalysis comes near to [denial's] elusive quality...
>
> Stanley Cohen (2001: 24)

> But I can feel it ... Or have I sinned? I did this to so many ... Is it all coming back to me?
>
> Anwar Congo, *The Act of Killing* (2012)

> How could vomiting be 'thinking'?
>
> Jonathan Lear (1990: 7)

In this chapter, I extend the discussion of guilt and responsibility to consider their relation to denial. It is one thing to establish that a person may experience mature guilt from which they come to see the need to take responsibility. It is another to acknowledge the difficulties in this process and to see how the road to moral development can be blocked. I argue that denial may be understood psychoanalytically in a way that is related to the mature guilt and responsibility developed in the last three chapters. The underlying issue in developing from guilt to taking responsibility involves the same kind of moral and psychological identification we traced from Herbert Morris to Hans Loewald. Lurking behind denial in a psychoanalytic frame is the thing denied and the human capacity to atone. This chapter analyses how this happens and reflects on a case study which shows it happening.

In the first two sections, I consider what is meant by denial in both its moral and psychological forms and how the latter may be developed and defended against criticism. Stan Cohen's *States of Denial* (2001) is a landmark account of the importance and difficulty of understanding denial in contexts of systematic violation such as genocide. For Cohen, moral and psychological denial are both real but not straightforward. They may involve a question of moral bad faith (*moral denial*) or a matter of psychoanalytic understanding (*psychological denial*). The interest in Cohen's account comes from its ambivalence regarding the latter. While he accepts psychological denial (see the first quote above) as something more than moral evasion, he remains deeply sceptical, questioning indeed whether it is plausible. Does the existence of unconscious motivation undermine personal responsibility? How could we know whether a person was involved genuinely in psychological denial or was simply dissembling? Is the psychological understanding of individuals important in comparison to the sociological determination of thought and action? Is it possible to think coherently about the relationship between what is consciously known and what is unconsciously denied? In the next section, I follow Cohen's development of a plausible account of psychological denial and then in the following section, sharpen it by exploring his ambivalent questioning.

In the third section, I draw on this refurbished understanding of psychological denial to consider a case study: Joshua Oppenheimer's stunning and perturbing film *The Act of Killing* (Oppenheimer 2012). I argue the film shows psychological denial in action and how it may be addressed even in the most unpromising of situations. *The Act of Killing* explores the mindset of a group of political gangsters and murderers during the 1965–66 genocide in Indonesia and in the early 2000s at the time of making the film. It reflects on how they deal with denial of what they did forty years ago. I consider three central characters in the film. Two of these men have been feted as national heroes and never challenged, yet their mental processes are organised around a suppressed guilt which they confront as they participate in the film. The film itself acts as a form of therapeutic practice. Invited to tell their story in their own very strange way, they come inadvertently to face what they did.

In this way, I argue that the film shows how psychological denial may begin to be addressed even in the most unpropitious of settings. Denial fractures as a central figure wonders about his guilt in metaphysical terms (second quote above) and eventually breaks down in a physically dramatic way. Dry vomiting becomes a way of expressing moral thought, a phenomenon that may be understood, and perhaps can only be understood, in metapsychological terms (third quote above). I argue that the film shows how psychological denial can be challenged in a dynamic psychoanalytical process. That *The Act of Killing* is a highly unusual kind of therapeutic process does not detract from its general significance in showing how guilt and its denial go deep even where it appears on the surface to be non-existent. I suggest finally that the film contributes a new and deeper meaning to the idea of 'transitional justice'.

The Nature of Denial: Disavowal and Splitting

Cohen describes denial as being both moral and psychological with the latter involving unconscious defence. In this section, I set out his account of the latter in terms of two linked concepts. The first is what Freud called 'disavowal', which is the unconscious disowning of an engagement with the world. The second concerns the form disavowal takes, and here Freud (and Cohen) speak of 'splitting'.

Moral and Psychological Denial

Denial of wrongdoing can mean that one denies one's act or denies it was for some reason wrong. This can take either a moral or psychological form.

The first is straightforward being close to everyday experience and witnessed frequently, for example, in the moral evasions of political discourse. It is convenient to deny wrongdoing to avoid blame or its consequences. A person makes a false statement or does a bad act and claims it was not him, or it was by mistake or accident, or that he did nothing wrong or even something right. Here, we are in the realm of lies, moral failure and bad faith. Such actions and claims are subject to scrutiny and can be criticised for their failings.

The second form of denial is more complex. It is where a person represses or denies wrongdoing through the functioning of unconscious psychological process. What someone did lies somehow below the level of consciousness, either in terms of 'the facts' or their moral significance. What happened is said not to have occurred or is understood in different, less challenging, terms, but the person is not consciously or deliberately lying. Because this experience borders that of moral failure or bad faith and can be interpreted in such terms, it may be seen as a way of avoiding them. Psychological denial as a phenomenon is therefore more contentious and likely to be challenged. Its plausibility may be questioned outright: 'you are lying! You know perfectly well what you did'. It may rather conveniently deny the idea of personal responsibility: 'even if I did such and such, I can't remember it, so how can you hold me responsible?' Moral and psychological denial may be distinguished and the latter may be seen as just a way of avoiding – denying – the former.

This is broadly the terrain pioneered by Freud and investigated in the early part of Cohen's *States of Denial*. We shall see that Cohen is both convinced by psychological denial, with only 'psychoanalysis com[ing] near to the elusive quality of the concept' (Cohen 2001: 24), and thoroughly wary of its implications. Two key ideas here are 'disavowal' and 'splitting'.

Disavowal

Freud's word for denial is 'disavowal' raising the question why he preferred this term. 'Denial' has perhaps more direct connotations as in 'I deny the validity of your statements' (Cohen 2001: 25). Another reason could be that disavowal is closely related to its converse, avowal, in a way that does not work with denial. A person who is engaged in psychological self-deception is ignoring an aspect or commitment he would otherwise be expected to own (avow) as part of his being. Cohen quotes Herbert Fingarette's view that there is here a self-deception in which 'the self-deceiver is one who is in some way engaged in the world but who disavows the engagement, who will not acknowledge it even to himself as his' (Fingarette 1969: 67; quoted in Cohen 2001: 39). A slightly fuller account of how disavowal leads to defensive tactics to maintain its terms is as follows: 'The self-deceiver is engaged in the world in some way, and yet he refuses to avow the engagement as his. Having disavowed the engagement, the self-deceiver is then forced into protective, defensive tactics to account for the inconsistencies in his engagement in the world as acknowledged by him' (Fingarette 2009: 213).[1]

Denial (disavowal) in this view might be seen as the performative refusal of what should be owned (avowed). Failure to own what one has done in this sense occurs when owning it would lead to 'intensely disruptive, distressing consequences [which are] unmanageably destructive to the person' (Cohen 2001: 217). Such a person is not in control of himself and may 'show signs of shame or intense guilt' while nonetheless outwardly disowning an action by not speaking of it as his and seeming sincere in his view. He 'accepts no responsibility' (Cohen 2001: 218) despite plainly showing at some underlying level signs of discomfort which bespeak affirmation of what he denies. Disavowal as failure to own involves a disconnection between what is shown in experience and expression and the existence of an underlying psychological state. It is this denial of an underlying owned (disavowed) connection that is understood as splitting (Cohen 2001: 224).

Splitting

Psychological denial for Freud involves the paradox of connection and disconnection, of 'knowing and not knowing', and this is splitting as how humans manage the 'need to be innocent of a troubling recognition' (Cohen 2001: 25).[2] Freud gave the example of a child who denies that a parent is dead while revealing in other ways that it knows this is the case. The child holds onto a belief necessary for its self-organisation while recognising in its actions the reality that denies it. Confronting the traumatic loss of the parent, the child's ego is disturbed and split by 'two contrary reactions to the conflict' (Freud 1984: 461). As noted, some may dismiss such ideas in other contexts as too convenient or as subterfuge, and Cohen will himself offer doubts that we examine in the next section. Nonetheless Cohen points out that it is not unusual for people to 'describe and explain … denial as being an unconscious defence mechanism. Uncomfortable truths are too threatening to "know", so they are unconsciously banished to some inaccessible zone of the mind' (Cohen 2001: 23).

It has become commonplace to say that someone is 'in denial' of something, and we recognise the grain of truth in the phrase. We understand in a lay way that this can happen. The human psyche must therefore be seen as 'complex enough to accommodate both denial as unconscious defence and self-deception as bad faith' (Cohen 2001: 41). We need a psychoanalytic conception to get close 'to the elusive concept' of unconscious denial whereby people handle knowledge that is 'too threatening to confront, but impossible to ignore', leading to the 'compromise solution … to deny and acknowledge them at the same time' (Cohen 2001: 27). Splitting is the mental process which keeps the dualities of knowing and not knowing (denying, disavowing) in place

[1] For a fuller elaboration, see Laplanche and Pontalis 1973: 118–21.
[2] Cohen quotes here from the psychoanalyst Christopher Bollas (1993: 167).

(Cohen 2001: 40–41). Yet Cohen is ambivalent. Accepting Freud, he nonetheless finds it astonishing that so disturbing an idea 'is so readily accepted.... How can it be? How can we deny the existence of a fact, yet simultaneously, apparently in another "part" of the mind, acknowledge that this fact does indeed exist?' (Cohen 2001: 28–29). How can it be that 'vital information is both registered and denied' (Cohen 2001: 32)?

How Can This Be?

Cohen's thoughtful answer to his own questions is that we need to avoid seeing the conscious and the unconscious in terms that maintain too much separation between them. On the one hand, we cannot think of the psyche operating as a kind of homunculus, a mind manager making decisions to direct mental traffic down one route or another while standing above the fray. That simply displaces the question of consciousness (and responsibility) to a deeper level in the psyche. On the other, we should not think of the unconscious as completely disconnected from the conscious. We need a more dynamic relationship between the two such that what is repressed is pushed below the line of consciousness, say by a traumatic event, yet able *still* to disturb or trouble the conscious mind. Think for example how dreams establish troubling connections between a person's day knowledge and those undercurrents which break through in wakeful sleep. Cohen notes that the psychoanalytic model allows

> a partial awareness ... of disturbing perceptions being banished to the zone of unawareness. After this initial awareness (which may be denied), the 'loss' of information over time is unconscious. This sequence sounds more plausible than invoking a mysterious inner barrier, its working impenetrable to conscious thought, that so effectively censors the information as to render it inaccessible...'. (Cohen 2001: 29–30)[3]

I think this is the way out of objections which rely on overstating the distinction between the conscious and the unconscious. It must be remembered that the relationship between the conscious and the unconscious is ongoing and interconnected, so that the unconscious is never completely disconnected from the conscious and 'loss' of information to the unconscious is never complete.[4] The two realms are dynamically interconnected and interactive, working together in a psyche which struggles for overall control.

3 c.f. Trunnell and Holt (1974: 771): 'Disavowal or denial as originally described by Freud involves, not an absence or distortion of actual perception, but rather a failure to fully appreciate the significance or implications of what is perceived.'

4 Cohen's formulation is perhaps not entirely clear. The unconscious, he says, is not impenetrable to conscious thought, but once an unconscious thought is up and running, information 'loss' is unconscious over time. This *may* suggest an unconscious mind that is ultimately (over time) impervious to conscious thought. There are two ways to develop an account of their ongoing interrelation. The first is through Freud's concept of the 'preconscious', which mediates the conscious–unconscious relation, and which tends to

If we put together disavowal and splitting, we construct a plausible account of psychological denial. It involves a splitting of mental activity into what is consciously maintained and what lurks unstably below the level of consciousness. There is a failure to own past and present thoughts and actions which remain sequestered in the unconscious part of mind. These may be traced back to events that are psychologically elemental and traumatic. What is held unconsciously in the psyche may disrupt otherwise smoother pattern of conscious thoughts in dreams or 'slips'. We have now followed Cohen's reconstruction of an argument for psychological denial while noting his reactive ambivalence to it. In the introduction, I noted that Cohen both makes an argument in favour of psychological denial and then submits it to a sceptical challenge in terms of its implications for thinking about guilt and responsibility for wrongdoing. It is to those challenges I turn now.

Three Challenges to Psychological Denial

In thinking about psychological denial, Cohen draws on the Freudian position, but his account is interlaced with sceptical discussion, identifying problems which, if accepted, would significantly undermine it. In this section, I identify three problems canvassed by Cohen.[5] These are, first, that the psychological account of denial threatens a basic understanding of human responsibility for action. Second, he raises the epistemological question of whether we are ever able to know if the Freudian psychological account is correct. The third objection is that the psychological model puts undue emphasis on the psyche and denies the importance of social and cultural aspects which are more important. Put together, these criticisms threaten to undermine the psychological model, even if Cohen's initial argument was in its defence. Let us consider them.

Is Human Responsibility Denied?

Cohen's concern rests on the relationship between the conscious and unconscious control of action. I begin by looking at his argument and then consider how it goes wrong.

'cluster in articulated structures of propositional thought' (Lear 2015: 219). This conception of the preconscious involves incomplete or inchoate ways of thinking that express the conflict between the conscious and the unconscious without being in a position to manage it. See further Loewald 1980: 169–70. The second is not to isolate unconscious and hidden thoughts and wishes from how other 'elemental forms of mental activity … dominate one's life' as a whole (Lear 2015: 53), holding in place and repeating problematic relations between the conscious and unconscious. Thus, the love of and need for the dead parent in Freud's example holds in place the split between knowing and not knowing the parent is dead. In *The Act of Killing*, discussed below, such 'elemental forms' exist as trauma and fear-induced repressions of extreme violation, which, buttressed by forms of social acceptance, govern how a person knows and does not know the past.

[5] The fourth, that we cannot coherently conceive of a relationship between the conscious and the unconscious, is discussed in the previous section.

Responsibility Depends on Conscious Control

For Cohen, the possibility of psychological disavowal raises the question of personal responsibility. How can we find any person responsible for what lies in their unconscious? One possible but ultimately unhelpful answer is that responsibility is always there, just hidden. Freud once noted that denying reality by splitting 'almost deserves to be described as artful' (Freud 1984: 464). Cohen suggests that this 'hints at some conscious intent in a process supposed to be unconscious' (Cohen 2001: 28). This is unlikely to have been Freud's meaning – his 'almost' more likely indicates a metaphor, an uncanny 'as if,' rather than an underlying psychological reality. Such a view would in any case take us back to the idea of a hidden mind manager, with whom responsibility ultimately resides. If we were to follow this line, the problem of non-responsibility would not really exist. The challenge to responsibility comes if there is no such directing part of the mind but rather a dynamic relationship between the conscious and unconscious. Where that exists, how can a sense of human responsibility be maintained? How can someone be responsible if 'the denying "portion" of yourself is entirely *unconscious* and split off from reality testing' (Cohen 2001: 30)?

It should first be noted that Cohen's question is not quite right because, as we saw, the dynamic relationship does not posit a complete split of conscious and unconscious, holding rather that the conscious and the unconscious are *not* entirely separate. Cohen's concern remains nonetheless valid for if the unconscious remains central to psychic experience, it means we 'go on thinking that we are doing something quite different from what we acknowledge' (Cohen 2001: 39). Psychological denial, then, *denies responsibility*, for we are 'not responsible for this evasion' (Cohen 2001: 39). Splitting thus involves a 'radical denial of responsibility' by attributing 'your action to another, autonomous part of the self' (Cohen 2001: 92), and this is a major problem for responsibility practices. Again, this is not quite right for the Freudian model does not presuppose that the unconscious is autonomous, only that it is not properly connected to the conscious psyche. Still, even on the idea of an interplay between conscious and unconscious agency, the master assumption is that the unconscious plays an irreducible part, and *it is that irreducible part* for which we are not responsible. Disavowal and splitting, it is true, leave traces of what is repressed, in dreams, memories or echoes of the past, but consciousness of this disconnect is not sneakily hiding in the background waiting to claim responsibility. Freud said that managing the relationship between what is known and unknown can *almost* be said to be artful, but this is not like the 'Artful Dodger', who did know what he was doing. Psychological denial in the Freudian manner does then appear to render responsibility hostage to the unconscious and the resulting lack of conscious control.

Taking Responsibility versus Holding Responsible

Cohen's account, however, is wrong insofar as it plays out with regard to responsibility. The reason is that to have unconscious knowledge is not to be irresponsible for it once we see that responsibility operates in a different way. Consider that Freud himself wrote that we are responsible for that staple element of our unconscious, our dreams. They are, he said, *our* dreams, part of *our* being, so who else, he asks, could be responsible for them?[6] Humans must take responsibility for them. Of course, the assertion does not explain why this is so given Freud's account of the unconscious. We can understand Freud's position if we see how he might configure the meaning of responsibility so that it is compatible with his psychological model. Here, Hans Loewald is helpful when he writes that personal responsibility stems from the possibility of personal agency linked to the nature of the superego. It will be recalled that we discussed the superego previously in relation to the idea that it represents an 'atonement structure' seeking to reconcile and make at one the different influences on the person (see Chapter 7). It does this because it takes responsibility for its unconscious impulses: 'Responsibility to oneself ... is the essence of superego as internal agency ... It involves appropriating or owning up to one's needs and impulses [even where] we appear to have been born with [them] or [they] seem to have taken shape in interaction with parents during infancy' (Loewald 1980: 392).

It is important to see that the psyche's responsibility for the unconscious is not based here on the presence or absence of a governing *conscious* process which if present establishes responsibility, if absent negates it. It operates rather in something like the following way. First, a person has to acknowledge that acts she committed but denies, disavows or sees as not a part of her, were nonetheless done by her, and because this is so, they are, like her dreams, a part of her. In that regard, she is responsible for them. Second, being responsible in a situation of denial, disavowal and so on means recognising that, where relevant, something subterranean was happening in her psyche, so that her thinking is or was divided (split). Third, her responsibility is then to come to understand how her actions are linked to the conscious and unconscious aspects of her mind. She has to come to terms with this as her overall psychological state, which she should address. Her responsibility, then, is dynamic, developmental and organisational: to start with being responsible for her thoughts and actions, and from there to work out how these became possibilities for her in an overall, holistic way. Conscious control of the unconscious is thus the end product of a process of self-analysis, which may or may not be possible, not the initial starting point from which all else flows.

Being responsible means taking on board the psychic conflict between one's conscious and unconscious processes, and not, pace Cohen, being responsible

[6] 'What else is one to do with them? Unless the content of the dream (rightly understood) is inspired by alien spirits, it is part of my own being. If I seek to classify the impulses that are present in me according to social standards into good and bad, I must assume responsibility for both sorts; and if, in defense, I say that what is unknown, unconscious and repressed in me is not my 'ego' then I shall not be basing my position on psychoanalysis, I shall not have accepted its conclusions.' (Freud 1925: 133)

only for those things that are known in one's consciousness. To think that is to revert to a non-psychological model of thought and action which ignores the complex psychological relation between the conscious and the unconscious in the mind. In Freud's account, the actor may still be held to account for what she did, meaning to acknowledge her acts (as with her dreams) *and* to address the psychological relation that led to them. This is 'taking responsibility', a psychological process involving dialogue with oneself and others to work through splits between one's conscious and unconscious being. It involves 'active engagement in an undertaking that takes time and involves real change' (Reeves, Norrie and Carvalho 2019: 396; Reeves 2022). Such an approach to responsibility is different from the static moment of being 'held responsible' by a legal or moral judge for one's conscious acts, which generates another, more superficial, understanding of being 'held to account' or culpable for what one did. Such a model underpins Cohen's objection. A person may not have been in conscious or rational control of past action but still not simply ignore the reality of the wrongs they have done (Reeves, Norrie and Carvalho 2019: 396). The focal point is not on whether a person was conscious but on bringing out the relationship between a psyche's conscious and unconscious elements, *both of which* are ownable and ought not to be disavowed.

If one sees that responsibility is not just about conscious control, but about working through the relationship between conscious and unconscious motivations, then Cohen's complaint can be nullified. The argument here is that where disavowal is psychologically real, appreciating this gives rise to a better way of dealing with perpetrators. Where straightforward moral or legal accusations are met with equally straightforward denials, a person may end up being punished while they continue to disavow their actions. Offending and punishment then become part of a repetitive cycle in which nothing is learned. Getting at disavowal as a conscious–unconscious reaction that is in principle capable of change through superego development is important to get moral accounting and responsibility going, rather than a way of avoiding it. That, I think, is one of the lessons of *The Act of Killing* (below), where we will see how splitting the present from the past, or the different sides of a personality, does not stop a perpetrator from taking responsibility. The question is how he might be able to come from a place of denial to avow what he has done.

How Can We Know Denial Is Psychological Rather than Moral?

This raises a second question for Cohen which is particularly significant where atrocities have been committed. If psychological denial is possible, how could we distinguish outcomes that are morally denied from those where trauma, repression and disavowal are involved? The analyst may be able to spot disavowal by observing symptoms, dreams and slips of the tongue, but the investigator into a past atrocity cannot know if a witness saw what they claim not to have seen (Cohen 2001: 28). There is 'no way to "show" any of this'. For the innocent, if I claim not to know and 'am told that I am deceiving myself or in denial, I have no convincing way to deny this' (Cohen 2001: 39). My denials are evidence of the depths of my denial. This is an important question in terms of distinguishing for example those who are complicit in violence from those who are themselves victims as bystanders. With a perpetrator like Adi Zulkadry in *The Act of Killing* (see below), it is hard to know whether he demonstrates only moral bad faith or something deeper.

The question of knowledge about psychological denial has echoed through the history of psychoanalysis, linking back to Sir Karl Popper's argument that psychoanalytic claims are unfalsifiable (Popper 1963). But, as Jonathan Lear (1998: ch 2) argues, and Cohen acknowledges, hidden motivations are a part of daily life, reading which we learn either to trust others or not to take them at face value. We all learn to judge if a person is straightforwardly lying or stating a belief we know to be wrong for undisclosed psychological reasons. It is no different in situations involving atrocities where judges and juries must find on facts: is this person lying or speaking from a conviction that has its roots in denial? Psychoanalysis develops a particular expertise in reading people and builds on this to posit mechanisms at play in the mind. Philosophies other than Popper's deal better with understanding the mind as a structure and how we explain this. Of course, such knowledge claims can be subject to error – and also abuse (Lear 1998: ch 2), but the Popperian criterion of falsifiability does not accommodate processes of deduction from apparent mental states to underlying structures of the mind which shape knowledge (Bhaskar 1979; Collier 1994; Norrie 2020). Difficulty of deduction and unfalsifiability are not the same thing.

The question then is whether a person is in a more simple moral sense denying or in a more complex psychological sense in denial. To answer it, one would look for evident manifestations in the form of dreams or slips, or particular signs that psychological disavowal rather than moral denial exists. Were witnesses to a massacre traumatised into not seeing, or did they see and conveniently 'forget' what they saw? Is the perpetrator simply rationalising his role or is he stuck, perhaps despite himself, in his rationalisation? Both moral bad faith and psychological disavowal are possible, and there will be borderline cases. This is to acknowledge difficulties in practice but draw the sting of the philosophical argument. A phrase here that covers both possibilities is 'turning a blind eye', which can apply to a moral case (think Nelson at Trafalgar), but also a psychological one (think Oedipus).[7] Yet to say that there are difficult and borderline cases

[7] Cohen discusses what Oedipus knew, or did not know, concerning his mother and wife, as he sought his father's killer. Space prohibits proper discussion of this intriguing subject, but Cohen suggests that 'turning a blind eye' conveys 'the right degree of ambiguity as to how conscious or unconscious the knowledge is' (Cohen 2001: 33), and how much Oedipus's ignorance about his mother was consciously or unconsciously motivated. He draws on John Steiner's (1993) work, which itself reveals an important ambivalence about Oedipus when one compares his different readings of what he did or did not know: contrast Steiner 1993 with Steiner 2020: ch 8. These two readings amply indicate the difficult borderline.

suggests that distinct and different cases falling into the two camps are possible. As we move to *The Act of Killing*, we will have reason to consider how we distinguish moral and psychological denial in these practical cases. With two of the three main characters, Anwar Congo and Suryono, it seems clear that we are in the realm of psychological denial, while in the third, it is unclear whether the perpetrator, Adi Zulkadry, is a man with or without psychological depth.

Psychological versus Sociological Determinants

The gist of the third question posed by Cohen concerns the relationship between social and psychological determinants of action. Surely, he suggests, perpetrators learn to kill by means of social scripts in social contexts which make their actions possible, and not by means of questionable psychological mechanisms like splitting and disavowal. Cohen challenges here Robert Jay Lifton's thesis that Nazi doctors dealt with the disjuncture between what they did and their roles as 'humane physician, husband, father' (Lifton 1986: 419) by splitting, and what Lifton extended to call 'doubling'. By this, he meant to include how the psychological organisation of a brutal self is kept apart from the humane self operating in other settings. A person in short splits in order to lead a double life.

For Cohen, this 'is not a convincing explanation of the Nazi doctors or similar perpetrators' (Cohen 2001: 92), for it is 'impossible that a doctor on weekend leave with his family could either be unaware of his actions during the week or assign these actions to another part of the self' (Cohen 2001: 93). What Cohen describes as the doctors' 'ideological autism' was, he argues, 'in harmony with the social reality of others' at the time, so that 'the subtleties of splitting are hardly needed to explain how these doctors deluded themselves into thinking that they were doing noble medical and scientific work' (Cohen 2001: 93). There were professional and ideological supports so that while not all doctors were true Nazis, they 'seemed to know what they were doing' even if they 'preferred' at the time or later 'not to see their behaviour as indicative of their "real" selves. Ordinary people do not become unreflective serial killers for years because of splitting and doubling' (Cohen 2001: 93). The language is 'too dramatic to convey the everyday forms of role distancing, compartmentalisation and segmentation by which people separate themselves from what they are doing…'. Such states 'result from publicly available, even clichéd cultural denials, such as "My job is not me"' (Cohen 2001: 93). Given widespread social and institutional motivations and supports for denial in 'late-modern cultures', people can act viciously according to normal social prompts.[8]

[8] A variant on this theme is provided by Slavoj Zizek (2013: 44–46) writing on *The Act of Killing*. He finds no crisis of conscience in the film, focusing instead on the power of global capitalism as the 'big other' to sustain the Indonesian death squads. He is right to point to this, but the issue should not be formulated as an 'either/or'.

The doubling thesis misidentifies this social possibility as a psychological one, and it has the dangerous consequence of suggesting a moral escape route into 'the unconscious' for doctors who really knew what they were doing.

For the reasons given above, I do not think psychological denial offers an escape route from accountability, only a better appreciation of what is needed to turn external blame into internal understanding and taking responsibility. I also think this overstates the way that social and cultural effects interact with individual psychological states. People do tend to compartmentalise, but they do not all become mass killers, and it is not clear that this is only for lack of opportunity or supportive social context. If we 'late moderns' *were* all potential mass killers, the question is still raised, how would we comfortably spend our weekends with our families or balance our commitments to care and health *without* splitting off our thoughts and actions. If we accept Cohen's phrase of 'ideological autism', we should note it is already a psychologically freighted term and ask how it *combines* strong social influence with psychic effects. Of course, Cohen's invocation of the sociological is entirely valid at its own level but his opposition of it to the psychological is overdrawn. Indeed, Cohen himself recognises this later in his book when he writes that denials 'invariably contain some elements of splitting, dissociation and distancing' and that these 'may be states of mind, but they are also indicators of wider cultural patterns' (Cohen 2001: 95). It seems more accurate to identify conjunctions at different levels in this way rather than in either/or terms. Certainly, when it comes to confronting people who are in denial (and whether it is moral or psychological) with what they did, it only makes sense to do so if we think that there is some dialogue and change to be had.

As argued in Chapter 3, we rightly assume that people are moral agents and not simply the product of sociological conditions. As we now leave Cohen's criticisms and follow through on his intuition that psychological denial is important, we come to our case study *The Act of Killing*. Here the relationship between the social and the psychological domains becomes important because the situation in Indonesia was one of consistent support for the role of the gangster and mass killer. The perpetrators there continued to have every social and political reason to think they had done the right thing, right up to the present. Yet this did not stop at least one of them, Anwar, the film's central character, from developing an awareness of his guilt, at the heart of which lurked his growing struggle with denial.

Challenging Denial in *The Act of Killing*

It is always challenging to make theoretical arguments as I have done above, but it is something else to show the relevance of the argument to actual experience. I have always wanted to link the two in this work, for example by exploring in Chapter 4 (and in earlier work: Norrie 2017c) the connection between Karl Jaspers and Primo Levi. Central to my motivation in how this book develops is both the practical and metaphysical experience of forgiveness in *The Forgiveness Project* (Chapters 4 and 5). Atonement (at-one-ment) in Chapters 6 and 7 is both morally practical and psychoanalytically grounded. My argument in this section is that the experience of violation of the main actors in *The Act of Killing* is explicable in terms of a sense of psychological denial, disavowal and splitting, so that the discussion of Cohen and Freud above has theoretical significance for the practical experience of the case study.

On *The Act of Killing*

The director Joshua Oppenheimer has made two films about the Indonesian genocide, *The Act of Killing* (2012) and *The Look of Silence* (2014). The accompanying text for both films states that they 'investigate the long shadow cast by Indonesia's 1965–66 genocide' but that 'neither is an historical documentary'. They explore 'what happens when perpetrators of genocide win, and build a society based on fear and violence' (Oppenheimer 2014). *The Look of Silence* concerns a young man seeking the murderers of his family and is in a more recognisable documentary style. *The Act of Killing* is more unconventional, exposing 'the consequences for all of us when we build our everyday reality on terror and lies'. It stretches boundaries, and 'may not be a documentary at all, but something altogether new: a non-fiction fever dream about escapism, fantasy – and guilt' (Oppenheimer 2014). These elements indicate something of its psychoanalytic quality.[9] The text describes the film's strangeness, whereby genocide perpetrators are given licence 'to be stars in their favourite film genres – gangster, western, musical. They write the scripts. They play themselves. And they play their victims. *The Act of Killing* is a nightmarish vision – a journey into the memories and imaginations of the unrepentant perpetrators and the shockingly banal regime of corruption and impunity they inhabit' (Oppenheimer 2014).

The viewer's initial disgust at the nature of this vision and its sense of indulgence to mass murderers gives way to appreciation of what the film can tell us about these perpetrators of cruelty. Reference to a 'banal regime' links the film to Arendt's 'banality of evil' (Arendt 1964), and one wonders if a world in which the Nazis had won would look similar. There is however an underlying current of unease in the film, and this increases as it progresses towards

[9] The film has attracted attention in film studies (Film Quarterly 2013; Meneghetti 2016); in memory studies (Dragojlovic 2018); in human rights (Kennedy 2016); critical Asian Studies (CAS Roundtable 2014). Nicole Rafter (2014) views it as an exercise in film as public criminology.

its dramatic conclusion. These men are not brought to account for their past actions by a film process that accuses and holds them responsible. Rather they may come through their play-acting to see for themselves what they have done. This is a kind of film-based psychodynamic process which brings them towards their guilt and to take responsibility as the film encourages them to address their past.

There are many actors in *The Act of Killing* who participated in the 1965–66 genocide. I focus on three: Anwar Congo, the film's central character; Adi Zulkadry, his co-killer; and Suryono, who as a young boy was a victim of the events, but who in the film has identified himself with the perpetrators. We cannot be sure why. We witness how these three actors react to their past psychological experience. Their emotional reactions reflect what it means to take responsibility in the sense discussed above. Without doubt, it depends and is shaped by the social settings in which they operate, but how they react is nonetheless related to their individual psychological standpoint. How do we know that their reactions engage deep psychological meaning in their lives which they would otherwise deny and not simple moral dissembling? In one case, I think we cannot be sure, while in the other two, it is their loss of emotional control shown in bodily reactions that suggests this is the case. Denial and its overcoming are seen to be not just a matter of moral bad faith, but rather are linked to how they process the past and the unconscious comes to consciousness.

As we discussed in the last three chapters, the ground state for guilt and responsibility is the possibility of moral and psychological identification with others. With Anwar and Adi, it is identification with their dead victims; with Suryono, it is identification with his murdered stepfather and what happened to him and his family. These are complex stories of individual identification and dynamic psychological development. With Anwar, we witness a developing capacity to experience guilt and an eventual taking of responsibility where previously there had been disavowal and splitting. With Adi, the psychological split permitted by disavowal between the emotional reality of the past and the normalisation of the present is retained, albeit shakily. Guilt may in the end be experienced, but he brushes it off. Alternatively, his position may thought to be a more simple case of moral denial, the ambiguous line between the two being brought out in his case. Suryono as a past victim is in a different situation though the underlying psychological process is similar. He reconnects to his own past victimhood which he has seemingly managed to 'forget'. His present links (and identification) with perpetrators force his past disowned experience back into consciousness. In all three cases, the importance of the social setting in supporting perpetrators remains crucial, as Cohen would expect, but the film shows how even in a thoroughly supportive setting for denial, psychological development of the unconscious is possible.

Anwar's Guilt and Responsibility

Anwar is the perpetrator who finally identifies with his victims through entering enthusiastically into making the film. On the surface, he is reflecting nostalgically on his glorious youth, but he is retelling a story in which he will revisit his past and assume film roles as killer, torturer and victim. Some scenes reenact historical events like burning a village, others are imaginative dramatic accounts of nightmares in which victims return as ghosts or severed heads that haunt him. Other scenes are bizarre fantasies involving dressing up in 1960s Hollywood film gear and more besides. These are interspersed with footage of the actors speaking among themselves and to the film director. In the process, Anwar's engagement with the past leads him to identify with what it would have meant to be a victim, though this is mixed up in his head with celebration of his achievements as a feted killer. His daily life is supported by the respect, fear and celebration of his community as the killer of communists. At mass rallies for Pancasila Youth, a paramilitary organisation, he is a guest of honour. He is admired by local and national politicians and becomes the star on a television chat show where the female presenter lauds him for inventing a way of killing communists 'efficiently'.

A scene of appalling fantasy brings out a delusional mentality: before a waterfall, with young women swaying to the film song 'Born Free', Anwar's ghostly dead victims thank him and place a medal around his neck. All this he takes as his due. At points, we see the cold killer: speaking of Chinese shopkeepers whom he used to extort, he explains matter-of-factly that if they gave money they didn't get killed, otherwise they did. 'They couldn't have it both ways'. Hearing the call to prayer of an Imam who had been a political opponent, he comments: 'Lucky he didn't fall into my hands or he'd be dead'. Yet Anwar teaches compassion to his grandson for injuring a duckling: 'Sweet little duck. Don't! You'll hurt her again. She's weak because you broke her leg … She's a baby. Say I'm sorry, duck'. Having played a torture victim in a graphic scene, he calls his grandsons to see the rushes of 'grandpa being tortured', placing an affectionate arm around them as the film starts. Anwar is a character in whom split and disavowal are revealed and start to unravel in five central scenes.

'Killing Happily'

Early in the film, Anwar takes Joshua Oppenheimer (JO), the film's director, to a first-floor room above a shop where he murdered people.

> There's many ghosts here, because many people were killed here. Unnatural deaths…. At first we beat them to death … but there was too much blood … so when we cleaned it up it smelled awful. To avoid the blood, I used this system. Can I show you? … See this pole? I'd tie wire to the pole. [*Demonstrates how people were strangled using the wire; looks into the camera with open smile*]. This is how to do it without too much blood.

Anwar is happy to recall his past yet is haunted by it. He has

> tried hard to forget all this with good music ... dancing ... feeling happy ... a little alcohol ... marijuana ... ecstasy. Once I'd get drunk, I'd fly and feel happy. Cha cha. [*Mimes dance steps, smiles and laughs happily*].

This 'happy' persona returns Anwar to what the killing life was like:

> When we'd watch happy movies, like Elvis movies – we'd leave the cinema smiling, dancing to the music ... Still dancing ... still in the mood of the film ... If girls passed, we'd whistle. We loved it. We didn't care what people thought. Here was the paramilitary office where I always killed people. I'd see the guy being interrogated.... I'd give him a cigarette. I'd still be dancing, laughing ... It was like we were killing ... happily.

And yet, he is deeply uneasy about this: 'I know my bad dreams come from what I did ... killing people who didn't want to die. I forced them to die'.

The Eyes of a Victim

The weight of the past is seen in his recollection of a murder that haunts his dreams, and a connection seared on his mind:

> I remember I said 'get out of the car'... I kicked him as hard as I could in the stomach. I saw Roshiman bringing me a machete. Spontaneously, I walked over to him and cut his head off ... And I heard this sound [*mimes a choking sound*]. His body had fallen down. And the eyes in his head were still open [*mimes open, mimes body shuddering, legs jerking and heaving*]. On the way home, I kept thinking, why didn't I close his eyes? And that is the source of all my nightmares. I'm always gazed at by those eyes I didn't close. That's what always disturbs me so very much.

Burning a Village

In this scene, the former perpetrators recreate the burning of a village and the murder of its inhabitants. Many enlisted to act, especially the young and women, look traumatised. Anwar is seen standing back, looking disengaged and awkward. The horror of what he has seen depicted has crossed a line in his mind:

> What I regret ... honestly, I never expected it would look this awful. My friends kept telling me to act more sadistic – but then I saw the women and children. Imagine those children's future. They've been tortured. Now their homes will be burned down ... What future do they have? They will curse us for the rest of their lives. This was so very, very, very ... [*sentence breaks off, Anwar looks distressed*].

Anwar Plays the Part of a Torture Victim

This scene depicts Anwar being tortured in a film noir setting. As it progresses, he appears more upset by what is being 'done' to him. The filming is suspended while he is offered a drink. It is this scene he invites his grandchildren to watch ('Come and see grandpa being tortured'), and after the playback, he discusses what happened with JO:

> Did the people I tortured feel the way I do here? I can feel what the people I tortured felt. Because here my dignity has been destroyed … and then fear comes right there and then. All the terror suddenly possessed my body. It surrounded me and possessed me.
>
> (JO): Actually, the people you tortured felt far worse because you know it's only a film. They knew they were being killed.
>
> [*Anwar looks bewildered, incredulous, pained*] But I can feel it Josh. Really, I feel it. Or have I sinned? I did this to so many people, Josh. [*He starts choking emotionally*] Is it all coming back to me? I really hope it won't Josh. I don't want it to Josh.

Remorse as Vomiting

At the end of the film, Anwar returns to the killing room above the shop. Now there is no smiling, dancing or pride at showing a new killing method. While he talks of being required to kill, his visceral response belies his words:

> This is where we tortured and killed … I know it was wrong but I had to do it. [*He bends over, makes a deep vomiting noise from the depth of his bowels, but nothing comes up*]. Why did I have to kill them. I had to kill. My conscience told me they had to be killed. This is one of the easiest ways to take a human life. And this was used to take away the human beings we killed. Because without this maybe people would know. [*He vomits deeply again*].

Adi's Resistance

Adi appears later in the film, flying in to meet with his former co-killer Anwar. Adi has created a geographical distance from the past and not responded to Anwar's phone calls. He descends from the plane wearing a tee shirt with the word 'apathetic' on it. He is hard to read, with a mild face and a relaxed manner. He does not engage fully with the film, arriving late and leaving early. He is accompanied by his wife and daughter and spends time looking bored in shopping malls. What kind of distance has he established from the past? In an initial scene, he challenges the other gangsters' view that they were in the right. 'It's easy to make the communists look bad after we destroyed them', but 'the communists were not more cruel than us. We were the cruel ones!' One is tempted to think that Adi will have a more detached and critical view, but that would be to ignore the tee shirt. Four scenes depict his attitude.

'It's How You Think about It'

Talking with Anwar, Adi considers how wrongs done in the past might be addressed. He sees the need for political acknowledgement:

> Sometimes I think … if my dad was a communist and was killed – I'd be upset. That's normal right? … There's been no official apology – but what's so hard about apologising? The government would apologise, not us. It would be like medicine. It would reduce the pain.

At a personal level, however, he suggests what is necessary is better management of the self. Anwar 'feels haunted because your mind is weak'; he suggests he go to a psychiatrist for medication since his nightmares are 'just a nerve disturbance'.

Killing His Girlfriend's Dad

With Adi, everything seems intelligible, reasoned and controlled. Yet an underlying, disconnected cruelty shows when he reminisces fondly about a past girlfriend's father:

> Remember the 'Crush the Chinese Campaign' in 1966? All along Sudirman Street, I killed every Chinese person I met. I stabbed them! I don't remember how many, but it was dozens. If I met them I stabbed them. All the way to Aria Street, when I met my girlfriend's dad … 'Crush the Chinese' became 'Crush my Girlfriend's Dad!' (*Adi laughs*). So I stabbed him too! Because he was Chinese! He fell into a ditch. I hit him with a brick. He sank.

Managing the Film's Impact

In the scene that will eventually lead to Suryono's torture (below), Adi returns to the need to be in control: 'Killing is the worst crime you can do. So the key is to find a way not to feel guilty. It's all about finding the right excuse.… That's the perspective we must make ourselves believe'. After Suryono's torture, Adi addresses the film's political dangers:

> Listen, if we succeed in making this film it will disprove all the propaganda about the communists being cruel … We were the cruel ones … It's not about fear. It's 40 years ago … so any criminal case has expired … It's about image. The whole society will say: we always suspected it. They lied about the communists being cruel … It's not a problem for us. It's a problem for history … If we succeed with this scene … the consequence is that everything Anwar and I have always said is false … I'm absolutely aware that we were cruel. That's all I have to say.

After this scene, Adi left the project.

'Start with the First Murder'

Adi is with Oppenheimer in a car to the airport, and some polite but challenging questions produce a less controlled response. Adi explains that what he had done was in a war and Oppenheimer points out that the Geneva Convention establishes war crimes. Adi responds that he doesn't 'necessarily agree with … international laws' that are the product of politics and shifting times:

> When Bush was a power Guantanamo was right. Saddam Hussein had weapons of mass destruction. That was right according to Bush, but now it's wrong. The Geneva Convention may be today's morality but tomorrow we'll have the Jakarta Conventions and dump the Geneva Conventions.

His explanation then takes a more personal and defensive note:

> 'War crimes' are defined by the winners. I'm a winner. So I can make my own definitions.... And more important, not everything true is good. Some truths are not good. Like re-opening this case.

Oppenheimer suggests it is good for the truth to come out for millions of victims' families, to which Adi's response becomes angry and grandiose:

> Fine, but start with the first murder, Cain and Abel. Why focus on killing communists. Americans killed Indians. Has anybody been punished for that? ... for me reopening this case is a provocation to fight. I'm ready. If the world wants continuous war, I'm ready ... I'd go [to the Hague]. I don't feel guilty, so why would I go? Because I'd be famous. I'm ready! (*Laughs angrily*) Please, get me called to the Hague.

Finally, it seems that a nerve has been struck, but his airplane awaits.

Suryono's Grief and Betrayal

Anwar's neighbour Suryono has become involved in a scene in which someone will be tortured and killed. Anwar is there with Adi and other younger members of Pancasila youth. In a friendly conversation prior to shooting the scene, Suryono suggests he tell a story of the past. He is open, affable, respectful, smiling broadly and with humility, seemingly very pleased to be involved. Yet his story is of his stepfather's murder and how as a child he became a victim of people like Anwar. The scene makes for uncanny, Pinteresque drama that as fiction would risk seeming unrealistic. There are two parts, one in which Suryono tells his story, and a follow-up scene in which Suryono plays the victim in a torture scene. It is unclear why he got this role, but it seems the story-telling was poorly received.

A Story Doesn't Go Down Well

The scene starts in a promising and well-established dramatic way:

	But if you want a true story I have one.
(ANOTHER):	Tell us because everything in this film should be true.

Suryono quickly admits it is his story:

> There was a shopkeeper. He was the only Chinese person in this area. To be honest, he was my stepfather. But although he was my stepfather, I lived with him since I was a baby' [*Anwar looks interested: where is this going?*]. At 3am someone knocked on our door. They called my dad. Mum said, 'it's dangerous,

> don't go out!' But he went out. [*Anwar smiles at Suryono in an encouraging way; Suryono speaks like he is telling an amusing tale*]. We heard him shout 'Help!' then silence. They took him away. We couldn't sleep until morning.

(ANOTHER): How old were you?

> 11 or 12 [*Anwar looks serious and alert*]. I remember it well. It's impossible to forget [*laughs*]! We found his body under an oil drum. The drum was cut in half and the body was under it. His head and feet were covered by sacks but one foot poked out like this. That same morning, nobody dared help us [*Anwar smiles watchfully*]. We buried him like a goat next to the main road [*Anwar smiles and nods*]. Just me and my grandfather, carrying the body, digging the grave … No one helped us. I was so small. Then all the communist families were exiled [*Suryono laughs broadly, gestures largely like it was all a crazy time*]. We were dumped in a shanty town at the edge of the jungle. That's why, to be honest, I've never been to school. [*He laughs again*]. I had to teach myself to read and write [*Anwar laughs with Suryono*].

The story has been told as a blackly humorous tale. From a desire to be one of the group, Suryono has both bared his soul and betrayed his family experience. He is too far inside his tale to withdraw, though he realises it has not gone down well:

> Why should I hide this from you? We should get to know each other, right [*smiles at others*]? I promise I'm not criticising what we're doing [*Anwar looks distant and appraising*]. It's only input for the film. I promise I'm not criticising you.

But the others now take their distance, and the story is shelved:

(ANOTHER): [*cool and dismissive*] Look everything has already been planned.
(ANOTHER): We can't include everything….
(ANWAR): And your story is too complicated. It would take days to shoot. Maybe we can work it in….

Suryono Plays the Part of a Torture Victim

After his revelations, Suryono plays the blindfolded torture victim. His torturers seem now to identify him as an enemy who should be submitted to a hyper-realistic depiction of torture in which he might really believe he is to be killed. Given the situation, why should Suryono, and indeed the film's audience, not believe this possible? Anwar and Adi take a backseat, dispassionate experts on torture and death:

(ADI): Give him water and a cigarette. He's scared.
(ANOTHER): We believe this man's a communist.
(ADI ASIDE): I tried to make them accept they were going to die.
(ANOTHER): Anwar, show us how to torture him.
(ANOTHER): It's ok if he really dies.
(ANOTHER): It's ok, we'll kill him for real.

(Anwar):	He can't see the wire. All of a sudden he's being strangled. [*Suryono looks increasingly distressed as he's pushed and forced to drink water*].
(Another):	Drink! Just drink! [*Takes cup and pours water over Suryono's head*]
(Adi):	Let him smoke.
(Anwar	[*a moment of realisation*]): It's sadistic Adi.
(Suryono):	Have mercy on me [*weeps copiously*]. Please sir. [*Mucus and tears stream from his face*].
(Another):	Should we kill him?
(Suryono):	Wait. Would you give a message to my family?
(Another):	Sure.
(Suryono):	Or could I speak to them one last time?
(Another):	No way.
(Adi):	He's dead. Take him away.

Later, Adi says 'this film will show we were the cruel ones', and Anwar repeats, as if it has just dawned on him, 'We're the cruel ones'. Suryono looks on, crumpled, withdrawn, destroyed. Adi then explains that 'It's not a problem for us, it's a problem for history. Not everything true should be made public'. Suryono's face is caught in an agonised, tear-stained, crumpled, grimace. He has relived his and his family's victimhood, betrayed that experience to perpetrators and been re-victimised for his trouble.

The Nature of Denial

Having identified the three main protagonists in *The Act of Killing*, I now consider how their conduct may be understood in terms of the two forms of denial, moral and psychological, identified in the first two sections. Psychological denial involves disavowal and splitting, whereby a person both knows (owns, avows) and does not know (denies, disavows) things too threatening to confront, but impossible to ignore. These are banished to an unconscious zone beyond the mind's cognitive or rational control. Splitting entails living at two levels where things are denied either in terms of their existence or their import, but the resulting lack of integration between the conscious and unconscious levels of the psyche threatens to undermine the person. This is disavowal, a failure to own what is one's to own, requiring defences which may break down with disruptive effects on the psyche. In terms of Cohen's three objections to Freud, this psychological process is, first, compatible with psychological responsibility for things banished to the unconscious, though this involves a more complex route of discovery than if a person was simply denying responsibility morally by lying. Second, establishing whether we are in the presence of psychological denial involves attending to speech and conduct and whether it manifests slips, absurdity, contradiction, obvious defensiveness or acute disruption when challenged. Third, it works alongside, but is not reducible to, social processes which may support it.

In Anwar's case, there are many signs of psychological disavowal. There is real disconnection to the moral weight of past acts. The split is between seeing multiple killing as logistical achievement and its underlying reality as murder in the form of blood, staring dead eyes, severed heads and ghosts. Lifton's idea of doubling where a person functions to a degree of competence such that one self is bracketed off from another looks relevant. With Anwar, the callous killer eventually clashes with the kindly grandfather, blithely disconnected from what is obvious to the viewer. This is the man who can call his grandchildren to 'see grandpa being tortured'. The burning village, torturing Suryono and playing the torture victim build up the conflict between the unconscious and the conscious self. What disrupts the split is the understanding finally that these were people like him with whose suffering he can finally identify. In the final scenes, the extreme disruption the film brings about as Anwar re-enters and comes to own his past forces a visceral reaction. The psychosomatic loss of control vindicates the film's method by signalling its ability to challenge disavowal. It offers a route not only to uncovering guilt but also to taking responsibility.

In contrast, is Adi's seemingly measured psychological control for real? When Oppenheimer corners him in the airport car, perhaps he was just in a bad mood or tired rather than inherently defensive and angry. His cynical view of the selectivity of the International Criminal Court would not be without its supporters, but his is the typical perpetrator's rationalisation and it is delivered with heat. Perhaps Adi is simply one who rationalises cynically and coolly, a man comfortable and uncaring in his skin, as his tee shirt reveals. His role in the film as one accepting his moral bad faith may be to give the contrast between moral and psychological denial. But Adi is also the man whose psychological state permits him to recount with warmth and humour how he murdered his girlfriend's father. He is the one who becomes angry and grandiose when finally challenged. What begins as a superficially rational but cynical critique of the laws of war descends into self-depiction as a superhero criminal ready to take on the world. Anger is perhaps the defence mechanism that keeps disavowal in place until he can jet off somewhere that doesn't include the past. Adi sits on Cohen's difficult borderline between moral and psychological denial.

Suryono's pathos is the film's most disturbing moment. Burying his murdered stepfather and everything that followed has become the subject of humorous anecdote. We see a man who has also buried past violation in a psychological sense and sought to identify with the violators. He has betrayed his family past even as he is forced to relive it in a repeated experience of victimhood. That this humble, unctuous man should choose to step back into the lion's den to become again the victim, but now also the betrayer, is a harsh and disruptive collision with a disavowed past. What psychological motives led him to seek this encounter, what did he hope to achieve and what instigated his reinvolvement? His identification with them comes at the cost of reliving murder, exile, poverty, fear and lack of education. This disconnection cannot be the product of simple moral bad faith. As with Anwar's gut-retching, the experience of psychological disavowal forced into the open is quite literally embodied in Suryono's physical undoing, the streams of mucus and tears, the crushed and depleted face. For both him, the victim and Anwar, the perpetrator, the most telling evidence of psychological denial is the psychosomatic experience in which the conscious mind is so emotionally destabilised that it loses bodily control.

The Act of Killing as Moral–Psychological Engagement

In this final section, I consider how a psychological reality of disavowal and split such as in *The Act* of *Killing* was successfully confronted. I suggest that the film succeeds not just because of its dramatic qualities but also because it works as a kind of psychoanalytical engagement, confronting denial and exposing guilt and responsibility among its *dramatis personae.*

The Film as Psychoanalysis

The aim of psychoanalysis is to assist someone to come to terms with things in their past and held as unconscious and troubling motivations in their present. It helps resolve past conflicts by allowing someone to take responsibility for them and address how they live now. Psychological denial is a deep-seated mechanism whereby a person disowns (disavows) acts by splitting the past from the present. It is a position defended against the past that may be disturbed by bringing denial and reality together, as happens for the actors in the film. But psychoanalysis does not operate by means of direct confrontation in which an analyst tells a patient what is wrong and then expects the patient to sort things out. The psychoanalyst seeks rather to get inside the patient's psyche and become part of her internal mindset. A well-defended psyche will dismiss external direction as so much noise, so the analyst must seek to participate in the analysand's world with its intimate and 'peculiar meanings' (Lear 1998: 71). The analyst thereby both 'lend[s] it substance' (Lear 1998: 71) and retains a critical distance. This works through a process of 'transference', whereby a patient projects their meanings onto the analyst and so includes her as an extension of his mental world.

Lear gives the example of someone who sees the analyst as a mother figure, permitting the analyst to talk to him like a mother. In this way, the analyst comes to occupy a position conforming to the inner meanings of his psyche and can then no longer be dismissed as an outsider. Yet, it turns out that this mother figure does not entirely conform to expectation. She speaks differently: 'Mother', as Lear puts it, 'has somehow changed her tune' (Lear 1998: 74).[10] In

[10] 'It is as though the analysand is trying to bring together an experience of recognition – Mama, it's you! – with an experience of irredeemable strangeness – Mama, what has come over you?' (Lear 1999: 75)

this way, the analyst puts together an insider's understanding of what a particular aspect of the psyche looks like with an outsider's appreciation of how it works as a complex and conflicted whole. The analyst is both inside and outside the analysand's defences: 'At every stage, in every role, the analyst is trying to import self-conscious understanding into the heart of a world which must, for its survival, remain opaque to itself. However, the basic means of preserving opacity is no longer available. The analyst is no longer outside the world, making comments on it' (Lear 1998: 75).

I suggest *The Act of Killing* works like this. It has nothing of the investigatory and accusatory quality of a typical documentary investigating genocide. It does not seek to accuse, confront or punish perpetrators, save insofar as *they* conclude they might have things to address. It enables them to face a buried feeling and so becomes for them a 'holding environment'. 'Thought and feeling [become] "delayed action", that is, activity that lingers … instead of being a short circuit' (Loewald 1980: 391). The film supports and engages the perpetrators' mindsets by engaging with their ongoing self-understanding, their film fantasies and their imagined rectitude while administering a dose of reality in which internalised values and external truths clash. Oppenheimer is not Anwar's 'mother' but he is his empathetic film-making friend, the willing listener to his experience, the seemingly indulgent recorder of his creative imagination. At the same time, he is the one who points out the inconvenient truths: that Anwar's victims were really going to die, that Adi's acts were war crimes. When Anwar returns to the torture place and his stomach heaves, this is an emotional distress the film has enabled by running with his fantasies to the point where they come into contact with his past and evolving emotional present. Adi going to the airport keeps the door barred on an emotional reality that perhaps also threatens him, but again the film's process and the director's insider status have taken him to the point of challenge. With Suryono, the film process alone does the work of confrontation. His imagined present of a bond with perpetrators runs up against the realisation that there is no way to make friends with gangsters who destroyed and traumatised his past. No one tells Suryono that this is so; tragically, he learns for himself how disavowal has betrayed him.

Change and Transitional Space

Here is a second way of exploring the film as a psychoanalytic enterprise. In *Playing and Reality*, Donald Winnicott writes of transitional objects and spaces in the lives of infants as they separate themselves from their parents and negotiate an external environment which seems threatening (Winnicott 2005). Transitional objects exist beyond the infant, but are still a part of it, like a favourite teddy bear. They have an intermediate position between internal and external reality and provide a secure transitional space in which the infant can try out relations with external reality. Play with transitional objects creates a secure place in order to accept something otherwise threatening. The teddy bear is treated like the real person with which the infant will eventually engage.

This idea may seem rather remote from the psychological process in *The Act of Killing*, but we should note that Winnicott saw infantile transitional processes continuing in adult life in play, artistic work, religious feeling and dreams. As adults, we may also play with illusions to address uncomfortable realities. Pushed to extreme, such play 'becomes the hallmark of madness when an adult puts too powerful a claim on the credulity of others, forcing them to acknowledge a sharing of illusion that is not their own' (Winnicott 2005: 4). This brings us to *The Act of Killing*, for the perpetrators' aesthetic choices in dress and performance do indeed provoke the thought that madness, or at least ghastly weirdness, is afoot. It is easy to see their cultural imagination as vulgar and kitsch, the product of lives caught in a deathly past. Yet presenting themselves as colourful cowboys, Hollywood gangsters, in drag, or as directors of dancing girls ('eye candy') looks a lot like forms of playful fantasy through which uncomfortable realities might be addressed. This may suggest an additional inflection to the transitional psychological method at work in the film. Perhaps Anwar takes to play so readily in order to face a reality that is otherwise unbearable. In the process, it becomes a rather unique form of transitional justice.[11]

Generalising from the Unique

It may be said that *The Act of Killing* and the experience it reflects is so extraordinary that it has no general relevance. The peculiar circumstances in which Joshua Oppenheimer came to have access to these men together with the invention of so strange a dramatic representation give the film its undoubted fascination but make it hard to draw lessons from. Where we have other groups of perpetrators enjoying substantial impunity, it can hardly be a generalisable response to give them all a film crew and invite them to tell their own story as they see fit. Yet there is an overall significance in this psychological journey in that, even when the sociological factors tilt heavily in favour of forgetting, there are situations in which some feel the need to remember, and in remembering challenge what they had unconsciously sought to forget. *The Act of Killing* is about how a perpetrator's denial may be overcome not by direct moral confrontation but by a conversation which draws the perpetrator into

[11] By this I mean to connect Winnicott's idea of transitional space to what Phil Clark calls the deep objectives of transitional justice: truth, peace, justice, healing, forgiveness and reconciliation (Clark 2010: ch 1). From their breadth, one can see how transitional justice at its most ambitious involves a mature process of change with the aspiration for reconciliation as the end goal. In relation to healing, transitional justice stresses the dehumanisation of victims but also of perpetrators, and it is here that *The Act of Killing*'s use of transitional space represents an unusual form of transitional justice.

a psychological space of identification with his victims. Denial is no longer so possible after what was suppressed is brought by internal process into consciousness.

The generalisable point is the one that occupied us in the first half of this chapter. It is that there is something in denial as psychological process no matter if this is an uncomfortable truth in terms of the more obvious verities of moral and legal discourse. To get at psychological denial requires a method that is not simply accusatorial, blaming and punitive but involves ways of dealing with deniers that get inside their defences. Accusations and blame in such situations are likely only to strengthen the barriers against taking responsibility. Because Indonesia's regime of impunity renders standard moral and legal approaches to accountability redundant, it opens a window to an alternative psychological process at a deeper level. This rests upon a metapsychology of atonement such as is developed in this book. We are unlikely to replicate the circumstances in which *The Act of Killing* was made, but its story reflects an underlying truth about the human capacity for change, even under the most unpropitious of circumstances. For the human animal that thinks and loves, responsibility for its actions may still lie deep inside, under encrusted mechanisms of denial.

10

Violation, Mourning and Melancholia

On Patricio Guzmán's *Nostalgia for the Light*

> I spent all morning with my brother's foot. We were reunited. It was a great joy and ... disappointment.
>
> Vicky Saavedra in *Nostalgia for the Light* (2010)

> ... mourning ... that loss ... of ... unitary single-mindedness ....
>
> Hans Loewald (1980: 329)

This chapter is the second of the three 'case studies' which extend and apply the moral psychology developed earlier in the book. Whereas the previous chapter extended guilt to denial and how it may be overcome, here I am concerned with how an ethics of forgiveness based on love is grounded in metapsychology. What is it for a human being to have to deal with the experience of violation as a victim? The case study concerns Patricio Guzmán's luminous film *Nostalgia for the Light* (2010) about the aftermath of General Augusto Pinochet's dictatorship in Chile between 1973 and 1990. Its focus is on survivors of the terror and in particular a group of women searching for the remains of disappeared and murdered family members in the Atacama Desert. I consider here the experience of three women survivors of the dictatorship, two who search in the desert, the third who is the now adult survivor of parents taken in that time. These women explain their thinking and motivation as they come to terms with what happened against the backdrop of Guzmán's own reflections on the period.

As we turn back to the victim after time spent with the perpetrator (Chapters 6–10), it may be worth explaining how this chapter sits in the overall argument. Two moral–psychological states lie at its heart, that of the perpetrator and the victim. We started exploring the territory of the victim in Chapter 2, with young Hegel's account of violation, grief and loss. There he identifies both the similarities and the differences between the perpetrator and the victim with the important common ground that both grieve because of violation. Grief for perpetrators is for disturbing the moral order of which they are a part, while for victims, it is in the loss felt in submission to violation. After an initial development of perpetrator guilt (Chapter 3), we then turned to forgiveness and the ethical nature of love (Chapters 4 and 5). The following three chapters then returned us to the perpetrator's guilt and developed the link between a moral metaphysics and a metapsychology of guilt. By the end of Chapter 8, a full moral psychology of guilt had been developed, showing its ethical and metapsychological levels in a comprehensive view. This was then taken a step further in Chapter 9 by investigating perpetrator denial as a moral and psychological experience.

Left out of the picture to this point is the connection between the victim's ethical metaphysics of violation and forgiveness in Chapters 2, 4 and 5 and its metapsychological dimension. Moral psychology on the side of victims is thus incomplete, and this chapter aims to complete it. Here I consider the metapsychological position of the victim of violation in Freud's terms of mourning and melancholia (Freud 1984). The chapter has four main sections. In the first, I develop a moral psychology of mourning, building on the account of mature guilt developed in Chapters 6–8. It may seem odd to commence the moral psychology of victimhood, mourning and forgiveness with reference to guilt, but there is a common root in moving from the ethics and metapsychology of victimhood to that we traced in guilt. I argue that the idea of metapsychological identification leading to atonement as 'at-one-ment' is common to both the feeling of guilt and the victim's need to mourn. This is the gist of the quotation above from Loewald.

In the second section, I then consider the positions of three women who are the main protagonists in *Nostalgia for the Light* and I show how their thoughts and actions reflect an ethics and metapsychology of grief and mourning. In a third section, I link these ideas around mourning to the idea of melancholia as the other titular term in Freud's famous essay (Freud 1984). I show how the psychological contrast between mourning and melancholia is central to an understanding of what the women are doing searching in the desert. I then conclude by thinking more generally about the moral and psychological relevance of the film, and how it operates as an effective depiction of the metaphysical and metapsychological dimensions of the struggle to address grief at violation.

Moral Psychology: From Guilt to Mourning

I argue in this section that the moral–psychological experience of violation for a victim is linked to that of a perpetrator by a common ground seen in both an ethical and a metapsychological approach. In both, the key issue is identification with another leading to the wish to be at one. For perpetrators, this may be coupled with grief and a desire to atone, in the sense of making oneself whole ('at one') again. In the case of the violated victim, the aim is to come back to wholeness through the grieving which mourns loss. Mourning in this sense is not disconnected from the moral and psychological processes we have already examined which establish guilt. Hence the development from ethical to metapsychological guilt outlined in Chapters 6 and 7 constitutes a prototype for understanding the place of victims of violation who mourn their loss. I make this case here, first, at the ethical level with Herbert Morris and then at the psychoanalytical level with Hans Loewald. Both elements, the ethical and the metapsychological, help build a composite picture of the moral psychology of victims of violation who grieve and mourn.

Common Ethical Ground

I discussed Morris's work in Chapter 6 as the philosopher of identification, atonement and guilt who took philosophy to the brink of psychoanalysis. The same argument can be developed to consider what is ethically at stake for a victim. As we saw, Morris starts with identification with others which 'implies … that we suffer when they do, just as we are pleased when they are. We imagine their feelings, thereby "entering into" them' (Morris 1987: 239). The idea of ethical connection as 'entering into' another indicates the proximity of Morris's view to the psychoanalytic view. He emphasises that this is more than mere sympathy, for it leads us to 'have the feelings we imagine [the other] to be having as contrasted with our merely responding in an appropriate way, say with sympathy, to [them]' (Morris 1987: 239).

Guilt through Identification

Entering into the experience of another by identifying with them, making it our own, links to guilt where we hurt another. In a passage, we met already in Chapter 6, here is Morris's account of how identification with another one has harmed comes back to bite the perpetrator:

> In cutting oneself off from others one comes to see oneself as being cut off, not whole, as if one had destroyed what one loved and thus also destroyed a part of oneself. This image of cutting off and being cut off, not whole, finds support in our view of the guilty person as not being able to function as a whole person could and does, not being able to enjoy life fully…. (Morris 1976: 99–100)

Morris notably explains the sense of loss the perpetrator feels to how it feels emotionally to lose a loved one:

> To be cut off from what we love is intensely painful, and the pain of separation involved in guilt resembles this … I have suggested that in union, best exemplified in love, there is an intensely satisfying feeling of wholeness or completeness. In seeing oneself as cut off from others one feels a sense of incompleteness, as a lover who loses a loved one may feel that a part of him has been taken away or torn from him. The person feels that peculiar pain and uneasiness when feeling guilty of cutting off a part of himself…. (Morris 1976: 99)

The emphasis on the loss of wholeness is important to the feeling of guilt, but feeling lost and cut off by one's guilt is participating in a more general ethical experience of wholeness that comes from love. Guilt feelings are thus part of a broader ethical mindset.

Grieving Loss

The comparison of guilt to loss of a lover points to a common link. Guilt addresses a lack of wholeness and the need to be at one as between oneself and one's world. The moral experience of guilt is then one type of moral experience in which the core element is losing a sense of wholeness. Being relieved of guilt 'is to feel again that one is joined together with others and with oneself, to no longer be divided within and at war with ourselves and others'. But victims of violation may feel something similar. The core of guilt is the 'need to make amends, to mend what has been damaged, and to be at one again with others and oneself' (Morris 1976: 100), but there may be two different kinds of moral experience wrapped up in this statement. It is one thing to 'make amends', another 'to mend what has been damaged'. The latter is what victims feel. There is for them the same sense of loss of wholeness, in their case because of their loss of the loved one or through an injury to themselves. To be sure, the two kinds of redemptive activity are not the same. There is a big difference where the aim of the victim is to understand, to come to terms and to mend. This is not the same as to make amends, but the key ethical similarity lies in loss, grief at loss and a desire to be at one again. These have a common ground of 'mending' in an ethics of love and identification.

Guilt 'by Association'

An ethical position that sheds light on the common ground is that of neither the perpetrator nor the victim but the person who feels guilt for what a loved *other* has done. An example here might be that of the relationship in a family, where a child discovers that a loved parent had been a war criminal in an earlier period. Here again identification is at stake. In the following passage, Morris describes why one might feel guilty for what a beloved friend or family member, or even one's country, has done:

> [T]he process of identification, once operative, carries a psychological momentum so that, in identifying with the person engaged in wrongdoing, one imagines how one would oneself feel.... [These] feelings connected with identificatory processes are often perfectly normal, and it is their total absence that may occasion concern.... Because they have defined themselves in a manner that reveals identification with others, the actions of those others are granted a power over them.... Individuals may in these circumstances believe themselves guilty. (Morris 1987: 239–40)

Linked however to such a feeling of shared *guilt* is the ethical possibility that one also feels *betrayed* by what the loved wrongdoer has done, so that participating in guilt is accompanied by a sense of one's own victimhood at the wrongdoer's hands. In this case, the identificatory loving relation makes the person both a co-perpetrator and a collateral victim. There is a double loss of wholeness in knowing that the loved person did bad things in which the individual feels complicit and in so doing also feels betrayed and victimised because of a shared identificatory love. That I can feel at the same time both complicit guilt with a perpetrator and betrayal as a collateral victim is only possible because my lost wholeness extends to both situations at the same moment. In both, a broken loving identification with the perpetrator is at stake, whether I feel complicit (guilty) or betrayed (a victim), or both at once.

The Underlying Metapsychology

From the common ground in ethics established by identification and the need to be at one, I turn now to the metapsychological bond. In his essay *Mourning and Melancholia* (Freud 1984), Freud writes of mourning in terms that seem straightforward:

> It is regularly the reaction to the loss of a loved person.... Profound mourning ... [involves a] painful frame of mind ... loss of interest in the outside world ... loss of capacity to adopt any new object of love ... and the same turning away from any activity ... not connected with ... [the loved person] ... Each single one of the memories and expectations in which the libido is bound to the object is brought up ..., and detachment of the libido is accomplished in respect of it ... [W]hen the work of mourning is completed the ego becomes free and uninhibited again. (Freud 1984: 251–53)

Loss of a loved person involves coming to terms with that person's place in one's life, grieving the loss and then becoming free of it. When he wrote *Mourning and Melancholia*, Freud had yet to develop the idea of the superego. While the paper is regarded as leading to discovery of the concept, it was melancholia rather than mourning that was important in the development (Lear 2015: ch 6). If guilt and atonement, as I argued in Chapters 7 and 8, are directly connected to superego development, and mourning shares common ground with guilt, Freud's position at the time he wrote *Mourning and Melancholia* will not provide us with what we need to understand how guilt and mourning are related. We need to go back to our earlier argument of Part III and the line pursued by Loewald.

Love 'Enformed'

Here is a brief recap on the argument of Chapters 7 and 8. Freud's later structural theory is the key to understanding the human psyche. We start with the state of 'primary narcissism', which is not as we understand the idea of narcissism generally, as a view of self that exaggerates its importance. At the earliest stage of human life, it represents the position of unformed love, or the life force, libido or Eros, which becomes enformed through developmental processes of ego and superego formation. This unformed life force is given form and organisation through the loving attention of parent and other figures, who make self-identification, individuation and self-differentiation possible. The infant, which has the material potential to develop into the child and adult, 'takes in' the example and the model of the parent figure through identification ('the earliest expression of an emotional tie' (Freud 1985: 134–35)). Paradoxically, it is through identification with another that one becomes oneself, and this process of identification is then the basis for loving oneself and others. It binds inchoate primary narcissism from birth with the evolving sense of self in relation with and to others, and especially as the infant develops an ego and then, pushing towards its independence, a superego.

Guilt and Atonement

As developed by Loewald, Freudian identification with another also leads to a need to atone (to strive to be at one), and this lies at the heart of guilt – and mourning. Both appear in the crucial phase of the Oedipus conflict from which emerges the development of the superego. In the Oedipal struggle, the process of becoming independent involves breaking from parents and their constitutive place in the child's psyche. To be a person in one's own right, parental authority needs to be expelled from the inner sanctum of psychological being, but 'killing' one's parents leaves a residue of bad feeling, guilt, for having discarded those one loves. This is the Oedipal drama in which we create a sense of independence, the essential experience from which develops the superego. The superego is the basis for coherent organisation of an individual life, but it leaves a residue of regret as a template for the future. This is why Loewald calls the superego an 'atonement structure'. It has the default mode of seeking to restore a wholeness which started in the past but looks to the future. Thus the key psychological dimension is that our moral development stems from processes of identification with others, which we come to discard and then regret discarding. An accompanying desire to restore becomes a template for personhood.

Mourning and At-One-Ment

That developing a superego through the Oedipal struggle might be linked to mourning may already be sensed. We miss the comfort of what we have abandoned. Superego development is gain as emancipation from loved parent figures but also loss. We savour independence and wholeness but grieve for what has gone. We miss the security of the earlier loving relation and the experience of being at one in it. Feeling bad (guilt) then goes together with *feeling sad* (mourning) as concomitant emotions relating to the loss of earlier wholeness. This is painful, the pain is what we call grief and the process of experiencing loss and grief is what we call mourning, its aim being to come to terms with the loss we feel. Just like guilt, the mourning which accompanies the acquisition of a superego is an early template of how to react to loss seared on our experience: 'Mourning … has its prototype in the resolution of the Oedipus conflict. There, too, a complex process of relinquishing and identifying with love objects takes place, involving the transformation of the superego. We may say that the first mourning … takes place in the resolution of the Oedipus conflict' (Loewald 1980: 329).

Mourning hurts because there is a break and loss of loving relations, and every loving relation expresses the underlying human capacity to love, first seen in the primary narcissistic position: 'In some sense, the sadness and grief as mourning perhaps also concerns that loss, that giving up of the unitary single-mindedness of instinctual life that tends to preserve in some way the primary narcissistic oneness from which we have to take leave in the development of conscient life and secondary-process mentation' (Loewald 1980: 170).

From this structural standpoint, mourning is about both loss and growth. Loss of a loved person with whom one has identified involves coming to terms with the place that person occupied in one's life. The mourner must reckon with an emotional wholeness, an 'at-one-ness', that has been lost because the loved person is no longer present. This adjustment involves, as Loewald puts it, accommodation to the loss that involves both de-identification with and assimilation of the lost object. Mourning involves surviving loss while the lost object is carried forward in a new, internal way: 'Side by side with object relations, processes of identification persist and re-enter the picture…. Mourning involves not only the gradual, piecemeal relinquishment of the lost object, but also the internalisation … of aspects of … the relationship between the ego and the lost object which … become a relationship within the ego system' (Loewald 1980: 266).

To sum up, we can say that mourning and guilt are two distinct emotions which share a common metapsychological root. Both are striving for at-one-ment or the repair of loss. One seeks to mend, the other to amend or, better, to mend by making amends. Two processes are locked into the same moral–psychological development of the human animal in its psychological development. In this way, we can see how becoming the animal that thinks and loves, the metaphysical animal capable of ethical being grounded in metapsychological process, means to be at one with oneself in processes after violation that include *both* guilt of perpetrators and mourning of victims. These are derived from the same source and that is why what is grounded in metapsychology comes to have effect on ethical argument. The argument for interconnection works ethically (Morris) because it works metapsychologically (Loewald).

Violation and Mourning in *Nostalgia for the Light*

We see this search for wholeness in *Nostalgia for the Light*, where three women seek to make emotional sense of loss and to become at one again with their lost family members and in themselves. After some initial comments introducing the film, I examine the position of these women.

On *Nostalgia for the Light*

Nostalgia for the Light (Guzmán 2010) is about how people have reacted as victims of state violence in Pinochet's Chile. In contrast to *The Act of Killing* in the previous chapter, where the film fascinates for its emotional ugliness and dark humour, this is a strikingly beautiful film in emotional and aesthetic terms, and this is relevant to the film's ethical commitments. Here is the film's blurb, which, unusually, does not exaggerate and describes the women searching the desert while sketching how the film contextualises their acts:

> Patricio Guzmán travels 10,000 feet above sea level to the driest desert on earth … Here, the sky is so translucent that it allows astronomers to see the boundaries of our universe. Yet Chile's Atacama Desert climate also keeps human remains intact: pre-Columbian mummies; explorers and miners; and the remains of disappeared political prisoners from the years of the Pinochet regime. Women sift the desert soil for the bones of their loved ones, while archaeologists uncover the traces of ancient civilizations and astronomers examine the most distant and oldest galaxies. Melding celestial and earthly quests, *Nostalgia for the Light* is a gorgeous, deeply moving, and personal odyssey into astronomy, archaeology, geology and human rights.

The film's power is derived not only from the tragic and poignant nature of the women's quest, but from setting this in reflections on the desert, the universe and the long history of humankind. Also significant is the beauty of its images of desert, sky and the planets and its plangent soundtrack. What these women have to say and how the film presents them open the door to profound truths about how people survive violation and what it means to be human. The film makes us think about their ethical and emotional reactions to violation and victimhood, holding to account and resistance, and to underlying states of grief and mourning. The film explores why their search occurs, and how the moral and the psychological combine in those committed to it. The violation of forced disappearance has disconnected and rendered them incomplete, and they seek to restore themselves by their search. While the film focuses on a number of people, three in particular are discussed here. Two of them, Violeta Berrios and Vicky Saavedra, search the desert for remains while the third, Valentina Rodriguez, is herself the child of disappeared parents, who speaks about her experience. Considering the women helps us understand the moral psychology that underpins their struggle as victims of human rights violations.

Violeta's Implacable Search

Here first is Violeta Berrios speaking of her adamantine determination to search the desert in the face of official lies and resistance:

> For as long as I can if we must carry on searching I will do so. … They say they unearthed them, … and threw them in the sea. … At this point in my life, I'm 70, I find it hard to believe what I'm told. They taught me not to believe.… I

> never stop asking questions ... If someone were to tell me they threw them out on the top of that mountain, I would find a way of getting right to the top. I'm not as strong as I was 20 years ago. I'm not as healthy. It would be difficult. But hope gives you strength. I no longer count the times Vicky and I have gone into the desert. We set out full of hope and return with our heads hanging. But we always pick ourselves up, give ourselves a shake and set off again the next day....

To cover up their murder, the remains of the disappeared were buried in the desert, then dug up and disposed of elsewhere. In the process, the bodies were broken up and parts were left behind. The fragmentation of the bodies means that they can never be retrieved in their entirety, yet Violeta will not accept the few remains that have been uncovered. She feels compelled to continue a quest that cannot be successful:

> Some people must wonder why we want bones. I want them so much. And I'm not the only one. When they found one of Mario's jawbones, I told them I didn't want it.... [I said] 'I want him whole. They took him away whole, I don't want just a piece of him'. And I'm not saying it just for him, but for all the disappeared . ... I don't want to die ... before I find him.

Violeta acknowledges that her conduct may not be understood by others, and she must surely know that the demand that underlies her persistence cannot be met. There seem to be two aspects to her search. The first is to find Mario's body, to make it whole again, and in so doing to put together the broken parts of her own life with his. This is a form of mourning. The second is slightly different. It is a determination to press the state on its wrongdoing. Every time she goes into the desert her aim is to find Mario, but her implicit demand is against the state that took Mario away intact, and then murdered him and broke his body apart. Violeta's commitment and struggle is not just to find Mario, but the mortal remains of all the disappeared. These are political objectives and they raise an important question as to how we understand their linkage to mourning. I suggest below that Violeta's struggle concerns not only the need to mourn, but the need to affirm a political space for mourning. This links to the need not only to mourn but to resist mourning turning in psychological terms into melancholia.

Vicky's Ability to Mourn

Here is Vicky Saavedra describing her slightly different moral psychology concerning the mourning of body parts. When she finds pieces of her brother, she takes them home:

> [I found] a foot. It was still in his shoe. Some of his teeth. I found part of his forehead, his nose, nearly all the left side of his skull. The bit behind the ear with a bullet mark. ... They finished him off with a bullet in the forehead....

It is emotionally powerful to hear this gentle woman describe the brutal process whereby her brother was 'finished off' with a bullet to the skull. The contrast between his being and his end is summarised as Vicky continues to describe how she mourned him through those body parts she found:

> I remembered his tender expression and this was all that remained. A few teeth and bits of bones. And a foot. Our final moment together, was when his foot was at my house. When the mass grave was discovered, I knew it was his shoe. That night I got up and went to stroke his foot. There was … a smell of decay. It was still in a sock. A burgundy sock. Dark red. I took it out of the bag and looked at it. I remained sitting in the lounge for a long time. My mind was blank. I was incapable of thinking. I was in total shock. The next day my husband went to work and I spent all morning with my brother's foot. We were reunited. It was a great joy and a great disappointment because only then did I take in the fact that my brother was dead.

The contrast between Vicky's moving memory of her brother and being with his partial remains leads to her final acceptance of his death. Unlike Violeta, Vicky is able to mourn by accepting the parts of a skull and foot she finds. She continues to search for the rest of him, so the search for the whole body remains important, but memory and the competing emotions around loss are made possible by the sense of being reunited with his partial remains. Mourning is about loss and retrieving a sense of wholeness after the experience of loss, though the renewed self is not the same as it was. We see this occurring for the three women in *Nostalgia for the Light*. Vicky's experience of taking home the remains of her brother's body, of sitting with them, of remembering the whole person that had worn the same sock, the joy of being reunited, together with the pain of realising his death: these all depict the making whole, the at-one-ment, that is the working of the mourning process. Searching in the desert is the effort to mourn, to make whole; finding parts of the body, taking them home, holding them, these take the process forward.

Valentina's Wish for Wholeness

Finally, there is Valentina Rodriguez, who is in a different position as the surviving child of parents who were disappeared and murdered, and who was brought up by her grandparents:

> I am the daughter of detained and disappeared parents. First they detained my grandparents…. They threatened them relentlessly to make them reveal where my parents were, or else I, too, would disappear….

We can only guess as to the underlying dynamics and difficulties that might have followed this situation for both the child and the grandparents. Valentina however was raised well and educated to become an astronomer and she explains the impact of her training on her thinking about what happened to her and her parents:

> Astronomy has somehow helped me to give another dimension to the pain, to the absence, to the loss. Sometimes, when one is alone with that pain, and these moments are necessary, [it] becomes oppressive. I tell myself it's all part of a cycle … we are all part of a current, of an energy, a recyclable matter. Like the stars which must die … [What] happened to my parents … takes on another dimension … and frees me a little….

The emphasis here is on a 'little' freedom, for Valentina lives with an ongoing sense of absence that leaves her feeling incomplete:

> My grandparents … found a way to make my parents important reference points for me. [They] were able to overcome their pain so that I could have a happy healthy childhood. Sometimes I feel like I'm a product with a manufacturing defect which is invisible. I find it funny when people tell me that it doesn't show that I'm the daughter of disappeared prisoners. [My] children don't have this defect.… I … am happy that my son is growing up like this.

Valentina's thoughts are both philosophical and psychological. Metaphysically her astronomical reflections provide a coda and rationale for the film's focus on the universe and stars. They link her sense of loss to a universe in which life continues while constantly changing. They link directly to the aesthetic themes of the film, which focus powerfully on the beauty of the universe viewed from the Atacama, and the interconnected historical flow of life that is the universe's being. The film only focuses on recent man-made violations of the natural and historical order in its second half. The first expresses the sense of history's *longue durée* as the ethical setting in which the present and recent past occur. This locates what happened to the disappeared in a much bigger order of things, but it does not so much diminish recent suffering as magnify it. How can such ugliness manifest itself amid such beauty?

Metapsychologically, there is Valentina's sense of herself as a defective mechanism, that something is missing in her as a result of the loss of loving parents. Her words make it clear just how much her grandparents played a parenting role in her life, but without ever substituting for the parents she lost. What, though, was the psychological defect with which she was left? Her sense of a lost part of herself, a part that can never be constituted, also looks like a form of mourning. It is the experience of lost parents who loved her as a baby, which, though she cannot recall, was constitutive of her as a human being. The grace and loving attention of her grandparents to care for her and tell her of her parents were ways to give wholeness where wholeness was not possible. Perhaps the telling served to point up the lack. The unknown parents who have been lost are identified with in their absence, while Valentina must still acknowledge the absence in herself. This is a complex form of mourning that can hardly be completed, though it may be supported and redeemed in the evolving emotional relations Valentina develops in her own family life.

Mourning as Political Struggle

The words of the three women in *Nostalgia for the Light* convey strongly the sense of loss and the drives that ensue from it. The words only take us so far, and the women should be seen in the film as their actions, expressions and convictions animate what they say. For all three, mourning occurs but this is not all that is happening in the film, especially for Violeta and Vicky in the desert. A loved person dies or leaves, an identification is lost and repurposed in the psyche. This is everyone's human experience, and we all have to find ways of re-creating our sense of identity and of wholeness after loss as best we can. In the cases of Violeta, Vicky and Valentina, loss did not occur in the usual way. It was forced upon them by the violence of a dictatorship after a military coup, and the question is what difference this makes. Violeta refuses to give up the search for remains because she demands the whole body be returned to her, and she searches on behalf of all victims. The state took her family member away, the state must return him intact. In her case and that of the others, just by appearing in the film, the work of mourning, of finding wholeness after loss, involves by implication political commitments to hold the state to account, and to bear witness to what it did.

Mourning as a search for at-one-ment is irreducibly political in this setting. We witness it in the tangible form of the struggle to get up and go out into the desert, to bear disappointment, and to renew commitment. Mourning cannot be pensive and private in this setting. It involves an active fight to maintain the conditions of, and the possibility to, mourn. Mourning becomes a citizen's right against a state, and without the assertion of that right, wholeness cannot be achieved. What would be the alternative to the struggle to mourn? To answer that question, I turn now to the other half of Freud's famous essay on mourning and melancholia and consider how the struggle to mourn relates to melancholia in the film.

Violation, Mourning and Melancholia

Thus far, we have considered how understanding identification and atonement could link together the ethical experience of the guilty person and the victim, for both seek to find a wholeness that has been lost – on the one hand by the perpetrator of the violative act, on the other in the experience of that act by a victim. In both, there is a sense of identification with a violation and a loss which must be addressed. The three women in *Nostalgia for the Light* are in this position but they must also face the fact that the perpetrators have done all they can to obstruct the process of mourning. This invokes the possibility of what Freud would call a melancholic response, which they must resist. Considering this aspect takes us back to Freud's essay on *Mourning and Melancholia* (Freud 1984).

The Nature of Melancholia

For Freud, melancholia is a reaction to a process of mourning that cannot be or has not been properly worked through. It involves an element of distorted psychic change as a person absorbs the negative characteristics of a situation in which a loved other has been lost. These include 'all those situations of being slighted, neglected or disappointed, which can import feelings of love and hate into the relationship…' (Freud 1984: 260). Melancholia translates a situation of external loss in disturbing or traumatising circumstances into an internal, negative re-organisation of the self. Of course, any loss in a situation of violation or victimisation occurs in difficult and challenging circumstances. It is not easily addressed, processed and absorbed. Rather, Freud's point is that it can become a negative element in the psychic organisation of the person so affected. Where mourning involves an external 'loss in regard to an object' which may be processed, melancholia 'points to a loss in regard to [the] ego' (Freud 1984: 256), one which travels inwards to affect the organisation of the psyche:

> The melancholic displays something else besides which is lacking in mourning – an extraordinary diminution in his self-regard, an impoverishment of his ego on a grand scale. In mourning it is the world which has become poor and empty; in melancholia it is the ego itself. The patient represents his ego to us as worthless, incapable of any achievement and morally despicable; he reproaches himself, vilifies himself and expects to be cast out and punished. He abases himself before everyone…. (Freud 1984: 254)

The external loss becomes translated into an internal subjective adjustment of a negative kind. In this way, 'the shadow of the object [falls] upon the ego' (Freud 1984: 258) and the negativity of this development can lead a person to hating the self, 'abusing it, debasing it, making it suffer and deriving sadistic satisfaction from its suffering' (Freud 1984: 260).

Of the two conditions, mourning and melancholia, Freud recognises many similarities. In both, there is painful dejection, cessation of interest in the world, loss of capacity to love and inhibition of activity. What melancholia has that mourning does not is, first, a lowering of feelings of self-worth to the extent of self-reproach, self-reviling and the expectation of punishment, and second the feature of a withdrawal of the problematic complex from conscious understanding. The person who mourns is more or less aware of the loss she must work through, while the melancholic loses sight of this, importing the loss as a more or less unconscious part of her self-organisation. The comparison with the Oedipal struggle is important here. Under normal circumstances, the outcome of the struggle is positive in that the ego develops a further element that provides it with greater overall power and coherence. In melancholia, the ego also develops such a further element, but here it is constricting and negative (Lear 2015: ch 6). In both, there is the creation of a 'special agency' (Freud 1984: 258) within the ego, but in melancholia 'one part of the ego sets itself over against the other, [and] judges it critically' (Freud 1984: 256), replacing potential reproaches against the lost external object (which could be worked through in mourning) with internal self-accusations. While superego development offers the promise of positive and emancipatory change, melancholia offers only negative self-criticism.

Melancholia and Violation

If we think about how melancholia might affect the person who has been victimised or violated, by another, what might this look like? Freud's account suggests that the triggers for melancholia are not that terrible, including situations where a person is done down by a slight, neglect or disappointment. Freud seems to have in mind situations where a relationship has broken down and a lover been discarded (Freud 1984: 257). This is small beer considering the types of violation we are considering with the murdered and the disappeared and the effect on their families. One might however think that there is more scope for self-blame and hatred where the 'shadow of the object' falls as an extreme form of victimisation. From *The Forgiveness Project* reports discussed in Chapter 5, here is one woman's account of the psychological effects of her sexual violation as a teenage girl. First, Madeleine Black describes the rape:

> When I was 13, in a flat belonging to my friend's mother who was away for the weekend, I was attacked by two teenage American students. They held a knife to my throat and tortured and raped me many times over, for about four or five hours. I begged them to stop, but they just kicked me and laughed at me. I remember wishing they would kill me to make it all end ... Near to the end one of my attackers urinated on me and out of everything they did, this felt the worse and it was one of the images that haunted me for years to come. Before they left, the most violent of the pair punched me in the chest, held the knife to my throat again and said if I told anyone he would find me and kill me. I believed him ... I lived in fear that the two young men who had raped me would kill me one day. (Black 2015: 63–64)

Then there is a description of her psychological reaction to being violated:

> I felt worthless, totally degraded, and empty. I thought it was all my fault, and most of all I felt so dirty and contaminated. I would spend ages in the bath for many years afterwards scrubbing my skin with cleaning products.... I started to become very promiscuous as I had no self-respect and if a boy approached me I just let him do whatever he wanted because I thought if I resisted he would hurt me. At the same time I started drinking and taking drugs. I also stopped eating as that was the only thing I felt I could control. (Black 2015: 64)

The effects are not just a loss that needs to be absorbed and overcome in a process of mourning, though that is ultimately what Black seeks and achieves. But something is in the way here. As a victim and survivor of this violation, she also 'takes in' a sense of her own worthlessness, deduced from how she has been treated, and permits it to structure her mental self-perception, with profound effects on how she then lives her life. This is melancholia brought about by violation that obstructs mourning.

Relating this discussion to the words and actions of Violeta Berrios and Vicky Saavedra, their thoughts and actions may be seen as not only mourning but more. The struggle in the desert represents not just the effort to mourn but also an insistence on their right to mourn. Further, they assert the right not just for itself but because in so doing they reject the imposed internalisation of melancholia by refusing to accept the way the state treats them. Viewed as worthless by the state, there is a fourfold violation of their being. First, there were the initial acts of violation against their family members, their disappearance and murder; second, there was the subsequent hiding and re-hiding of the remains; third, there is the present refusal to reveal what happened to the bodies, so that the women may mourn; and fourth there is the refusal to recognise the women's need to mourn, seeing them, as Violeta puts it, as 'lepers'. Their desert searches are accordingly not just in the way of mourning nor just actions insisting on their right to mourn. They are also means to resist the imposition on them of a sense of their lack of worth and unworthiness to mourn. To accept the state's denial would be to accept its treatment of them with its implicit understanding of them as worthless. To struggle to mourn is also to resist melancholia.

Mourning or Melancholia?

In the Introduction to a collection of essays on loss, mourning and remains, David Eng and David Kasanjian follow Walter Benjamin in writing of the importance of 'active mourning' as a means of establishing an active and open relationship with history. The struggle to attend to physical and other kinds of remains 'generates a politics of mourning that might be active' (Eng and Kasanjian 2002: 2), and not wrapped up in the complacent hegemony of history's present victors. The description seems apt for the women in *Nostalgia for the Light* but mourning raises for them the question underlying this chapter, that of the relationship between mourning and melancholia. Eng and Kasanjian wonder whether Freud's distinction between the two holds in anything like the way he thought. Though they are not discussing our film, what they say helps us clarify our terms and what is happening in it.

For Eng and Kasanjian, Freud's account in 'Mourning and Melancholia' is problematic because he treats mourning as normal, while he pathologises melancholia. They also object because in Freud's account, mourning closes and kills off the past. It 'abandons lost objects by laying their histories to rest'. They however see melancholia in contrast as the state which 'creates a realm of traces open to signification, a hermeneutic domain of what remains of loss' (Eng and Kasanjian 2002: 4). 'Unlike mourning, in which the past is declared resolved, finished, and dead, in melancholia the past remains steadfastly alive in the present' (Eng and Kasanjian 2002: 3–4), and therefore the way to an open future politics. If this were the way to distinguish the two terms, it is hard to see how Freud could assist Benjamin in thinking through the idea of active *mourning*, for it is melancholia that must play the active role. It alone goes beyond 'a fixed notion of the past [in favour of] a continuous engagement with loss and its remains' (Eng and Kasanjian 2002: 4).

That mourning and melancholia are interconnected is unquestionable, but in my view Eng and Kasanjian both overstate the deathly purpose of mourning and understate the pathologizing quality of melancholia, with its negative attack on subjectivity. With regard to mourning, we can draw on Loewald's development of Freud's account to see more clearly how mourning operates. For Loewald, mourning is about developing and enriching identity through a subsequent holding of the past in a way that enables growth and does not close off relevance. Melancholia in contrast leaves the person trapped in the circumstances of the loss:

> When we speak of the internalisation of object relations, such as in the resolution of the Oedipus complex and in the work of mourning, it is not, if the processes are brought to completion, a matter of maintaining identification with the objects to be relinquished; the latter is the case in melancholia where the object and the identifications with the object cannot be given up. In internalization it is a matter of transforming these relations [by] increasing and enriching psychic structure. (Loewald 1980: 83)

In this account, mourning does not kill or close, for successful completion and relinquishing are transformations, increases and enrichments carried forward in an enhanced and open psychic structure. There is new development in the psyche of the person who mourns. Mourning is about coming to terms with loss in the sense of both letting go and carrying forward. It is melancholia on the other hand which represents the kind of stasis and repetition in the subject Eng and Kasanjian impute to mourning in Freud.

Neither Freud nor Loewald had in mind the kinds of experiences of violation seen in *Nostalgia for the Light* though Freud was clear that mourning extended beyond the personal and into the social.[1] In the film's setting, the contrast between an enriched and an impoverished ego structure around mourning and melancholia needs to be maintained. The three women we have focused on need to mourn in the ways described: to cradle a detached, decomposing foot in its burgundy sock; to know lost parents and what kind of people they were; to press the activity of mourning against the continuing violation visited on them. The beauty of a brother's smile, the proud love of hopeful young parents, these become a part of Vicky Saavedra's and Valentina Rodriguez's lives and enrich them by allowing them to go on. At the same time, the *struggle to mourn* as a creative and demanding political process should be recognised

[1] Mourning is the reaction to the loss of a loved person, 'or to the loss of some abstraction which has taken the place of one, such as one's country, liberty, an ideal, and so on' (Freud 1984: 252).

and honoured. The resistance displayed in the desert is animated by mourning and the need to mourn. They do not feel negative about themselves in the desert, indeed being there keeps negativity at bay, representing the fight against it. There is a refusal to accept or 'take in' a negative self-definition based on 'being slighted, neglected or disappointed' (Freud 1984: 260), and so much more: being violated, ignored and treated with contempt, like lepers.

Through the need to mourn and to contest its denial, the women in the desert keep critical politics alive that would otherwise be lost to a melancholy future. In a brief Afterword to Eng and Kasanjian's collection, Judith Butler is closer to the mark when she writes that melancholia involves a deadening of the emotions pursuant to the failure of mourning. On a recent visit to Chile, I was told more than once that ordinary people no longer show a commitment to politics that involves any sense of social solidarity but focus on their work and immediate family. There is a shutting down of communication. That, it was suggested, was Pinochet's continuing influence on society. If this is so, then this is the kind of melancholia in action which comes from accepting the failure to be allowed to mourn, to enrich in both personal and social relations through the experience of loss.[2] With the three women, what is not lost is the vitality of the emotions, and that is why theirs is a struggle both *to* mourn and *against* melancholia. Butler muses that the distinction between mourning and melancholia may not ultimately hold because they are 'experienced in a certain configuration of simultaneity and succession' (Eng and Kasanjian 2002: 472). Certainly in the Freud–Loewald account, there is common ground that links guilt, mourning and melancholia but this seems rather a reason to maintain than to discard the terms. That the relationship between mourning and melancholia can generate configurations of 'simultaneity and succession' indicates a productive pairing. That it can illuminate the moral strength of the women in *Nostalgia for the Light* is also good reason to maintain it.

Nostalgia for the Light as Moral-Psychological Struggle

In this concluding section, I start with a critical view of *Nostalgia for the Light* relating to the idea of nostalgia in its title. I then move on to summarise its metapsychological and metaphysical aims.

In Defence of Nostalgia

In 2012, Guzmán gave an interview for *Film Quarterly* about the film, which starts with a review of the film by the interviewer, Rob White. The review praises the film, but 'arguably – though not obviously' sees it as 'much more ambiguous

[2] This was just before the demonstrations of 2019–21 which indicated the ongoing potential for resistance to a melancholic present. For discussion see Charney, Marshall and Christodoulidis (2021).

and despairing' (White 2012: 3) than Guzmán's previous work. It raises questions about my view, that the film depicts a moral–psychological and ongoing political struggle against the state. This is perhaps also called into question by the film's title. 'Nostalgia' is often taken to mean looking back as a means of avoiding the present. Is this what the word means in *Nostalgia for the Light*?

Nostalgia as Evasion?

In his review, White targets nostalgia writing of the women's desert search that if 'disavowal is one way of deactivating the past, then nostalgia is surely another'. Perhaps, 'noble as they are, the aging women who tramp the Atacama in their quest for victims' remains are some kind of nostalgists too' (White 2012: 3). Of Valentina and her 'manufacturing defect', White suggests that this is 'possibly an even sadder expression of the national tragedy' (White 2012: 3–4) than the stony faces of her grandparents (as seen in the film), without a sense of redemption. There is also an early scene in which a 1960s suburban house and kitchen are bathed in an intense sunlit glow as the director recalls warmly the Chile of his childhood before the dictatorship. Then, the light begins to be affected by thousands of motes which float across it as the picture dissolves. These are 'the most sinister images in *Nostalgia for the Light* because … they most directly express distraction and the way a field of vision begins to blur' (White 2012: 4). The coup was 'a phenomenon of psychic repression' (White 2012: 2) and these scenes depict the success of the repression, while the film's galactic vision starts to turn the coup's terrorism 'secret again' (White 2012: 3).

It is possible to depict *Nostalgia for the Light* as participating in 'the calcification-like process whereby Pinochet's … coup gains protection for itself – whereby abuses of power are gradually, numbingly accepted' (White 2012: 3). The film aids forgetting, and its title suggests the accompanying psychological mindset, nostalgia, which makes this possible. Strangely, White's ensuing interview with Guzmán reveals a man committed to working with memory and against denial and to teaching a new generation of Chileans about their suppressed history. Guzmán notes that while 'Pinochet governed with terror' and 'victims were traumatised by … a tremendously powerful oppression' (White 2012: 5–6), fear and repression is not the fate of young Chileans today. 'Only now is there no fear. Some victims are beginning to talk, finally. We're seeing again a student movement, which is not only fighting for a better education, health, working conditions, but also for the memory' (White 2012: 6). Psychological repression is the fate of the previous 'lost' generation who grew up in the coup's shadow, 'many of whom detest me'. For the young, Guzmán says, 'I'm not old and there's a meeting point and a rapport' (White 2012: 6). If White is right about nostalgia and deactivating the past, did Guzmán's film backfire regarding the young? Much hinges on how we understand nostalgia, the pain of return, to operate. Does it deactivate like the disavowal examined in Chapter 9? Of course, nostalgia *can* operate as escape, and so be complicit in denial, but does it have to be, and is it so in the film?

Memory, History and Nostalgia

The first of these two questions takes us to the relationship between nostalgia and memory and the complex of emotions that make these terms part of human moral psychology. The animal that thinks and loves is an animal in history and it is so because it is capable of thought and memory. Memory for the psychoanalyst 'has something to do with separation, loss, mourning, and restitution, *and often carries with it a sense of nostalgia*' (Loewald 1980: 148, emphasis added). The development we have discussed in this and earlier chapters of the self as an emergent synthesis of love and organised mentation enables humans to demarcate time and understand their history. Through memory, humans hold onto the past, give meaning to the present and shape the future. Memory gives a sense of continuity as 'the activity by which, above all, some sort of order and organisation and ... permanence, as well as of movement and change, come into our world' (Loewald 1980: 149). Through it, we make sense of the past as an ongoing process of interpretation and assimilation of what happened. We 'become a truly historical being [capable of] history-creating activity' (Loewald 1980: 172). We are able to contemplate our futures, understanding where we are and how we got here. Given memory, we can also think about the past and mourn loss. In this setting, nostalgia as the pain of return is an obvious complement to mourning. And since looking back, say, to childhood experience reflects our understanding in an earlier time, when the world was not less complex but was more suffused with the experience of early love, nostalgia is both bitter (because of loss) and sweet (because of love).

All this is central to human self-formation. 'In such memorial activity,' Loewald writes, 'which weaves past, present and future into a context of heightened meaning, each of us is on the path to becoming a self' (Loewald 1980: 172). He was writing here of the nature of psychoanalytic conversation, but this depicts what is happening in *Nostalgia for the Light.* It is what the women of the film and its director seek. Guzmán's personal investment is seen in that early scene in the 1960s kitchen:

> The shots evoking my childhood were images of a kind of paradise, the magical world of objects in which I lived as a child ... I found the house we filmed in a provincial town ... and I couldn't believe it. All the things I had had in my home were there ... I'm interested in these different kinds of time. (White 2012: 9)

Do these shots then represent a retreat to a prelapsarian time trapped in consoling memory? Alternatively, are they reflective of the time in the director's own life when love began productively, as it should do for each human being? Do they then represent the possibility of an ethical anchor point from which to witness what then happened? There is a love at the heart of the human psyche, that may be deflected but remain undefeated, and which may be seen in the making of a film or the mourning of women who remember and protest their disappeared family members. Memory and nostalgia are central to such love and Guzmán's personal investment in the film aligns him with the struggle to mourn and for a better Chile. This is the struggle of Violeta Berrios, Vicky Saavedra and Valentina Rodriguez.

Metaphysics and Aesthetics

Nostalgia for the Light offers perspectives on the Atacama Desert and its place in human history across millennia, but also its place in the universe. Aesthetically, the film could not be more beautifully shot, with views of the desert and the planets, and these are matched by the plangent soundtrack. The word 'gorgeous' in the film's blurb is often over-indulgent, but not here. These aspects along with other techniques, including the 'haptic' quality (Ribeiro de Menezes 2019) of the desert's sights and sounds – the scrape of tools, the sound of wind interacting with antique human artefacts and the acuity of colour – all establish its beauty. This provides the setting for women involved in human struggle, one that has sensuous life, history and the universe 'on their side'. It is not until the film's second half that the women in fact appear, but this decentring only makes their small, individual struggle the larger. It indeed becomes central not just to the film, but to all those things the film contains: history's *longue durée*, time and the universe.

If nostalgia in the service of mourning and resisting melancholia stems from the possibility of human identification, wholeness and atonement, the film is itself invested in the struggle to achieve it. The special earthly beauty of the Atacama Desert, its link to the galaxies, the sublime aesthetic quality of the images and music, all indicate a sense of cosmic wholeness. This goes far beyond the microcosmic struggle for dignity and human rights of Pinochet's victims, but the micro represents, expresses and enlists the macro as a world is caught in a grain of sand. The film's aesthetic indicates it is on the side of the struggle to mourn because mourning is its part and parcel. Identification and atonement, mourning and nostalgia, are all affirmed as at once personal, political and universal. This is what makes Valentina's comment towards the end of the film pivotal: 'we are all part of a current, of an energy, a recyclable matter. Like the stars which must die … [What] happened to my parents … takes on another dimension … and frees me a little ….' It summarises its metaphysics and what it seeks to achieve, but it does not shy away from what Guzmán calls the 'big contradiction, [that] happiness can live with sadness and pain…. You can be happy but still be the victim of a tragedy at the same time. That's how life is' (White 2012: 10). That is what *Nostalgia for the Light* expresses in terms that are at once political, metaphysical and metapsychological.

The Film and the Argument

Nostalgia for the Light perfectly captures this book's understanding of what human beings are. The three women search for their lost loved ones in order to mourn and through mourning to become at one with themselves in their social and historical setting. How they feel about their loss goes to the emotional heart of who they are. It is observed equally in a practical search and politics, in the expression of love and grief, in reflection on death and the disappeared, and on the Atacama and the human place in the solar system. Many animals can express the sense of attachment and loss that we call grief, but only an animal that thinks and loves could express these in quite this way. The organisation of the film adds a further layer to the metapsychology and metaphysics on display with sound, vision, narration and its synthetic relation of different images. In these ways, the film explores how the metaphysical is grounded in the metapsychological on the side of the victims of violation in ways that are different from but also the same as for perpetrators. For all the difference between the two sides of violation, an ethics of love and forgiveness, which is now linked to mourning, is grounded in a metapsychology of love, identification and atonement just as is a perpetrator's moral guilt.

My overall argument is that being human is naturally to be a social animal that thinks and loves and this involves the ethical capacity to think of oneself in universal terms. Our thoughts and feelings combine enabling us to express ourselves in terms reflecting an underlying ethics of love. This metaphysical quality of thought and being is grounded in our real animal nature as creatures with a metapsychology based on a drive to live and love which Freud called both libido and Eros. As we saw in Chapter 4, he linked Eros to the 'language of the poets', to Plato and to Paul (Freud 1985: 119–20), signalling how metapsychology and metaphysics were united in human nature. How this comes about as humans develop from the primary narcissistic state to become 'enformed' and structured entities with organised functions of thought and action is described in Chapter 7. Paradoxically this development is only possible because we are born into and out of a community. We can only be active and thoughtful creatures by virtue of what we take in from parents and others from whom we learn. To be a metaphysical animal is to be this thinking, loving, social creature grounded in a metapsychology that responds to violation from the heart.

11

Guilt, Freedom and Reconciliation

On Jimmy Boyle's *A Sense of Freedom*

> I hated everyone…. They made it plain that they felt the same….
>
> Jimmy Boyle (2016: 179)

> In the studio that day … I created my first sculpture through … love.
>
> Jimmy Boyle (2016: 294)

> … what was happening … had consequences wider than … the penal system….
>
> Jimmy Boyle (2016: 295)

In this third 'case study', I return to the perpetrator's moral psychology of guilt and develop it in relation to two further concepts in a moral psychology of violation: freedom and reconciliation. Here I focus on moral development beyond guilt and its denial. The study this time is not of a film but of a prison autobiography, Jimmy Boyle's jail memoir, *A Sense of Freedom* (Boyle 2016).[1] This recounts his life in Scottish prisons in the late 1960s and early 1970s in a time of upheaval and change. His and others' violent resistance to a violent regime led to a radical penal experiment based on the idea of a therapeutic community.

The regime Boyle joined was established as a Special Unit at Barlinnie Prison in Glasgow in 1973. His book analyses his time there as part of his overall life story in and out of prison. He describes what he went through as a boy and young man growing up in a Glasgow slum, how he became a gangster, fought the prison system to a standstill and then changed his life at Barlinnie. The book offers an acute analysis of what prison meant to him and how he developed morally and psychologically in and beyond it. The book's title summarises a key element in his development, the emergence of a 'sense of freedom'. Becoming free from and reconciled with the past and present are the elements that inform his prison experience and shape his life. I draw here on *A Sense of Freedom* to concretise freedom and reconciliation and show their practical relevance to the moral psychology of change after violation.

Barlinnie Special Unit deserves to be remembered as an effective alternative and challenge to the prison system because it adopted a radically different approach to the moral psychology of violation. It enabled freedom and

[1] It was originally published in 1977 and made into a film in 1981. See also his later prison diaries (Boyle 1985).

reconciliation to grow. This chapter explores its approach in three main sections. In the next section, I examine how Boyle's 'sense of freedom' evolved, representing a dialectic in which the meaning of freedom progresses. It becomes more complex and complete, moving from a strongly negative quality (first quote above) to something ultimately very positive, based on a deepening and flourishing sense of self and place (second quote above). In the subsequent section, I then consider how reconciliation develops as an adjunct to freedom in Boyle's moral psychology. I examine the intricate relationship between the individual and the social dimensions of that psychology in which there is also a dialectic (third quote above). In a concluding section, I link ideas of freedom and reconciliation to their earlier development in this book and consider the overall implications of Boyle's account of the Special Unit for thinking about prisons and the question of penal abolition.

Developing a Dialectic of Freedom

What is the sense of freedom referred to in *A Sense of Freedom*? The title hints at something only half-grasped or needing development and the book in fact discloses several different meanings. After some introductory comments, I outline the evolution in Boyle's account. This section charts a deepening and progressive dialectic, or dialectical phenomenology, of freedom. As the author's experience grows, the sense of freedom changes so that the book discloses an immanent moral logic. I begin with some general comments.

Jimmy Boyle and Barlinnie Special Unit

Republication of *A Sense of Freedom* in 2016 reminds us of a time in recent British penal history that seems to belong to a different era. Jimmy Boyle now lives as a recognised sculptor and writer in the South of France, far from the Scotland of the 1960s and 1970s where he made his reputation as a 'hard man' and became an uncontainable prisoner. In the early 1970s in Glasgow, a new form of imprisonment was developed to take prisoners that the system could not hold. These prisoners had refused to accept the prison regime. They met the violence with which it maintained itself with counter-violence, introducing the spectre of ungovernability into the system. The Barlinnie Special Unit was based on a different model of imprisonment, drawing upon ideas of a therapeutic community. It had an impressive effect, producing not only a way of calming and containing prisoners (Whatmore 1987; Cooke 1989), but unleashing creative ideas and artistic practices in an environment that was built on social and democratic premises, albeit in the prison setting (Carrell and Laing 1982; Nellis 2010, 2014).[2] It changed the lives of those in it but the outcome of such success was not what a contemporary reformer might have hoped for.

[2] For recent discussions of the Barlinnie Special Unit, see Bird 2017; Oliver 2017; McGeachan 2019; Anderson 2024.

Barlinnie Special Unit was always seen as an experiment on the edge of the system. As its achievements became well-known and linked to public, media-led controversy, politicians and prison authorities sought to distance themselves and to marginalise it further. Leading figures in the Unit, including Boyle and committed prison officers, were moved out. In the end, it was shut down in the early 1990s, now regarded as redundant, as in a way it had become because of how it had been handled (Sparks 2002). In its early days, however, it established a radical theory and practice that succeeded in producing creative citizens out of troubled, violent and angry young men. In an Afterword to the new edition, Boyle observes: 'I would write, study, sculpt, create a physical fitness regime and, in general, live a productive life. In making myself socially literate everyone was benefitting. I was learning how to use my leadership skills in a positive way. Isn't that the purpose, expected by the public, of the prison system?' (Boyle 2016: 302).

What of Boyle himself? Born in 1944 into one of the poorest areas in Britain, Glasgow's Gorbals, Jimmy Boyle grew up in an educational system offering, as he saw it, training only in social inferiority, and a street culture encouraging gang violence. He became a leading 'hard man' involved in local racketeering and with connections to London gangsters. The story is so familiar as to seem a cliché, of a society which does little to make things better for its poorest and most disadvantaged members, and so often leads to the criminal justice system.[3] Boyle was one of those victims of social neglect who victimise others as we discussed in Chapter 3. That many people in similar circumstances did not follow Boyle's route is often presented as proof that what he did was a matter of personal choice and responsibility, but that misses how decisions and actions meld with circumstances in individual cases. The route for Boyle and many like him led only to one place, crime and the prison. Eventually he was given a life sentence for a crime he has always maintained he did not commit, though he acknowledges he committed others. Reflecting on his younger self, he writes that he was 'out of control and if it hadn't been this particular crime it would have been something else' (Boyle 2016: 309). In prison, it seems likely that his sense of injustice at his life sentence had something to do with how he fought the system, but he was a man with purpose, strength and pride as well as anger and what he now describes as a 'warped belief system' (Boyle 2016: 299).

If he was unused to backing down, the prison system was unrelenting in its insistence that prisoners accept a regime that dehumanised them. For the prisoner who resisted, punishment cells and even 'cages' existed, but what would happen if obdurate prisoners fought back and fought the system to a standstill? This was the setting in which the Barlinnie Special Unit was created and in which Boyle conducted his struggle for freedom. The sense of freedom to which Boyle refers first reflects a negative breaking away from and fighting

[3] A pithy summary introduces the new Afterword: 'Fact: From the age of eleven until I received my life sentence, I had been inside institutions for all but twelve and a half months'. He adds: 'All those years inside had taught me nothing' (Boyle 2016: 299).

against persecutory and oppressive social environments in the main prison system. Later, at the Special Unit, freedom connects with love, trust, solidarity and creativity in a more mature form of psychological development.

The Dialectic of Freedom

In Boyle's account, we can chart a progressive phenomenology of freedom involving nine different elements which move from the negative to the positive, leading ultimately to the flourishing and emancipatory, and linking freedom to love.[4] Noticeable also is that this dialectic of freedom incorporates both individual and social experience.

Negativity: Freedom as Refusal

The first time Boyle mentions freedom is to describe his rejection of the life offered to children in his social position. In school, he felt a bond to the other kids, but he was aware of how he and his classmates were not given nurturing or support. Teachers put them down, punished them and generally treated them as having no future. They predicted criminal careers, and Boyle recalls how at school he graduated from petty to larger crime with its accompanying celebrity. In the following passage, Boyle talks about his experience of leaving school and its similarity with hindsight to prison life: 'At fifteen I left school and in every way it was like leaving prison. I had no regrets. I felt a real *sense of freedom*. The school didn't have a very good success story, as I continued to meet guys from my class in prison' (Boyle 2016: 72–73, emphasis added).

Boyle cites four members of his class later sentenced to long-term imprisonment on murder charges. In school, kudos and empowerment came not from achievement but from rule-breaking. The freedom of which he speaks is that of a simple reactive negation in breaking away from an institution that treated him at best with indifference, at worst with contempt. School had provided his first taste of a persecutory environment. As a form of oppression, it was a denial of freedom, which he then himself denied. School was something from which he was eventually set free, but he was heading only to more and worse of the same.

Deepening Negativity: Freedom as Resistance

In a second sense of freedom as rejection, Boyle has moved on from the school to the prison. Here, he writes of the prison as a persecutory environment, and the effect this has on the emotional life of the prisoner:

> The fact is that prison eats your insides out, and ties your stomach in knots, leaving your heart very heavy. All of this takes place when you are alone, but it wouldn't be the done thing to let this be seen by other people … I returned

[4] In what follows, I have highlighted passages where Boyle talks explicitly of freedom, and I also refer to passages where freedom is at stake but not specifically invoked.

> to the punishment cell and decided that I hated all bastard screws. What I couldn't accept was their rendering me absolutely helpless before coming in and attacking me.... (Boyle 2016: 122)

Prison eats the soul, forcing the prisoner to contain and swallow the negativity of the environment. Prisoners are non-people who must 'suck it up', not betraying their inner anguish, or showing weakness. Boyle found himself in a dynamic in which he met violent control with anger, hatred and violence. Prison represents in his experience a triple denial of freedom: being contained in lock up, being physically beaten and being denied meaningful human relations. A sense of freedom in this environment could only be achieved by detaching, opposing and hating. Hatred represents an active negative withdrawal and resistance to a negative setting, a second negation of a negation.

Purifying Negativity: Freedom as Withdrawal

In a third move in the prison, Boyle doubles down on resistance to a system that had treated him without respect. He begins to generalise his negativity and to see his experience as part of an overall life available to someone in his situation:

> Being a Life prisoner meant looking at prison in a totally different perspective ... Certainly, I had lost my life, but not my will to live, to fight. The whole of my thought processes were undergoing a dramatic change. It dawned on me for the first time that my life sentence had actually started the day I left my mother's womb. Strangely enough I now found a new *sense of freedom*, which I had never experienced before.... I decided I would now live by my laws, not giving one fuck for society or the laws of society. Their very representatives, the media, were labelling me 'Animal', 'Maniac'... I hated everyone and distrusted everyone. They made it plain that they felt the same about me, so we all knew where we stood. (Boyle 2016: 178–79, emphasis added)[5]

Boyle could not walk away from the prison as he could from the school, but he found freedom in understanding the system as a whole and setting himself outside it. This takes things to a deeper level in terms of his comprehension of the system and his standing in it, providing a more totalised sense of negativity and a concomitant freedom. This is existential freedom to live outside the law, aligning his experience in the criminal justice system with how society had treated him as a slum child. Sentenced to life imprisonment, the past and the present are seen as a coherent set of negative experiences, which he will in turn negate in their totality. Freedom is another word for nothing left to lose, for nothing more could be done to him. 'Death was all that would stop me' (Boyle 2016: 236).

[5] '... left my mother's womb': in terms of the importance of the primary narcissistic state (Chapter 7) for ethical development, this statement reflects the significance of being born into a world of poverty and constricted life chances, which of course does start from day one. But birth for Boyle was also associated with his mother's love.

This is a dialectic of negative freedom taken to its logical conclusion. It should be noted however that the position is complex. It *still* contains a positive element in affirming the freedom to stand against the system, even if this is only in terms of pure negativity. For Boyle, 'I had endured all that they could throw at me and come out all the stronger for it' (Boyle 2016: 236). This is an existential freedom *to be*, independent of all negative restrictions which are pushed outside one's essential being. It is couched in purely negative terms though these have been clarified and justified. The question then is where could this sense of real but purely negative freedom lead, and on what could it build?

Countering Negativity: Freedom as Abstract Ideal

A fourth view then starts to become apparent. While a negative sense of freedom as rejection dominated his life at this point, Boyle also experienced something very different. In the following passage, Boyle has been sentenced to life imprisonment and is being transported across country, to Inverness in the north of Scotland, to start his sentence. It juxtaposes the pure resolve to meet negation with negation with something else:

> I was dragged from the court feeling hate, hate, hate … [Being driven across country, there] were occasions when we passed a house and would catch sight of families sitting at a table eating. Fleeting glances that showed me the beauty of home life. Seeing these things really twisted my guts causing me terrible nostalgia. The countryside showed me *total freedom*, with deer running in the distance, and here was I travelling in this prison, manacled, squashed between two screws and three other cars. (Boyle 2016: 183–84, emphasis added)

The passage contrasts positive ideas of family love and nature, senses of 'total' freedom related to natural being and belonging, with the outlaw freedom described above. Boyle writes warmly throughout his memoir of his family and especially his mother. Mother and family love is the root of these feelings. It may be idealised but 'total freedom' captures a deep sense of how Boyle might really imagine a positive freedom, albeit one expressed in abstract terms. This is not the negative freedom to stand outside the system, but the sense of positive human freedom as belonging in a loving family or a natural setting. It stands in contrast to these, and there is a sense both of nostalgia and real utopian possibility. These are not things Boyle imagines as actual possibilities on his own life journey, yet they reflect wishes with which most of us could identify. Could there be a way in which these abstract ideals of free life might become real and concrete?

Developing Freedom: Emancipatory Social Agency

An element of actual freedom appears in the following situation in Inverness jail. Boyle and others were placed in a newly built set of cells with iron bars built inside bigger cells, creating a cell within a cell structure. Known as the cages, they were constructed to control those whose troubled nature, anger and resistance the system could not handle. The prisoners realised that the cement had not properly hardened in the cell walls, and they were able overnight to dismantle them. This felt like a huge, collective, victory against the prison. When Ben, another prisoner in solitary confinement, broke through to the others, he

> greeted us with wild joy and all of us hugged and embraced each other over and over. We laughed at this beautiful victory and knew this was the ultimate dream ... It was agreed that we should knock down all the walls and use the bricks to build a fortress for us to hold off the screws in the morning ... Although still very much in prison, there was this glorious *sense of freedom* about us sitting there together, talking quietly and able to say what we wanted. (Boyle 2016: 212, emphasis added)

The sense of freedom here is based on a positive victory against the system. To have broken down the walls of the cells allowed the prisoners to reaffirm their humanity in a system that caged them as if they were non-human. Affirmed too was their group solidarity and power to act together, and this was an important element in achieving their sense of freedom. Of course, the victory was extremely limited, since they were still in prison, but the sense of freedom here combines elements from the others we have examined. It remains only the negative freedom to resist a system that retains its power, but this was an actively deployed negative freedom. It was achieved with a sense of acting for emancipation and empowerment through a small and reversible victory against an overwhelming persecutory system.

The ability to resist and act together, with a sense of solidarity and collective action, suggests a more positive vision in which people come together, affirm their humanity and resist oppression. Of course, this sense of freedom is a world away from families gathered together or deer roaming in the wild, but it confirms a possibility of collaborative moral agency leading to emancipation no matter how limited the triumph. In another setting, could prisoners act cooperatively in a way that did not pit the power to hate against a hated power? Could they find a more positive way of overcoming the prison system, and what might the broader social implications be if they could?

Developing Freedom: Trust and Collective Empowerment

This leads to the sixth sense of freedom, which comes with an overall change in the institutional setting. Unable to deal with him, the Prison Service eventually transferred Boyle to Barlinnie Special Unit. Though very suspicious of the new environment, the first thing that struck him was that a prison officer handed him a pair of scissors to perform a task, where in the mainstream system scissors would be viewed as a dangerous weapon. He was to be trusted to act freely, responsibly and without violence, reflecting a setting that was housed inside a prison but operated along non-punitive, cooperative lines. The following passage describes the way in which decisions were taken and how these undermined residual punitive elements. Like the mainstream system, the

Unit possessed punishment cells to control prisoners, a system that sat uneasily with a therapeutic ethos. These were eventually scrapped by means of a collective resolution of staff and prisoners:

> The most important development taking place at this time was through the staff/inmate meetings. I suggested that we should do away with the punishment cell with the double door. The presence of the punishment cell meant that sooner or later one of us was going to be taken in front of the Governor and given solitary and that would be the beginning of it. By doing this the real problem wasn't being faced … Eventually they conceded and allowed the extra door to be taken from the cell … and a big cheer went up. By doing this it gave potence to the meetings and … meant that any problems we did have would have to be absorbed by the group meetings. (Boyle 2016: 275)

Trust, responsibility and discussion fed into how decisions were reached. Whereas the Inverness punishment cages had been destroyed by a move of negative resistance that did nothing to change the system, Barlinnie Special Unit got rid of its punishment cells by an act of collective agreement between prisoners and staff. Albeit in the prison setting, this was emancipatory and reconciliative collective action to diminish punishment. It was initiating a sense of democratic decision-making and the freedom it could offer. Aligned here are two forms of positive freedom: the ability to look at solutions in progressive ways, and the ability to achieve this socially and democratically. Both involve nurturing group trust and responsibility, but how could this environment change the mindsets of the prisoners themselves?

Developing Freedom: Taking Responsibility and Self-knowledge

Alongside these positive aspects of a setting built on freedom, and emanating from them, was a seventh sense of a deeper freedom. This was becoming free psychologically, as a new, responsible, reflective person worthy of respect:

> Accepting responsibility was the crucial [problem] as that entailed making decisions, having to consider others, and looking at my own life in relation to others … In order to be able to do this and to understand others I had to find out more about myself. This is what made the Special Unit such a tough place to live in – the fact that every single one of us had to look at himself … [M]any of us, staff and inmates, began to realise we really didn't know who we were. I personally felt that the best way for me to adjust … was to look on it as a rebirth … I was experiencing lots of things for the first time in my life. (Boyle 2016: 277–78)

Being in the Barlinnie Special Unit and voluntarily submitting to a regime based on democratic dialogue with others was hard. It involved answering to the group for what one had done in a way that the normal prison does not. The freedom here was to rethink what one did, what this meant, and how one might become a different person. Boyle's experience of personal development through dialogue with others leads to a sense of freedom as 'rebirth'. To be free means to accept responsibility for what one is and has done, but that involves knowing who one is; and when this leads to fundamental regret, being responsible involves accepting this is so, and being willing to change. Barlinnie Special Unit began to mine a seam in Boyle and others of freedom to act on an understanding of what he had done and been and could become. Freedom was fundamentally linked to progressive moral–psychological change and it was achieved only in an environment which included others.

Developing Freedom: Becoming Alive

The following quote pursues the theme of rebirth, of finding the freedom to become a different kind of person and one can link what is said here to Boyle's more abstract utopian understanding of what freedom might mean on the drive to Inverness. Importantly, it links change to internal creative development:

> Violence is no longer my means of communication. I was becoming articulate and learning how to use it effectively … Small parts within me were blossoming and I was experiencing the glory of being alive. Things looked and felt differently and in a way I was gaining a *form of freedom*. This was *freedom of the mind*, a sense of awareness and the pain that goes with it. The sculpture took on a vital importance, not only in the sense that it was a medium to channel all my aggressions but a medium in which to build and repair the damage to my inner self … I was developing with each piece … I was purging myself of the past. (Boyle 2016: 283–84, emphasis added)

Freedom is not another person's family life, or the freedom of animals to run wild, though these turn out to be real harbingers of something actualised as concrete and personal. It is the freedom of *this person* to pursue and experience life, and the depth of its possibilities. In the language of Chapter 4, it is the ethical experience of a person as a concrete universal/ singular. In Boyle's case, this meant learning how to bring out his potential as a sculptor and to work through his negative passions in creative artistic work. It involved rejection of what he had been in the view of what he could be. Boyle calls this a freedom of the mind, which it is, but it is also a freedom that sets emotional, embodied affect free at a deep and synthetic level. In Boyle, it is freedom through authentic artistic expression, and it is coming alive, becoming an animal that thinks and loves.

Developing Freedom: Love and Creativity

This becoming free could still achieve more. In the following passage, Boyle describes a poignant moment in Barlinnie Special Unit, when he discovered a friend and fellow prisoner, Larry Winters, unconscious in his cell from a drug overdose. Winters was a troubled man who had developed the ability to express himself in poetry, and he and Boyle were close. Later, Winters would try again to kill himself and succeed. Here, Boyle describes an emotional transition as he reflects on sculpting, worried that Winters should survive:

> One morning by sheer chance I happened to look into Larry's cell; he was lying on the floor unconscious from an overdose. He was hovering between life and death … I spent the day sculpting in my makeshift studio, expecting to hear any minute that he had died … It was while working in the studio that day with all this in my mind that I created my first sculpture through the feeling of love. Until this period it had been motivated by feelings of anger and hatred. Later that day I was told that Larry was out of danger. (Boyle 2016: 292–94)

In this passage, the dialectic of freedom is pushed towards expressing love of another and the link between emotional involvement and creative process. That *any* Scottish male could write in these terms, far less in a Scottish men's prison in living memory, gives pause for thought. Of course, this is all happening in a prison, but how far the setting could take a prisoner in terms of the expression of a sense of freedom is clear. In this setting, Boyle was able to unify love for another with creative artistic practice. In his life after prison, Boyle would go on to marry and raise a family, continue his artistic practice, pioneer an exchange system for people leaving prison and set up a scheme for dealing with AIDS in a working-class area of Edinburgh, while remaining an active critic of the society of the day. Such commitments took him beyond the kinds of freedom developed in Barlinnie, and in so doing revealed the limitations of how far freedom could go in prison. These were all perhaps ways in which his 'sense of freedom' expanded in personal and social terms after release. Yet their makings began in the moral–psychological journey towards freedom started in family life in the Gorbals and unusually pursued for all its limits in a Scottish prison.

Freedom and Reconciliation

In this section, I look at the need to reconcile that accompanied the sense of freedom discussed above. I consider reconciliation as both an aspect of individual moral–psychological development and as something that happens in a social process. I begin by looking at the grounds of reconciliation in Boyle himself and then consider how the Special Unit worked with these. I end by reflecting on the substantive nature of moral wrongdoing in a case like this.

Ingredients for Reconciliation

Reconciliatory processes of moral–psychological development were evident even in Boyle's time of angry violence in the mainstream prisons, indeed the two mind states came to be starkly juxtaposed. Among elements conducive to reconciliatory change were Boyle's openness to family love, his ability to experience 'the enemy' as human and that he could generalise from his experience to others similarly placed. These all suggested a capacity to develop a mature view of himself and his position even in an environment set to crush it.

Family Love versus Dehumanisation

When he was transferred to the Special Unit in Barlinnie, what initially kept him going was his family who were now more able to visit him (Boyle 2016: 264–65). Inverness and Peterhead (the other high-security prison where he was held) were far from Glasgow in the north of Scotland. On the cusp of change but still in these mainstream prisons, he describes how his children and mother sustained him and made him rethink:

> I had a visit from my ma … and it was beautiful to see her and the two children. She was looking terribly old and I knew that bringing the kids all this way was too much for her … We had a very emotional and heart-breaking discussion. I loved her as I'd always done and she was my world; her loyalty to me never faltered … She wrote to me each week and kept me in touch with all the family and the growth of my children … After this visit I went back to my cell and thought, and thought, and thought. (Boyle 2016: 216)

Boyle's survival strategy was to dehumanise himself to cope with a hostile environment. Visits with loving family caused great pain because they 'confronted me with almost everything that had been beautiful in my life, and the part that would never be again' (Boyle 2016: 202). Speaking to his mother 'opened up the parts I was trying to kill; the cherished parts of me that made me feel human in an inhuman situation' (Boyle 2016: 202). If we were to put this in Melanie Klein's terms (see Chapter 8), we might say that Boyle's prison experience maintained the persecutory (paranoid–schizoid) psychology he had lived with as a hard man. It kept him from the place in which he could act reparatively, based on loving connection (Klein's depressive position). In prison, 'Something had died within me. I was now animalised and felt nothing….' (Boyle 2016: 251). By the time he got to Barlinnie Special Unit, Boyle was quite paranoid as to staff intentions, with a heightened animal sensibility that he 'could actually smell people … from a good distance away' (Boyle 2016: 260). He had become 'a stranger to myself, so many things had changed within me that utter chaos and confusion dominated by very primitive survival instincts were what I lived on' (Boyle 2016: 258). Yet, the pain that he experienced in the face of his mother's love reveals that something mature and reconciliatory jostled with the primitive in his psyche.

Recognition of the Human in the Enemy

Even in punishment cells or the 'cages', where his anger, defences and violence were at the maximum, Boyle could still be wrong-footed by a human gesture:

> One night…, the door opened quickly and a small paper bag was thrown towards me, then the door shut immediately. I was startled and opened the bag to find two small chocolate biscuits. This almost broke my heart. It seemed that two of the screws had left … and the third … had opened the door and thrown in the biscuits … Although it was obviously the human in him, why did he do this? It confused the picture, as it brought something human back into me and

> I would have preferred to think of us all as animals in the one jungle. This guy had no idea what he had done … I didn't ever say anything to him nor him to me, but he had got to me. (Boyle 2016: 182)

An overheard conversation where an officer talked about his sister 'stopped me dead as I had become so alienated … that I somehow couldn't imagine this guy having a sister, or even being human' (Boyle 2016: 206). In Barlinnie, Boyle would confront the same problem of seeing prison staff as human beings and his ability to respond would slowly overcome his initial hostility and paranoia. Though there was 'a great amount of hatred in me for all screws,… some of the unit staff would approach me in a way that was so natural and innocent' that it would 'tell me that there was something genuine within them' that 'I didn't really want to recognise' (Boyle 2016: 266). Even in the most violent times, when he had most supressed it, there was this other side to Boyle that could accept human interaction. This ability to recognise the common connection between self and other is a key element in love and reconciliation, which we discussed in Chapter 5 as one of the five forms of love. It is also central to identification with the other that we discussed in Chapter 7.

Reflecting on the Other

In prison, Boyle generalised from personal experience, aware that his life course was the same for others from his background. Most had trouble with the law, many ended up in jail like him. There was a terrible repetition as people in the same situation followed the same path, each one a 'primitive rebel' against the system and repeating his mistakes. Boyle identified with this shared fate, and that this could include his own children growing up in the same environment:

> I often thought of the vicious circle of staying in places in the Gorbals and how I had always looked up to all the hard men in my street … Then the kids looked up to me and saw me as the game guy … And yet if only they could have seen me in that cage with no future nor even a cotton vest to cover me … I could see all the traps that I had fallen into … and I felt passionately for those younger kids about to step into them. I would have given anything to stop them doing so … My feelings … were heightened … as I had children of my own and was fearful for their future. (Boyle 2016: 269)

This ability to generalise, to feel outrage and commitment to others, is also a key ethical moment in the development of human love. I described it in Chapter 5 as a moment in the dialectic of love involving self and other in the wider community.[6] It operates like Boyle's recognition that prison officers were human and could be different in another environment. Identification with others from his community and with prison officers, and the resulting sense of

[6] It is also present in the account of identificatory guilt in Chapter 6 and anticipatory guilt in Chapter 7.

the interchangeability of experience, both pushed him towards reconciliation in his own psyche and his social commitments.

Developing a Mature View of Self

Even when Boyle was at war with the system, something was changing in him, though it would be stymied by the prison setting. A psychological force for 'inner transformation [was] taking place' (Boyle 2016: 207). Even in solitary confinement after his period in the Inverness cages, Boyle took up yoga intensively in both its physical and mental aspects. It was a period

> when I reflected on my whole being. Self-analysis became a daily habit as I was trying to find out more about myself…, where I had come from and where I was going. I looked at myself critically and thoroughly till the pain was at times unbearable, and shook my very soul. What was I doing in this place? Was this my life? What was my life all about? … I went through a period of deep shame about the life I had led … I had suffered … but hadn't a clue about anything as I was so dumb and inarticulate and here I was, now an adult, feeling pain like I had never done before. (Boyle 2016: 214)

There is a striking juxtaposition at this point in Boyle's story. He thinks maturely about his situation, leading to shame, torment and pain about the past. He comes to feel he can now 'pull myself together and prepare myself for the future. I had come out of this experience stronger and felt the power surging through my body' (Boyle 2016: 215). Yet, he has just come out of the cages and is still in a punitive and hostile environment. The potential for change in this setting is repurposed as the old power to resist: 'I was living in a jungle and there seemed to be no alternative but to live like an animal in order to survive…' (Boyle 2016: 215). This stark contrast between two ways of being represents an impasse between mature progression and primitive repetition, so how could things move forward?

A Reconciliatory Process

We do not know how things would have developed in the mainstream because at this point, Boyle's resistance led to the Special Unit at Barlinnie. It would provide the setting that could take the ingredients for growth and reconciliation and develop them in three ways: through democratic governance and responsibility, artistic creativity and generalising moral experience.

Democracy, Responsibility and Reconciliation

As we saw already, the Barlinnie Special Unit took decisions democratically, albeit in a prison setting, and a key mechanism for running the Unit was the 'hot seat'. This was important both because it developed relationships in a community and because it stressed that persons take responsibility for their actions before the group. Boyle describes the hot seat as harder than any punishment he had had to bear. Having to face your friends and acknowledge you have done something that will affect them was 'very heavy'. In terms of our discussion in Chapters 8 and 9, this was not about 'holding a person responsible' in the sense of blaming them, but of supporting the person to 'take responsibility' for who he was, what he had done and for reconciliation. If conduct was the result of problems that a person was experiencing, the group would 'reach out and touch him' (Boyle 2016: 276), otherwise, it would require him to respond to criticism for his behaviour. The Unit emphasised the importance of community, but underlying this was a commitment to an individual taking responsibility:

> Parts of me had changed and for the first time in my life I was thinking not as a victim but as a person who had been responsible for doing things I shouldn't have … The reason … was that the unit was allowing me to function responsibly and in order to achieve this one had to think responsibly … I was growing and developing, seeing things through new eyes and a clear mind. (Boyle 2016: 282–83)

What was required was reconciliation of responsibility to oneself and to the group, and this had implications both for how one viewed one's past life and how one would live in the future.

Creativity, Emotion and Reconciliation

One day an art therapist left a 7 lb bag of clay in the Unit, and Boyle began to work with it. Quickly he developed a skill and 'was knocked out by my depth of feeling when I completed a piece of sculpture. The only thing I could compare it to was when I'd won a victory when fighting in the past'. Now Boyle was 'creating an object that was a physical symbol, yet perfectly acceptable to society'.[7] The clay became the medium into which he poured 'the expressions of my soul with pain/ anger/ hate/ love/ despair and fears embodied in it' (Boyle 2016: 282). In this way the strong emotions he felt could be channelled constructively, holding onto them but giving them a new artistic form:

> The sculpture took on a vital importance, not only in the sense that it was a medium to channel all my aggressions but a medium in which to build up and repair the damage to my inner self. I was developing with each piece and the work I was creating was a very strong symbolic statement relevant to my past. I was purging myself of the past. (Boyle 2016: 284)

Note the distinction Boyle makes here between channelling aggression and working through the past. Sculpting allowed both but it was particularly the latter which developed him. He was building himself as a creative and responsible person, living and working with others. In so doing, he was launched on a project of reconciliation between past, present and future and

[7] Though not entirely so as the subsequent media criticism, marginalisation and closure of the Unit revealed.

between self and other. Sculpting was part of the process of reconciliation because it permitted psychological wholeness, what both Herbert Morris and Hans Loewald call from their different points of view atonement (see Chapters 6 and 7). As we shall now see, this promise of reconciliation as atonement through art and democracy was something Boyle thought could be generalised in the broader society.

Generalising beyond the Prison

With Boyle's creative development went opportunities to have his artwork shown in galleries, and to act as an ambassador for the Special Unit. In a time of prison rebellion in Attica, Parkhurst and elsewhere he thought that the Scottish Prisons Department 'had achieved a tremendous breakthrough in penology'. Generalising, he became committed to 'changing the whole decadent system' (Boyle 2016: 285) by promoting the Unit as a radical alternative. His belief was that progress could be made 'by expanding the unit's philosophy into the penal system' (Boyle 2016: 286) with the Prisons Department's support. When he went out to a gallery exhibition, he felt a 'tremendous amount of responsibility' towards making his visit a success both for himself and for the Unit. He could show how people in hopeless situations could 'act responsibly and through their own experience, give something back to society'. What he had done could be done by 'every long-term prisoner' (Boyle 2016: 289–90) given the chance to develop.

The history of how the Barlinnie Special Unit fell prey to a change in government[8] and decisions to transfer out committed staff has been mentioned already. It is not hard to see how Boyle's and others' commitment to generalising its experience proved too challenging for the system, even though the logic of expanding the Unit's benefits in terms of creativity and responsibility was valid:

> All of us knew that what was happening in the Special Unit had consequences wider than that of the penal system, and that some of the lessons learned here could be applicable to society in general. We had greatly expanded our policy of inviting members from the general public in, also people working in the socially deprived areas of Glasgow and the west of Scotland. We felt it was our duty to show what could be done, and is being done. (Boyle 2016: 295)

Perhaps it was this desire to take a 'model that could be used anywhere' (Boyle 2016: 296) to the prison system as a whole, and even to the broader society, that was too much to accept for those in power in politics and the media of the day. If so, the problem lay not with the idea of creating mature, responsible individuals who could reconcile with each other with respect in a community, but with a society organised in ways that could not permit this experience to be generalised.

[8] To a Labour government, it should be noted.

Moral Reconciliation in a Grey Zone

A Sense of Freedom is no trite tale of one who was once lost but now is found. That would ill describe the violent and conflicted route Boyle followed, where the reconciliative impulse is already forming in the most punitive of circumstances, and where its growth is juxtaposed with violence. Nor would it help with the complex moral accounting involved in a case like this. A sober account shows how individual moral psychology can falter or grow as social context and psychological process interact, but how a violent prisoner can nonetheless become a creative artist and social activist. The process is not linear but messily dialectical, since the angry and violent and reconciliatory sides of the person are juxtaposed and jostle; yet a valid development can occur in unpromising circumstances.

Dialectical complexity is also seen in the moral analysis that accompanies change. The later reconciled, or at least reconciling, person has to take up the social and moral truth that was contained in the earlier violent struggles. When Boyle looks back on his past, he sees a time when he was 'out of control' (Boyle 2016: 309), and when in jail he had a 'warped belief system that all cops, screws and authority were bastards and that we, the bad guys, were actually the good guys' (Boyle 2016: 299–300). He stresses that his book 'is not intended to be an apologetic account' and acknowledges he had 'caused much suffering…' (Boyle 2016: 297). The later parts of the book are full of expressions of pain, self-hatred and a desire to change. His Afterword describes him as 'a good person who is deeply sorry for anyone I may have hurt in my life' (Boyle 2016: 309).

Yet Boyle's authentically redemptive appeal reveals a point of real complexity. In addition to being sorry for the past, Boyle takes a philosophical view of his own agency in everything that happened. He caused suffering and suffered himself while being part of a 'disease … much larger and older than me' (Boyle 2016: 297). He asks himself now 'what was all of that about? All that violence, theft, anger and hatred for territorial or material gain, when in fact none of us own anything' (Boyle 2016: 309). He regrets that nothing has changed in the penal system which 'seems to be a lost cause', perhaps is even worse through the impact of drugs, and with rehabilitation viewed as a dirty word (Boyle 2016: 309–10). That society and its politicians have failed points to the structural issues that underlie crime and violence and lead others into the same mistakes he made. They confirm his observation that his criminal career had been 'that of an inarticulate rebel against what was being done to us in places like the Gorbals, and now in prison' (Boyle 2016: 223).

What he did and what was done to him: his, we might say, was a 'primitive rebellion', but in the broader setting, it contained its own moral truth. Putting this in terms of reconciliation, we might also say there could be no genuine settlement with the past that did not see that Boyle's resistance contained such an element. In a very different context, Primo Levi described what he called a moral 'grey zone', which was also a situation where victims victimised others (Levi 2013: ch 2; Chapter 3).[9] It would not be morally truthful to overlook the contradictory moral issues alive in Boyle's struggle with his past. Without seeing this, we would not understand the broader implications of what it might mean to achieve genuine reconciliation for a psychologically evolving person put in the position of a victim who has victimised others in a society that does not itself change. Put another way, a genuine reconciliation requires the entwinement of individual atonement ('at-one-ment') and substantial social reform.

A Sense of Freedom, Moral Psychology and Abolition

In this final section, I reflect on how *A Sense of Freedom* develops a moral psychology aligned with the arguments of this book. I then consider what its broader implications are for the nature of the prison in terms of its punitive form before linking this to an argument for what I call 'deep abolition'. While abolition involves wide-ranging issues and requires a much fuller consideration, I argue that the moral psychology of this chapter indicates the underlying ontological ground on which an abolitionist argument rests.

Metaphysics and Metapsychology in *A Sense of Freedom*

As he acknowledged, Boyle adapted to prison by acting like a cornered animal, but like every human being, he was an animal with ethical capacity, a metaphysical animal, one that is able to think and love. The dialectic of freedom apparent in his account deepens his understanding of himself and reunites his early experiences with his emerging mature orientation. The dialectic of reconciliation seeks wholeness at two levels: internally, in a person's individual psychological self-understanding, and externally, as it broadens out from individual to social commitments. These dialectics in action connect Boyle's story to the underlying moral psychology of this book.

The Metaphysics of Violation

In the 2016 Afterword, Boyle asks himself 'what was all that about? All that violence, theft, anger and hatred for territorial or material gain, when in fact

[9] Levi was discussing the situation of Jews who collaborated with the Germans in the Holocaust to save themselves. Such people did wrong, but it was difficult or even impossible to judge them depending on their situation. In such cases, moral issues of right and wrong became grey and ambiguous. A similar 'problem structure' operates where people become criminals who lack practical choices to act differently. A truthful reconciliation must recognise the case of the victim who victimises another. This makes authentic reconciliation difficult without genuine social change. See also the case of the reconciliative dialogue between Patrick Magee and Jo Berry discussed in Chapter 4. This is another kind of grey case involving a structural blockage rooted in Magee's grief at what he did while continuing to believe he was right in the circumstances to do it.

none of us own anything. In life we are passing through, guardians of what we have….' (Boyle 2016: 309). His writing shows how he increasingly thought in universal terms about the human condition and its place in the world, and this connects him to the young Hegel's view of love and fate, as discussed in Chapter 2. In Hegel's terms, Boyle rediscovered his fate, the point when the 'feeling of a life disrupted must become a longing for what has been lost' (Hegel 1948: 230). Such a fate 'finds itself again' through a love with which it 'is reconciled' (Hegel 1948: 232). A need to find himself drove Boyle to contemplate his life in high-security jails and the pain he had caused and experienced. In terms of reconciliation, we can also think of the phenomenology of love developed in Chapter 5, where we examined the spreading of love between self and other, their mutual relationship and the link to the wider community. This leads to the final stage of love for the 'concrete universality/singularity' of the other, and I think it was such a point that Boyle describes in his close relationship with Larry Winters. This expanding and deepening of love informed his longing for reconciliation with self, family, victims and society while facing its injustices.

The Metapsychology of Violation

How does this drama of love, guilt and its resolution come to be the fate of a human animal? In Chapter 3, we first considered how a metapsychological argument might underpin a metaphysical one. We can relate Boyle's account here to Jessica Benjamin's contrast between identificatory relations based on mutuality and those based on domination (Benjamin 1988, 2018). In a healthy parent–child relationship, and then extending into adult life, mutuality provides the basis for recognising the other. Relations of domination make recognition of the other (and the self) impossible, whereas relations based on mutuality lead to respect for oneself and the other. Where there is domination, we can speak of an experiential split between the 'doer' and the 'done to', whereas healthy individual and social relations are based upon 'co-doing'. The orthodox prison is a clear example of a regime based on doer/done to relations. In Chapter 3, I suggested that the need to be free of guilt rests with the person who dominates while sensing the need for mutuality, for co-doing as a better moral option. At a deep psychological level, Boyle could recognise the other, and this began to emerge even in the punitive mainstream prison. Boyle's psychological position, like that of others in his situation, was complex. As in Chapter 3, he was a victim who victimises, one who both dominates and is dominated, a doer and a done to in the one person. It was this sort of complexity in the victim/victimiser relation that I spoke of as a grey zone in the previous section.

What sustained Boyle and led to his pursuit of freedom and reconciliation was an early life that included a loving family and more broadly a warm and close social community. These were marginalised by his educational and institutional experiences, but they began to re-emerge in the prison. In Chapter 3 and again in

Chapter 8, I suggested that underlying a metapsychology of recognition would lie something like the object relations theory of Melanie Klein with its paranoid–schizoid (persecutory) and depressive (reparative) developmental positions. The penal system maintained Boyle's psyche at a persecutory and paranoid level, but there was a reparative dimension at work in him even under these circumstances. At the point, he most rejected the punitive system, the psychological ground was clearing for potential reparative change to emerge. Reparative change as the root of freedom and reconciliation was beginning, though it would only evolve under the different circumstances of the Special Unit.

We need, however, something more than relations of recognition (Benjamin) or the cultivation of a reparative position (Klein) to understand the need to be free and reconciled, and in Chapters 6–8, I sought to show how a desire *to atone* might be relevant as we moved from Herbert Morris's philosophy to the Freudian psychoanalysis of Hans Loewald. The meaning of atonement in both is to be at one with oneself and others. Morris's ethics knock on the door that Loewald opens to the psychological core of the metaphysical animal. It is in Loewald that we see how freedom and reconciliation (being at one) lie at the heart of human being. Our human psyche's nature lies in that it becomes free and autonomous while retaining a wish to be in a more complex way at one with that from which we separate. Formed in the Oedipal conflict as a struggle for independence and accompanying adult relations thereafter, freedom *and* reconciliation are the two central aspects of what it means to be autonomous. Guilt, as Loewald says, is 'not a troublesome affect that we might hope to eliminate…, but one of the driving forces in the organisation of the self'. The self, he writes, 'in its autonomy, is an atonement structure, a structure of reconciliation, and as such a supreme achievement' (Loewald 1980: 394).[10] Applying this to *A Sense of Freedom*, we might say that Boyle's journey to autonomy lay at the heart of his attempt to be free from a punitive environment. The act of writing the book is itself an exercise in overcoming and changing the world of which he had been a part and in that sense part of a reconciliation with it.

Competing Elements in the Modern Prison: Towards Abolition

Describing Boyle's own emancipatory journey through the prison represents only one side of his book. We also need to look more closely at what he faced in taking on the penal system and especially the prison.[11] What does his

[10] This achievement is never something the individual psyche does alone. It emerges as a form of being-in-relation as the infant experience within the mother–child matrix, the first social bond out of which individuality must emerge. The individual starts as the incomplete potential of a being that still needs to individuate itself as its powers develop. Herein lies the force of love as both a bond with others and a grounding drive of the self.

[11] Penal systems are of course multifaceted and not just made up of prisons. They also include ways of diverting offenders away from the prison, so the prison is far from the whole story. Yet prisons represent the apex punishment of the system and have an overall importance, casting a huge, one might say melancholic (in the sense of Chapter 10), shadow over it.

experience of the mainstream and of the Special Unit tell us more generally; in particular, what does it tell us about the question hovering over his account, about the nature of penal abolition?

The Persecutory Impulse and the Emancipatory Trace

In thinking about the modern prison, we cannot brush aside Klein's strictures on punitiveness when this is given so powerful a setting as the prison. The brute reality Boyle faced was that of an institutional system that punished, controlled and dehumanised its occupants. This is partly about the buildings and design of the industrial prison (the medium is the message), partly about prison cultures and political policies of deterrence, incapacitation and security, and partly about the social desire to punish and to be punitive. Ultimately it is about a society and polity that takes a punitive and fear-inducing approach to crime control as the means of promoting what Henrique Carvalho and Anastasia Chamberlen call 'hostile solidarity' (Carvalho and Chamberlen 2024). More than a matter of policy choices, this is a sociological and historical question of how a society which sediments forms of structural violence thinks about punitive practices.[12] As Michel Foucault observed, the industrial prison accompanied industrial capitalism from the beginning while failed attempts to reform it are as old as the system itself. This baleful repetition reflects the nature of an antagonistic, structurally violent, society where prison is primarily a place for the poor, disadvantaged and marginalised (Foucault 1977; Wacquant 2009; Fassin 2018). There, a persecutory dehumanisation delimits the penal universe, working through psychological tropes which maintain human beings in their least developed, most vulnerable and hostile states. In metapsychological terms, it reaches not for reparative or mature responses in prisoners, but sees them, in Klein's terms (see Chapter 8), as 'all-bad objects' (Klein 1998; Reeves 2019; Reeves, Norrie and Carvalho 2019) needing to be placed in fear, even 'terrorised' for the greater social good (Sim 2009) and the instruction of the law-abiding (Foucault 1977; Carvalho and Chamberlen 2024).

Yet this overall picture is too black and white. Barlinnie Special Unit was after all also a feature of British prison life, albeit for a short time and in the face of much opposition. If a persecutory, punitive tendency is to the fore, rehabilitative ideas continue to operate in the penal system and in particular prisons (Norrie 2022b) though politicians are generally reluctant to say so. It is true that political promises to rehabilitate may become ways of expanding the prison estate as a whole (Carvalho and Chamberlen 2024: 100–1), though this is not to deny that many prisoners rely heavily 'on the support offered to them via teachers, psychologists, artists and third sector organisations … to survive and resist their objectification and punishment' (Carvalho and Chamberlen 2024: 102–3). Even their strongest critics have noted that prisons

[12] A point made earlier in regard to Jeffrie Murphy's discussion of retributive punitiveness in Chapter 8.

can be organised around both punishment and limited reform, an emancipatory or humanising trace in the system. Didier Fassin for example notes the historical, religious and democratic impulses behind a humanising strategy in western penal systems, which 'perhaps even [offer] potentialities for the future' (Fassin 2018: 55–58; see Norrie 2019b). Angela Davis, arguing for abolition in the United States context, similarly points to the role of writing and educational programmes in delivering change for prisoners in the 1960s and 70s, though she notes how these were subsequently closed down (Davis 2003: ch 3).[13] These observations acknowledge the possibility of at least *some* reparative and reconciliative elements in a penal system, and, therefore, the need to think about their relation to its overall punitive structure.

Relating Impulse and Trace: A Structure in Dominance

I suggest we think of the modern penal system, especially as it is manifested in the prison, as punitive and persecutory, but with a humanising element, that is, as persecutory in the major and reparative in the minor key (Norrie 2019b). It is not that movements to reform the prison or to ameliorate and develop its practice do not exist and have their own validity, but that they must always battle against an overall structure which limits and undermines them, even using them to expand the overall punitive network (Carvalho and Chamberlen 2024: 92). Nonetheless, attempts at treating the prisoner as a whole person rather than as an object of control and discipline remain present in the system, but in a way that is dominated by the overarching punitive structure. This major/minor key analysis accounts for the reforming strain in modern prisons' discourse. It explains, to take a couple of recent examples, how it can be claimed that new forms of institutional design may permit prisoners' voices to be heard to their moral benefit. Prisoners may join in 'co-producing' prison social order, at least in a way that ameliorates their lives inside (Weaver 2018). It explains how a prison manager can criticise prison managerialism and target setting in favour of honesty, transparency and integrity – a politics, indeed, of love (Bennett 2019). If not merely rhetorical or performative, these suggest a limited move beyond doer/ done to practices which needs to be recognised as part of prison reality. Such recent views of how prisons should work reconstructively and reparatively are plainly pale echoes of what occurred at Barlinnie, but they reflect the humanising trace in a penal system alongside its focus on punitiveness and control.

That said, the overall punitive setting remains, and the shutting down of educational programmes described by Davis, the eclipse of reform in favour of punitiveness noted by Fassin (2018), and of course the fate of Barlinnie Special

[13] Compare Boyle, looking back in 2016, on the fate of rehabilitation in jails today: 'If anything, things have got worse. The prison system seems to be a lost cause. No one cares … It is a dereliction of duty by the authorities when a prisoner's only chance of getting off drugs is when they are released.' (Boyle 2016: 309–10)

Unit itself show how major and minor keys are co-related. This systemic co-relation is important because it indicates that however major key punishment and minor key reform are drawn in particular periods, an underlying structural arrangement is in place. This is necessarily linked to the nature of social control of the poor and marginalised in structurally unequal modern western societies. We could perhaps draw here on what Louis Althusser (1970) called in another context a 'structure in dominance', by which he meant the way in which a structural whole operates to regulate the parts from which it is made.[14] With regard to the penal system, we could talk of how a dominant punitive and persecutory approach to control defines the space in which reconciliative practices are permitted, subjected to monitoring and control and shaped or made to conform to overall punitive considerations. This acknowledges the existence of reform approaches while noting that they operate on a limited and constrained terrain.

Moral Psychology as 'Deep Abolition'

Is this structure in dominance of the punitive over the mature and reconciliatory inevitable? This brings me finally to the question of abolition, and here I want to consider how *A Sense of Freedom* and Barlinnie Special Unit relate to claims to abolish the prison.

Reform or Abolition?

The experience of the Special Unit is fascinating because it can be read as either a demand for prison reform or for prison abolition. As regards reform, it seems to show how a radical revamping of the prison could permit it to do what penal reformers always thought it should, rehabilitate prisoners. It thereby might be taken to consolidate the prison's importance and value. When Boyle writes (in 2016) that 'Rehabilitation shouldn't be a dirty word; it should be one of civic pride' and that 'Most prisoners are looking for a way out of a lifestyle in which they feel trapped' (Boyle 2016: 310), he appears to take this view. Yet he was also aware of the radical challenge Barlinnie Special Unit posed to the prison system as a whole and to the broader society of which it was a part. That its promise should be treated as marginal and shut down suggests that political actors who pay lip service to rehabilitation could not see it as valid because it challenged the system as a whole.

There are echoes of this in Davis's account of the role of prison writing and education in the United States, which might be seen as only ameliorative reforms. Yet these became for black prisoners, including amongst their number Malcolm X, 'a transformative experience' encouraging 'individual prisoners to acquire autonomy of mind' (Davis 2003: 56–57). Davis depicts

[14] For discussion of the ideas of structured or holistic totality and causation, see Norrie 2010: 93–96.

the move to disestablish such programmes as showing prisons' disregard for rehabilitative strategies, but that may have been only one element in their thinking. They too may have been concerned about the radical implications of prisoners understanding too much. The potential in processes of creative self-development inside the prison are of course ways of rehabilitating offenders but they also tend to generate an immanent critique of the system that houses them. This kind of reform from within at some point pushes towards more radical, abolitionist implications. This is not of course the whole story, but it does reveal the importance of freedom and reconciliation being initiated inside a prison.

Abolition's Theory

In the United States, penal abolition is linked to race as well as class and gender issues. The need to abolish prisons addresses what Davis calls the 'prison industrial complex', a system whereby prison-building and mass incarceration have become big business (Davis 2003; Roberts 2019). Davis's work is important for stressing the complexity of the tasks involved in challenging the prison while supporting its inmates through reforms and pressing for non-punitive alternatives.[15] How a movement for prison abolition should be developed, how it would operate in different countries and what its ultimate aims should be are all important practical questions still to consider. I do however think that the experience of the Barlinnie Special Unit raises the fundamental question, why should we see prison abolition as a real human possibility?

For Dorothy Roberts, it is necessary to 'imagine and build a more human and democratic society that no longer relies on caging people to meet human needs and solve social problems' (Roberts 2019: 7–8), but this is quite general. She notes that abolitionists tend to avoid definitional questions and cites a number of rhetorical devices they have used. Abolition is 'a form of consciousness', 'a theory of change', 'a long-term political vision' and 'a spiritual journey' (Roberts 2019: 6–7). She also quotes Dylan Rodríguez, who 'lyrically' describes abolition as 'a practice, an analytical method, a present-tense visioning, an infrastructure in the making, a creative project, a performance, a counterwar, an ideological struggle, a pedagogy and curriculum, an alleged impossibility that is furtively present' (Rodríguez 2019: 1578). Later, Roberts argues that a 'guiding [abolitionist] philosophy cannot be invented theoretically but must emerge from the practice of collectively building communities that have no need for prisons' (Roberts 2019: 44). There is something in this concerning the relationship between theory and practice and her words might be seen as a caution against the kind of theorisation I argue for. It should however be noted that the moral psychology developed here draws precisely on prisoners collectively and individually building a community by seeking the germ of 'a

[15] For further work on abolitionism apart from that cited here and in Chapter 12, see Christie 1977; McLeod 2013, 2019; Brown and Schept 2017; Langer 2020

more human and democratic society' inside the prison itself. Figurative and rhetorical devices should be grounded in an understanding of what human beings are, and the naturalistic moral psychology here is an attempt to provide such a position.

Deep Abolition and the Loving Prison

Barlinnie Special Unit held up the possibility of change as radical self-emancipation, albeit in a setting that left its logic necessarily 'unfinished' (c.f. Mathiesen 2015). It also required broad social change to complete it (c.f. McLeod 2015, 2017; Davis 2003). It showed just how human beings may relate to each other humanly given space to do so and how they may develop 'a sense of freedom' and reconciliation, even inside the prison. In terms of the prison and its punitive structure in dominance, the Barlinnie Special Unit represented a way of thinking and practising the inversion of that structure, in favour of the human and democratic, the emancipatory trace over the persecutory impulse. While this may seem counter-intuitive and even paradoxical, and while the regime was no doubt imperfect, it put love, solidarity, democratic action, reconciliation, individual respect and responsibility, human creativity and loving concern at the heart of the prison.

A more philosophical way of taking it would be to describe it as a concrete and real utopian practice of the loving prison. It established that it was possible for people to develop their moral psychology away from anger and violence. It revealed how reform of the prison could have an inside–outside direction of travel rather than the reverse. Society did not need conventional ways to reform the prison, rather the prison could become an engine for change for itself and for the exterior world. Of course, this was only part of the story, and of course the Special Unit was introduced by social and political agents for their own purposes. Yet the nature of what happened in creating a self-acting process for change is an important element that is too easily missed. Boyle and others including prison officers in the Unit saw this and their experience chimed with the cultural politics of the time. Their mistake was not to misunderstand what they were doing, but to underestimate what would be needed to bring about the broad structural change that could enable the loving prison to be generalised. The loving prison established a huge stress line between the mainstream and the margin, between prison form and emancipatory content. Yet for a brief period, it offered an alternative that was *both* a logical corollary of prison reform *and* a radical challenge to the existing system. It did not fail in its own terms.

I return to the question of abolition in the final chapter, but the experience of Jimmy Boyle in the Barlinnie Special Unit can be seen as the basis for a deep abolitionist tendency in penal practice grounded in human nature. It carried out in practice the theoretical inversion I developed in Chapter 8 of mature retributivism in which giving each his due, a *suum cuique tribuere*, was associated with each taking responsibility for who they were, what they owed and what they might do. This was not a superficial matter of legal requital, romantic assertion or political choice. It was inscribed in the nature of the human metaphysical animal with its capacity to think and love as it met the prison system and its reform tendency. Even in very antagonistic times, when the punitive impulse was highly pronounced in the mainstream prison, and in Boyle as a mainstream prisoner, the other side of reconciliation and the search for freedom could emerge. The Special Unit gave space for human ontology, positing as its immanent logic that the punitive approach to criminal justice is inadequate for developing real human potential. If the penal system took its cue from the kind of understanding the Special Unit began to practice, it would at the least open doors to a better version of itself. So doing it would also reveal its own inner tendency towards abolition.

Part V
Mature Retributivism as Abolition

Introduction to Part V: From Moral Psychology to Penal Abolition

The aim of this book has been to develop a naturalistic moral psychology of violation around concepts of grief, forgiveness, guilt, denial, mourning, freedom and reconciliation. It has done so at the two interconnected levels of what it is to be a human animal: the level of ethics and metaphysics, and that of human metapsychology. The former allows us to express moral feelings meaningfully and to engage with others accordingly. The latter grounds such moral expressions and provides the human psychological experience that needs to be expressed, as pain, loss, grieving and anger, as feeling 'rotten, depleted of energy, and tense' (Morris 1976: 99). The two levels unite mind and body, 'the flesh made word' (Lear 1990: xii), through the developmental life force that is libido, love and Eros. The outcome is the 'enformation' of the human as a metaphysical animal working at both ethical and metapsychological levels, as an animal that thinks and loves.

The natural consequence of human ontology in its developed form is a set of responses to violation which seek to restore our being to a sense of being at one with ourselves and others, and this is true both for perpetrators and victims. To be at one with oneself is to be in a state of 'at-one-ment', a way of being that is taken too narrowly when we speak of atoning in the sense of paying back for our misdeeds. Punitive payback shrinks atonement to a primitive, punishing relationship which does not take the perpetrator or the victim forward. Atonement in this narrow sense fails to address the victim's position since the victim is not the one with something to atone for, though to be back 'at one' with self and world is precisely what *is* needed. Since both the doer and the done to have a need to restore a sense of at-oneness, and since what lies in the way of restoration is a violative relation that denies this, at-one-ment may be assisted by a process of reconciliation between them.

This moral psychology of atonement as at-one-ment and reconciliation lies at the heart of this book. It establishes an understanding of what human beings are and are capable of which contrasts with how violation is dealt with in existing criminal justice systems. With us today, the dominant mode (the 'structure in dominance': Chapter 11) is an approach that is ethically punitive and psychologically persecutory. The contrast between a primitive and a mature approach to violation generates what I call an ERIC critique, one that is both ethically real and institutionally critical. It is based on a mature retributivism that retrieves the term from its melancholy association with punitiveness by linking it to *suum cuique tribuere*, a broader sense of giving to each his own that can be aligned with at-one-ment (Chapter 8). Such a mature retributivism constitutes the theoretical basis for thinking about an alternative to punishment. As such it constitutes the positive moral and psychological position that can give substance to the otherwise negative concept of abolition. To abolish is to absent or to negate, but what will take punishment's place? The negative concept of abolition does not in itself provide an answer.

In Chapter 11, an example of mature retributivism in action was provided by examining the work of the Barlinnie Special Unit. Jimmy Boyle's account of the metaphysics of freedom and reconciliation with its metapsychological links to loving creativity and relationships shows the developmental possibilities in a mature environment. It suggests alternatives to punishment in the very heart of the prison system grounded in the nature of the human condition. I describe this as a deep or tendential abolition, meaning a potential for love, creativity, solidarity, democratic action, reconciliation, individual respect and responsibility that can develop even at the heart of the prison – if given the space to do so. That is precisely what mature retributivism based on a moral psychology of guilt, forgiveness and at-one-ment after violation aims for. In the final chapter, I push forward ideas about what mature retributivism and deep or tendential abolition entail. I focus on the law's relationship to the vindictive, the vindicative and the validatory, to the idea of dispositional-relational responsibility, and to the difference between imminent and immanent abolition.

12

Mature Retributivism as Abolition

> It is not necessary at the outset to take account of the obstacles which lie in our way – obstacles which perhaps do not necessarily arise from the true character of human nature, but rather from the previous neglect of true ideas .... For there is nothing more pernicious and more unworthy of a philosopher, than the vulgar appeal to a so-called adverse experience, which indeed would not have existed, if those institutions had been established at the proper time and in accordance with ideas....
>
> Immanuel Kant (1993: 246)

In this final chapter, I bring together the mature retributivism identified in Chapter 8 and the deep or tendential abolitionism developed in Chapter 11. The first hurdle to negotiate in arguing for an abolitionist position is that the term is essentially negative. To abolish is to absent, cancel or negate, so it begs the theoretical question of what will come in its place. One answer might be that nothing needs to be put in place of punishment, but the question of what to do about violation and how we respond to it does need to be answered. A mature retributivist position, based on atonement as at-one-ment, and utilising a naturalistic moral psychology of guilt, forgiveness and reconciliation offers a way forward. Combining reconciliative requirements at both the individual and the social level and linking its ethical realism to institutional (what I call ERIC) criticism of what is presently done, it offers a non-punitive alternative to fill the theoretical space left by abolishing punishment. Existing abolitionist texts do offer practical alternatives, many of which are in line with the argument here, but they do not offer an overall theory.[1] My claim is that the mature retributive and deep or tendential abolitionist positions are in essence complementary. Mature retributivism as the moral psychology for repairing violation becomes a way of fleshing out what abolition means. Working from within the terms of retributive theory, it turns a justification of punishment into its negation in the name of an alternative substantive practice.

The chapter has five main sections which reflect the fact that the argument brings together the two concepts of mature retributivism and deep or

[1] See the discussion in Chapter 11 and in this Chapter's fourth and fifth sections.

tendential abolition. The first three move from mature retributivism to abolition seeking to develop the latter's ethical space. The last two start from abolition and consider how mature retributivism can be engaged with existing abolitionist positions. I begin in the first section in what follows by defending the idea that punishment as we understand it is primitive and persecutory and argue that punishment cannot be defended as combining primitive and mature retributive sentiments. We need to move decisively beyond punishment and to that end I argue in the second section for a model of mature authority which aligns the idea of law's public vindicative power with a broader moral, social and political response to violation. In the third section, I extend the analysis of mature retributivism to look at the model of responsibility it suggests for an abolitionist social control practice.

In the fourth and fifth sections, I consider what abolitionism looks like in terms of the deep or tendential model I have been developing. In the fourth, I explore Kant's broadside against 'adverse experience', which heads this chapter, and how abolitionism deals with such difficulties. I argue that the abolitionist argument must involve a real utopian position so that the slogan 'abolition now!' must distinguish the ethically *immanent* from the practically *imminent* in violation's reconciliation. From there, we can then see how abolitionism may operate both inside the actually existing system and as its radical alternative. In the fifth section, I argue that an abolitionist position must recognise that it is the violative relationship between a perpetrator and a victim that lies at the centre of abolitionist practice. However, in line with the argument for mature responsibility, this must generally be connected to the broader social setting in which violation occurs.

In general, any theory that seeks to deal with violation must touch upon a number of points. First, what is valuable in a theory that means that it should be adopted over others? Second, how does this theory relate to the position of an overall authority, such as is represented by law? Third, what conception of responsibility does it deploy? Fourth, how does it connect with the actual social conditions in which it must operate? Fifth, what is its central focus? Though this is no doubt an incomplete list, these are the questions I seek to answer here. My answers will also, I am sure, provoke further questions and appear incomplete.

Primitive and Mature Retributivism Compared

The overall value of mature retributivism as the basis for a deep or tendential abolitionism is that it replaces a primitive, punitive and persecutory approach which tends to the repetition of violence with a mature moral psychology of guilt, forgiveness and reconciliation which permits for resolution and change. But this begs some questions which I seek here to address. I begin with a brief consideration of the language of the punitive and the persecutory I have used to discuss existing criminal justice, and whether it is valid to equate the punitive with the persecutory. I then move to consider an argument that the punitive may be in fact related not to the persecutory but to mature outcomes, considering Antony Duff's theory of secular penance. I then complete the section by considering how restorative justice fits with the picture of a mature retributivism.

The Punitive as Persecutory

In Chapter 8, I described two kinds of retributive theory, one that is persecutory and punitive the other that is mature and reconciliatory, and it is on the basis of that distinction that I have developed the argument for abolition. The distinction, it may be said, is too stark. It may be thought an unfortunate outcome of drawing moral psychology and criminal justice together that two terms (the persecutory and the punitive) have been inappropriately brought together. It is important to distinguish them since they come from different fields, with one rooted in psychoanalysis and the other in law and penology. To punish, in short, is not to persecute, the latter entailing a degree of negative affect not to be found in the former.

Against this, we could see the persecutory and the punitive as different terms with different nuances, but as combining at different levels in criminal justice practice. We could describe punishment in its own terms, as for example the infliction of just deserts, or to deter or control the dangerous. We could then say that an underlying aim of punishment is to cause pain, inspire fear and condemn, and we could add that it aims to isolate and, pushing our argument forward, to alienate and dehumanise, particularly in the prison setting. Of course, as we get to isolation, alienation and dehumanisation, these might be rejected by a criminal justice system theorist or practitioner, and it is not my argument that all criminal justice personnel subjectively endorse the worst aspects of the system. Chapter 11's analysis of its two keys (persecutory in the major, reparative in the minor, but with the former as a structure in dominance) allows for different subjective viewpoints on criminal justice practice. That however would not be an end to the matter for a complex system may have both manifest and latent functions (Shelby 2022: 91–95). Punishment could be articulated in penal theory in a more positive and hopeful way, or be practiced with good intentions, yet take institutional forms which extend its negative quality, and which embed an underlying persecutory psychological function.

If we look more deeply into the punitive experience, we might also detect the possibility noted by Nietzsche, that justice's noble appearances do not exclude underlying persecutory elements delivered through the penal sentence, including the wish to annihilate the 'all bad' other.[2] In modern criminal justice, we somehow manage the gap between the seemingly benign authority of the law

[2] 'Whoever fights monsters should see to it that … he does not become a monster. And when you look long into an abyss, the abyss also looks into you' (Nietzsche 2000: 279 (para 146)).

and the reality of the prison, while punishment may still 'please' us at a deeper psychological level we would prefer to disavow (Carvalho and Chamberlen 2018; Reeves 2019). This is seen especially around the desire for the death penalty or in some kinds of populist political discourse about punishment or 'law and order', where negative affect is riled up. While this may or may not find its way into the articulated sentence of a judge in a court, or a theory of punishment's benign outcomes, it is not unfair to consider a persecutory psychological dimension as informing punitive sentiment or practice. Whether expressed or not, its effects run through punitive practices like the prison where isolation, deterrence and containment remain criminal justice's major key (see Chapter 11).

I argue therefore that speaking of such practices as a primitive and persecutory response in contrast to a mature one is defensible. So long as the Victorian industrial prison or its modern high-security equivalent remain as the apogee of the penal system, and the model of punishment remains to contain and 'warehouse' prisoners according to a deterrent (fear-based), a dangerousness or a condemnatory logic, we are working with a primitive and persecutory moral psychology. I do not deny that other kinds of penal sanction are available in the criminal justice system, but the prison remains the answer to the worst crimes and the solution when other sanctions fail. This means that the punitive as persecutory is constitutive of the penal system as a whole and casts a long shadow over it. I also accept that various kinds of rehabilitative or restorative ideology offer a different perspective on the prison. These do play a role there as in the system as a whole, but they are always the minor to punishment's major key (see Chapter 11). The moral psychology of the prison is ultimately focused on the repetition of the past and what David Scott describes as the lingering, living death of the prisoner-subject, not the prospect of a new and different life.[3] This can then be contrasted with the kind of mature moral psychology of violation, grief, guilt, making amends, atonement (at-one-ment) and reconciliation elaborated in this book. An abolitionist position must identify the existing system for what it is and move beyond its persecutory punitiveness in the direction of mature reconciliatory process.

The Punitive and the Reconciliatory: Synthesis or Hybrid?

My argument is that the punitive and the reconciliatory operate according to different logics and cannot be reconciled.[4] A counterargument from Antony

[3] Scott writes persuasively of the prisoner as a 'death-bound subject' that is one who in the 'prison place' is 'haunted by past trauma and drained of hope in the present and the future' (Scott 2020: 139).

[4] In recent work, Halil Cesur has developed an analysis of what he calls legal and ethical retributivism. Drawing on a range of theorists from Hegel to Hampton, Murphy, Duff, Brudner, Lacey and myself, he argues that legal retributivism as the dominant modern ('neo-classical') justification of punishment is defined against a broader ethical approach which it unsuccessfully denies: see Cesur (forthcoming).

Duff is that they can be effectively combined so that a punitive element operates as part of a reparative or reconciliatory approach. Punishment may constitute an ethical communication leading a wrongdoer to a 'secular penance' in the form of repentance, reform and reconciliation (the 'three Rs') (Duff 2001). The argument is attractive for its identification of mature moral responses to crime but raises the question whether it synthesises punishment with these or involves a hybrid between conflicting approaches.

What Is Punishment Really Like?

In work on the relationship between punishment and restorative justice, Duff (2003a; 2003b) argues that the aim of punishment is not to make the offender suffer 'just for its own sake', but 'to induce an appropriate kind of suffering – the suffering intrinsic to confronting and repenting one's own wrongdoing and to make reparation for it' (Duff 2003b: 53–54). The discussion concerns the role of mediation within a criminal justice system, that is, a process whereby a person is confronted with the moral damage she has done and brought thereby to repentance. Differences exist with more standard forms of punishment, but these do not substantially alter the core moral process of dialogue. Imprisonment for example operates to communicate that a crime has made it 'morally impossible for [a person's] fellow citizens to live with him in ordinary community' (Duff 2003b: 58). In taking these positions, Duff acknowledges he is 'not seeking to justify our existing penal practices, or anything very like them' (Duff 2003b: 55), so that there is a gap between the normative position he endorses and what is factually the case. This is seen then as a matter for ongoing normative criticism of existing practices, but it does not indicate an underlying, necessary, *structural* gap between what theory portrays and penal institutions deliver. If, however, the system was in fact structurally disposed to provide suffering 'just for its own sake', it would mischaracterise the situation to see it as one that is open to normative reform by means of better argument. Further, to argue for the validity of punishment according to an ideal conception of what it could be when its essential reality runs counter to that conception lends support to maintaining it as it is, not to changing it.

I have argued already that imprisonment, the apex punishment of the criminal justice system, with the shadow it casts, does indeed involve suffering 'just for its own sake'. This can be thought of both in terms of how imprisonment *feels* and what it has been *designed* to do (Carvalho and Chamberlen 2024: 95). As regards how it feels, a long line of literature has depicted how its isolation of the offender in a total institutional setting alienates and dehumanises.[5] In terms of how it was designed, the position is complex. In the early days, a religious conception of the prison as a place of reflection and penitence vied with more

[5] Carvalho and Chamberlen (2024: 94–98) and Scott (2020: ch 6) discuss and develop this extensive literature. Key works include Sykes (2007 [1958]), Cohen and Taylor (1972), Matthews (1999), Medlicott (2024 [2001]) and Liebling and Maruna (2005).

hard-nosed ideas of the 'mill to grind rogues honest', the panopticon and the economic argument for 'lesser eligibility'. There is an underlying 'theological' dimension to the prison with both pain-imposing and redemption-seeking aspects (Fassin 2018: 55–59). The late nineteenth-century idea of the prison as a place of rehabilitation also deflects from the idea of imprisonment as a place of punishment for its own sake, but operates, as indicated in Chapter 11, as prison's minor key. If we give the prison's original architects the benefit of the doubt, recognising they might have had mixed motives, we have had long enough now to know how it works, both manifestly and latently, and how it fails. If the prison and its punitive effect are still accepted as central to the working of criminal justice in light of such knowledge, we can only say that those who support it know what they are supporting. As a matter of fact, how prison punishment feels and what it is designed to do are two aspects of the same overall persecutory process, and they look at its core like punishment for its own sake.

Can modern punishment really lead to the 'three Rs'? Michel Foucault's point that carceral punishment has been seen from its inception, that is for 200 years, as failing to improve its inhabitants should be recognised (Foucault 1977). For Duff, punishment can provide an opportunity which a wrongdoer might take to change, so we may hope, but not necessarily expect that it will work. The argument is, correctly, that a liberal society must leave it to the individual to make his own decisions (Duff 2001: 107–12), but might this not also be in part acknowledgement that the prison cell is less a place of quiet contemplation for change and more one of dehumanisation, a place that 'eats your insides out, and ties your stomach in knots, leaving your heart very heavy' (Boyle 2016: 122). Linking modern state punishment and the 'three Rs' together establishes a hybrid in which the two elements make strange bedfellows. At the root of Duff's position is the relationship between the ideal and the actual. Of course, we can relate an ideal to an actual, but only if the two are intrinsically connected so that the ideal might critically interrogate the actual. It is not possible for a land-based animal to fly (at least by itself) and no amount of constructive criticism will help.

Punitive Burdens Are Not Always Needed

In another way, Duff's argument is compelling. There is much in his moral psychology of penitence, repentance, reform and reconciliation to think that the underlying drive in his argument is reconciliatory, and indeed towards penal abolition. Against that, he argues that some kind of punishment as the imposition of a 'burden' is always required. There is a necessary connection between standard retributive and restorative justice, such that the latter is a form of the former (Duff 2003b). The language of 'burdens' euphemises the reality of modern punishment but it does not do away with it. In any case, is the imposition of punishment always necessary? Where a wrongdoer and a victim are reconciled without imposing such a burden, or a hug, gift or other reparative token would do, it seems unnecessary. In such cases, Duff argues that the wrongdoer still owes an obligation to the community represented by the law and state, which must also be satisfied, so the punitive burden is still needed. Yet the community too might feel that what has passed between wrongdoer and victim is sufficient. It might also feel that censure and punishment are not owed because it itself has been at fault, and a more relational response is needed.

An interesting short exchange between Duff and John Braithwaite (Braithwaite 1999: 20; Duff 2003b: 52) illustrates the point. The example is offered by Braithwaite of villagers giving rice to a thief for shame that he should be so poor as to have to steal. It illustrates the interconnectedness of wrongdoing, of the perpetrator and victim, of the judge and judged in a mature and reconciliatory social setting. In the process, punishment or burdens are seen either to be distributed more broadly, or as rendered otiose by a relational moral accounting. Duff's admittedly brief response presses the punitive response to violation with regard to what the perpetrator owes the victim, but in making the argument for punishment's necessary burdens, he abstracts this relationship from the wider social and moral relations where the debt goes the other way.[6] The problem is that a mature account of the 'three Rs' has to be able to deal with moral psychology in both its individual and its social terms, while marrying such a mature moral psychology to a legally based perpetrator–victim relationship will pull the discussion back to the punitive and its 'burdens'. Yet such 'burdens' are non-necessary from a mature psychological point of view emphasising the relational. A properly reconciliative position based on ideas of repentance, reform and reconciliation must move beyond punishment and in the direction of abolition.

What of Restorative Justice?

Mention of Braithwaite's work raises the question how far the current approach is linked to arguments for restorative justice. This book does not come out of such an approach, though it is sympathetic to its underlying ethical impulse. The problem is that while restorative justice 'draws upon … a definite set of ethical ideas about how we should relate to other human beings' (Johnstone 2002; Johnstone, 2003: 6), it is hard to find a developed, synthetic account of what it means in ethical terms. Gavrielides and Artinopoulou (2013) see the philosophy of restorative justice as emergent from its practices. They agree that there is no single ethical account available and assert the value of an exploratory journey over firm theoretical foundations. Meredith Rossner (2017) emphasises the variety of value- and practice-based explanations. Emblematic of this lack is the contrast between Braithwaite's (1989, 1993) foundational work for restorative justice on shame and reintegration, which takes a sociological and historical route, and Bernard Williams's (2008)

[6] Some of the ways in which the punishment relationship is undermined by social justice issues in Duff's work are discussed in Chapter 3.

account of the ethics of shame (first published in 1993). Williams's work has had some influence on the restorative justice literature (e.g. Harris, Walgrave and Braithwaite, 2004; Harris and Maruna, 2006), but not much. In any case, his emphasis on shame over guilt is problematic and indicative of the need for deeper enquiry (Wilson 2020), while his call for a deeper moral psychology of guilt and blame has not been taken up (see Chapter 6).

Restorative justice remains underdeveloped theoretically, drawing pluralistically on a variety of cultural, historical and religious resources to inform practical reflections (see e.g. Johnstone 2003; Sullivan and Tifft, 2006; c.f. Pavlich 2003). While the emphases on pluralism and practice may seems a strength, it leaves a gap for a moral theory that could critically inform what is happening. This may however be hard for restorative justice to grasp. Amanda Wilson (2021a; 2021b; 2022) has argued that theorists have not only failed to pursue deep ethical questions in favour of a simplified sociological and historical approach, but also that their emphasis on shame in contrast to guilt is misplaced and shaped by the misunderstanding that guilt is necessarily law's domain. Restorative justice, it is believed, must avoid guilt if it is to offer a practical alternative to criminal justice.

The problem here is that guilt is understood only in punitive terms, and the possibility of mature guilt, which would be an appropriate foundation for restorative justice, is not seen. Theorists too readily accept the opposition between retributive and restorative justice so that the possibility of a mature retributivism based on a moral psychology of reconciliation is lost. Restorative justice both acts and thinks in the shadow of law, condemning itself to be law's junior partner and tailoring its concepts to this role. One might suggest that the focus of liberal modernity has been so intensely on law and punishment that alternative approaches have had to draw on fragments of what has been marginalised such as first nation experience, religious tradition or 'informal' social practices. So doing, theorists cut themselves off from a theoretical understanding that could ground their practical and ethical claims. In this way, restorative justice theorists think in a way that hybridises the relation between the restorative and the punitive, because understanding the former takes place while accommodating the latter. My proposal would be that the conception of mature guilt and retributivism argued for here is appropriate to understand what restorative justice involves, and to press its case as an alternative to legal punishment. This claim takes us to an exploration of how mature retributive guilt handles what I call the vindictive, the vindicative and the validatory.

Mature Retributivism as Vindicative and Validatory

I argue that two kinds of retributive theory are possible, one that is persecutory and punitive, the other that is mature and reconciliatory. The distinction is valid and the attempt to combine the punitive with the reconciliatory produces a hybrid form that does not reconcile its main elements. Could it *still* be claimed that the existing legal, retributive, punitive and persecutory approach contains a deeper ethical significance through the recognition of right and the condemnation of wrong? Would a mature retributivist position eschew this and would something be lost in the process? What is at stake here might be made clear in considering an argument by Jeffrie Murphy. At the point in his career when he was most impressed by punishment, he pressed a point in favour of what he termed 'retributive hatred'. This might seem an unlikely argument to attract a mature retributivist arguing for abolition, but there is something here that should be observed.

For 'Retributive Hatred'?

Murphy wrote of a case of rape where the victims sought maximum punishment for the perpetrator:

> These women were outraged at the thought that this vicious man, utterly unrepentant, could soon continue to lead a free life … I sympathised with their anger and hatred, having no inclination at all to call them petty or spiteful … *This* is the kind of case that must be discussed and made central in any comprehensive attack on the nature and justification of … the kind of hatred I have called retributive in nature. (Murphy and Hampton 1988: 92)

On the one hand, Murphy's language has the appearance of a primitive reaction. The perpetrator is 'vicious' and 'utterly unrepentant,' the response of the victims naturally characterised by anger and hate. On the other, there is in Murphy's conviction the sense of an experience that needs to be addressed and vindicated, that is, made right by punishment. Though not everyone reacts in this way, it is perhaps hard not to feel something like this in some terrible cases. Here was a serial rapist preying over time on all the women of an entire community and placing them in fear. Does moral rectitude not lurk in the most punitive sentence of a court faced with such egregious wrongdoing? Is not the criminal court doing something right here in expressing a properly punitive sentiment? Murphy's point deserves further discussion and can help us see better what is at stake in mature retributivism and abolition. An answer to his challenge should consider two complex things. The first is the relationship between three moral elements in criminal punishment, what I shall call the vindictive, the vindicative and the validatory. The second concerns the nature of anger as a moral emotion.

The Vindictive, the Vindicative and the Validatory

Criminal justice involves a complicated ethical moment that draws on three different elements in what might be termed a 'justice complex'.[7] First, there

[7] For a fuller development of this argument, see Norrie 2023.

is the 'vindictive', by which I mean the primitive, punitive and persecutory practice discussed earlier as being at the core of modern punishment. This is about inflicting fear, pain and payback, its ultimate modality being the prison. The second is the 'validatory', which in contrast involves a broad understanding and reconciliation of the complex issues and responsibilities, including individual and social responsibilities, which need to be understood if a violative act is to be properly acknowledged and dealt with. This involves the possibility of expressing moral guilt, seeking and finding forgiveness, working through violation, and ultimately individual and social reconciliation. To validate the reality of violation and support recovery from it is to engage with it in a mature way for perpetrators, victims and the community as a whole. It leads to broader social reflection on how the wrong came about and what would be needed socially to stop such things from happening again. Of such reconciliative possibilities, especially pertaining to victims, Murphy writes sharply that he would find it 'indecently insensitive and presumptuous had anyone charged them with the vice of failing to forgive and love their enemies' (Murphy and Hampton 1988: 92). The validatory position is not however a question of imposing an expectation to forgive. Rather it involves reflecting naturalistically on the human psychology of grief and mourning for people faced with violation and how they might survive it, repair themselves and live better in its wake in a social setting.

If the vindictive and the validatory represent the primitive and mature poles of a response to violation, there is a *third* possibility that sits between them that is important in law, that I called above the 'vindicative'. This is the moral and legal declaration by a supportive community that a victim has been violated, one which publicly upholds what is morally right and condemns what is morally wrong. In the hands of a judge with weight in her pronouncement, this is a point of formal vindication, and it is when criminal justice looks in principle most morally meaningful.[8] The public declaration that a victim was violated and that a wrong was done is a moment which contains ethical value. I think this is the moral nub of the issue Murphy was trying to get at in supporting the rapist's punishment.

There is however a question not just about criminal justice's best, vindicative moment, but how it fits into the overall 'justice complex' involving also the vindictive and validatory. On the one hand, the vindicative *extends towards the validatory* in that it recognises and condemns the violation that has occurred. It declares against the violation, and this may be a necessary, or at least supportive, element in reaching towards a broader validation of the effect of wrongdoing and its overcoming. On the other hand, the result of a vindicative criminal justice decision is likely to be a prison sentence, which links the moral condemnation to a persecutory and punitive disposal, that is, *to a vindictive*

[8] Of course, what is so 'in principle' is not necessarily so 'in practice'. Weighty moral declarations from the bench are undermined by conditions of social injustice, as discussed in Chapter 3 (and see Kelly 2018). They are also undermined by tying vindication to vindictive punishment, as discussed next.

outcome. Vindicative judgement may ring in the perpetrator's ears, but his future will be organised along vindictive lines. Vindication occupies a middle ground between two contradictory positions. It beckons towards validation by virtue of its moral declaration, but it falls back into vindictiveness by virtue of its punitive outcome. Its ultimate reliance on a primitive and persecutory disposal drains substance from the fine, mature words of moral vindication that may have struck a chord in Murphy. The problem is that extant criminal justice combines the vindictive with the vindicative, while what is needed is that the vindicative should be combined with the ethically broader validatory.

Anger's Bivalence

Underlying Murphy's concern is a second element, concerning the complex nature of anger and how humans deal with it. There is more at stake here than Martha Nussbaum allows (see Chapter 4). For her, anger is a problem in relation to violation because it is associated with the vindictive as 'payback', the primitive desire that things should go badly for the perpetrator (Nussbaum 2016: 23). The exception to this is what she calls 'Transition-Anger', but this only allows anger its moral place where it is converted quickly into a commitment to social change. There are two possible kinds of anger according to the moral psychology developed in this book (Chapters 7 and 8). In the perpetrator, a mature anger leads to the desire to restore (Klein) or to work through guilt (Freud and Loewald). In the victim, anger can be either vindictive or validative. In the former, it is either annihilatory (Klein) or fear-inducing (Freud). In the latter, it would be an anger based on the desire to restore or on grief at violation of a love-invested life that has been disrupted, which seeks for at-one-ment and may eventually lead to a commitment to social change. Anger, in other words, is part of a mature ethical response to being either the violator or violated. It is the natural moral accompaniment to a disturbed life that seeks to be restored (made again at one). Yet, such mature vindicative anger is likely only to be part of an initial angry reaction, which will include an impulsive response to violation. A *vindictive* element flares up initially, but then may transform into a *vindicative* desire to condemn the wrong, and then to view it as part of a holistic, mature, *validatory* response. The moral quality of the anger modulates over time.

The upshot is that Murphy is correct to claim there may be a rightfully expressed anger at play in responding to serious violation. This may however go in two directions, either towards the vindictive ('I want to see you suffer') or towards the vindicative and the validatory ('This is wrong and should not happen'). The latter anger may lead to transitional motivations for social change, but it has an authentic, subsisting moral ground in how a victim (or perpetrator) might deal with violation. The overall point is that at an experiential level, anger is anger, an eruption of deep feeling in which the primitive desire to hit back and the mature desire to address things more roundedly are fused. These can hardly be distinguished initially, either by the one feeling it or by the observer. A victim's vindictive–vindicative anger at violation has a natural foundation which deserves respect and space. Yet to say so is not to support what Murphy calls retributive hatred, the desire to hit back. In its initial reactive form, rightful anger may reflect such a desire, but it is also in that same moment the harbinger of a deeper vindicative–validatory response to violation. The question then becomes how anger develops and whether it animates a desire for payback or a desire for moral affirmation, recovery and change.

In its early stages, it would be easy to identify initial anger with retributive hatred, but an immanent ethical anger may unfold as vindication and a broader moral validation.[9] This is, I believe, an important aspect that drives the commitment to mature retributivism as abolition. It is the sense that punishment does not take seriously enough what is wrong with violation so that a better and broader human solution is possible. A properly reconciliative position must move beyond vindictive punishment towards an approach which holds onto the vindication of right and wrong while seeing that these function in a broader validatory process. A role for public authority remains possible here, but one that separates the vindicative from the vindictive.[10]

Mature Retributivism and Taking Responsibility

A third issue concerns the nature of responsibility in a mature retributivist approach. One anxiety that might be triggered concerns the relationship between an approach that draws upon Freudian metapsychology and the thought that this is a 'therapeutic' approach. Of course it depends on what that means but does it bring the argument too close to the idea of a therapeutic state, an old and discredited idea and one that discards the key concept of individual responsibility? In fact, the argument counterposes two models of responsibility, where one is deeper than the other.

Holding Responsible and Taking Responsibility

Putting the problem in a very concrete way, how can a model of human conduct which locates springs of action in, say, a person's unconscious enable us to find that person responsible for their acts? For Victor Tadros,

[9] In Chapter 10, I see Violeta Berrios as expressing a vindicative moral anger which continues to inform her search in the desert. In Chapter 11, I suggest that Jimmy Boyle's anger in refusing to accept the mainstream prison system mixes vindictive and vindicative elements, while a validatory response begins to emerge en route to the Special Unit.

[10] A possible image of the state that could eschew vindictiveness and reflect vindication and validation is what David Scott calls the 'non-coercive mediator state' that 'prioritises life, acknowledges human dignity and looks to handle troubled people through mediation, repair and redress' (Scott 2020: 228). The model here is drawn from the guild socialism of GDH Cole (1920).

the rational explanation required for legal responsibility 'involves psychological states at the level of consciousness' and excludes 'deep level and hidden desires of the agent'. Such explanation is 'precisely to be distinguished from explanation in terms of the agent's "unconscious self", if indeed there is such a thing' (Tadros 2005: 28). If there is not, of course, there is no problem, but my premise is that there is. Beyond law's 'radically incomplete ... picture of any person we know' (Moore 1984: 112) lies something like the metapsychology established in this book. That can be discussed in terms of a person's unconscious, though that is not all that is at stake. I therefore need to consider whether individual responsibility is at risk here, and what is at play in distinguishing 'rational explanation' from deeper elements in a person's selfhood.

A starting point is Sigmund Freud himself (see Chapter 9). Writing of dreams, a central locus of the unconscious, Freud was clear that the dreamer was responsible for them:

> What else is one to do with them? Unless the content of the dream (rightly understood) is inspired by alien spirits, it is part of my own being. If I seek to classify the impulses that are present in me according to social standards into good and bad, I must assume responsibility for both sorts ... (Freud 1925: 133)

Freud's point is that one is not responsible for one's dreams in the simple sense that one should blame oneself for having a bad dream or congratulate oneself for a good one. The dream rather shows the dreamer something about herself that should be of interest in her waking thoughts. Through it, she may learn about her unconscious thought process, relate it to how she conducts her conscious life, and understand more fully what that life is. Taking responsibility for one's dreams is not about being 'held responsible' and censured for them, but about a process of learning and change by taking the dream seriously. What does the dream tell me about aspects of myself that are there but partially hidden from my conscious understanding?

We could apply this question to a violative act, where what has been done reflects my underlying sense of self, and it is this that needs to be thought about and addressed. It is about linking the act to who I am, why it was wrong, what its effects were, how I came to do it and what I would need to do to not repeat it. In its fullest form, this is what Amanda Wilson describes as addressing a 'quantum guilt' (Wilson 2021a; see Chapter 6), that is, a responsibility that takes in my past as well as my present, and how I react unreflectively in ways that are problematic for me and other people's lives. It may also involve addressing the social environment which made the act possible, and what I would need to do to try to repair a violation. So doing I would have the chance of atoning and reconciling, of being at one with myself and others. All these things are included in a much deeper sense of responsibility than a simple legal approach to what one 'rationally' can grasp. Nor do they cancel an overall conception of what is rational, but rather expand it in the way suggested in Chapter 6, as part of developing a fuller sense of what an examined life can mean.[11] Responsibility is thus central to the moral psychological position, though it is not the kind of responsibility usually considered by law. Law's account involves a formal abstraction of the individual which then looks for the connection between mind and act at a point in time, in technical legal terms a conjunction of mens rea and actus reus. This model at the level of consciousness is 'punctualist' in that a mental state and act are caught at their intersection in time and are linked to formal requirements of capacity, choice and fair opportunity. Simple requirements of consciousness, voluntariness, intention, awareness plus non-insanity and absence of duress then complete the picture (Norrie 2014).

A Dispositional-Relational Approach

Here it is interesting to note that broader conceptions based on character or its dispositions (e.g. Lacey 1988; Tadros 2005) are available, but these must still be limited to a focus on the act or they risk losing their purchase on the choice. They then risk the claim that the individual was not responsible at all since we do not choose our character. Character and its particular dispositions and how these make an act mine are attractive supplements to choice and capacity models, but they may threaten the punctualist view of responsibility needed to hold a person decisively responsible and punishable in law. My approach is related to this dispositional account but with a significant difference in that I argue for a model of responsibility that is both dispositional *and relational*.

With regard to responsibility for ourselves understood in a broad and more complex way, Freud's comment about dreams can be linked to Loewald's account of ego and superego formation where the superego is a means inter alia of self-monitoring, understanding and living with one's dispositions in order to make sense of them, develop one's capacities and live holistically with their effects (see Chapter 7). The superego is the reason why we should seek to take responsibility for our dispositions, but not in the standard way of being held responsible for an act. This is not responsibility in law's punctualist manner, leading to individual blame and punishment, but about taking responsibility for what one has done in a process of seeking to find wholeness, a process of being 'at one' by developing mature judgement. This is about relating a violative act to who I am, how I could have done it and what I would need to do to not do it again. It is about addressing behaviours which may be

[11] Like Tadros, Tommie Shelby has recently taken such a position to argue against penal abolition. The abolitionist is caught in a contradiction, he claims, because she cannot wish to deny 'the capacity for rational and free action' (Shelby 2022: 61) even as she argues that 'the agency of the oppressed has been compromised by the structural violence of unjust institutions' (Shelby 2022: 63). The point of the dispositional–relational approach to responsibility discussed in what follows is to agree about the value of human reason but to argue that rationality is more complex than is usually allowed in legal theory. Abolitionism, on a dispositional–relational approach, must consider how responsibility is *taken* – realised, accepted, developed and acted upon, and not just imposed through blame and punishment.

sedimented in one's personality and prone to be repeated. It is about finding, in psychoanalytic terms, a balanced relationship between superego and ego functions. Dispositional responsibility is about experiencing, reflecting upon and understanding one's dispositions, adjusting or reorganising them in the light of developed understanding and responding to them. In that process of discovery and adaptation, taking responsibility for one's dispositions is about connecting what I did to who I am in a deeper, moral psychological, sense.

This broader sense of responsibility is also about understanding the social–relational component in the forming of dispositions. Individuals' violative actions, as with all actions, are never just about individuals, but about the relationships which inform their actions. Human agency is from the start social in its nature since human ego formation is always about what we take in from role models as our ego ideals (Chapter 7). These become ours as we move from the ingestion of ideals to their overall organisation in individual identity formation, but the social is always there at the heart of what we do and see as ourselves. This process starts in childhood and is ongoing in adult life as we deal with social and cultural messages and changes. Insofar as such messages encourage violative actions, the link between what a person did and the social setting in which they did it remains ever present, and that is why responsibility is dispositional–relational and shared between a person and a context.

Think for example of the way social and cultural messages about sex and gender may reflect misogyny, and how male perpetrators come to understand how to behave in relations with women. This is why the 'dialectic of forgiveness' explored in Chapter 5 moves from self and other to the wider community in the experience of a victim of sexual violence like Jayne Stewart. Through a theory of responsibility in which the individual and the social remain ultimately inseparable, we find another reason why a commitment to individual change leads to the need for social change.[12] A properly reconciliative position must move beyond holding people responsible in the sense of blaming and censuring them and find ways in which they can reflect upon their past behaviour and take responsibility for it.

Deep or Tendential Abolitionism Today

A fourth question concerns how we connect mature retributivism qua deep or tendential abolition to the social world in which we advocate it. The question is

[12] These comments illustrate a broader point about how we come to change our mind about serious questions of right and wrong and the implications for a sense of responsibility (Norrie and Wilson 2024). This concerns how real historical change in a person's thinking and self-identity can affect her understanding of what she has previously done. It is central to grasping how people come later to accept responsibility for past wrongdoing and what they should do about it. What may have seemed moral, socially accepted and indeed rational conduct at one time is very different looking back. The argument is that such change can be understood within the dispositional–relational approach adopted here, but not in law's or standard philosophy's abstract and formal approach.

whether in speaking of penal abolition one talks in an impractical and utopian way, one that should be dismissed for its idealism.

The Problem of the 'Adverse Experience'

'It's a nice idea, but it can't work' is the basic charge and responding to it takes us to Kant's comment at the head of this chapter about thinking impractically. Interestingly, he related his position there to the possibility of no punishment in the ideal state, which he took to be a plausible position.[13] Since his political writings are a foundation for the modern justification of punishment (see Chapter 3; Norrie 1991: ch 3), this comment from the *Critique of Pure Reason* is surprising. We should however welcome his assertion that philosophers must think boldly and outside the box while noting a parallel and irony between his time and now. Kant wrote in a period of great historical change when forces of enlightenment addressed the dismal weight of a punitive past, just as we consider the failures of punishment that bear down on us today. The irony is that the modern retributive system of punishment he proposed has become the basis for the problems we now face.

Yet his words about the need for bold thought are as true now as they were then. To repeat them, there is 'nothing more pernicious and more unworthy of a philosopher, than the vulgar appeal to a so-called adverse experience', especially where it 'would not have existed, if those institutions had been established at the proper time and in accordance with ideas…' (Kant 1993: 246). After 200 years of dealing with violation badly, we do indeed use our accumulated 'adverse experience' to carry on as before (Foucault 1977; Carvalho and Chamberlen 2024). Those who offer radical philosophical criticism are dismissed as idealists and required to come up with practical answers before their criticism may be considered. Yet the philosopher's privilege to think laterally and creatively is also a responsibility and there is no reason to cite today's adversities as justification for repeating them tomorrow. As a first salvo, critics of radical change should take Kant's view seriously both in itself and in terms of a philosopher's responsibility.

One practical way of expressing the 'adverse experience' would be to ask how one would deal with people who commit serious crimes who are simply reactive, unthinking or immature in their understanding. Taking up the key theme of victims who victimise others (Chapter 3), those who come to the criminal justice system from disadvantaged backgrounds may not have had the space or support to develop emotionally or psychologically. Crime affecting ordinary people and their communities is often a product of damaged, uncared for or unsupported people acting or reacting badly around money,

[13] 'The more legislation and government are in harmony with this idea, the more rare do punishments become, and thus it is quite reasonable to maintain, as Plato did, that in a perfect state no punishment at all would be necessary' (Kant 1993: 246).

violence, drugs or gangs. It may be said, however, that the criminal justice system must deal with people as they are, and not as an ideal theoretical model would like them to be. Moving from perpetrators to victims and the broader social audience, nor can we dismiss the strongly punitive reaction of many for whom anger and a desire to pay back a perpetrator are significant. *Bien pensant* liberal desires for reform are more easily entertained by those who are not at the sharp end of violative conduct. Punitive reactions may be stoked for political purposes, or to hide a lack of positive social reform, but they still have to be faced as the reality against which a reconciliative alternative is posed.

My response to this picks up the distinction between a vindictive, a vindicative and a validatory reaction to violation and how they are all contained within the initial anger at the kinds of violation we see most days in the news. In its initial spontaneous form, such anger fuses the violent desire to hit back and the more considered moral recognition that something wrong has happened that should be addressed and resolved. Most people, regardless of their social position, can reflect broadly on what has happened[14] and see that a punitive response involves mainly repetition of violence. Locking people up provides a sense of instant satisfaction and protection but the problem of crime is only deferred, in different ways, for the perpetrator, the victim and the wider community. It is one thing to enjoy the moment of vindication in the courtroom, another to realise that its outcome will be the vindictive locking away of someone who may be poor and inadequate, who will languish for many years without support to change, while receiving ongoing tuition in the ways of violence and crime. It would be better for all concerned that a vindicative reaction be upheld but aligned with a validatory rather than a vindictive response to crime. It should be especially the responsibility of the impersonal state and its law, unhampered by an initial angry reaction, to reach for the morally validatory approach.

A second way of expressing the problem is in terms of institutional possibilities. It would be ‘unrealistic to expect institutions to realise and mobilise all the subtle dynamics of interpersonal life’ (Lacey 2024: 9) such as a mature retributivist position requires. Certainly, if our model is that of a formal legal system operating according to abstract rules to allocate punishment, this is not an institutional approach that easily accommodates interpersonal experience; indeed it is specifically developed not to do so (Norrie 2014). Yet, even within our existing legal systems, we are aware that the legal field is broad enough to incorporate other more interpersonal approaches, in terms of rehabilitative and restorative aims and processes, or those aimed at young people. Though limited, and operating against the increasingly punitive flow, humane judges can look precisely for a personal truth, for example, about a person’s likelihood of reoffending in a custodial sentencing decision (what has been called

[14] Julian Roberts and Mike Hough (2011a) and their international collaborators (Roberts and Hough 2011b) have shown how public opinion in contrast to its political representation often favours mitigatory, non-custodial, community-based or rehabilitative punishments as opposed to more punitive options.

the 'beckoning candle' philosophy: Norrie 2014: 356). Pressed to the maximum, a penal system can also come up with a mature retributive response, as we saw in Chapter 11 in the case of the Barlinnie Special Unit. Of course, these may then be marginalised or become places through which power dynamics flow, but it is not clear that institutional responses must be formalistic in a way that denies attention to interpersonal life. Legal institutions designed to punish represent only one kind of institutional design. The overall problem here is not that of designing processes to be sensitive to individual needs but of living with a system based on the abstract and formal allocation of punishment in a socially divided world.

Real versus Ideal Utopias

There is, however, a deeper philosophical question at stake here, concerning the utopian nature of the argument because we know how the world of 'law and order' politics works. Why should we think it could have any force in a world whose institutions have been pre-programmed for 200 years to reject it? My response is that the argument is institutionally relevant today *because it is ethically real.* This is an ERIC argument rooted in the naturalistic human ontology of the animal that thinks and loves. It may be utopian, but it is realistically rather than idealistically so, and the two must be distinguished. The human metaphysical animal looks something like the moral psychology this book describes, and it is this ontological reality that renders the criminal justice system unfit for human purpose. To deal with violation maturely is humanly possible and it is therefore morally compelling even if, and indeed because, the institutional design is wanting. The Freud–Loewald–Lear (Chapters 7 and 8) or the Klein–Benjamin (Chapters 3 and 8) routes from immature to mature responses are true of and for human moral psychology. They show that the primitive persecutory response must fail to address violation in the way that is needed for it to be overcome. This does not cease to be true if politically influential voices say otherwise or 'adverse experience' sits heavily on our shoulders. To not seek to go down the route of mature response represents a failure of human being, a denial of human capabilities.

The argument of this book is an exercise in real utopianism, in that it corresponds to what is ontologically true of and for human beings. Throughout, I have related the argument to actual human experience, from Primo Levi experiencing survivor guilt, to those practicing forgiveness like Jo Berry or Marian Partington, to those seeking wholeness through mourning like Violeta Berrios, Vicky Saavedra and Valentina Rodriguez, to those confronting, however haltingly, their own denial like Anwar Congo, and those working from guilt to change like Patrick Magee and Jimmy Boyle. One can be a utopian in either a realist or an idealist sense. The former is based on real powers that can be actualised and developed. The latter rests on a false belief that something could happen when in reality it cannot. At my age, I cannot become a concert pianist but I could still climb all the Scottish Munros (though time is running out). I do not intend to do either, so in both the wish is utopian, but one ambition is idealistic, the other realistic. Likewise, it is realistic, though utopianly so, to consider that humankind could start to live and deal with violation maturely under present social conditions. We have considered examples of this, though they may appear marginal today and hard to broaden out in social and institutional processes. Much would have to change, and not just to the penal system itself, before we could see the 'adverse experience' for what it really is: something that 'would not have existed, if those institutions had been established at the proper time and in accordance with ideas…' (Kant 1993: 246). It is the weight of social, political and historical experience that renders the proposal utopian rather than the real nature of human moral psychology. It is a mistake to conflate being utopian with being an idealist.[15]

Immanence and Imminence

This idea of a real and immanent possibility also helps us resolve some concerns within existing abolitionist thought. My argument for a mature retributivism is in effect abolitionist, but in a deep or tendential form. It is insistent because immanent to human being even where it is ignored or discounted in favour of a primitive, persecutory or punitive approach to violation. Powers can operate as real potentials even where they remain un- or under-actualised (Bhaskar 1975, 1979). Where processes dealing with violation take a persecutory direction in the major key (Chapter 11), there is generally a related, though lesser, tendency in another, restorative, one.

Abolitionist argument sometimes takes the form of claiming that abolition should happen 'now' (Davis et al. 2022), but what does this mean? What 'abolition now' claims commit to is both an overall desire to do away with the primitive, persecutory and punitive approach to dealing with violation and a present need to push for change that is possible here and now in the direction of mature and restorative process. Abolitionist work is necessarily ambivalent as between short- and long-term strategies, with campaigns to close prisons operating alongside, for example, teaching classes in them, supporting restorative justice processes and organising around parole hearings (Davis et al. 2022: 5). For Angela Davis and her co-authors, the 'now' in the title of their recent book 'is meant to encourage thoughtful and principled action … not … to suggest that there is an answer within reach at this moment' (Davis et al. 2022: 172). In the process, abolitionist practice may appear contradictory and ambiguous

[15] In this regard, it may be those theorists who repetitively look to reform a punitive penal system who are the idealistic utopians. Think for example of the claims for penal parsimony in a system that gets ever more punitive; or where a 'just deserts' model designed to limit punishment becomes the vehicle for its increase; or consider the 'just deserts in an unjust society' problem, which is so rooted in modern conditions that, even if noted, it must remain unaddressed.

because the 'signposts between reforms that work to shrink and end our reliance on carcerality and those that deepen and grow its reach are not so obvious' (Davis et al. 2022: 158). Acting prospectively and viewing with hindsight may lead to different judgements as to what should be done. 'Abolition now!' describes a situation where the abolitionist imperative is present and operative, yet not always obvious in its aims while remaining a drive immanent within the world of human capabilities.

Such immanence is what I mean by deep and tendential abolition and it answers a problem raised by Tommie Shelby. Against abolitionist calls for a moratorium on imprisonment, he argues that the 'tragic truth' in the modern United States is that it is often the oppressed who 'are vulnerable to violent aggression … at the hands of ordinary citizens, many of whom are oppressed themselves. It is the unjustly disadvantaged who are most vulnerable to being physically threatened, beaten, raped, or killed, sometimes by co-ethnics, neighbours, friends, intimate partners, and even family' (Shelby 2022: 114). One response here is to say that existing systems do not protect, the poor and marginalised or ethnic minorities and women anyway. Yet, where resort to a highly imperfect criminal justice system is effective, which is not always the case, the call to suspend punishment ('abolition now!') looks like a bad idea. Shelby is discussing here the problem of the victim who victimises another (see Chapter 3), and I will say more further on this, but he is surely still to some extent right in his claim. Yet to make this point is not to go against an abolitionist position if abolition is a tendency or drive *immanent* in social life, rather than presented as an *imminent* requirement in any particular social moment. Shelby's scenario may be one where principles must be thought through without offering easy answers, but it is not an objection to abolition per se.

Inside and Outside

Immanence is also the reason why abolitionist practice must function both inside and outside the penal system. Carvalho and Chamberlen (2024: 83) point to the ambivalent role of therapeutic and arts-based initiatives functioning in the modern UK prison system. Are these to be supported by abolitionists? Dilemmas of this kind, echoing the larger experience of Barlinnie Special Unit (Chapter 11), are possible because of the contrast between a real ontological basis for ethical change and the structurally dominant institutional setting change confronts. Just as 'now' human beings are capable of developing in more mature ways, so prisons and punishment also operate 'now' in their actually existing primitive forms. Their concrete and increasing weight through securitisation and expanding the prison estate means that 'abolition now' involves an insistence on the possibility of the non-punitive in ongoing and extending punitive environments. It may involve contributing support to prison reform initiatives in the 'minor key', while recognising how this may be seen to contribute to the system's 'major key' punitive purposes.

Abolitionist approaches must both intervene in the actually existing system (teaching class, arguing parole, pushing restorative solutions) and maintain a wider abolitionist objective. Prison reform programmes may seem a way of doing things better and more humanely while being cooptive, a way of pushing greater use of the carceral by appearing more caring. These are the practical dilemmas of abolitionism where the primitive, persecutory and punitive are structurally dominant. Abolitionist advocates seek to distinguish non-reformist reforms which challenge the system from reformist ones which simply enable it to function better, and they seek to recognise when the one turns into the other, but the lines are not always obvious (Mathiesen 2015: 230–2). Nonetheless, the claim for 'abolition now' operates as an ERIC practice, that is, the claim is both ethically real and institutionally critical with regard to actually existing practices and is relevant both inside and outside the system.

Abolition's Central Moral Focus

Fifthly and finally, there is the question of abolitionism's central focus and here I argue that the core concern of an abolitionist approach should be the violative relation between a 'doer' and a 'done to'. This is not always the case. Abolitionism has many different concerns and these relate to the wider social setting, to the need to address the 'prison industrial complex' (Davis 2003: ch 5), and the social environment which is the backdrop to crime and the problem of victims who victimise others (Chapter 3). The broader social and political setting is necessarily central to abolitionism, but I will now argue that this cannot mean prioritising social justice over the vindicative and validatory, mature retributive, justice that lies at the centre of addressing violative relations.

The Violative Relation

In Chapter 3, I parsed the question of 'just deserts in an unjust society' as the problem of the victim who victimises another. It is the one who has been damaged in psychological and emotional terms who proceeds to damage another. Alternatively, a person's conduct could simply reflect available life choices and youthful error in a poor social environment, or it could be a combination of interpersonal and social features. However it comes about, it is obvious 'to anyone who has spent five minutes in a court or prison' that 'the damage has already been done' (Cohen 1979: 35, 41), and that criminal behaviour is socially skewed towards those who experience significant disadvantage. Yet orthodox criminal justice theory's abstract and punctualist categories of responsibility leave little space for the moral backstory. What matters is that the victimisation occurred, while the thought that the victimiser was himself a victim is marginalised.

If the orthodox normative approach ignores the 'upstream' story of damage that leads to violation here and now, it seems sometimes that the abolitionist approach marginalises the 'downstream' violation in favour of accentuating the victimised victim's history. Drawing on Enrique Dussel, David Scott's victim is one who has been 'excluded, marginalised, denied dignity' and the need is to 'challenge the validity of such denials from the perspective of the victim' (Scott 2020: 46). The victim here is, however, not the actual or direct victim but the one who victimises. Scott argues that this does not mean 'ignoring victims of criminal harm', but his standpoint is that of 'the broader community of victims of injustice' with a 'much wider definition of victimhood' (Scott 2020: 47). In the process, the *relationship of violation* between the victimiser and the victim tends to get relegated to the margin. If liberal theory focuses too narrowly on acts of victimisation, this approach focuses too broadly on the overall social nature of victimhood. What is missing in both cases is the dialectical relation implicit in being *a victim who victimises.*

Scott's argument is at its most powerful when he analyses just how negative the experience of the prison is for the prisoner. The emotional constellation is one of abandonment, of 'sadness, melancholia, insecurity and a sense of loss' (Scott 2020: 130). Prison life involves a hopelessness and deathliness based on isolation and dehumanisation. There is a sense of grief and mourning for the prisoner, which he describes as that 'generated by the loss of a previous home' (Scott 2020: 130). This is a very human description of an inhuman environment, but Scott does not say much about the sense of grief and guilt an inmate might experience for violating another. Prisoners are 'haunted by past trauma and drained of hope' (Scott 2020: 139), but is such trauma related to what happened to the prisoner or what the prisoner did? Scott's emphasis is on neglect in the prisoner's past, on 'the absence of care and love as both children and/ or adults', the experience of 'different forms of physical and psychological harm, injury or trauma' (Scott 2020: 157), and how this makes the isolation and persecution of the prison environment much more a living death. The prisoner has been a victim of his previous and his present life, but there is only limited acknowledgement that prisoners may 'themselves have engaged in problematic and troublesome conduct' or may experience 'guilt-ridden forms of trauma' (Scott 2020: 157). 'Problematic conduct,' it should be remembered, may involve doing serious violence to another human being. Focusing on the previous social and psychological development of the perpetrator as a victim, and how the prison then re-victimises him, the argument overshoots the immediate violation, the victimisation of another which brought the person to the prison.

The Micro and Macro

To this concern, it might be countered that the overriding problem is the structural social conditions which sediment victimisation and the overall institutional way in which the state deals with it. The commitment is to radical change at the societal level, where 'the social' is the macro, 'the individual' the micro. Sort the system and you will sort the individual. Against this, any commitment to a radical social alternative must recognise that change takes place at both levels. The old problem of 'state socialism' is precisely one in which individual hearts and minds are not changed by macro processes. More than this, the abolitionist cannot ignore the here and now problem of how human relationships can be restored or reconciled as part of a commitment to change. The social and the individual cannot be opposed to each other but must rather be combined so that we can see how social change might support individual reconciliation, and individual reconciliation might support social change. The issue is both structural and agential (Bhaskar 1979; Archer 2003) so both must be present. This book has emphasised at various points (e.g. Chapter 4 on Nussbaum's work) that the individual and the social must work together just as they do initially in the formation of each individual psyche (Chapter 7), or in the diagnosis of the problem of just deserts (Chapter 3).

A coda to the discussion and a crucial test case is provided by Scott's discussion of relations between men and women, and how violence against women may be addressed, often in ongoing relationships. Here structure and agency come together, and Scott begins to consider how an approach based on mature psychological development might occur. What is important is to restore the dignity of both the victim and the wrongdoer, to 'repair what is broken and encourage the non-repetition of such harmful behaviours in the future' (Scott 2020: 221). Cognitive behavioural therapies 'can help in taking back … emotional control', yet many men 'require extensive therapy, aid and assistance … in terms of addressing the impulse to violence' (Scott 2020: 221). Consideration needs also to be given to 'social, structural and cultural contexts as well as the significant difficulties that men face in reconstructing their masculinity without ongoing and long-term networks' (Scott 2020: 222). The problem here links the macro and the micro and it engages the perpetrator of violence, the actual victim herself, the perpetrator as himself a victim and the relationship between the two both in themselves and in the broader social context. It is about both taking responsibility and reconciliation.

Deep or tendential abolition (mature retributivism) is at its core about developing a human way of relating that can address violation through dialogue, understanding and emotional development that recognises the underlying potential in human relations. In dialogues around partner violence, the reconciliative ambition is to deal with both the immediate violation and its victim, and the perpetrator of the violation, who may himself be a victim. There are two victims here, we may say, but it will not resolve the relational difficulty if we bypass one in favour of the other, elide the difference between them, or ignore their asymmetry. None of these things should happen even if it nonetheless makes sense to treat the violence relationally, holistically and in a reconciliative way. Though domestic violence constitutes a specific and troubling problem, the way to deal with it reflects broader questions about how an abolitionist approach should and can deal with violation. As we saw in Chapter 5, with the work of *The Forgiveness Project*, questions of taking responsibility and reconciliation are not confined to close familial relationships.

Abolition as Mature Retributivism

To seek to resolve the situation of men and women in a violent relationship is to be committed to an abolitionist position around responsibility and reconciliation where the alternative is to be punitive. Such a mature retributive possibility exists because human beings are at heart metaphysical animals who deal best with violation by addressing what they have done, or responding as best they can to what has been done to them. Out of this, a reconciliation may be possible that stems from the deep moral psychological potential immanent in human lives. Once this is recognised, we have an effective way of supporting or moving towards reconciliative approaches and leaving behind those that are primitive, punitive and persecutory.

Taking this position yields a mature retributivism that is open to restoring wholeness through atonement (at-one-ment) of those who have violated or been violated. Recognising that the positions of the victim and the victimiser (including the victim who victimises) are not the same, we still note the common root of violation and the need to restore, albeit differentially, in a manner that turns an asymmetrical violative relationship towards forgiving and reconciliation. Mature retributivism may be argued for theoretically by pushing the bounds of philosophy in line with the ancient Socratic injunction to know ourselves (see Chapter 6). This includes however the modern commitment to understand ourselves, in terms of our nature as animals that think and love. Humans possess a psyche in both the modern psychological sense and the ancient Greek understanding of a soul, and it is this double sense that makes us metaphysical animals (see Chapter 7). Such an approach pulls us away from punishment as it is expressed in standard retributive theory as a primitive return of pain for pain, and so in the direction of its mature abolition. Punishment to extinguish guilt 'does not work … and more … is needed' (Loewald 1980: 391).

I began this chapter with five questions that should be addressed by any theory seeking to deal with violation. With regard first to the overall value of a mature retributive approach in contrast to a model of punishment as primitive and persecutory, the former takes us forward and offers the possibility of change, where the latter offers repetition of violence both in the state's punitive response itself and as the outcome of a system which fails to change behaviour. The punitive–reconciliative hybrid position does not work because the reconciliative always operates in the shadow of punishment. Second, I developed an alternative account of the role of the state and law that delinked law's morally vindicative significance from its relationship with punitive vindictiveness. In the analytical difference between the vindictive, the vindicative and the validatory, I turned it towards a broader sense of moral validation if perpetrators, victims and a broader community are to deal with violation and reconciliation to be possible.

This was then linked, thirdly, to an account of responsibility which deepens it by developing its dispositional and relational quality. It allows the violator to own what he has done and move beyond it, rather than to be blamed and punished for it in a repetitive action that remains in a cycle of pain and anger. That this may look, fourth, like an ideal solution to an actual problem cannot be gainsaid. It is no doubt the case that Kant's 'adverse experiences' are abundant. Nevertheless, we are dealing here with a *real* ideal, one that is immanent in human powers, and this makes it more than a simple fantasy. A real utopian position invites us all, proponents and critics, to think and act with moral seriousness about how we deal with violative relations. What is certain, fifth, is that the violative relation between 'a doer' and a 'done-to' must remain at the core of the possibility of change both at the individual micro-level and in the broader social macro-sweep, so that a virtuous feedback loop between the two may operate. That the possibility of social reform often looks a distant possibility does not detract from the value of the argument that change at both levels is necessary.

Let us return briefly and finally to the idea of a real utopian abolitionist position, the fourth point mentioned earlier. Armed with a vindicative–validatory conception of authority, a dispositional–relational account of responsibility and a focus on violative relations in both their individual and social aspects, mature retributivism qua abolitionism must negotiate the difficult practical and theoretical terrain where real utopian solutions engage with actually existing problems. Questions of what is possible inside and outside the existing system rear their head as inevitable practical dilemmas. Abolitionism as mature retributivism must keep its eyes on what is humanly needed in the longer term while dealing with what is possible here and now. The possibility of 'adverse experiences' guarantees a necessary mismatch between ideals and actualities which can only be negotiated under present social and institutional conditions. This leaves many questions unanswered, and it would be presumptuous to say that the theoretical argument presented here addresses abolitionism's many different and difficult practical implications. This is to be expected since the idea of 'abolition now!' is 'meant to encourage thoughtful and principled action … not … to suggest that there is an answer within reach at this moment' (Davis et al. 2022: 172). It is immanent but not necessarily imminent.

Similarly, from within the existing penal field, there will be a raft of 'what if' or 'what about' type questions, which contrast the real utopian theory with existing practices. Possible 'adverse experiences' will fly in from all directions. I have tried to deal with some of these, but others will come, as they must in a world where the punitive and persecutory remain our structure in dominance (see Chapter 11). Perhaps one overall anticipatory response would be to say: if the theory presented here holds, then practical answers are a matter for us all, and not just those who argue for an abolitionist position. After all, we are all these metaphysical animals who think and love and so we all have an obligation to consider problems and ways of bringing about change. Those who ask the 'what if' or 'what about' questions which foreground the 'adverse experience' are also obliged to come up with answers.

From within abolitionism itself, there is a range of different and contested approaches to abolition that lie beyond the scope of this book (see e.g. Mathiesen 2015; Scott 2020; Coyle and Scott 2021; Davis et al. 2022). My contribution concerns what it means to think through mature retributivism as the theoretical core of a deep or tendential abolition. This is both connected to and different from existing abolitionist debate. It provides an ethically real basis for institutional criticism, what I have called an ERIC position, which scans the existing field and provides a basis for thinking about change. Critiquing the existing penal field, it could have as a further step an enquiry into the relationship between deep or tendential abolition and existing *abolitionist* practices, as well as those punitive practices which the book has focused on. However such thinking develops, this book has established an ontological basis for, and a moral psychological theory of, mature retributivism as a deep and immanent abolitionist tendency in human being. It has taken a concept central to punishment and turned it into its abolitionist opposite by distinguishing mature from primitive retributivism. Given its central argument, which started with the young Hegel, it has been quite literally a labour of love, for the metaphysical animal that thinks and loves.

References

Allais, L. (2021) 'Frailty and Forgiveness: Forgiveness for Humans', in B. Warmke, D. Nelkin and M. McKenna (eds.) *Forgiveness and Its Moral Dimensions*. Oxford: Oxford University Press: 257–84.

Altham, J. E. J. and Harrison, R. (1995) *World, Mind and Ethics*. Cambridge: Cambridge University Press.

Althusser, L. (1970) *Reading Capital*. New York: Pantheon.

American Friends Service Committee (1971) *Struggle for Justice*. New York: Hill and Wang.

Anderson, K. (2024) *The Barlinnie Special Unit: Art, Punishment and Innovation*. Hook: Waterside.

Andrew, M. and Waldron, R. (2007) *The Poems of the Pearl Manuscript*. Exeter: University of Exeter Press.

Archer, M. (2003) *Structure, Agency and the Internal Conversation*. Cambridge: Cambridge University Press.

Arendt, H. (1964) *Eichmann in Jerusalem*. London: Penguin.

Aristotle (1984) *Nicomachean Ethics. Complete Works: Volume 2*. Princeton: Princeton University Press.

Ashworth, A. and Zedner, L. (2014) *Preventive Justice*. Oxford: Oxford University Press.

Benjamin, J. (1988) *The Bonds of Love*. New York: Pantheon.

Benjamin, J. (2018) *Beyond Doer and Done To*. Abingdon and New York: Routledge.

Bennett, J. (2019) 'Against Prison Management', *Prison Services Journal* 247: 4–13.

Bernhardt, D. (2017) "It's Over. Let's Let It Go': Wilma Derksen Wrestles with Emotions after Mark Grant Acquitted', *CBC News*, 19 October. www.cbc.ca/news/canada/manitoba/candace-wilma-derksen-verdict-1.4361709.

Bhaskar, R. (1975) *A Realist Theory of Science*. Leeds: Leeds Books.

Bhaskar, R. (1979) *The Possibility of Naturalism*. Brighton: Harvester Wheatsheaf.

Bhaskar, R. (1993) *Dialectic: The Pulse of Freedom*. London: Verso.

Bhaskar, R. (2012) *The Philosophy of MetaReality*. London: Routledge.

Bhaskar, R. (2016) *Enlightened Common Sense*. Abingdon: Routledge.

Bird, J. (2017) 'Spatial Autonomy and Desistance in Penal Settings: The Barlinnie Special Unit (1973–1994)', in E. Hart and E. van Ginneken (eds.) *New Perspectives on Desistance: Theoretical and Empirical Developments*. London: Palgrave Macmillan: 111–37.

Black, M. (2015) 'I Used to Think They Were Evil', in M. Cantacuzino (ed.) *The Forgiveness Project*. London: Jessica Kingsley: 63–64.

Boraine, A. (2000) 'Truth and Reconciliation in South Africa: the Third Way', in R. Rotberg and D. Thompson, *Truth v Justice: the Morality of Truth Commissions*. Princeton: Princeton University Press.

Bollas, C. (1993) *Being a Character*. London: Routledge.

Boyle, J. (1985) *The Pain of Confinement* London: Pan.

Boyle, J. (2016) *A Sense of Freedom*. London: Ebury Press.

Braithwaite, J. (1989) *Crime, Shame and Reintegration*. Cambridge: Cambridge University Press.

Braithwaite, J. (1993) 'Shame and Modernity', *British Journal of Criminology* 33(1): 1–18.

Braithwaite, J. (1999) 'Restorative Justice: Assessing Optimistic and Pessimistic Accounts' in M. Tonry (ed.) *Crime and Justice: A Review of Research*. Chicago: University of Chicago Press.

Brooks, T. (2021) *Punishment: A Critical Introduction* (2nd ed.). Abingdon: Routledge.

Brown, M. and Schept, J. (2017) 'New Abolition, Criminology and Critical Carceral Studies', *Punishment and Society* 19(4): 440–62.

Brudner, A. (2009) *Punishment and Freedom*. Oxford: Oxford University Press.

Burton, G. (2014) 'Tributum', in S. Hornblower, A. Spawforth and E. Eidinow (eds.) *Oxford Companion to Classical Civilization* (2nd ed.). Oxford: Oxford University Press.

Cantacuzino, M. (2015) *The Forgiveness Project*. London and Philadelphia: Jessica Kingsley.

Cantacuzino, M. (2022) *Forgiveness: An Exploration*. London: Simon and Schuster.

Carrell, C. and Laing, J. (1982) *The Special Unit Barlinnie Prison: Its Evolution through Its Art*. Glasgow: Third Eye.

Carvalho, H. (2017) *The Preventive Turn in Criminal Law*. Oxford: Oxford University Press.

Carvalho, H. and Chamberlen, A. (2018) 'Why Punishment Pleases: Punitive Feelings in a World of Hostile Solidarity', *Punishment and Society* 20(2): 217–34.

Carvalho, H. and Chamberlen, A. (2024) *Questioning Punishment*. London: Routledge.

CAS Roundtable (2014) 'Indonesia Roundtable: The Act of Killing', *Critical Asian Studies* 46: 145–207.

Cesur, H. (forthcoming) *Legal and Ethical Retributivism: A Restorative Analysis*. Abingdon: Routledge.

Charney, J., Marshall, P. and Christodoulidis, E. (2021) 'It Is Not 30 Pesos, It Is 30 Years': Reflections on the Chilean Crisis: Introduction', *Social & Legal Studies* 30(4): 627–68.

Chiao, V. (2018) *Criminal Law in the Age of the Administrative State*. Oxford: Oxford University Press.

Chodorow, N. (2003) 'The Psychoanalytic Vision of Hans Loewald', *International Journal of Psychoanalysis* 84(4): 897–913.

Christie, N. (1977) 'Conflicts as Property', *British Journal of Criminology*, 17(1): 1–15.

Clark, P. (2010) *The Gacaca Courts, Post-Genocide Justice and Reconciliation in Rwanda*. Cambridge: Cambridge University Press.

Cohen, S. (1979) 'Guilt, Justice and Tolerance: Some Old Concepts for a New Criminology', in D. Downes and P. Rock (eds.) *Deviant Interpretations*. Oxford: Martin Robertson.

Cohen, S. (2001) *States of Denial: Knowing about Atrocities and Suffering*. Cambridge: Polity.

Cohen, S. and L. Taylor (1972) *Psychological Survival: The Experience of Long-Term Imprisonment*. London: Penguin.

Cole, G. D. H. (1920) *Guild Socialism Restated*. London: Parsons.

Collier, A. (1994) *Critical Realism: An Introduction to Roy Bhaskar's Philosophy*. London: Verso.

Collins, H. (1997) *Autobiography of a Murderer*. London: MacMillan.

Cooke, D. (1989) 'Containing Violent Prisoners: An Analysis of the Barlinnie Special Unit', *British Journal of Criminology* 29(2): 129–43.

Cornell, D. (2014) *Law and Revolution in South Africa: uBuntu, Dignity, and the Struggle for Constitutional Transformation*. New York: Fordham University Press.

Coyle, M. and Scott, D. (2021) *The Routledge International Handbook of Penal Abolition*. Abingdon: Routledge.

Davis, A. (2003) *Are Prisons Obsolete?* New York: Seven Stories.

Davis, A., Dent, G., Meiners, E. and Richie, B. (2022) *Abolition. Feminism. Now*. London: Penguin.

Deambrogio, C. (2023) *Judging Insanity, Punishing Difference: A History of Mental Illness in the Criminal Court*. Stanford: Stanford University Press.

Deigh, J. (1996) 'Remarks on Some Difficulties in Freud's Theory of Moral Development', in J. Deigh (ed.) *The Sources of Moral Agency*. Cambridge: Cambridge University Press.

Derrida, J. (2001) *On Cosmopolitanism and Forgiveness*. London: Routledge.

DeValve, M. (2015) *A Different Justice: Love and the Future of Criminal Justice Practice in America*. Durham: Carolina Academic Press.

Dostoyevsky, F. (1997) *Crime and Punishment*. London: Penguin.

Dragojlovic, A. (2018) 'Violent Histories and Embodied Memories: Affectivity of "the Act of Killing" and "The Look of Silence"', in K. McGregor, J. Melvin and A. Pohlman (eds.) *The Indonesian Genocide of 1965*. London: Palgrave: 269–85.

Duff, A. (2001) *Punishment, Communication, and Community*. Oxford: Oxford University Press.

Duff, A. (2003a) 'Restorative Punishment and Punitive Restoration', in G. Johnstone (ed.) *A Restorative Justice Reader*. Cullompton and Devon: Willan.

Duff, A. (2003b) 'Restoration and Retribution', in A. von Hirsch, J. Roberts, A. Bottoms, K. Roach and M. Schiff (eds.) *Restorative Justice and Criminal Justice: Competing or Reconcilable Paradigms?* London: Hart.

Eng, D. and Kasanjian, D. (2002) (eds.) *Loss: The Politics of Mourning*. Berkeley: University of California Press.

Farmer, L. (2016) *Making the Modern Criminal Law*. Oxford: Oxford University Press.

Fassin, D. (2018) *The Will to Punish*. Oxford: Oxford University Press.

Film Quarterly (2013) 'Special Dossier on The Act of Killing', *Film Quarterly* 67(2): 8–56.

Fine, R. (2001) *Political Investigations*. London: Routledge.

Fingarette, H. (1969) *Self-Deception*. London: Routledge

Fingarette, H. (2009) 'Self-Deception and the 'Splitting of the Ego", in R. Wollheim and J. Hopkins (eds.) *Philosophical Essays on Freud*. Cambridge: Cambridge University Press.

Foucault, M. (1977) *Discipline and Punish*. Harmondsworth: Peregrine.

Freud, S. (1925) 'Some Additional Notes on Dream Interpretation as a Whole', in J. Strachey (ed.) *Standard Edition of Complete Works of Sigmund Freud*. Volume 19: 127–38.

Freud, S. (1927) *The Future of an Illusion*. New York: W. W. Norton & Company.

Freud, S. (1964) 'New Introductory Lectures on Psychoanalysis', in J. Strachey (ed.) *Standard Edition of Complete Works of Sigmund Freud*. Volume 22: 1–182.

Freud, S. (1984) *On Metapsychology: The Theory of Psychoanalysis*. Penguin Freud Library, Volume 11. London: Penguin.

Freud, S. (1985) *Civilization, Society and Religion*. Penguin Freud Library, Volume 12. London: Penguin.

Freud, S. (1990) *The Origins of Religion*. Penguin Freud Library, Volume 13. London: Penguin.

Gamper, A (2021) '*Suum Cuique Tribuere* – A Common Narrative of Federalism and Equality?', in E. Belser, T. Bächler, S. Egli, and L. Zünd (eds.) *The Principle of Equality in Diverse States: Reconciling Autonomy with Equal Rights and Opportunities*. Nijhoff: Brill.

Gavrielides, T. and Artinopoulou, V. (2013) *Reconstructing Restorative Justice Philosophy*. London: Routledge.

Greenberg, J. R. and Mitchell, S. A. (1983) *Object Relations in Psychoanalytic Theory*. Cambridge: Harvard University Press.

Griswold, C. (2007) *Forgiveness: A Philosophical Exploration*. Cambridge: Cambridge University Press.

Guzmán, P. (2010) *Nostalgia for the Light* (Film). Brooklyn: Icarus Films.

Harris, N. and Maruna, S. (2006) 'Shame, Sharing and Restorative Justice: A Critical Appraisal', in D. Sullivan and L. Tifft (eds.) *Handbook of Restorative Justice*. London: Routledge.

Harris, N., Walgrave, L. and Braithwaite, J. (2004) 'Emotional Dynamics in Restorative Conferences', *Theoretical Criminology* 8(2): 191–210.

Hartwig, M. (2007) *Dictionary of Critical Realism*. London: Routledge.

Hearty, K. (2016) 'Legislating Hierarchies of Victimhood and Perpetrators: The Civil Service (Special Advisers) Act (Northern Ireland) 2013 and the Meta-Conflict', *Social & Legal Studies* 25(3): 333–53.

Hegel, G. W. F. (1948) *Early Theological Writings*. Philadelphia: University of Philadelphia Press.

Hegel, G. W. F. (1977) *Phenomenology of Spirit*. Oxford: Oxford University Press.

Hegel, G. W. F. (1979) *System of Ethical Life*. Albany: State University of New York.

Hegel, G. W. F. (2008) *Outlines of the Philosophy of Right*. Oxford: Oxford University Press.

Honneth, A. (1995) *The Struggle for Recognition*. Cambridge: Polity.

Hugo, V. (1976) *Les Misérables*. London: Penguin.

Inwood, M. (1992) *A Hegel Dictionary*. Oxford: Blackwell.

Jaspers, K. (2000) *The Question of German Guilt*. New York: Fordham University Press.

Johnstone, G. (2002) *Restorative Justice: Ideas, Values, Debates*. Cullompton and Devon: Willan.

Johnstone, G. (2003) *A Restorative Justice Reader*. Cullompton and Devon: Willan.

Kant, I. (1991) *Political Writings*. Cambridge: Cambridge University Press.

Kant, I. (1993) *Critique of Pure Reason*. London: Dent.

Kelly, E. (2018) *The Limits of Blame: Rethinking Punishment and Responsibility*. Cambridge: Harvard University Press.

Kennedy, R. (2016) 'Remembering the Indonesian Killings', in L. Bond, S. Craps and P. Vermeulen (eds.) *Memory Unbound: Tracing the Dynamic of Memory Studies*. New York: Berghahn: 47–64.

Klein, M. (1997) 'Notes on Some Schizoid Mechanisms (1946)', in M. Klein (ed.) *Envy and Gratitude*. London: Vintage.

Klein, M. (1998) *Love, Guilt and Reparation*. London: Vintage.

Lacey, N. (1988) *State Punishment: Political Principles and Community Values*. London: Routledge.

Lacey, N. (2016) *In Search of Criminal Responsibility*. Oxford: Oxford University Press.

Lacey, N. (2024) 'Institutionalising Forgiveness in Criminal Justice'. LSE Working Papers 1. London: London School of Economics.

Lacey, N. and Pickard, H. (2013) 'From the Consulting Room to the Court Room? Taking the Clinical Model of Responsibility Without Blame into the Legal Realm', *Oxford Journal of Legal Studies* 33(1): 1–29.

Lacey, N. and Pickard, H. (2015) 'To Blame or to Forgive? Reconciling Punishment and Forgiveness in Criminal Justice', *Oxford Journal of Legal Studies* 35(4): 665–96.

Langer, M. (2020) 'Penal Abolitionism and Criminal Law Minimalism', *Harvard Law Review Forum* 134: 42–77.

Laplanche, J. and Pontalis, J.-B. (1973) *The Language of Psychoanalysis*. London: Karnac.

Lear, J. (1988) *Aristotle: The Desire to Understand*. Cambridge: Cambridge University Press.

Lear, J. (1990) *Love and Its Place in Nature*. New Haven and London: Yale University Press.

Lear, J. (1998) *Open Minded*. Cambridge and London: Harvard University Press.

Lear, J. (2003) 'The Idea of a Moral Psychology: The Impact of Psychoanalysis on Philosophy in Britain', *International Journal of Psychoanalysis* 84(5): 1351–61.

Lear, J. (2004) 'Psychoanalysis and the Idea of a Moral Psychology: Memorial to Bernard Williams' Philosophy', *Inquiry* 47(5): 515–22.

Lear, J. (2015) *Freud* (2nd ed.). Abingdon: Routledge.

Lear, J. (2017) *Wisdom Won from Illness*. Cambridge: Harvard University Press.

Levi, P. (2013) *The Drowned and the Saved*. London: Abacus.

Liebling, A. and Maruna, S. (2005) (eds.) *The Effects of Imprisonment*. London: Willan.

Lifton, R. J. (1986) *The Nazi Doctors*. New York: Basic Books.

Loewald, H. (1980) *Papers on Psychoanalysis*. New Haven: Yale University Press.

Mac Cumhaill, C. and Wiseman, R. (2022) *Metaphysical Animals*. London: Chatto and Windus.

Mathiesen, T. (2015 [1974]) *The Politics of Abolition Revisited*. Abingdon: Routledge.

Matthews, R. (1999) *Doing Time: An Introduction to the Sociology of Imprisonment* (2nd ed.). London: Palgrave.

McEvoy, K. and McConnachie, K. (2012) 'Victimology in Transitional Justice: Victimhood, Innocence and Hierarchy', *European Journal of Criminology* 9(5): 527–38.

McEvoy, K. and McConnachie, K. (2013) 'Victims and Transitional Justice: Voice, Agency and Blame', *Social & Legal Studies* 22(4): 489–514.

McGeachan, C. (2019) '"A Prison within a Prison"? Examining the Unfolding Spatialities of Care and Control in Barlinnie Special Unit', *Area* 51(2): 200–7.

McLeod, A. (2013) 'Confronting Criminal Law's Violence: The Possibilities of Unfinished Alternatives', *Harvard Unbound* 8: 109–32.

McLeod, A. (2015) 'Prison Abolition and Grounded Justice', *UCLA Law Review* 62: 1156–239.

McLeod, A. (2017) 'Beyond the Carceral State', *Texas Law Review* 95: 651–706.

McLeod, A. (2019) 'Envisioning Abolition Democracy', *Harvard Law Review* 132(6): 1613–49.

Medlicott, D. (2024 [2001]) *Surviving the Prison Place: Narratives of Suicidal Prisoners*. Abingdon: Routledge.

Meneghetti, M. (2016) 'Self-Exculpatory Imaginings: Reenactment and Observation in The Act of Killing', *Canadian Journal of Film Studies* 25(2): 39–61.

Mitchell, S. (1998) 'From Ghosts to Ancestors: The Psychoanalytic Vision of Hans Loewald', *Psychoanalytic Dialogues* 8(6): 825–55.

Mitchell, S. and Black, M. (1995) *Freud and Beyond: A History of Modern Psychoanalytic Thought*. New York: Basic Books.

Momigliano, A. and Cornell, T. (2014) 'Tribus', in S. Hornblower, A. Spawforth and E. Eidinow (eds.) *Oxford Companion to Classical Civilization* (2nd ed.). Oxford: Oxford University Press.

Moore, M. S. (1984) *Law and Psychiatry*. Cambridge: Cambridge University Press.

Morris, H. (1976) *On Guilt and Innocence: Essays in Legal Philosophy and Moral Psychology*. Berkeley: University of California Press.

Morris, H. (1987) 'Nonmoral Guilt', in F. Schoeman (ed.) *Responsibility, Character and the Emotions*. Cambridge: Cambridge University Press.

Morris, H. (1988) 'Murphy on Forgiveness' *Criminal Justice Ethics* 7: 15–19.

Murphy, J. (1979) *Retribution, Justice, and Therapy*. Dordrecht: Reidel.

Murphy, J. (2012) *Punishment and the Moral Emotions*. Oxford: Oxford University Press.

Murphy, J. and Hampton, J. (1988) *Forgiveness and Mercy*. Cambridge: Cambridge University Press.

Nellis, M. (2010) 'Creative Arts and the Cultural Politics of Penal Reform: The Early Years of the Barlinnie Special Unit 1973–1981', *Journal of Scottish Criminal Justice Studies* 20: 47–73.

Nellis, M. (2014) 'The Arts and Imprisonment: Some Reflections on the Barlinnie Special Unit', *Scottish Justice Matters* 2(2): 27–28.

Nields, J. (2003) 'From Unity to Atonement: Some Religious Correlates of Hans Loewald's Developmental Theory', *International Journal of Psychoanalysis* 84(3): 699–716.

Nietzsche, F. (2000) *Beyond Good and Evil*. W. Kaufmann (trans), *Basic Writings of Nietzsche*. New York: Random House.

Norrie, A. (1991) *Law, Ideology and Punishment*. Dordrecht: Kluwer.

Norrie, A. (2000) *Punishment, Responsibility and Justice*. Oxford: Oxford University Press.

Norrie, A. (2005) *Law and the Beautiful Soul*. London: Glasshouse Press.

Norrie, A. (2010) *Dialectic and Difference*. Abingdon: Routledge.

Norrie, A. (2011) 'Legal Form and Moral Judgement: Euthanasia and Assisted Suicide', in R. A. Duff, L. Farmer, S. E. Marshall, M. Renzo and V. Tadros (eds.) *The Structures of Criminal Law*. Oxford: Oxford University Press.

Norrie, A. (2014 [1993]) *Crime, Reason and History* (3rd ed.). Cambridge: Cambridge University Press.

Norrie, A. (2017a) 'To Flourish or Destruct: A Personalist Theory of Human Goods, Motivations, Failure, and Evil', *Journal of Critical Realism* 16(4): 423–30.

Norrie, A. (2017b) 'Criminal Law and Ethics: Beyond Normative Assertion and Its Critique', *Modern Law Review* 80(5): 955–73.

Norrie, A. (2017c) *Justice and the Slaughter Bench: Essays on Law's Broken Dialectic*. Abingdon: Routledge.

Norrie, A. (2019) 'Beyond Persecutory Impulse and Humanising Trace: On Didier Fassin's The Will to Punish', *Criminal Law and Philosophy* 13: 681–88.

Norrie, A. (2020) 'The Flesh Made Word: Critical Realism, Psychoanalysis, and the Ontology of Love', *Journal of Critical Realism* 19(4): 341–61.

Norrie, A. (2022b) 'Restoration, Abolition and the Loving Prison: Jimmy Boyle and Barlinnie Special Unit', *The Howard Journal of Crime and Justice* 61(1): 103–16.

Norrie, A. (2023) 'Crime and the metaphysical animal'. *Journal of Critical Realism* 22(5), 904–21. https://doi.org/10.1080/14767430.2023.2265689.

Norrie, A. (2024) 'Dialectical Critical Realism, Complexity and the Psychology of Blame'. *Journal for the Theory of Social Behaviour*: 1–18. https://doi.org/10.1111/jtsb.12411.

Norrie, A. and Wilson, A. (2024) 'On Dispositional-Relational Responsibility: From Punishment to Reconciliation', in T. Crofts, L. Kennefick, and A. Loughnan (eds.) *Routledge International Handbook of Criminal Responsibility*. Abingdon: Routledge.

Nussbaum, M. C. (2004) *Hiding from Humanity: Disgust, Shame, and the Law*. Princeton: Princeton University Press.

Nussbaum, M. C. (2013) *Creating Capabilities: The Human Development Approach*. Cambridge: Harvard University Press.

Nussbaum, M. C. (2014) *Political Emotions: Why Love Matters for Justice*. Cambridge: Harvard University Press.

Nussbaum, M. C. (2016) *Anger and Forgiveness*. New York: Oxford University Press.

Oliver, V. M. (2017) 'Understanding Historical Changes in Social and Penal Arts Programs', *Journal of Offender Rehabilitation* 56(8): 511–33.

Oppenheimer, J. (2012) *The Act of Killing* (Film). London: Dogwoof.

Oppenheimer, J. (2014) *The Look of Silence* (Film). London: Dogwoof.

Partington, M. (2016) *If You Sit Very Still*. London: Jessica Kingsley.

Pashukanis, E. (1978) *A General Theory of Law and Marxism*. London: Ink Links.

Patel, P. per BBC (2019) 'Home Secretary Priti Patel: I want criminals to feel terror', BBC, 3 August. www.bbc.co.uk/news/uk-49213743.

Pavlich, G. (2003) 'Deconstructing Restoration: The Promise of Restorative Justice', in G. Johnstone (ed.) *A Restorative Justice Reader*. Cullompton and Devon: Willan.

Plato (1997) *Complete Works*. Indianapolis: Hackett.

Popper, K. Sir (1963) *Conjectures and Refutations: The Growth of Scientific Knowledge*. London: Routledge and Keegan Paul.

Rafter, N. (2014) 'Film Review: The Act of Killing', *Theoretical Criminology* 18(2): 257–60.

Ramsay, P. (2009) *The Insecurity State*. Oxford: Oxford University Press.

Ramsay, P. (2016) 'A Democratic Theory of Imprisonment' in A. Dzur, I. Loader and R. Sparks (eds.) *Democratic Theory and Mass Incarceration*. Oxford: Oxford University Press.

Reeves, C. (2019) 'What Punishment Expresses', *Social & Legal Studies* 28(1): 31–57.

Reeves, C. (2022) 'Responsibility beyond Blame', in M. Matravers and K. Lernestedt (eds.) *Criminal Law's Person*. London: Hart.

Reeves, C., Norrie, A. and Carvalho, H. (2019) 'Criminal Law: Between Persecution and Reconciliation', in E. Christodoulidis, R. Dukes and M. Goldoni (eds.) *Research Handbook on Critical Legal Theory*. Cheltenham: Edward Elgar.

Ribeiro de Menezes, A. (2019) 'Memory beyond the Anthropocene: The Tactile Rhetorics of Patricio Guzmán's Nostalgia de la luz and El botón de nácar', in B. Jung and S. Bruzzi (eds.) *Beyond the Rhetorics of Pain*. London: Routledge: 101–19.

Roberts, D. (2019) 'Abolition Constitutionalism', *Harvard Law Review* 133(1): 1–122.

Roberts, J. and Hough, M. (2011a) 'Custody or Community? Exploring the Boundaries of Public Punitiveness in England and Wales', *Criminology & Criminal Justice* 11(2): 181–97.

Roberts, J. and Hough, M. (2011b) *Changing Attitudes to Punishment*. Abingdon: Routledge.

Rodríguez, D. (2019) 'Abolition as Praxis of Human Being: A Foreword', in Developments in the Law – Prison Abolition, *Harvard Law Review* 132(6): 1575–612.

Rossner, M. (2017) 'Restorative Justice in the Twenty-First Century', in A. Liebling, S. Maruna and L. McAra (eds.) *Oxford Handbook of Criminology*. Oxford: Oxford University Press.

Scott, D. (2020) *For Abolition*. Hook: Waterside.

Shelby, T. (2022) *The Idea of Prison Abolition*. Princeton: Princeton University Press.

Sim, J. (2009) *Punishment and Prisons*. London: Sage.

Simon, J. (2007) *Governing through Crime*. New York: Oxford University Press.

Smith, C. (2015) *To Flourish or Destruct*. Chicago: Chicago University Press.

Sparks, R. (2002) 'Out of the 'Digger': The Warrior's Honour and the Guilty Observer', *Ethnography* 3(4): 556–81.

Steiner, J. (1993) *Psychic Retreats*. Abingdon: Routledge.

Steiner, J. (2020) *Illusion, Disillusion, and Irony in Psychoanalysis*. Abingdon: Routledge.

Sullivan, D. and Tifft, L. (2006) *Handbook of Restorative Justice*. London: Routledge.

Sykes, G. (2007 [1958]) *The Society of Captives: A Study of a Maximum Security Prison*. Princeton: Princeton University Press.

Tadros, V. (2005) *Criminal Responsibility*. Oxford: Oxford University Press.

Trunnell, E. and Holt, W. (1974) 'The Concept of Denial or Disavowal', *Journal of American Psychoanalytical Association* 22(4): 769–84.

Volf, M. (2005) *Free of Charge*. Grand Rapids: Zondervan.

Volf, M. (2006) *The End of Memory*. Grand Rapids: Eerdmans.

Wacquant, L (2009) *Punishing the Poor*. Durham and London: Duke University Press.

Weaver, B. (2018) 'Co-production, Governance and Practice: The Dynamics and Effects of User Voice Prison Councils' *Social Policy and Administration* 53: 249–64.

Warmke, B., Nelkin, D. and McKenna, M. (2021) *Forgiveness and Its Moral Dimensions* Oxford: Oxford University Press.

Whatmore, P. (1987) 'Barlinnie Special Unit: An Insider's View', in A. Bottoms and R. Light (eds.) *Problems of Long-Term Imprisonment*. Aldershot: Gower.

White, R. (2012) 'After-Effects: Interview with Patrizio Guzman', *Film Quarterly*, 12 July. https://filmquarterly.org/2012/07/12/after-effects-interview-with-patricio-guzman/.

Whitebook, J. (2004) 'Hans Loewald: A Radical Conservative', *International Journal of Psychoanalysis* 85(1): 97–116.

Whitebook, J. (2017) *Freud: An Intellectual Biography*. Cambridge: Cambridge University Press.

Williams, B. (1981) *Moral Luck*. Cambridge: Cambridge University Press.

Williams, B. (1993) *Shame and Necessity*. Berkeley: University of California Press.

Williams, B. (1995) *Making Sense of Humanity*. Cambridge: Cambridge University Press.

Williams, B. (2002) *Truth and Truthfulness: An Essay in Genealogy*. Princeton: Princeton University Press.

Williams, B. (2011) *Ethics and the Limits of Philosophy*. Abingdon: Routledge.

Wilson, A. (2020) 'Shame, Guilt and Martha Nussbaum's Immaturing Process: Alethic Truth and Human Flourishing', *Journal of Critical Realism* 19(4): 380–97.

Wilson, A. (2021a) 'Guild beyond Guilt: From Political Theory to Metaphysics with Herbert Morris', *Modern Law Review* 84(1): 89–117.

Wilson, A. (2021b) 'General Terms of Comparison: Two Cores of the Restorative Justice Apple', in T. Gavrielides (ed) *Comparative Restorative Justice*. New York: Springer.

Wilson, A. (2022) 'What a Shame! Restorative Justice's Guilty Secret', *The Howard Journal of Crime and Justice* 61(1): 39–52.

Wilson, R. (2001) *The Politics of Truth and Reconciliation in South Africa*. Cambridge: Cambridge University Press.

Winnicott, D. (2005) *Playing and Reality*. London: Routledge.

Winnicott, D. (2018) *The Maturational Processes and the Facilitating Environment*. Abingdon: Routledge.

Zizek, S. (2013) 'Slavoj Žižek on *The Act of Killing* and the modern trend of "privatising public space"', *The New Statesman*, 12 July. www.newstatesman.com/culture/2013/07/slavoj-zizek-act-killing-and-modern-trend-privatising-public-space.

Zweig, A. (1967) *Kant, Philosophical Correspondence 1759–99*. Chicago: University of Chicago Press.

Index

For EU product safety concerns, contact us at Calle de José Abascal, 56–1°, 28003 Madrid, Spain or eugpsr@cambridge.org.

www.ingramcontent.com/pod-product-compliance
Lightning Source LLC
LaVergne TN
LVHW062206200926
848484LV00006B/1335